The Limits of Familiarity

TRANSITS:

LITERATURE, THOUGHT & CULTURE, 1650–1850

Series Editors
Kathryn Parker, University of Wisconsin—La Crosse
Miriam Wallace, New College of Florida

A long running and landmark series in long-eighteenth-century studies, *Transits* includes monographs and edited volumes that are timely, transformative in their approach, and global in their engagement with arts, literature, culture, and history. Books in the series have engaged with visual arts, environment, politics, material culture, travel, theater and performance, embodiment, writing and book history, sexuality, gender, disability, race, and colonialism from Britain and Europe to the Americas, the Far East, and the Middle East. Proposals should offer critical examination of artifacts and events, modes of being and forms of knowledge, material culture, or cultural practices. Works that make provocative connections across time, space, geography, or intellectual history, or that develop new modes of critical imagining are particularly welcome.

Recent titles in the *Transits* series:

The Limits of Familiarity: Authorship and Romantic Readers
Lindsey Eckert

"Robinson Crusoe" after 300 Years
Andreas K. E. Mueller and Glynis Ridley, eds.

Transatlantic Women Travelers, 1688–1843
Misty Krueger, ed.

Laurence Sterne's "A Sentimental Journey": A Legacy to the World
W. B. Gerard and M-C. Newbould, eds.

Hemispheres and Stratospheres: The Idea and Experience of Distance in the International Enlightenment
Kevin L. Cope, ed.

Rewriting Crusoe: The Robinsonade across Languages, Cultures, and Media
Jakub Lipski, ed.

Narrative Mourning: Death and Its Relics in the Eighteenth-Century British Novel
Kathleen M. Oliver

Lothario's Corpse: Libertine Drama and the Long-Running Restoration, 1700–1832
Daniel Gustafson

For a full list of *Transits* titles, please visit our website: www.bucknelluniversitypress.org.

The Limits of Familiarity

AUTHORSHIP AND ROMANTIC READERS

LINDSEY ECKERT

Bucknell University | University Press
LEWISBURG, PENNSYLVANIA

Library of Congress Cataloging-in-Publication Data

Names: Eckert, Lindsey, author.
Title: The limits of familiarity : authorship and Romantic readers / Lindsey Eckert.
Description: Lewisburg, Pennsylvania : Bucknell University Press, 2022. | Series: Transits: literature, thought & culture 1650–1850 | Includes bibliographical references and index.
Identifiers: LCCN 2021039294 | ISBN 9781684483907 (paperback) | ISBN 9781684483914 (hardback) | ISBN 9781684483921 (epub) | ISBN 9781684483938 (mobi) | ISBN 9781684483945 (pdf)
Subjects: LCSH: Romanticism—England. | Authors and readers—Great Britain—History—18th century. | Fame—Social aspects—Great Britain—History—18th century. | Books and reading—Great Britain—History—18th century.
Classification: LCC PR457 .E25 2022 | DDC 820.9/145—dc23
LC record available at https://lccn.loc.gov/2021039294

A British Cataloging-in-Publication record for this book is available from the British Library.

∞ The paper used in this publication meets the requirements of the American National Standard for Information Sciences—Permanence of Paper for Printed Library Materials, ANSI Z39.48-1992.

www.bucknelluniversitypress.org

Distributed worldwide by Rutgers University Press

Manufactured in the United States of America

For my brother Scott

It is not easy to write a familiar style.
—William Hazlitt, "On Familiar Style"

CONTENTS

ILLUSTRATIONS

ACKNOWLEDGMENTS

There have been times while writing this book when, to quote William Hazlitt, "I have felt my subject gradually sinking under me as I advanced, and have been afraid of ending in nothing." That my efforts have come to something speaks to the support that I received from so many.

My biggest intellectual debt is to Deidre Lynch, who has been familiar with this project since its inception; I am beyond thankful for her ongoing generosity and mentorship. Heather Jackson and Daniel E. White helped guide my research at the University of Toronto, and David Taylor and Sonia Hofkosh offered critical ideas for its development. My kind colleagues at Georgia State University supported the early stages of this book and my professorial life. I especially want to thank Michael Galchisnky, Randy Malamud, Jay Rajiva, and the faculty members of the Work in Progress Group at GSU. During my time in Atlanta and since, Gina Caison has read more of this book than most, and I value her friendship even more than her incisive feedback. My current colleagues at Florida State University have encouraged and supported me, and I offer my particular thanks to Anne Coldiron, Perry Howell, Michael Neal, and Gary Taylor. I feel lucky to have joined the faculty at the same time as Jacki Fiscus-Cannaday, Frances Tran, and Joel Smith—the latter whose position in the Chemistry Department we don't hold against him. Members of the Coffeehouse Writing Group—Holly Horner, Meegan Kennedy, Molly Marotta, and Judith Pascoe—have offered feedback and conviviality. Judith, in particular, has been a model mentor and friend.

Beyond FSU, many others have offered support and asked important questions: Gerard Cohen-Vrignaud, Katherine D. Harris, Michelle Levy, Tom Mole, Jonathan Mulrooney, Megan Peiser, Dahlia Porter, Kate Singer, Helen Williams, and Jonathan Sachs. My research has been enriched by more sustained conversations with and feedback from Claire Battershill, Nicholas Mason, Brittany Pladek, and Andrew Stauffer. Julia Grandison has been a friend, critic, and accountability partner since grad school, and she embodied all three roles with particular dedication in the final months of this book's completion. During the pandemic, I've been bolstered by academic communities on Twitter and through the Zoom events of "Romanticism in the Meantime," organized by Emily Rohrbach and Jonathan

Mulrooney. I first read Coleridge at Kenyon College, and it is James Carson's fault that I am a Romanticist.

Miriam Wallace saw this book's potential for the *Transits* series and offered important feedback and encouragement early on. I want to thank my two anonymous readers whose detailed, gracious reports helped me hone my ideas. Suzanne Guiod at Bucknell University Press has been supportive throughout this process. I would have been lost without Pam Dailey's help with questions about production and permissions and Michelle Scott's guidance during the final stages of publication.

I thank the British Library Board, the E. J. Pratt Library, the Robertson Davies Library at Massey College, the Wordsworth Trust, and the Yale Center for British Art for granting permission to reproduce images from their collections. Quotations from the Lovelace Byron Papers, currently on deposit with Bodleian Libraries, are reproduced by permission of Paper Lion, Ltd., and the Proprietor of the Lovelace Byron Papers. Part of chapter 3 first appeared as "Lady Caroline Lamb Beyond Byron: *Graham Hamilton*, Female Authorship, and the Politics of Public Reputation," *European Romantic Review* 26, no. 2 (2015): 149–163, and a version of chapter 5 appeared as "Reading Lyric's Form: The Written Hand in Albums and Literary Annuals," *ELH* 85, no. 4 (2018): 973–997. I thank Taylor & Francis and Johns Hopkins University Press for permission to publish revised versions here. I presented parts of chapters 2 and 5 at invited talks at the University of Tennessee, the University of Georgia, and the symposium "Manuscripts, Print, and the Organization of Knowledge" held at the Wordsworth Trust's Jerwood Centre in Grasmere. The participants and audiences at these events offered critical insights that helped shape my arguments.

A grant for summer research from Georgia State University and a First Year Assistant Professor Program Grant from Florida State University supported my writing; an Arts and Humanities Program Enhancement Grant, also from FSU, supported the book's completion and production. Fellowships at Chawton House Library and the Centre for the History of the Book at the University of Edinburgh allowed me to consult primary materials essential to my arguments. Of course, consulting research materials depends on the work of those who keep libraries and archives running. David McClay was the curator of the John Murray Archive when I did the bulk of my research there, and his knowledge of everything Byron- and Murray-related was immensely helpful. I would also like to thank Darren Bevin at Chawton House Library, Jeff Cowton at the Jerwood Centre, Rachel Duke at FSU Special Collections, Roma Kail at the E. J. Pratt Library, P. J. MacDougall and Julia Warren at the Robertson Davies Library at Massey College, Kirsty McHugh at the John Murray Archive, and the many people who've offered assistance at other libraries, including the Bodleian Libraries, British Library, New York Public Library, Thomas Fisher Rare Book Library, and Florida State University Libraries. I am in awe of FSU's humanities librarian, Mallary Rawls, whose MacGyvering helped me access materials during the extended COVID lockdowns of 2020–2021.

In a book that is, in many ways, about the line between sharing and oversharing, I am anxiously aware of the personal nature of much of the support that I've received, which I'd nonetheless like to acknowledge publicly. My lawyer, Richelle M. Marsico, deserves her own sentence here for helping secure my sense of safety at home and on campus so that I could complete my book in peace. Friendships with Laura Chaffee, Tracy Johnson, Katie Goehner, Laura Miller, and Sarah Waltz continue to sustain me even though I am the only one of the group no longer in Minnesota. My riding community in Tallahassee has provided camaraderie and the occasional mimosa. The animals who lived with this project—Sir Leoline, Roland, Gracie, and Lafitte—showed an active indifference to my research that was necessary to its completion. My brother Scott Eckert, to whom this book is dedicated, always finds the humor in everything from action movies to academic publishing. My life and this book are so much richer because of him and his family—Vanessa, Jenny, and Jack.

I owe my deepest debt of gratitude to my parents, Jane and Steve, who, as my mom likes to point out, taught me to read in the first place, and whose support of my bookishness—and everything else—has been endless. This is a debt that cannot be repaid but only acknowledged here with love.

ABBREVIATIONS

BLJ	*Byron's Letters and Journals*, ed. Leslie Marchand, 13 vols. (London: Murray, 1973–1994)
CPW	*Lord Byron: The Complete Poetical Works*, ed. Jerome McGann, 7 vols. (Oxford: Clarendon, 1980–1993)
ECCO	Eighteenth Century Collections Online
JMA	John Murray Archive, National Library of Scotland, Edinburgh
Letters	*The Whole Disgraceful Truth: Selected Letters of Lady Caroline Lamb*, ed. Paul Douglass (New York: Palgrave Macmillan, 2006)
RR	*The Romantics Reviewed: Contemporary Reviews of British Romantic Writers*, ed. Donald Reiman, 9 vols. (New York: Garland, 1972)
RWWR	*Romantic Women Writers Reviewed*, ed. Ann R. Hawkins, 9 vols. (London: Pickering and Chatto, 2011–2013)
SWWH	*The Selected Writings of William Hazlitt*, ed. Duncan Wu, 9 vols. (London: Pickering and Chatto, 1998)
WWR	Women Writers in Review (Northeastern University Women Writers Project, 2016), https://wwp.northeastern.edu/review/

The Limits of Familiarity

INTRODUCTION

Familiarity's "due bounds"

> The present age has discovered a desire, or rather a rage, for literary anecdote and private history.
>
> —Walter Scott, "Memoir of the Early Life of Sir Walter Scott"*

IN EARLY 1791, LONDON BUZZED with tales about the young and beautiful Elizabeth Gunning, niece of the famously attractive Gunning sisters. The sisters had, in the mid-eighteenth century, made advantageous marriages to men whose wealth and rank far exceeded their own. Perhaps wishing to replicate her aunts' matrimonial successes, Gunning entered London society and began her search for a rich husband. Shortly thereafter, she found herself embroiled in a complex scandal involving young love, forged letters, and a tyrannous father worthy of a Minerva Press novel. In 1790, Gunning had caught the attention of the Marquis of Blandford, wealthy heir to the Duke of Marlborough.[1] According to one of her contemporaries, soon "the report of Miss Gunning's marriage with Blandford was the general topic of conversation in all the enlightened and all the enlivening circles."[2] Among these enlightened and enlivening circles it was common knowledge that Blandford and Gunning had begun an intimate correspondence. That their supposed epistolary familiarity did not end in a marriage proposal shocked London's elite as well as the readers who followed society gossip in the pages of the periodical press. Instead, it was discovered that Blandford's letters as well as those between the male heads of each family had been forged. London went mad for information. Horace Walpole, whose correspondence throughout 1790 and 1791 describes the scandal, complained, "One has heard of nothing else for these seven months!"[3] Who forged the letters? Had Gunning been jilted? Did she love Blandford? Who was to blame?

We may never know definitive answers to these questions, but we do know that Gunning's supposed siege on Blandford's heart and her attempt to obtain an aristocratic title failed. While she most certainly was not repelled by feces, as James

Gillray's caricature "The Seige of Blenheim" would have it, the explosion of publicity forced Gunning and her mother, Susannah, to flee to France in disgrace (figure I.1).

The center of Gillray's image, one of three that he produced about the scandal, depicts Gunning and her mother unsuccessfully attacking Blandford's familial Oxfordshire residence, Blenheim Palace.[4] Susannah Gunning uses a quill pen to light a cannon, a reference to her career as a novelist and the related suspicion that she authored her daughter's scandal. The cannon shoots forth correspondence, including a "Letter from Marq. Blan[dford] written by Myself," a "Forged Love Letter," and a "Letter forg'd by myself." Elizabeth Gunning's naked thighs astride the phallic cannon and its orgasmic explosion of letters signal gendered ideas about female sexual impropriety and shameless social reaching. Gunning's vulnerable position—the fact that she is falling off the cannon that she presumably believed she could control—reflects the gendered volatility of publicity in the Romantic period.

The Limits of Familiarity: Authorship and Romantic Readers argues that the volatility of both publicity and professional authorship hinged on the decorous limits of familiarity—a cultural value as important in the Romantic period as it was unstable. Widely recognized as a social virtue, familiarity—a feeling of emotional closeness or a quality of comforting predictability—could also be dangerous, uncouth, or boring. Lawrence Klein's conclusion that a "mobility of meanings increases the complexity of mapping discourse" applies here; eighteenth- and nineteenth-century attempts to negotiate and define familiarity reveal its polysemy.[5] According to Samuel Johnson, *familiarity* is "easiness of conversation" and "affability." Likewise, he defines *familiar* as "domestick, relating to a family," "easy in conversation," and "unceremonious; free, as among persons long acquainted."[6] Class and gender informed choices about one's appropriate familiars, effectively creating a moving target. George Crabb's *English Synonymes Explained* (1818) clarifies the tensions inherent in familiarity in his description of the relationship between *acquaintance*, *familiarity*, and *intimacy*. Crabb explains that *familiarity* is "produced by a daily intercourse, which wears off all constraint, and banishes all ceremony." While banishing all ceremony could be beneficial in some instances, in others, indiscriminate familiarity could be vulgar or immoral, especially as *familiarity* was also used as a byword for sexual intimacy. Crabb continues, "'Too much *familiarity*,' according to the old proverb, 'breeds contempt.' The unlicensed freedom which commonly attends *familiarity* affords but too ample scope for the indulgence of the selfish and unamiable passions."[7] In addition to contempt, familiarity could also breed boredom and indifference. No man, Crabb cautions, "can be *familiar* without being in danger of obtruding himself to the annoyance of

Figure I.1 James Gillray, "The Seige of Blenheim, or the New System of Gunning, Discover'd" (London: H. Humphrey, March 5, 1791). Courtesy of the Yale Center for British Art, Paul Mellon Collection.

others."[8] Because of its negative associations, *familiar* also became an accusation that reviewers leveled at works containing repetitive language and tired literary tropes. In order to overcome familiarity's associations with banality and annoyance, Romantic authors sought new ways, as Samuel Taylor Coleridge put it, to combine "the sense of novelty and freshness, with old and familiar objects."[9]

It is the slippery nature of familiarity with which this book is concerned, and I suggest that the cultural value of familiarity—especially its dual associations with interpersonal closeness and, if overextended, banality and vulgarity—framed the affective relationships between Romantic-era readers and the authors they read. I explore how authors, editors, and public figures like Gunning attempted to negotiate and exploit familiarity's social and commercial limits. Uniting reception studies, celebrity studies, and literary history, I reveal how anxieties about familiarity shaped both Romanticism and conceptions of authorship. In turns, familiarity was a banality to overcome, a quality to court, and a characteristic to avoid. It could connect people and, this book argues, authors and readers in particular. However, familiarity also had the worrying potential to disrupt social and literary codes, and debates about familiarity played out against a backdrop of political and social unrest during the French Revolution, the Napoleonic Wars, and their aftermath. "All the decent drapery of life," Edmund Burke laments in *Reflections on the Revolution in France*, "is to be rudely torn off," leaving only "the defects of our naked shivering nature."[10] Throughout the Romantic period, many authors and commentators removed the drapery of private life, as literalized in Gillray's print featuring Gunning's hiked petticoat and bare legs. Parallels between Burke's ideas and his contemporaries' reactions to authorial familiarity connect political and literary revolution. In both cases, rapid changes upended traditional assumptions about hierarchy and propriety that governed both literary and social spheres. On the one hand, familiarity helped foster Romantic publics through feelings of sharedness and sympathy. On the other, as an element that could level distinctions between social groups, it facilitated unruly relationships in both public and private life. *The Limits of Familiarity*, then, enriches reconsiderations of the Habermasian public sphere that recognize the messy, overlapping nature of the "private" and the "public." As familiarity's traditional, decorous limits began to buckle under Romanticism's social, political, and technological changes, concerns about familiarity's potential to connect and to disgust, to build community or to disrupt it became all the more pressing.

Familiarity's competing possibilities are on full display in the Gunning scandal, and the episode demonstrates the difficulties of evoking familiarity's more positive associations in private and in public. People following the scandal sought to understand if, how, and by whom familiarity's decorous limits had been crossed.

Had Gunning really been on familiar terms with Blandford? Did the matriarchs of Blandford's own family mistakenly encourage Gunning to misread mundane politeness for romantic familiarity? (Blandford's grandmother, offering shelter underneath her skirts in Gillray's image, had welcomed Elizabeth and Susannah Gunning into her home at the height of the scandal, causing some to wonder if Blandford had a measure of culpability.) Did Gunning's father, slinking off the left side of the print, use the scandal to mask and then excuse his own carnal familiarity with another man's wife?

Answers to such questions varied. Many thought the Gunnings uncouth for seeking familiar connections with aristocrats above their social station. Referencing the drastic social climbing that Gunning's marriage to Blandford would have entailed, Walpole observed that it was "an idea so improbable, that even the luck of the Gunnings cannot make one believe it."[11] The scandal seemed to reveal Gunning's déclassé desire for wealth and status, an idea supported by her father's accusation that Elizabeth "avoid[ed] all acquaintance and familiarity with gentleman beneath a certain rank" so that she could trade her beauty for "an earldom at least."[12] Gunning's supposed vulgarity was compounded by reports that she falsified her familiarity with Blandford both by forging his letters herself and by circulating gossip about their courtship.[13] Rumors of the pair's romantic attachment likely exerted pressure on Blandford to propose; wanton familiarity with a young unmarried woman suggested rakish impropriety—a quality that Blandford was as disinclined to court as, it seems, he was Gunning. Others believed that the invented proposal was meant to prompt Gunning's cousin to propose out of jealousy.

The salacious story prompted press coverage in periodicals and newspapers as well as numerous pamphlets. Gunning's mother and father each entered the pamphlet war surrounding their daughter, and their revelations signaled a shocking, overly familiar relationship with the public whose opinions they tried to manipulate. Airing embarrassing anecdotes and launching vitriolic accusations of familial betrayal, these pamphlets relayed information that should have, by almost all moral measures in the period, remained within the bounds of the family. Public demand for information was such that Susannah Gunning's pamphlet about her daughter sold out the same day it appeared and went through four editions.[14] Gunning's mother's career as one of the prolific novel-writing Minifie sisters led to speculation that the scandal was a marketing ploy to increase sales of her fiction.[15] Even if the scandal bolstered Susannah's authorial career (and, later, Gunning's own), it also damaged their reputations and ability to manage them. As Gillray's Gunning loses control of her epistolary cannon she cries, "Mother! my mask'd Battery is discovered & we shall be blown up!" The event did blow up in newspapers, periodicals, pamphlets, and prints throughout 1791 and 1792, leaving little of Gunning's personal life masked. As one pamphleteer describes it, "No circumstance has occurred in the variegated circle of Fashion, for a long series of years, that has excited the public attention, in so high a degree, as the recent dissentions which have prevailed in the family of General Gunning."[16] The whole affair seemed too salacious to be real.

And maybe it was. Gunning and the figures surrounding her became caricatures more informed by melodramatic novels than by actual events. The intrigue drew public attention partly because the events mirrored familiar tropes from popular fiction. As Walpole observed of the scandal, "It is lost time for people to write novels, who can compose such a romance as these good folks have invented."[17] Gunning was alternately presented as a coquette, a wronged woman, and an innocent pawn in her mother's marriage game. The parties involved and the press at large obscured distinctions between fiction and reality. One newspaper quipped that new details about Gunning's family would "make an excellent *dénouement* to the GUNNING NOVEL," pointing to the scandal's almost unbelievable developments as it ricocheted through different media forms and genres.[18] To recall Crabb's definition of *familiarity*, Gunning's life had become the "daily intercourse" of the periodical press, and the publicity surrounding her wore "off all constraint, and banishe[d] all ceremony."[19] In the words of one eighteenth-century commentator, Gunning had experienced "the theft of her own Narrative."[20]

Gunning took back the story of her life by writing about it herself.[21] Because her life and her seeming disregard for class- and gender-based notions of familiarity had already been publicly exposed, she had little to lose by becoming even more familiar with interested readers. In 1794, when memories of the scandal would have still been fresh in the public mind, Gunning published *The Packet*, the first of her nine novels.[22] In *The Packet* Gunning capitalizes on her bad name much in the same way that, as we shall see in chapter 3, Lady Caroline Lamb did following her infamous affair with Lord Byron. Using references to the scandal surrounding her, Gunning's novel embraces her prior public exposure through further public exposure, and she frames her relationship with readers as "unceremonious; free, as among persons long acquainted."[23] Across the novel's four volumes Gunning offers tantalizing allusions to her own life and to her previous treatment in the press, making her novel, according to Pam Perkins, "a deliberate and rather clever move in an eighteenth-century public relations game."[24] *The Packet*'s preface explicitly acknowledges that Gunning's notorious name attracted readers: "In the circles of high life I know my book will be read, if only for the novelty-sake of *that* name which has already afforded my *dear friends* a great deal of subject for conversation."[25] The italics emphasize Gunning's sarcasm and seeming frustration that intimate details of her life—details that should have remained in her familiar circle—became public fodder. While appreciating that her authorial success largely depends on readers eager for scandal, *The Packet* repeatedly attacks the gossip culture that these same readers perpetuate. In her most scathing condemnation, she describes one of her characters opening a newspaper to find "several anecdotes of fashion, or, to speak with greater propriety, of fashionable people—a most excellent species of amusement this, where thousands are to be diverted at no greater expence than the sacrifice of a good name, or a blameless reputation!"[26]

The Romantic-era literary marketplace traded on diverting stories like Gunning's. Willingly shared, borrowed, or sometimes downright stolen, (auto)biographical information played a central role in eighteenth- and nineteenth-century literature. Increasingly, readers wanted to feel as though they were on familiar terms with public figures and authors. This was the age of a Peeping Tom public hungry for sordid biographical details, and the author turned exhibitionist often willing to oblige. The demand for information was so heightened that, according to Julian North, almost no one seemed "safe from the voracious alliance of biographers, readers, and publishers, eager to market lives."[27] What did William Wordsworth wear, and where did he walk? Who was Byron's new mistress, and how did his marriage fare? Did William Hazlitt sleep with prostitutes, and did he actually have pimples? To an unprecedented degree, answers—sometimes accurate, sometimes not—were tantalizingly at the ready for Romantic readers. Confessional poetry, romans à clef, silver-fork novels, memoirs, familiar essays, gossip columns, and facsimiles of manuscript materials gave readers exceptional access to well-known authors.[28] But how close was too close? Or, rather, at what point did familiarity become overfamiliarity? *The Limits of Familiarity* argues that these questions shaped literary production and reception in the Romantic period. As Lord Chesterfield famously explained, "I know nothing more difficult in common behaviour than to fix due bounds to familiarity: too little implies an unsociable formality; too much destroys friendly and social intercourse."[29] Here I attempt to illuminate these difficulties and their relevance to Romantic studies.

From the mid-eighteenth century onward, establishing familiarity's "due bounds" was especially challenging for authors. Byron's familiar style, for instance, encouraged the romantic adoration of his fans, while Lady Caroline Lamb's familiarity with readers in her novel *Glenarvon* proved commercially successful but morally repulsive. Analyzing both readerly responses to authors and their works as well as the techniques that authors used to shape these responses, I demonstrate that becoming familiar with readers was an elusive but fundamental aspect of Romantic authorship. The case studies presented in *The Limits of Familiarity* indicate that the constant danger of familiarity was that it could quickly shift from an asset into a liability. Authors had to balance autobiographical forthrightness with decorum and discretion. Apart from Byron, whose reception during the years of fame I consider in my second chapter, the authors examined here largely got this balance wrong. They demonstrate how easily familiarity could become untoward overfamiliarity, making one an object worthy of public interest—the modern-day celebrity train wreck one cannot help but watch—but not sustained sympathy.

As I track familiarity's limits across this book, I make three interventions in Romantic scholarship. First, I complicate understandings of Romantic-era reception by revealing familiarity's role in evaluations of literature by reviewers, publishers, and common readers. Drawing on a variety of published and archival evidence, I argue that familiarity and the resulting emotional attachments that writers evoked in their readers governed contemporary evaluations of literary works, particularly works with autobiographical undertones. Shifts in the Romantic-era literary marketplace and the reading public deepened tensions between high and low literary culture. Perceptions of a work's (over)familiarity with different readerships, in turn, shaped perceptions of a work's (and its author's) literariness, and I suggest that historical definitions of authorship depended on one's ability to negotiate successfully familiarity's shifting boundaries. Crossing the line into overfamiliarity excluded one from the category of author, and many readers and reviewers described Charlotte Smith and Lady Caroline Lamb as hacks, Byron as an immoral radical, Hazlitt as a Cockney scribbler, and those who wrote for literary annuals as authorial prostitutes.

Second, I reconsider the emphasis on Byron that characterizes foundational research in celebrity studies and, relatedly, author-reader relationships in the Romantic period. Influential work by scholars such as Tom Mole, Ghislaine McDayter, Eric Eisner, and Corin Throsby historicizes celebrity and its ability to ease, in Mole's words, "the sense of industrial alienation between readers and writers" in Romanticism's rapidly changing print market.[30] This insightful scholarship reimagines Habermasian theories of the public sphere within burgeoning celebrity culture. However, a continued focus on Byron risks both overestimating the novelty of the poet's relationship with his audience and forwarding a Byron-centric understanding of early celebrity culture. My work questions this emphasis on Byron and his seemingly unique relationships with readers. I acknowledge that Byron was in many ways at the center of debates about the social, moral, and literary consequences of readers' passionate feelings for authors. As such, Byron is an influential force throughout this book. However, in seeing Byron as one figure among many, I build on Clara Tuite's *Lord Byron and Scandalous Celebrity*, which examines the poet's celebrity in the context of his famous contemporaries, including Lady Caroline Lamb, Stendhal, Napoleon Bonaparte, and Lord Castlereagh.[31] Studying Byron alongside authors that employed similar strategies of semi-autobiographical revelation helps explain what made Byron unique in degree though not, I suggest, in kind. It also enables us to see his indebtedness to his female predecessors like Charlotte Smith, whose connections with readers and literary tactics for establishing those connections were arguably as influential as Byron's.

Finally, *The Limits of Familiarity* seeks to show how the language of sympathy central to Romanticism intersects in previously unrecognized ways with debates about familiarity and, in turn, with the writing and publishing practices that familiarity animated. Recognizing familiarity's influence in the eighteenth and nineteenth centuries, then, demands a reconsideration of key concepts that have long interested scholars of Romanticism: sympathy, sensibility, authorship, and the public sphere.[32] Overall, this book's analysis of familiarity's social and literary import necessitates a revision of not only the history of Romantic-era author-reader relations, but also what Pierre Bourdieu terms "the literary field" of Romanticism. Examining "the mood of the age," Bourdieu explains, is necessary to historicize the system that engenders the material production as well as the symbolic production of literary works.[33] The arguments set forth here assert that familiarity formed a crucial component of the mood of the Romantic age and the literary field it created.

Romanticism's literary field partially comes into focus through an examination of reception history. However, reception history is, as book historians have long known, difficult to document and assess. Books are destroyed; letters and journals lost or burned; marginalia erased or effaced.[34] Still, evidence awaits those able to plough through the sort of archival material central to my arguments: letters and anonymous fan mail, manuscript albums, publishers' papers, notes on the flyleaves and in the margins of books, and published reviews. As important as historical records of Romantic-era readers are, Jon Klancher, in a retrospective on his field-changing book historical work in *The Making of English Reading Audiences, 1790–1832*, cautions against the "larger, more ontological claim" of the "myth of the real reader."[35] Heeding Klancher, my work explores real readers alongside the audiences that authors, critics, publishers, and other readers imagined—readers evoked in the content of Romantic texts and implied by the material attributes of texts that conjure particular types of readers and reading experiences. For this reason, the terms *reader* and *audience* necessarily shift throughout this book, at times signaling historical readers who have left evidence behind and at others signaling the audiences that contemporaries imagined. Even though prominent Romantic figures' ideas about readers did not necessarily reflect the actual publics around them, as Andrew Franta has shown, these imagined readers still influenced how and what writers wrote.[36] From Charlotte Smith pitting her ideal, sympathetic readers against hard-hearted reviewers to Byron's critics fretting about the "Byromania" supposedly infecting readers' minds, imagined Romantic audiences feature in my analysis alongside tangible evidence of real readers.[37]

Examining the affective ties that readers—real and abstract—had with authors and authors' literary strategies to secure those ties, this book reveals how sympathy and revulsion were shaped by the language and social expectations of familiarity. Throughout, and particularly in the first, second, and fourth chapters, I argue that familiarity was integral to the period's moral philosophy and theories of sympathy, and I seek to refocus scholarly work on emotion and literary history. Since Adela Pinch's influential *Strange Fits of Passion: Epistemologies of Emotion, Hume to Austen*, scholars have explored how eighteenth- and nineteenth-century theories about sentimentality and emotional closeness influenced literary history.[38] More recently, works like Andrew Stauffer's *Anger, Revolution, and Romanticism*, Nancy Yousef's *Romantic Intimacy*, Melissa Sodeman's *Sentimental Memorials: Women and the Novel in Literary History*, and Deidre Lynch's *Loving Literature: A Cultural History* have examined representations of emotion in Romantic-era literary works and the moral philosophy contemporaneous with them.[39] As important as this work is to my own research and to Romantic studies generally, its focus on sensibility bypasses other influential social values like familiarity that organized Romantic-era life and literature. For instance, Pinch has shown that in the Romantic era, questions about "whether someone's language is suited to their passions" quickly slid into questions about "whether that person's feelings are suited to their situation—whether their feelings are authentic or false."[40] Yet such questions, informed by a shift away from Enlightenment ideals and new concerns in the 1790s about how ungoverned passions might undermine government itself, are only part of the story. In the eighteenth and nineteenth centuries philosophical questions about the passions often became questions about whether a person's familiar language was suited to a particular audience. The same language could feel authentic or false, polite or vulgar, genial or degenerate, and the sympathetic charge of one's communication depended on complex dynamics surrounding decorous familiarity as well as its gendered and classed applications. In other words, the revelations and rhetoric used in a letter to a friend might not evoke the same feelings of closeness when shared with what Coleridge called "the multitudinous PUBLICS."[41] Indeed, this was the case with Gunning's autobiographical novels, which drew voyeuristic readers but not their lasting sympathy.

FAMILIARITY IN CONTEXT

Familiarity features prominently in discourses surrounding literature and sociability; it appears in reviews and in works that considered the moral limits of (auto)biographical exposure. Most famously, Sir Walter Scott's review of the fourth canto of *Childe Harold's Pilgrimage* describes the pride that Byron's readers should feel in "being called as it were into familiarity with a mind so powerful."[42] Wordsworth, too, acknowledged a growing "class of poets, the principal charm of whose writings depends upon the familiar knowledge which they convey of the personal feelings of their authors."[43] In his *Dissertation on Anecdotes* (1793), Isaac D'Israeli similarly claimed that readers valued anecdotes and memoirs because they offer "a familiarity, which invites us to approach" great people; knowing "minute circumstances," he explains, "familiarize[s] us to the genius of [those] whom we admire."[44] Throughout the Romantic period writers increasingly courted their readers' feelings of affectionate familiarity, and readers responded in droves. As Eric Eisner summarizes: "A memoir-mad public devoured the gossip about writers' private lives . . . and some adoring readers schemed to see in person, to get to know, even to sleep with the poets they idolized."[45] This memoir madness afflicted the marketplace more generally, with audiences keen to read (auto) biography into imaginative literature despite (and sometimes because of) authors' insistence that they should not. The end of the eighteenth century also saw a burgeoning culture of fan letters as readers sought to get even closer to the authors whom they admired and, in some cases, loved. According to Scott, the public had "discovered a desire, or rather a rage" for details that put them on familiar footing with authors and other public figures.[46]

Not everyone welcomed this new rage, and authors' numerous complaints evidence familiarity's prominence and, importantly, its contentiousness. Even D'Israeli acknowledged the limits of personal anecdotes, admitting that they could easily become "frivolous, insipid, and inconsequential."[47] Wordsworth was more direct in his criticisms of readers' frivolous, insipid curiosity. In *A Letter to a Friend of Robert Burns* (1816), Wordsworth rejects "the coarse intrusions into the recesses, the gross breaches upon the sanctities, of domestic life" that characterized many literary biographies.[48] Wordsworth was not alone in his grumblings against nosy readers. As Deidre Lynch observes, many contemporaries also feared that "the nineteenth-century public's appetite for writers' lives tended to outrun its eagerness to consume writers' works."[49] Public interest encroached on the private lives of authors, and Wordsworth's nostalgic desire for a division between authorial public life and the "recesses" of private life reveals that such binaries were unclear.

Readers' "gross breaches" into authors' lives were more than a matter of literary taste; they also reflect ethical concerns about relations between authors, their works, and their readers. Feeling familiarity's emotional closeness (and, conversely, overfamiliarity's disgust) for authors' lives colors both historical and current literary reception. However, questions remain about if and how much weight should be given to these emotive responses. For instance, were those who wept for Byron as much as they did for his character Childe Harold somehow less skilled readers than those who saw his hero as the true child of imagination? Relatedly, does my scholarship come into question if I admit my abhorrence for Hazlitt as a historical person? At what point does feeling for (or against) an author become either a liability or a potentially valid metric for understanding literature and literary history? And is it ethical to feel entitled to information about authors and public figures, especially if that information shows them in a poor light?

While such questions about the ethical and aesthetic implications of voyeurism and overfamiliarity are pressing today, they were newly intensified in the Romantic period when authors increasingly obscured distinctions between literary and private life. One of Gunning's critics, for instance, pointed to this very dynamic, advising her to "endeavour to forget *herself*, if she wishes to interest us in her characters"—a comment reminiscent of Crabb's claim that too much familiarity leads to a disgusting "indulgence of the selfish and unamiable passions."[50] The reviewer's complaint points to the marketplace conditions wherein fictional characters held readers' interest partly because they seemed based on real figures like Gunning. As with the preface to *The Packet*, the review notes that autobiography—not literary quality—piqued readers' interest in the novel, yet the reviewer also suggests that Gunning's life will not remain a literary draw for long.

Just over two decades later, Byron faced similar criticisms for sharing private information. The short-lived review *Farrago* objected to the personal content of Byron's *Poems* (1816), which included references to his acrimonious separation from his wife, Annabella Milbanke: "We are sorry to observe at page 21, the republication of a Poem ['Fare thee well'] which has a pointed reference to a subject wholly unfit to meet the public eye. The prerogative of public criticism, however unlimited in other cases be its power, cannot be fairly said to extend over the domestic conduct of living characters. By this we would not be understood as asserting, that on no occasion ought the veil which conceals private life to be torn away—but as merely condemning domestic criticism in general as cruel and disgraceful."[51] The reviewer struggles with the propriety of reviewing Byron's improper poems and attempts to solve the problem by criticizing Byron for exposing himself in the first place. However, reproaching Byron, the review participates in a culture that feeds on the poet's self-exposure. Even when condemning indecorous overfamiliarity, reviewers and social critics were put in the awkward position of pandering to readers' desire for it.

In an increasingly urbanized, unstable, and literate world, negotiating familiarity's confusing and even contradictory boundaries, in turn, shaped the boundaries of and corresponding debates about everything from sympathy and social class to the literary marketplace and politics. Note that both Wordsworth's observations about literary biography in *A Letter to a Friend of Robert Burns* and the *Farrago*'s review of Byron's *Poems* draw directly on Burke's conservative rhetoric in *Reflections on the Revolution in France*, with its references to the decent drapery of social and political life being torn asunder. Rising concerns about familiarity in the Romantic era coincide with the radical politics of the late eighteenth century, which I address in more detail below. While demonstrating the ubiquity of familiarity is one goal of *The Limits of Familiarity*, understanding the historical factors that made familiarity a guiding force in Romantic-era literary and social thought equally shapes my analysis. Revolutionary politics, the expanding reading public, debates about high and low literature, uncertain divisions between domestic and public life, and rapidly changing technologies that produced and disseminated print all intensified questions about if and how the desire for familiarity framed, sustained, and strained social relationships and literature.

Once one starts to look for familiarity in Romanticism, its pervasive presence becomes difficult to unsee. For instance, familiarity's formative relationship to poetry and poetic genius is a central, though underappreciated, theme of several of Romanticism's canonical literary treatises. In an oft-cited passage of "A Defence of Poetry," Percy Bysshe Shelley explains, "Poetry lifts the veil from the hidden beauty of the world, and makes familiar objects be as if they were not familiar."[52] For Shelley, poets can overcome the familiar to reveal hidden truths. Coleridge's earlier *Biographia Literaria* praises Wordsworth's ability to make the familiar strange and to breathe meaning back into the everyday. Coleridge even suggests that the primary manifestation of genius is the ability "to represent familiar objects [so] as to awaken in the minds of others a kindred feeling concerning them."[53] While, like Shelley, Coleridge acknowledges that the "film of familiarity" can cloud perceptions of the world, he also suggests that, in the hands of genius, familiar objects enable sympathetic human connection.[54]

In addition to the connective possibilities of familiar objects, eighteenth- and nineteenth- century moral philosophers explored links between familiarity and sympathy. In *Plays on the Passions*, Joanna Baillie asserts that the "sympathetick propensity of our minds" arises in part from our natural desire to become familiar with "what men are in the closet as well as the field."[55] Even more explicitly, Adam Smith's philosophical assertions about sympathy in *The Theory of Moral*

Sentiments are claims about familiarity's limits, though this connection, which I explore more fully in chapters 2 and 4, has gone underanalyzed by scholars. Smith explains that the more familiar we are with someone, the more sympathy we can anticipate from them: "[M]y imagination is more ductile, and more readily assumes, if I may say so, the shape and configuration of the imaginations of those with whom I am familiar."[56] Thus, familiarity does not simply facilitate "easiness of conversation" and "affability," as Johnson's *Dictionary* indicates; it promotes sympathy.[57] For Smith, evoking sympathy, like familiarity, depended on restraint and limitation. One's passions must be appropriately keyed to a particular audience—friend, acquaintance, stranger—in order to prompt sympathy. "[V]irtue," according to Smith, "consists not in any one affection, but in the proper degree of all affections."[58] In theory, familiarity could establish such affections and sympathetic connections. But in practice, Romantic-era authors and readers struggled to define what "the proper degree" of familiarity meant and what its boundaries were in literature.

Familiarity's simultaneous potential to numb and to connect informed not just poetry and philosophy but also debates about Romantic-era sociability and, significantly, sociability between classes. In the period, interpersonal familiarity could uphold class distinctions; the different degrees of familiarity that one might extend to members of various groups reflected good breeding and knowledge of one's place in the social hierarchy. Yet interpersonal familiarity could also signal an indecorous or, worse, a radical disregard for class. As we have seen, the seeming disrespect for class divisions negatively framed Gunning's familiarity with Blandford. One writer earlier in the eighteenth century bluntly explained that people should have "Familiarity with none but such as are eminent for some commendable Qualifications."[59] These "Qualifications" were often shorthand for wealth and rank. Hester Lynch Piozzi's *British Synonymy; or, An Attempt at Regulating the Choice of Words in Familiar Conversation* (1794) offers advice about proper conduct across classes: "[A]mong people where talents or fortune only make the difference, a strain of polished familiarity, or familiar politeness . . . is the behaviour most likely to attract affectionate esteem."[60] Like Adam Smith before her, Piozzi suggests that familiarity fosters emotional connection because it serves as an important social lubricant, yet, also like Smith, she believes it must be restrained. Her qualification that familiarity should be "polished" indicates the class awareness that should accompany sociability.

Cross-class familiarity proved especially problematic when it concerned servants and their employers. "We do not hold it proper to converse so *familiarly* with our domestics," wrote an observer in 1760, as "it is very far from our intention to introduce a *levelling Scheme*."[61] In 1825, another commentator similarly advised, "In your manner to your servants, be firm, without being severe, and kind without being familiar."[62] The "servant problem," which preoccupied commentators throughout the long eighteenth century, hinged on slippery familiar relations between family members and the domestics they employed.[63] Decreasing visual markers of class intensified concerns about familiarity as the clothing worn by servants began to mirror that of their masters and "blurr[ed] what the employing classes regarded as the appropriate hierarchical distinctions in a society where dress was expected to indicate rank."[64] Hazlitt, as we shall see more fully in chapter 4, complained about women who become "quite familiar with the maid, and chatter with her (upon equal terms)."[65] Even Mary Wollstonecraft's radical *A Vindication of the Rights of Woman* noted that "mixing them [women and servants] thus indiscriminately together" promoted a "gross degree of familiarity" detrimental to sociability, morality, and education.[66]

The period's shifting pedagogical practices also foregrounded familiarity's radical potential to efface traditional social divisions. Dissenting thinkers, for instance, sought to strengthen connections between sociability and political action through the pedagogy of "free and familiar conversation."[67] Michèle Cohen has convincingly argued that scholars have underestimated the power that the term *familiar* had in reframing education as "social, domestic and informal"; the term's appearance in the titles of eighteenth- and nineteenth-century didactic texts about everything from history to mathematics implied a pedagogy that welcomed "groups excluded from formal education."[68] Familiarity radicalized education by eliding distinctions between male and female pupils, between autodidacts and the formally educated, and between members of the middle and upper classes. One criticism of this new pedagogy, however, was that familiar conversation could easily become too free and even too feminine and, as a result, become frivolous and even dangerous.

To mitigate these dangers, didactic works offered advice about negotiating familiarity's limits. From the mid-eighteenth century onward, pupils looked to letter-writing manuals to learn to write in a proper familiar style and avoid the perils of its misapplication. The role of the familiar letter became especially pertinent as the development of Britain's postal system democratized epistolary exchange and allowed "letters to filter through the social spectrum" and become an "everyday activity."[69] The sizable market for manuals like *Newberry's Familiar Letter-Writer* (1788) and *The Complete Letter-Writer, Containing a Great Variety of Plain, Easy, Entertaining & Familiar Letters* (1808) demonstrates familiarity's framing role in interpersonal communication—communication inflected by class and, just as important, gender.[70] These manuals indicate the growing diversity of those who participated in epistolary sociability; however, they also reveal an interest in preserving social distinctions because "demonstrating a precise awareness of the [letter] writer's and reader's relative positions within the social hierarchy" was crucial to polite epistolary exchange.[71]

Concerns about class and decorous familiarity apparent in didactic texts also appear in the imaginative works from the period. Teaching by fictional example, novels, Clifford Siskin reminds us, acted as "conduct books of the most sophisticated kind" throughout the nineteenth century.[72] Many novels show familiarity's possibilities and pitfalls, suggesting that the dynamics of familiarity are an underrecognized crux of Romantic-era fiction. For instance, in Jane Austen's *Emma*, the title character's (mis)reading of the society in Highbury depends on her interpretations of familiarity; for Emma, the most obvious sign of Mrs. Elton's crassness is her inappropriately familiar behavior with those she barely knows.[73] Fears of overfamiliarity shape moral and social navigation in *Mansfield Park*, too; the danger of performing *Lovers' Vows* arises not only from the play's representation of illicit love but also from "the *more* than intimacy—the familiarity" with unsuitable male acquaintances of a lower socioeconomic status that the need for additional actors will invite.[74] While familiarity posed a threat if applied too liberally, novels also demonstrated how it could promote affection. *Pride and Prejudice*'s Charlotte Lucas recognizes love behind Darcy's familiarity, commenting, "My dear Eliza he must be in love with you, or he would never have called on us in this familiar way."[75] Beyond the marriage plot, other subgenres of the novel also focused on familiarity. One of the "things" that William Godwin explores in *Things as They Are; or, The Adventures of Caleb Williams* is the catastrophic consequences of familiarity gone wrong. Caleb acknowledges that his cross-class familiar relationship with Falkland pushed the bounds of propriety until there was no going back: "The longer this humble familiarity on my part had continued, the more effort it would require to suppress it."[76] Caleb's insatiable curiosity about Falkland's murderous past is fueled by their growing familiarity. Relatedly, Tyrell's suddenly shifting "affableness and familiarity" makes him especially volatile and frightening: "When his subjects, encouraged by his familiarity, had discarded their precaution, the wayward fit would seize him . . . and a quarrel of a straw immediately ensue[d] with the first man whose face he did not like."[77] Across genres, readers encountered examples of familiarity's social importance and its dangerous instability.

FAMILIARITY FOR SALE

The period's dynamic print culture contributed to the rising demand for literary works that thematized familiarity, as in Austen's and Godwin's novels, and also works that seemed to reveal intimate details about authors' lives, as in Gunning's novel. Three interrelated factors at the end of the eighteenth century shifted relationships between authors' private lives, their texts, and their readers. First, technological and legal changes in the literary marketplace created the conditions that circulated public and private information more widely and rapidly than ever before. An explosion of old and new reading material was available at lower prices to a growing mass readership.[78] Improved methods for papermaking and printing led to unprecedented print production. By the beginning of the nineteenth century wove paper largely replaced laid paper, and inventions like the Fourdrinier papermaking machine cut the time and human labor needed for paper manufacturing. More publishers used stereotype plates for popular works, which minimized typesetting costs for reprinting.[79] Publishers' bindings and novel technologies for producing illustrations put new emphasis on the mass-market, physical aspects of texts, while better transit capabilities and the postal service disseminated print from major urban centers like London and Edinburgh throughout the United Kingdom and its colonies.[80] News traveled fast in the Romantic period, and what qualified as "news" changed with equal rapidity.

Authors like Coleridge and Wordsworth worried not only about gossiping texts but also about how many people read them. Though offering different versions of the growth of print culture in the late eighteenth and early nineteenth centuries, scholars such as Jon Klancher, Deidre Lynch, H. J. Jackson, Patrick Brantlinger, and William St Clair have all noted the marked increase in numbers of both texts and readers.[81] As one commentator put it in 1829, "[A] great revolution there has been, from nobody's reading any thing, to everybody's reading all things."[82] The population growth of England and Scotland throughout the eighteenth century corresponded to an equally impressive boom in literacy; "a conservative estimate would suggest two million new readers over the course of the century."[83] David Allan's study of libraries in Georgian England equates the large number of commercial book-lending institutions with increased access to books and literacy, with more than two hundred active book lenders in London alone from the eighteenth century through the reign of George IV.[84] Ina Ferris's related work on rural book clubs proves that widespread reading and the sociability it encouraged extended beyond the metropolis.[85] Whether growing numbers of readers led to more print or the growth of reading materials spurred widespread reading, it is clear that throughout the period, both reading audiences and the availability of texts expanded exponentially.

A second factor that shifted Romantic-era author-reader relations was the growth of genres connected to private information. Both the type and sheer amount of available material, particularly periodicals, newspapers, and other forms of cheap print, differentiates the realm of late eighteenth-century print publicity from earlier forms of public exposure. The end of the eighteenth century witnessed the popular rise of gossip columns, fashion reporting, personal familiar essays, and crim. con. columns that revealed the latest lawsuits arising from adultery. Readers were titillated by tête-à-têtes in the pages of *Town and Country* and salacious courtesans' memoirs.[86] The public turned to silver-fork novels that claimed to give them access to the social habits and bad behavior of the upper classes and, much like romans à clef, invited readers to identify the real characters behind their fictional counterparts. These genres met the growing demand for the type of familiar information previously reserved for, to recall Gunning, one's "*dear friends.*" Though Coleridge grumbled about living in an "age of literary and political GOSSIPING," many authors, like Gunning, engaged directly the gossip surrounding them.[87]

But writing about one's self, while often lucrative, was not necessarily considered literary. According to Robert Southey, life writing had become the mundane expectation of the marketplace: "[B]ooksellers, public lecturers, pickpockets, and poets, [all] become autobiographers."[88] The trend had become so marked that in 1823 a contributor to *Blackwood's Edinburgh Magazine* wrote, "This is confessedly the age of confession,—the era of individuality."[89] In particular, Jean-Jacques Rousseau's *Confessions* marked a turn toward unabashed autobiography. According to Rousseau, "nothing," not even the fact that he urinated in a neighbor's cooking pot as a child, would "remain hidden or obscure."[90] Similarly, Samuel Johnson argued for the type of truthful biography found in his *Lives of the Poets*, where he notably commented on Richard Savage's drunkenness and laziness. Johnson's equally detailed revelations about Alexander Pope, including the suggestion that Pope's "weakness made it very difficult for him to be clean," made the poet's cleanliness as much of a concern as his literary craft.[91] Johnson's style decisively shifted the genre of biography away from panegyric, and after his death the unflinching honesty that he practiced was applied to him. James Boswell's anecdotal and at times unflattering biography of Johnson demonstrates that by the end of the eighteenth century all aspects of authors' private lives were considered (at least by some) to be appropriate and relevant to reveal. Importantly, "the age of confession" influenced a variety of genres and the ways readers approached them. Readers frequently mined works of imaginative literature—from Gunning's *The Packet* to Byron's *Childe Harold's Pilgrimage*—for biographical details about authors and their contemporaries.

A third, related element of the literary marketplace that made familiarity's limits particularly pressing in the period was the general explosion of consumerism. Theoretical concerns about sympathy, class, and gender that preoccupied Romantic readers and writers alike dovetailed with concrete monetary matters. Familiarity was not just an abstract cultural or literary value but also a commodity sold to voracious readers; authors' personal lives were on offer as one of the most lucrative products on the market. Fears that rapacious readers bought and read the wrong sort of literature reflected larger anxieties about commercialization. Wordsworth's famous invective against "sickly and stupid German Tragedies" in the Preface to *Lyrical Ballads* offers just one example of contemporary ideas about the commercialized literary marketplace—a marketplace worryingly susceptible to the tastes of women.[92] From Byron's complaint "That taste is gone, that fame is but a lottery, / Drawn by the blue-coat misses of a coterie" to Southey's belief that women who read literary annuals in the 1820s had killed the market for poetry, the supposed degradation of literature and a corresponding desire for familiarity was often laid at the feet of female consumers.[93] As such, gendered debates about moral and literary standards often returned to consumerism's worrying influence on both, with Coleridge disparaging the "Overbalance of the Commercial Spirit" that characterized the age.[94] This trend manifested itself in what Coleridge described in *Lay Sermons* as a "degrading appetite for scandal and personal defamation"—the same leering, peering tendencies of the public that Wordsworth criticized a year earlier in *A Letter to a Friend of Robert Burns*.[95]

While monetary motivations might vulgarize literature, even the most commercialized works could facilitate connections between authors and readers as well as between readers. Thus, semi-autobiographical works like those addressed throughout *The Limits of Familiarity* were both products of an expanding commercialized and depersonalized public sphere and a possible remedy to it. The growth of urban centers at the end of the century created cities populated by strangers—something Wordsworth notes in book 7 of *The Prelude*:

> Above all, one thought
> Baffled my understanding, how men lived
> Even next-door neighbours, as we say, yet still
> Strangers, and knowing not each other's names.[96]

Hazlitt voices a similar sentiment in his later essay "On Londoners and Country People." "It is a strange state of society (such as that in London)," he observes, "where a man does not know his next-door neighbour."[97] Information about public figures and authors helped offset this impersonality and anonymity. Oftentimes, familiar social relationships were founded not on local, personal gossip but on shared interests articulated in the public sphere of print. Seemingly anticipating Benedict Anderson's work on imagined communities and print capitalism, Hazlitt explains that "a community of ideas and knowledge (rather than local proximity) is the bond of society and good-fellowship."[98] Public figures and well-known authors "provid[ed] a topic about which anyone could take a view" so that, according to Mole, they "structured social intercourse and supplied a ligament of group identity."[99] This group identity was largely enabled by the explosion of print. Because, as Nicola Parsons has convincingly argued, printed "gossip is a participatory discourse, it creates a bond of intimacy between those who engage in its process."[100] The Romantic period gave rise to public, printed gossip focused on authors. In other words, feeling pride at "being called as it were into familiarity" with an author connected readers both to that author and to other readers.[101]

In his examination of fictional characters, David Brewer outlines how "imaginative expansion"—"an umbrella term of an array of reading practices in eighteenth-century Britain by which the [fictional] characters in broadly successful texts were treated as if they were both fundamentally incomplete and the common property of all"—created virtual communities of readers.[102] In the mid-eighteenth century these virtual communities arose from a "devotion to beloved characters, rather than authorial voice."[103] However, the Romantic period witnessed readers' striking insistence on the overlap between authors and their characters. Readers saw Childe Harold as Byron, *Glenarvon*'s Calantha Avondale as Lady Caroline Lamb, and *Liber Amoris*'s "H." as Hazlitt. Authors in the Romantic period, then, came to serve a similar function as the community-building fictional characters of the eighteenth century. They provoked, if not always devotion, then at least a desire for more that Brewer recognizes as a touchstone of imaginative expansion. Readers' refusal to limit their biographical interpretations to (auto)biographical texts effectively turned authors into characters, making them and their lives common public property, even at a time when "the very idea of the commons, whether real or metaphorical, seemed increasingly untenable."[104] From the perspective of authorial characters as commons, Wordsworth's complaints about the public invading domestic life read like unsuccessful attempts at enclosure. Virtual communities formed around authors and offered common ground for sociability as well as exploitation.

Despite the potential of literary works to foster feelings of familiarity between authors and readers and between groups of readers, the prospect of commercial exploitation loomed. Readers' desire to feel familiar with authors was colored by equally strong concerns that authors, publishers, and editors preyed on this desire in order to further profits. In the context of a commercial, industrial marketplace, authors' efforts to establish familiar relationships with readers could be seen as little more than an empty marketing strategy. Indeed, one of the most poignant effects of the expansion of the reading public was the effacement of the lingering remnants of eighteenth-century coterie author-reader relationships. No longer dependent on a single patron or circle of readers, Romantic authors were faced with numerous, nameless readers. Under these evolving market conditions, publishers, editors, and authors had to take new pains to present their familiarity with readers as personal rather than strictly commercial.

Authors most successful at evoking their readers' feelings of familiarity and counteracting the vulgarity of the literary marketplace shared personal information obliquely. They remained partially, tantalizingly hidden to readers. Describing intimacy, Lauren Berlant has noted the importance of incompleteness in promoting emotional closeness: "To intimate is to communicate with the sparest of signs and gestures, and at its root intimacy has the quality of eloquence and brevity."[105] Intimacy arises from the ability to intuit without being directly told—the idea that those most familiar with us "just know" what we're thinking. Similarly, literary familiarity relies on partial revelations. Though speaking of fiction, Deidre Lynch's comments about eighteenth-century characterization apply here, for "the fleshing out" of autobiographical figures similarly involves "the fine line between the more and the less" and "the difference between enough and too much." Lynch's explanation of the necessity of "deferring complete explication" in the creation of round characters attests to the importance of implication over detailed information.[106] Roundness is crucial for semi-autobiographical characters, too, and sympathetic responses to familiarity in literary works often depended on the *absence* of detail, thus giving readers room for the type of imaginative expansion that Brewer associates with eighteenth-century fictional characters. However, not all authors had the same opportunity to withhold information; by the time Gunning wrote her first novel, much of her private life had already been exposed in detail. Authors like Gunning faced problems of gauging how much more private information to share with readers and what literary strategies to employ. As I show in the following chapters, assessments of familiarity in Romantic-era literature were as much about the strategies of autobiographical revelation as they were about potentially overfamiliar content. In her work on eighteenth-century privacy, Patricia Meyer Spacks notes that "the preservation of privacy as a mode of self-protection depends less on the nature than on the tactics of revelation."[107] Importantly, these tactics were not equally available to all authors and not equally effective across genres. William Hazlitt's intertexual, revelatory style in his novel *Liber Amoris; Or, the New Pygmalion* was received rather differently than Byron's in his poem *Childe Harold's Pilgrimage*. This book strives to understand how the line between enough and too much familiarity was applied—often unevenly—to different genres and writers of different classes and genders.

THE CASES FOR FAMILIARITY

The case studies in my five chapters reveal that evoking familiar relationships with readers was a difficult task that required the balancing of seemingly conflicting expectations: of marketplace conventions and authorial originality, of a mass reading public and a coterie audience, of innovativeness and repetition, of sharing and exhibitionism. This book begins by detailing how philosophical concerns about sensibility informed late eighteenth-century discourses about repetitive, familiar modes of emotional expression in literature. It ends by arguing that the material forms that texts took shaped how readers and critics interpreted literary expressions of familiarity. In pairing literary analysis with both published and archival evidence of reception, my work attempts to model how dominant forces in the Romantic literary field—like familiarity—might productively be explored through a methodology that brings together threads of formalism, book history, and literary history.

Understanding how and why some authors' evocations of familiarity failed to attract readers' and critics' sympathy brings to the fore how the desire to feel close to contemporary authors was, to borrow from Lynch, "haunted by the spirit of mass consumption" and the associations of vulgarity and banality that frequently accompanied it.[108] While the works presented here all had reasonable market success, many were, like Gunning's novels, largely ridiculed as embarrassingly forthright, repetitive, or financially motivated. Readers devoured them, drawn by the autobiographical information that they purportedly revealed, but often readers (and, even more often, critics) were also disgusted by the overfamiliarity that the works represented. Critical responses to authorial overfamiliarity are important, for they depict the Romantic literary field with more accuracy than if we consider in isolation authors like Byron, who were lauded for calling readers "into familiarity."[109] As Bourdieu suggests, "The attacks that are suffered—can be used as the criterion establishing that a work belongs to the field of position-takings and its author to the field of positions."[110] In the railings against Charlotte Smith's repetitiveness, Lady Caroline Lamb's indecency, Hazlitt's exhibitionism, or literary annuals' derivativeness, the historical literary field takes shape, revealing that aesthetic evaluation in the Romantic period partly depended on the gendered and classed charges of familiarity.

Chapter 1 analyzes connections between familiarity, sincerity, and repetition in Charlotte Smith's *Elegiac Sonnets*. Smith's melancholy sonnets, many of which conformed to familiar tropes of sentimental suffering, appealed to a wide audience and went through numerous, expanded editions. However, some accused Smith's sonnets of borrowed banality, and she was charged with, in Smith's words, "*feigning* sorrow" for financial gain.[111] Answering charges that she revealed too much about her life while borrowing too heavily from other authors, Smith used her prefaces, notes, and the sonnets that she added to subsequent editions of *Elegiac Sonnets* to justify the authenticity of her familiar language and her autobiographical style. Smith's claims prefigure key statements about literary repetition by Coleridge and Wordsworth. I demonstrate how Smith, like Wordsworth in "Essays Upon Epitaphs" and *Lyrical Ballads*, theorizes the affective potential of repetitive language, which, according to Wordsworth, might outwardly seem "too familiar."[112] Smith's and Wordsworth's claims that familiar language signals sincerity mark Romantic-era struggles to establish an authentic, autobiographical style—a style that was both innovative and reassuringly familiar. My research looks beyond Smith's and Wordsworth's poetic practice to reveal connections between both poets' theoretical and moral thinking about repetition, familiarity, and emotional attachment. The chapter recognizes Smith as a poetic theorist rather than merely a practitioner.

The second chapter examines the poetic strategies that Byron uses to encourage his readers' feelings of familiarity as well as readers' and critics' reactions to these strategies. After examining Byron's own poetics of familiarity in *Childe Harold's Pilgrimage* and the Turkish Tales, the chapter turns to Byron's reception history, particularly the fan mail written to him. The similar sentiments and rhetoric in Byron's fan letters suggest that his literary style encouraged not only readers' feelings of familiarity but also their specific modes of familiar epistolary address. Notably, fans excuse their presumptive familiarity with Byron by pointing to his poetry. While fans flocked to Byron, contemporary reviews reveal uneasiness about his familiar style and his sway over the public. This uneasiness, I show, is often framed in the language of moral philosophy. The chapter argues that concerns about Byron's celebrity were not a general response to the burgeoning culture of celebrity, as previous scholars have posited, but rather a more abstract fear that Byron destabilized theories of sympathetic connection and its material manifestations.

Looking to Byron's biggest fan turned lover, chapter 3 considers Lady Caroline Lamb, with whom Byron had a disastrous affair in 1812. The reception of her infamously autobiographical novel *Glenarvon* (1816) demonstrates how notions of gendered propriety determined familiarity's proper limits. The chapter challenges pervasive beliefs about Lamb's narrow literary talents and her indebtedness to Byron, and I contend that her gender and aristocratic status, rather than *Glenarvon*'s supposed aesthetic weakness, provoked its negative critical reception. Drawing on unpublished archival material, I demonstrate that Regency readers thought that *Glenarvon* was well written and that its problems arose specifically from its exhibitionist overfamiliarity. The chapter analyzes *Glenarvon*'s autobiographical strategies and Lamb's attacks on the hypocritical gendered standards that delineated decorous familiarity in society and in print. The end of the chapter turns to Lamb's later career, and I show how she attempted to combat her poor public reputation that had become all too familiar—both banally predictable and indecorous.

Chapter 4 reveals that familiarity was not only a matter of personal morality but also one of philosophical import. Hazlitt was one of the period's most articulate theorists of familiarity. However, his autobiographical novel *Liber Amoris* (1823) goes against Hazlitt's own standards of proper familiarity. As with Lamb, Hazlitt's depiction of failed romance simultaneously intrigued and offended his contemporaries, and this chapter pinpoints why nineteenth-century readers found *Liber Amoris* to be, in the words of Henry Crabb Robinson, "disgusting . . . nauseous and revolting."[113] My work identifies the novel's connections to Adam Smith's *The Theory of Moral Sentiments* and Hazlitt's own ideas about familiarity detailed in his familiar essays from *Table-Talk* and *The Plain Speaker*. Hazlitt's essays about familiarity frequently allude to Smith, whose theories explore familiarity's importance for sympathy. Reading *Liber Amoris* in the context of Smith's theories of sympathy and Hazlitt's own ideas about familiarity clarifies why readers found the novel so objectionable, and the chapter presents new connections between the novel, Hazlitt's essays, and moral philosophy.

My final chapter argues that, by commercializing the culture of coterie manuscript exchange, the publishers of literary annuals in the 1820s and 1830s sought to place readers on familiar terms not only with famous contributors but also with sociable practices associated with manuscript albums. In the case of the annuals, familiarity was closely aligned with the volumes' physical, mass-produced forms. I show that printed literary annuals' manuscript-like elements—especially album verses that emphasized handwriting and facsimiles of authors' signatures—were essential to the medium's development and initial popularity. However, what I call the printed annuals' "manuscript ethos" became increasingly ineffective at simulating album culture and its affective, interpersonal associations. I suggest that annuals began to fail critically and commercially in the 1830s as they seemed increasingly common and banally familiar.

By addressing a variety of authors writing in diverse genres—sonnets, prose treatises, prefaces, long lyrics, semi-autobiographical fiction, familiar essays, and poetry found in literary annuals—I demonstrate how fears about familiarity's limits explicitly and implicitly shaped the content of Romantic texts and, just as important, their reading. There are many Romantic-era works that push the limits of familiarity—Godwin's *Memoirs of the Author of "A Vindication of the Rights of Woman,"* for instance, comes to mind. However, here I intentionally avoid works that fall under the category of "life writing" (such as memoir and biography) or works of nonautobiographical fiction (like Austen's or Godwin's novels mentioned above). Rather, I have chosen works that resist categorization—often with authors promoting their works' fictiveness and readers insisting on its grounding in an author's life. Studying imaginative works inflected with autobiographic elements creates a unique tension between writers and readers, between authors and their characters, and between different genres. The texts I study sit uneasily at the nexus of developing genre conventions and strategies for their reading. The contested zone of familiarity was made more volatile by Romantic-era genres like the familiar essay and album verse that themselves effaced distinctions between personal and public, private and print.

The case studies in this book, though thoroughly grounded in the Romantic period, gesture forward, and the questions that *The Limits of Familiarity* asks about how Romantic-era authors fostered feelings of familiarity encourage us to reflect on the conditions of our own historical moment, concerned as it is with celebrity culture and public displays of private life. This book offers a historical perspective on seemingly recent issues like "oversharing" and the phenomenon of "TMI" (too much information) that preoccupy both public and private discourse. Brian Glavey's recent work on post-WWII and contemporary American poetry evidences a growing scholarly interest in analyzing (and, by extension, historicizing) oversharing. For instance, Glavey argues that James Schuyler's "treatment of sexuality [in 'The Morning of the Poem'] refuses to adopt the rhetoric of confession, operating instead according to a nonmoralizing poetics of oversharing."[114] A similar lack of moralization characterizes many Romantic-era texts that cross the line into overfamiliarity; as we shall see, none of the authors I study convey a sense of guilt about sharing their lives publicly. One thing that makes oversharing and overfamiliarity in literature so striking and potentially uncomfortable is authors' refusal to apologize for testing the boundaries of acceptability. In doing so, their overfamiliarity implicitly challenges the validity of those boundaries, thereby destabilizing conventions of both literariness and sociability. Fears about destabilization shaped debates about familiarity in the Romantic era and mirror current discourse.

Debates about familiarity and overfamiliarity, concerns about how to evoke closeness without provoking disgust, and questions about new modes of autobiographical expression are as pressing now as they were in the Romantic period. Numerous twenty-first-century pundits on parenting, professionalism, and romance offer advice, criticism, and much hand-wringing about people's seeming disregard for traditional social boundaries.[115] For instance, an episode of the *New Yorker*'s *Outloud* podcast, "Memoir in the Age of T.M.I.," considers how current modes of self-exposure might change the contemporary literary landscape, and popular outlets from the *Economist* to *Psychology Today* have referred to ours as the "age of oversharing."[116] Yet *The Limits of Familiarity* shows that the age of oversharing and the age of TMI are rooted in the age of Romanticism—an age that, like ours, struggled with new technologies of textual dissemination, a shifting public sphere, and audiences with a sense of entitlement to and a voracious appetite for the lives of public figures. The story that this book tells clarifies the origins of debates that now seem a familiar part of daily life in the twenty-first century, and I reveal that Romantic authors' attempts to establish familiar ties with readers prefigure today's preoccupation with the line between telling all and telling all too much.

1

CHARLOTTE SMITH, WILLIAM WORDSWORTH, AND THE PROBLEMS OF READING FAMILIARITY

I am unhappily exempt from the suspicion of *feigning* sorrow for an opportunity of shewing the pathos with which it can be described—a suspicion that has given rise to much ridicule, and many invidious remarks.

—Charlotte Smith, Preface to vol. II of *Elegiac Sonnets**

WILLIAM WORDSWORTH CHAMPIONED the affective potential of literary familiarity—a style employing common language to describe everyday subjects. Yet Wordsworth also recognized that his new style carried risks. In the Advertisement for the 1798 edition of *Lyrical Ballads* Wordsworth anticipates the criticism the volume might face: "It will perhaps appear to them ['readers of superior judgment'], that wishing to avoid the prevalent fault of the day, the author has sometimes descended too low, and that many of his expressions are too familiar, and not of sufficient dignity."[1] On the one hand, Wordsworth acknowledges that his familiar expressions might seem banal and repetitive or, worse, vulgar and unpoetical. On the other hand, he claims that such expressions could convey "human passions, human characters, and human incidents" with a sincerity unattainable in what Wordsworth saw as the rigid style of earlier eighteenth-century poetry.[2]

In his later "Essays Upon Epitaphs" Wordsworth goes further, framing familiarity as a connective mode that allows both poetry and gravestones to reveal human nature and, in doing so, foster readers' sympathy. According to Wordsworth, attentive readers could see the "substance of individual truth" behind familiar phrases and boilerplate language.[3] Still, such expressions must be sincere to have power, for, as he explains, "[W]hen a Man is treating an interesting subject . . . no faults have such a killing power as those which prove that he is not in earnest, that he is acting a part, has leisure for affectation."[4] For Wordsworth, feigned emotion not only produces bad poetry and bad epitaphs but also "shocks the moral sense."[5] In other words, he suggests that a familiar style had both moral and aesthetic implications.

Wordsworth's contemporaries shared his concerns about familiarity's moral and literary limits. As much as Coleridge celebrated Wordsworth's ability to combine "the sense of novelty and freshness, with old and familiar objects," he also bemoaned "the film of familiarity" that made people less sympathetic and life less affecting.[6] Indeed, a moral crux of Coleridge's "Fears in Solitude" is his frustration that war reporting desensitized readers. He lamented that those who "would groan to see a child / Pull off an insect's wing, all read of war, / The best amusement for our morning-meal!"[7] Though cut from a different political cloth than Coleridge and Wordsworth, Edmund Burke was equally invested in the object of one's sympathy and the power of familiarity to dampen or distract it. In *A Philosophical Enquiry into the Origin of Our Ideas of the Sublime and Beautiful* Burke claims that "it is absolutely necessary" that one's passion "not be exerted in those things which a daily and vulgar use have brought into a stale unaffecting familiarity."[8] Burke elaborates, "Knowledge and acquaintance make the most striking causes affect but little."[9] Overexposure and familiarity, Burke believed, blunted emotional responses and undermined the beautiful and the sublime alike. Exerting one's passions on the wrong things—on familiar or vulgar things—revealed one's lack of taste and miscalibrated moral sentiments. From such a perspective, the entire project of *Lyrical Ballads* was misguided. The ideological differences between Burke's dismissal of familiarity and Wordsworth's appreciation of it reflect larger cultural debates about the social and literary role of familiarity. Whereas Burke rejects familiarity for its tendency to dull the sublime, Wordsworth recuperates familiarity for its revelatory and sympathetic potential.[10] But for neither man was familiarity as fraught as it was for women writers.

Well before Wordsworth made his famous claims about the power of familiar language and common poetic subjects, Charlotte Smith argued for a poetic style in which sincerity revealed itself through familiar topics and repetition. For instance, Smith celebrates the familiar in her long political poem *The Emigrants* (1793). Anticipating Coleridge's praise for Wordsworth's familiar style, Smith's opening dedication to William Cowper commends the "force, clearness, and sublimity" of *The Task* and celebrates "the felicity, almost peculiar to [Cowper's] genius, of giving to the most familiar objects dignity and effect."[11] Smith's comments about the familiar came when she herself had already been a familiar public figure for almost a decade; the first edition of *Elegiac Sonnets* appeared in 1784. Smith was acutely aware of the profitable possibilities and potential pitfalls of the familiar. Sharing her sorrows with readers in sentimental sonnets and offering increasingly specific clues about the origins of her pain in poems, paratexts, and novels, Smith risked becoming an overly familiar poetic object without "dignity or effect." Throughout her career, but especially in *Elegiac Sonnets*, Smith attempted to overcome Coleridge's "film of familiarity" and the associations of vulgarity in Burke's "unaffecting familiarity" by asking her readers to recognize authenticity behind her seeming emotional monotony. In this way, her work prefigures Wordsworth's later celebrations of repetition, common language, and the "monotonous language of sorrow."[12] However, her reception history reveals how Romantic-era perceptions of monotony and authorial sincerity were inflected by an author's gender.

While scholarship on Smith's poetry often points to its autobiographical ambiguity, this chapter argues that details of Smith's difficult life were common knowledge by the 1790s. Even in her political poem *The Emigrants*, Smith melds the mortifications of those fleeing the violence in revolutionary France with autobiographical references to "the o'erwhelming wrongs, / That have for ten long years been heap'd on me!"[13] As I explain below, most readers in 1793 would have recognized Smith's allusion in these lines to the ongoing litigation surrounding her father-in-law's will. As Smith's career advanced and as editions of *Elegiac Sonnets* were revised and expanded, Romantic-era readers encountered a wealth of information about Smith, so that in her case, familiarity came to signal what would now be termed *oversharing*—a form of exhibitionism arising from too much familiarity with too wide an audience. Her familiarity also produced a repetitive literary strategy that could connect and comfort readers or distance and disgust them. Critics' growing skepticism about the authenticity of Smith's sorrow, which her harshest readers thought a bathetic caricature of the archetypal sentimental woman, points to larger political anxieties about testimony and truth—anxieties intensified by women's relative lack of legal and literary authority.

Though conventionally viewed as a poetic practitioner rather than a poetic theorist, Smith deserves a place beside authors of famous Romantic-era treatises about poetry and language. This chapter shows, first, that *Elegiac Sonnets* attempts to align contrasting ideas of familiarity and, second, that Smith's works and reception history exemplify the literary, cultural, and moral problems of familiarity at the end of the eighteenth century, particularly in the tense political climate of the 1790s. Reading Smith and, in my final section, Wordsworth, this chapter reveals Romanticism's conflicted, gendered relationships between personal despair and published texts, between authorial success and aesthetic originality, and between authenticity and exhibitionism. Like Wordsworth, Smith sought to establish an autobiographical poetic style that was both authentically original in its emotional expressiveness and reassuringly familiar in its indebtedness to previous poets.

Because Romantic writers and readers alike had difficulty defining familiarity's literary and cultural limits, what the word *familiarity* meant throughout the period and in different contexts shifted. Familiarity could either be soothing and reliable or boring and repetitive; it could enable polite sociability or, if overextended, lead to reckless impropriety. Within one's social circle, familiarity tempered social awkwardness. However, in the broader world, familiarity risked vulgarity, and it could exacerbate the very social awkwardness it was meant to counteract if extended indiscriminately to too many people, particularly those of disparate classes. As Smith's career progressed alongside revolution and reactionary conservatism, tensions about familiarity's social, political, and literary importance grew. Dangerously overfamiliar relations between authors and readers and between different classes and groups suggested the loose morals of libertinism and the radicalism of Jacobin politics. As Burke's comments above indicate, habitual exposure could make familiar people, things, or literature stale, and in a volatile political context, misplaced familiarity could undermine distinctions between social classes and traditional hierarchies of power. Opposing senses of *familiarity* reveal that what could be welcoming and powerfully emotive in some cases could quickly become unaffecting and uncouth in others.

Smith negotiated these conflicting senses of familiarity throughout her career. *Elegiac Sonnets* was wildly popular at the end of the eighteenth century and was integral to the sonnet revival in England.[14] However, by the time the sixth edition of *Elegiac Sonnets* appeared in 1792, some readers believed that Smith was overly familiar on multiple fronts.[15] She was criticized for "*feigning* sorrow" for financial gain.[16] Critics thought the emotional and stylistic repetitiveness of *Elegiac Sonnets* revealed the type of affectation that Wordsworth would later decry in "Essays Upon Epitaphs," and Smith was accused of copying other writers as well as her own works. She was also attacked for her increasingly familiar relationship with the public because prefaces to new editions of *Elegiac Sonnets* and the autobiographical elements of her novels revealed Smith's personal life in progressively explicit terms.

This chapter begins by examining what one critic called Smith's "often-repeated repetition."[17] Smith's reliance on sentimental tropes and intertextual strategies inured some readers almost to the point of indifference. In short, it became unclear whether what one reviewer termed Smith's "wild melody of elegiac woe" should evoke sympathy or ridicule, and Smith's prefaces combat accusations of repetitiveness, insincerity, and vulgar familiarity.[18] Examining the negative responses that Smith received, I consider how the gender dynamics and historical context of the late eighteenth century—including a rapidly changing literary marketplace, fears of revolution, and debates about testimony and circumstantial evidence—shaped reactions to her pleas of authorial sincerity.

From the courtroom to the coffeehouse and from Parliament to the private library, Romantic readers were interested in, but inclined to question, authors' self-justifications, and I suggest that negative reactions to Smith's angry, detailed prefatory defenses should be read in the revolutionary context of the 1790s and debates about professional (female) authorship. I conclude by considering how the ideas about sincerity and familiar language for which Wordsworth is often celebrated are strikingly similar to the literary strategies for which Smith was condemned.

Focusing on Smith, this chapter challenges the uniqueness of Wordsworth's literary strategies and his defenses of them. Jacqueline Labbe, an astute critic of the relationship between Smith and Wordsworth, observes that at the turn of the century, "*Lyrical Ballads, with a Few Other Poems* . . . joins a debate rather than initiat[es] one."[19] More than a decade after Labbe's important work, there is still much to be done to understand Smith's role in that debate and to glean how familiarity helped define its contours. Examining the role of repetition in assigning familiarity's opposing valences, I interrogate why Wordsworth has been seen, in Matthew Arnold's words, as the poet who "make[s] us feel," while Smith has been faulted, in the words of her contemporary, as a poet who offers a "perpetual dun on pity."[20] Far more than Wordsworth, Smith deployed familiarity at her peril, and her career reveals the difficulty that Romantic authors, particularly women, had in negotiating familiarity's gendered expectations.

"A FREQUENT REPETITION": SMITH'S ECHOING STYLE

In comments mirroring the reviews of Elizabeth Gunning's semi-autobiographical novels that I addressed in this book's introduction, Anna Laetitia Barbauld claimed that Smith's "later publications would have been more pleasing, if the author, in the exertions of fancy, could have forgotten herself."[21] Smith knew the dangers of airing her problems publicly and repetitively. For instance, the preface to her novel *The Banished Man* (1794) acknowledges that "some Review" had "objected the too frequent allusion I made in it to my own circumstances."[22] A few years later the anti-Jacobin critic Robert Bisset noted that Smith's "own situation and private affairs" occupy "so much of her thoughts as to produce a frequent repetition of it under different forms to the public. . . . In her *Young Philosopher*, as in all her compositions . . . some of the most affecting parts are copies of what she has often drawn before."[23] Though more politically aligned with Smith, Mary Wollstonecraft was even more blunt, asserting that Smith "too frequently, and not very happily, copies."[24] Such assessments were compounded by the fact that

Smith reprinted sonnets from her novels in new editions of *Elegiac Sonnets* and borrowed images, phrases, and entire lines from fellow poets. Throughout her career, Smith was accused of copying from other writers, copying autobiographical versions of herself into her novels, and copying "affecting parts" from her oeuvre back into *Elegiac Sonnets* where they risked affecting readers little. Through their repetition, details of Smith's life—details traditionally reserved for one's familiar circle—became common knowledge, and the literary strategies she employed to share her life sometimes seemed derivative.

Aspects of Smith's life dovetailed with established literary tropes and archetypes of female suffering, which Smith frequently repeated. Judith Pascoe argues that throughout the multiple editions of *Elegiac Sonnets* "Smith evolved a poetic persona that shared much in common with the role women most commonly performed on stage, that of the tragic heroine."[25] Relatedly, Labbe observes, "In the sonnets, she appeals to her readers' familiarity with the roles women play, and writes poems accordingly: we see most often the distressed and needy woman, sometimes a romantic damsel, sometimes a devoted mother, sometimes a martyr to sensibility."[26] While Smith's association with familiar female roles gave readers an established framework through which to view her and allowed Smith to market herself accordingly, the predictability of her life and work veered toward Burke's "stale unaffecting familiarity."[27] She risked seeming unoriginal and, worse, insincere.

Drawing on sentimental archetypes, Smith's poetry challenges readers to determine who is speaking and whose emotions are being portrayed. Smith's multiple speakers and repetitive literary allusions blur lines between poet and lyric speaker and between sincere feelings and borrowed literary formations.[28] Adela Pinch has gone so far as to describe Smith's sonnets as "echo chambers, in which reverberate direct quotations, ideas, and tropes from English Poetry."[29] In many cases, though, it is Smith's own voice that echoes most loudly throughout *Elegiac Sonnets*, sometimes ventriloquized through other characters.[30] Much of *Elegiac Sonnets* seems to reflect Smith's autobiographical voice, yet, as Stuart Curran observes, when it "attained its final state in 1800, there were in all thirty-six poems in the collection distinguished as not being her personal expression."[31] For instance, Smith wrote four poems from Petrarch, one from Metastasio (an eighteenth-century Italian poet), and five poems voiced by Goethe's sentimental hero Werter.[32] Fusion between Smithian and fictional speakers intensifies in sonnets spoken by characters from Smith's own novels, such as "Supposed to have been written in America," voiced by Orlando Somerive from *The Old Manor House*. While *Elegiac Sonnets* is expressly dialogic, in practice, the multiple voices in the collection offer a chorus of Smith in a dynamic not unlike a pop star recording her own backing vocals. Romantic readers recognized Smith behind her speakers, foreshadowing, as we shall see in chapter 2, readers' insistence that Childe Harold's sorrows were, in fact, Byron's.

Smith's use of multiple voices aligns her with the ventriloquizing and intertextual tendencies of the sonnet sequence, yet her critical reception also reveals the deeply gendered stakes of such tendencies. Much in the way that familiarity could be both an asset and a liability, allusions, according to John Hollander, can be seen alternately as a "set of credentials" or "as props to the infirmities of unoriginality."[33] These alternative readings depended on the other (gendered) credentials a poet might have. Pascoe explains that the endnotes in Smith's *Beachy Head* display a "type of educational seal of approval" that it was just assumed many other male poets possessed.[34] This observation equally applies to *Elegiac Sonnets*, which from the third edition onward included notes identifying Smith's sources—a direct response to criticisms that she had plagiarized.

As a female poet, Smith struggled to show her familiarity with the canon without compromising her own originality. Though Michael Gamer argues that the "dual origins" of Smith's grief, "which are both experiential (personal) and aesthetic (impersonal),"[35] had a largely positive effect on Romantic-era readers, I recognize the interplay between personal and impersonal as a critical vulnerability—a vulnerability exacerbated by Smith's gender. In other words, Smith's ventriloquism, quotation, and intertextuality offered her a strategy for entering the male literary tradition while, at the same time, opening her to accusations of derivativeness. Fellow poet Anna Seward, for instance, criticized Smith's sonnets as "a mere flow of melancholy . . . full of notorious plagiarisms, barren of original ideas and poetical imagery."[36] Smith was caught in a double bind wherein the literariness of her work was used as evidence of hackneyed writing.

Smith's balancing of authenticity and repetition and of literary borrowing and plagiarism is most evident in her Werter-voiced sonnets. These five poems introduce two key themes that appear throughout the collection. First, the Werter sonnets place Smith solidly in a tradition of the sentimental hero—a popular type that she often deployed, though in this case male rather than female. Second, the Werter sonnets blur distinctions between fictional and autobiographical lyric speakers through intertextual allusions. References to mythology and literary quotations reverberate through *Elegiac Sonnets* regardless of speaker. "Supposed to be written by Werter," for instance, clusters allusions together:

> Like the poor maniac I linger here,
> Still haunt the scene where all my treasure lies;
> Still seek for flowers where only thorns appear,
> "And drink delicious poison from her eyes!"[37]

Beyond gesturing toward the Philomel myth through the reference to thorns, Smith also quotes Alexander Pope's "Eloisa to Abelard": "Still on that breast enamour'd let me lie, / Still drink delicious poison from thy eye."

However, Werter's speech is indebted to another poet: Charlotte Smith. "Supposed to be written by Werter" evokes two earlier poems in *Elegiac Sonnets*: the opening sonnet "The partial Muse has from my earliest hours" and "To hope," which feature Smith's autobiographical speaker. Both poems focus on painful images of thorns, so that evocations of Philomel in "Supposed to be written by Werter" also evoke Smith. Additionally, "The partial Muse has from my earliest hours" and "Supposed to be written by Werter" both point to Pope's "Eloisa to Abelard." Describing the pain that motivates her writing, Smith's autobiographical speaker laments, "Ah! then, how dear the Muse's favours cost / *If those paint sorrow best—who feel it most!*"[38] The third and fourth editions of *Elegiac Sonnets* highlight Smith's indebtedness to Pope by italicizing the borrowed line and adding "*(a)*" next to it to flag the corresponding endnote, which quotes the relevant lines from "Eloisa to Abelard."[39] Smith's ostensibly fictional speakers recycle the sentiments and literary allusions of her autobiographical speakers, so that the most important voice echoed throughout *Elegiac Sonnets* is Smith's own.

The three poems—"The partial Muse has from my earliest hours" and "To hope" (both voiced by a Smithian speaker) and "Supposed to be written by Werter"—are linked through shared connections to other sources. While these literary allusions point beyond Smith's volume, they also emphasize repetitions *within* it; this is especially the case with the first two editions of *Elegiac Sonnets*, before Smith added endnotes to record borrowed lines. Moreover, from the fifth edition onward, in-text endnote indicators disappear, shifting the emphasis from external intertextuality and back to the volume's internal intratextuality.[40] The most important common text, then, is neither the Philomel myth nor Pope's poem but Smith's own sonnets. In the Werter poems and throughout *Elegiac Sonnets*, Smith quotes herself quoting and alludes to herself alluding. Rather than see this repetition as a form of unoriginal, almost lazy copying, as Wollstonecraft and others did, I recognize Smith's repetition as an active canonizing practice wherein familiar phrases, tropes, and allusions signal both her authority and consistent emotional sincerity.

Smith's self-echoing is especially evident in two of the most strongly mirrored sonnets in the collection: "To the moon" and the third poem in the Werter sequence, "By the same. To the North Star." Though ostensibly representing distinct speakers, both sonnets feature a solitary, despondent figure seeking guidance in the night sky, and similar diction heightens the central image of each poem. "Fair, fav'rite planet!" in the Werter sonnet mirrors the "fair planet of the night" in the sonnet "To the moon."[41] Smith also repeats other images and phrases; "pale beam" (1), "shadow trembling in the stream" (3), and "floating clouds" (4) in "To the moon" become "bright beams" (1), "wild stream" (10), "trembling light" (11), and "swift clouds" (8) in "By the same. To the North Star." The similarities are so extensive that, in some ways, the latter poem reads as a revision of the earlier one. Notably both sonnets embrace death, and the trope of suicide here and throughout *Elegiac Sonnets* connects Smith's speakers. For example, in "To the North Star" Werter sees death as the only outlet: "So o'er my soul short rays of reason fly / Then fade:—and leave me to despair, and die!" (13–14). The punctuated anguish of this passage with its dashed caesura and exclamation mark aligns the poem with Smith's autobiographical speaker in "To the South Downs": "Ah! no!—when all, e'en Hope's last ray is gone, / There's no oblivion—but in death alone!"[42]

Connections between Smith, Werter, and her other speakers intensify in the second volume of *Elegiac Sonnets*, published in 1797; Smith's lament in the preface that circumstances "leave me with no hope but in the oblivion of the grave" echoes the many laments of her lyric speakers.[43] Like Coleridge's Ancient Mariner, Smith and her speakers are compelled to relive and retell, caught in a familiar narrative loop. Even in the first edition of *Elegiac Sonnets*, Smith's qualified claim that "Some very melancholy moments have been beguiled by expressing in verse the sensations those moments brought" invites readers to consider the moments that were not beguiled.[44] The alleviation that writing offers Smith seems so brief that poetry's anodyne properties appear almost inconsequential. Unlike other famous sonnet sequences, like that of Philip Sidney, which is shaped by the narrative thrust of Astrophil's desire for Stella, Smith's sonnets lack sequential force and instead offer a repetitive non-narrative of sorrow.[45]

While largely undermining a sense of narrative progression, Smith's repetition plays a crucial poetic and, I argue, theoretical role in the sonnets. Analyzing Smith's emotional iterativeness and literary debts, Gamer explains that "Smith's fondness for deep engagement not just with other poets but with her own verse" creates poems that "are at once self-conscious and self-referential."[46] That is, *Elegiac Sonnets* places familiar literary expressions and tropes alongside echoes and repetitions of Smith's *own* images and phrases. Smith uses the credentialing aspects of quotation and allusion to bolster her own authority, her own voice. Smith's literary strategies enact the type of self-canonization that has been more often associated with later female poets like Felicia Hemans and Letitia Elizabeth Landon.[47]

One example of this self-canonization appears in Smith's "The gossamer," published in the second volume of the sixth edition of *Elegiac Sonnets*. Smith weaves intertextuality into her description of the spider's gossamer, describing how "A thousand trembling orbs of lucid dew / Spangle the texture of the fairy loom."[48] Bethan Roberts notes that the poem's image of the "fairy loom" also "appears in

Smith's earlier sonnet 'To Mrs. ****,'" which laments that "Imagination how has lost her powers, / Nor will her fairy loom again essay / To dress Affliction in a robe of flowers."[49] Additionally, Smith's note to "The gossamer" cites another poem within *Elegiac Sonnets*: "The slender web of the field spider is again alluded to in Sonnet 77 ['To the insect of the gossamer']."[50] Here and elsewhere, Smith deploys familiar literary tropes and allusions, and, through repetition, she co-opts them to both participate in and bypass the literary tradition. Her allusions, quotations, and paraphrasing transform into self-quotation, so that she seems to be their originator. It is not unlike a Romantic-era version of a cover song played so much that it subsumes as its own the original's originality.

FROM FAMILIAR TO FORMULAIC

Some critics rebuked Smith for her repetitiveness. The *Critical Review*, for instance, observed that *Elegiac Sonnets* "contain[ed] a single sentiment."[51] Similarly, the *Lady's Magazine* praised Smith but also complained of "a want of variety in her images."[52] Seward famously described Smith's sonnets as "everlasting lamentables . . . made up of hackneyed scraps of dismality, with which her memory furnished her from our various poets. Never were poetical whipt syllabubs, in black glasses, so eagerly swallowed by the odd taste of the public."[53] The success of *Elegiac Sonnets* validates Seward's claims that readers "eagerly swallowed" what Smith wrote, familiar as it may have become later in her career.[54]

While critics' skepticism of Smith's repetition intensified, the final decades of the eighteenth century also saw numerous poems about or dedicated to Smith. Mostly by amateur or near-amateur poets beyond Smith's social circle, these sonnets point toward Romanticism's burgeoning fan culture and predate the sort of celebrity fandom typically associated with Byron, which I address in the next chapter. Take "Sonnet To Mrs. Smith on Reading Her Sonnets Lately Published" from the *European Magazine*. The author, "D.," praises the "plaintive eloquence" of Smith's poetry. Echoing Smith's sonnets, "D." claims that neither "time nor hope can heal" Smith's grief:

> Oh! could or fame, or friendship, aught impart
> To cure the cruel wounds thy peace has known
> For others sorrows, still thy tender heart
> Should softly melt;—but never for thine own!
> Till pitying all—and ev'n thy foes forgiven,
> *Thy candid spirit*—seeks its native heaven.[55]

Though presumably unknown to Smith, "D." asserts a familiar connection with her. In doing so, "D." aligns themself with "the few" readers who possess "sensibility of the heart" whom Smith addresses in her prefaces to *Elegiac Sonnets*.[56] Despite the sympathy and friendship that "D." offers, the poem ultimately reiterates what Smith's sonnets say: there is no lasting hope but in death. Yet it was this very lack of hope and the iterativeness of Smith's sonnets that critics found objectionable. Even those who appreciated Smith's sonnets recognized their repetitive nature, and another fan-authored sonnet by "T. B." urges Smith to "choose no more this sad ungenial theme."[57]

As Smith revised *Elegiac Sonnets*, she used her prefaces and poems to defend her increasingly predictable "ungenial theme." The preface to the sixth edition, for example, acknowledges her "apparent despondence, which, when it is observed for a long series of years, may look like affectation."[58] "I wrote mournfully," she explains, "because I was unhappy—And I have unfortunately no reason yet, though nine years have since elapsed, to *change my tone*."[59] Smith offers her repetitiveness as a sign of her sincerity.

The sonnets themselves argue that repetitive emotions are sincere emotions—a point which, I show in my final section, Wordsworth also makes. Smith suggests that sincerity is naturally repetitive by declaring her inability to be *in*sincere. "To Fancy" reveals Smith's failure to imagine herself beyond sorrow:

> Thee, Queen of Shadows!—shall I still invoke,
>   Still love the scenes thy sportive pencil drew,
> When on mine eyes the early radiance broke
>   Which shew'd the beauteous rather than the true!
> Alas! long since those glowing tints are dead[60]

Smith's appeals to fancy evidence not only her "murder'd Happiness" (8) but also her failed falsehood. The repetition of "still" in the opening lines indicates that this is not the first time she has invoked the "Queen of Shadows." Smith's rejection of the "false medium" of fancy (9) also distances her from professional authorship, and the poem's final lines denounce Smith's role as a professional poet. She concludes that she will no longer "seek perfection with a poet's eye, / Nor suffer anguish with a poet's heart!" (13–14). Praising the poet's unique ability to recognize beauty and feel intensely, Smith laments that she no longer has this power. However, abandoning fancy, Smith offers her readers recompense: sincerity. In doing so, Smith separates herself from the normative expectations of poetry, as Wordsworth later would. In the preface to *Lyrical Ballads*, Wordsworth asserts that his desire to write in "the language of men . . . has necessarily cut" him "off from a large portion of phrases and figures of speech which from father to son have long been regarded as the common inheritance of Poets."[61] Emphasizing his poetry's departure from traditional poetic diction, Wordsworth asserts the sincerity of his own common language. Similarly, Smith declares the authenticity of her monotonous melancholy strain by emphasizing her inability to write with a typical "poet's eye" or "poet's heart."

Throughout *Elegiac Sonnets* Smith repeats the idea that repetition reveals sincerity, and the personal apostrophes of some sonnets frame them as intimately confessional. Take "To Mrs. ****." Like "To Fancy," "To Mrs. ****" also denies fictionalized sentiments by calling attention to Smith's unfulfilled desire for them. Smith claims that she no longer "courts enchanting Fiction."[62] Reaching a rather dreary conclusion for a poet, she admits, "Imagination now has lost her powers."[63] By addressing her painful poem about artistic failure to the redacted name of a friend, Smith invites readers to see themselves as part of her inner circle. Smith's claims in the preface to the first two editions of *Elegiac Sonnets* that her poems "found their way into print" due to her friends' "partial indiscretion," presents her poems as personal pieces rather than poems intended for publication.[64] Even if exaggerated, the poems' supposedly private pedigree is important, for Smith could reveal her sorrows to a friend with candidness that might seem inappropriate for the public at large. Thus, poems like "To Mrs. ****" attempt to bypass improper, public overfamiliarity by highlighting their intimate origins. From this perspective, "To Mrs. ****" is confessional and even apologetic. The consistency of Smith's sorrows, the poem suggests, has made it impossible for her "wearied soul . . . to stray" beyond the doleful limits of her situation, despite her friend's urging.[65]

Not all readers believed the severity of Smith's distress or the appropriateness of her willingness to share it publicly. If we believe Burke's claim that "we have a degree of delight, and that no small one, in the real misfortunes and pains of others," then it seems logical that readers might feel betrayed when "real misfortunes" turn out to be fictional.[66] As the *Monthly Magazine* proclaimed in 1796, "Extreme sensibility, if real, is pitiable; if pretended, ridiculous."[67] In *Elegiac Sonnets*, Smith justifies the authenticity of her emotions and appeals to sympathetic readers in increasingly bold, defensive prefaces, and commentary on her publications drew attention to and expanded on the autobiographical information that she provided. Like opposing sides in a legal case, Smith and her critics attempted to sway readers about the correct way to interpret her sincerity based on the evidence before them.

SMITH'S "OFTEN-REPEATED REPETITION": AUTHORIAL INTENT AND PREFATORY DEFENSES

Smith's impassioned defenses against accusations of her feigned sorrow coincided with widespread debates about (false) sensibility and emotional contagion. In 1782, two years before *Elegiac Sonnets* first appeared, Hannah More summarized the period's conflicting ideas about sensibility by celebrating its "exclamations, tender tones, fond tears, / And all the graceful drapery" while also acknowledging the unsettling possibility that "These lovely symbols may be counterfeit."[68] This potential for counterfeit emotions preoccupied readers and writers, and Smith's work and reception history raise pressing questions: How can one write in the same mode without becoming predictable? And how can one live one's life and express one's experience authentically when that life and that experience sound like everyone else's?

One option was to offer more (auto)biographical information, the idea being that if readers were armed with details about an author's life, they could more accurately assess authorial sincerity. By the end of the eighteenth century, readers' knowledge of a poet's life was integral to the reception of their work. Paul Keen has shown that public interest shifted "from a focus on a cultural product (literature) to a group of producers (authors)."[69] Authors like Smith were in a tricky spot of wanting to appeal to readers' desire for autobiographical information without crossing the "due bounds" delineating familiarity and overfamiliarity that so concerned moralists like Lord Chesterfield.[70] As I have suggested, mismanaged familiarity could flatten boundaries between classes as well as between one's inner circle and mere acquaintances or, worse, the public at large. Concerns about these boundaries intensified during the political uncertainties of the 1790s. Motivations mattered: Did overfamiliarity arise from naiveté about familiarity's proper limits? Or, more concerning, was an author intentionally manipulating these limits to attract the paying public with untoward self-exposure?

As Smith's popularity grew, so too did readers' and critics' desire for answers to these questions. While some celebrated *Elegiac Sonnets* as a "small but valuable collection of poems, which breathe the genuine spirit of pathos and of poetry" and noted that "Smith's talent for poetry" was "universally acknowledged," others took issue with Smith's repetitiveness and increasing familiarity with readers.[71] A review in the notoriously conservative *Anti-Jacobin Review and Magazine* in 1798 linked Smith's repetitiveness to her garish autobiographical tendencies; her "desire of obtruding on the public her own private history," the review claims, "has given a sameness to her tales."[72]

The dire financial circumstances that pressured Smith to publish so much so quickly did, admittedly, produce "a sameness" in her poetry and novels. Her bad marriage to and separation from Benjamin Smith left her in a precarious position; Smith moved twenty-eight times in less than two decades, attempting to stretch her meager funds to support her large (and often sickly) family.[73] Her father-in-law's estate, which had been left to her children rather than to her abusive husband, was in litigation for more than twenty years, and she died before its resolution.[74] It was common knowledge that Smith wrote for money, and her correspondence reveals the extent to which authorship was often an obligation. For example, in September 1790 she confided in her publisher, Thomas Cadell, "I am extremely sick of *my trade* and am very anxious to leave it off. When ever my Childrens affairs are settled, I shall not need it for *them* & have at all events an independence for myself."[75] Her literary works, like a silversmith's wares, were produced to be sold. And produce she did. Smith authored multiple volumes of poetry, several children's books, and almost a dozen novels before her death in 1806. She made close to a thousand pounds from the various editions of *Elegiac Sonnets*, and her novels brought her more than twice that.[76]

Smith's commercial success and financial distress were central pieces of evidence that she and her detractors used to justify her (in)sincerity, (un)originality, and (over)familiarity. Critics of sensibility were quick to accuse authors of exploiting public sympathy and displaying private pain for monetary gain—charges that Smith, one of the most successful writers of the period, had trouble denying. Smith's foray into sentimental fiction intensified accusations that money, rather than taste, motivated her. Following the publication of her second novel *Ethelinde* (1789) one reviewer regretted that Smith had succumbed to the "pecuniary temptation of writing romances for the dangerous amusement of love-sick boys, and the delusion of boarding-school misses"—the very same audiences that Wordsworth would later decry.[77] Charges of "pecuniary temptation" were hard to deny since Smith herself, according to Barbauld, "represents them [her novels] as being written to supply money."[78]

If, according to Bourdieu, literary authenticity is often demonstrated "by the fact that it brings in no income," then it makes sense why Smith's prolific, profitable career gave some contemporaries pause.[79] Binaries between low commercial and high literary pursuits made blatant attempts to earn money the dirty underbelly of literary production—a tension to which I will return in this book's final chapter. Consider, for instance, Wordsworth's dismissal in the Preface to *Lyrical Ballads* of frantic, lucrative literary works in favor of his own supposedly more authentic poetry. (It is worth recalling, though, that *Lyrical Ballads* was as much an economic as an aesthetic venture; Wordsworth admitted in 1799, "I published those poems for money and money alone."[80]) Like a witch trial where innocence is proven by death, financial failure in some respects legitimized authorship in the Romantic era's increasingly commercialized literary field. Smith's marketplace success, then, seemed to confirm allegations that she manipulated public sympathy for financial gain. The long lag between the first and second volumes of the sixth edition of *Elegiac Sonnets* in 1797 only made matters worse; according to Smith, she was accused of "design[ing] to accumulate [income], by gathering subscriptions for a work" that she "never meant to publish."[81]

Such charges against Smith played out in the court of public opinion, and questions about Smith's authorial motivations mirror the increasing mistrust of personal testimony in legal cases at the end of the century. Smith's career developed alongside the French Revolution, the contentious impeachment trial of Warren Hastings (1788–1795), and numerous treason trials against those who, according to prosecutors, imagined the king's death.[82] The influx of French refugees prompted policies like the Aliens Act of 1793, which required officials at the Alien Office "to create and transcribe an intelligible narrative about each émigré" in order to assess whether they were a domestic threat; in practice, as Toby Ruth Benis explains, "Distinguishing the deracinated émigré from the covert insurrectionary proved difficult."[83] In an age of political volatility, the sincerity and veracity of personal narratives became a pressing national concern, and Smith's work was directly embedded in this context. In addition to her overtly political texts like *Desmond*, *The Banished Man*, *The Emigrants*, and *The Young Philosopher*, Smith's experimentations with the sonnet form in *Elegiac Sonnets* and her willingness to share her life with readers in ways that challenged familiarity's traditional limits "aligned [her] with a revolutionary impulse."[84] The changing political backdrop of Smith's career and her own shift away from her early radicalism complicated assessments of her monotonous literary style, insincerity, and supposed opportunism.[85]

How best to read sincerity and intention concerned authors, literary critics, and politicians alike. Alexander Welsh explains that throughout the late eighteenth and early nineteenth centuries, there was an open "distrust [of] direct testimony."[86] Burke's arguments in favor of admitting circumstantial evidence into the Hastings trial mark an important shift toward interpreting intent and action through an expanding body professional and private information. Though Hastings was acquitted in April 1795, his trial signals a historical turning point wherein public figures' private lives became central to political debate. This trend continued throughout the Romantic period, as demonstrated by the scandals surrounding George IV's debauched lifestyle, which brought his private debts and, in 1820, his marriage to Queen Caroline into parliamentary debate. Similarly, starting in 1809 the House of Commons addressed the Duke of York's relationship with his kept mistress, Mary Anne Clarke, who sold military promotions through her influence with the duke. Such events made separating domestic and public life increasingly difficult.

The critical reception of *Elegiac Sonnets* exemplifies the double bind of personal testimony and circumstantial evidence—one that for Smith was complicated by gendered legal and social restrictions about who could offer evidence in the first place. Smith's career demonstrates how testaments of innocence could be co-opted as indicators of guilt. Authors who defended their sincerity often saw those defenses turned against them by critics who, in Annette Wheeler Cafarelli's words, distrusted "the subject's own account as a reliable source of biographical information and impressions of character."[87] Smith's biography and repetitiveness were used both by Smith—who cited her personal difficulties and stylistic consistency to affirm the sincerity of her emotions—and by her critics—who drew on the same evidence to bolster claims that her works were monetarily motivated and unoriginal. Smith's prefaces, for instance, point to financial hardship as proof that she was not "*feigning* sorrow."[88] However, detractors used those same circumstances to argue that, because she needed money, she wrote poems to exploit the public's pity and their pocketbooks. The poet and educator Samuel Whyte certainly thought so. He included Smith in his poem about the contemporary literary marketplace:

> And wouldst, though with pleasing mingle pith,
> Read the Recess, and vie with Charlotte Smith,
> Author's emoluments who most excel,
> Their staple friends, the Booksellers can tell.[89]

Whyte highlights Smith's profitability, aligning her with mercenary booksellers. Such lines suggest the belief that Smith was, by the early 1790s, exaggerating her miseries or, at least, was wearying the public with them. When viewed skeptically, Smith's emotional consistency looked like formulaic feeling repeated for emolumentary gain.

To counter such narratives, Smith offered evidence to prove her misery. Her prefaces to *Elegiac Sonnets* became more explicit, and her descriptions of personal and legal troubles in the preface to the second volume (1797) were so aggressively detailed that the preface was removed from future editions. Labbe notes that Smith's preface to volume 2 "subverts the standard relationship between the individual and the law" as she represents herself as a litigant rather than as a wife in her attacks on lawyers litigating her father-in-law's will.[90] Frustrated by the lawsuit and hobbled by her legal status as her abusive husband's wife, Smith turned to public forms of testimony. Her explicitness strained the limits of decorous familiarity, and the more Smith divulged about her private life, the more she risked seeming loathsomely forthright, overfamiliar, and—problematically for a woman writer who had been labeled a Jacobin—angry.[91] Smith's impassioned defenses, then, became liabilities. Kerry Sinanan and Tim Milnes explain, "[I]ncreasingly urgent testimonies on behalf of sincerity have the curious effect of unsettling it."[92] In a political and legal climate that saw assertions of innocence as potentially duplicitous, Smith's repetitive—and progressively detailed—defenses of her sincerity were suspect.

Many of Smith's contemporaries would have been familiar with her challenging personal circumstances, a fact that can become obscured by focusing on her poetry alone. While early editions of *Elegiac Sonnets* may "preserve a sense of mystery" by "concealing the specific, biographical sources of the poet's melancholy," by the end of the 1780s, little about the sources of Smith's melancholy remained unknown.[93] Considering Smith's celebrity, Stephen Behrendt reminds us that "Smith's own situation became well known among the public, as a result of both what she said (and intimated) . . . and what her public commentators said about those works once they appeared."[94] Hints about unhappiness in early editions of *Elegiac Sonnets* become in later editions specific tirades against "the inhuman trustees" of Smith's father-in-law's estate who kept possession of her children's inheritance by "false and frivolous pretences."[95] Even Smith's notes point to her legal turmoil with barely veiled ambiguity: "[I]t has been my misfortune to have endured real calamities. . . . I have been engaged in contending with persons whose cruelty has left so painful an impression in my mind."[96] Recall, too, that readers of *Elegiac Sonnets* were likely aware of Smith's fiction. Her novels included exculpatory paratexts about the "*weazles*, *wolves*, and *vultures*" whom she claimed had wronged her.[97] The preface to *Desmond*, for instance, describes her finances "being most unhappily in the power of men who *seem to exercise all these with impunity*," and in *The Banished Man* she complains of "those who have detained the property of my children" and even threatens the future "necessity of giving the portraits at full length."[98]

The trajectory of Smith's career, then, is one that progressively pressed the decorous limits of familiarity as she referred to her personal circumstances with increasingly clarity. One reviewer in 1793 criticized *The Emigrants* for its public portrayal of Smith's "inconveniences of a narrow income or a protracted law-suit"—a comment indicating the extent to which Smith's private woes were common knowledge.[99] Tired of Smith's repeated complaints, reviewers reminded Smith that, whatever her misfortunes "may be, the public, by whom this lady's productions have always been peculiarly well received, is not answerable for them."[100] Negative public responses to Smith's testimony echo her private legal challenges. Curran describes "Smith's long years of effort, unable herself to join in litigation, to enlist help from powerful male allies in order to provide for her children's education. In the end her hectoring alienated most of these men."[101] As Smith's male allies became fatigued by her repeated calls for help so too did some readers grow tired of Smith's now-familiar melancholy. Smith's experiences show that in both the legal and literary worlds, a bond of familiarity that might initially promote sympathy and tangible help could, over time, numb others and even provoke their resentment.

By repeating her personal problems in poems that deploy repetitive literary tactics, Smith might have overestimated her readers' sustained "sympathetic curiosity," to borrow Joanna Baillie's term from *Plays on the Passions*.[102] As I explore further in subsequent chapters, eighteenth-century thinkers like Baillie grappled with the effect of emotional forthrightness on sympathetic connection. Adam Smith, for example, found immoderate emotions off-putting: "We are disgusted with that clamorous grief, which, without delicacy, calls upon our compassion."[103] One might listen to "importunate lamentations," but the prime motivator, according to Adam Smith and Baillie, is base curiosity rather than familiar, emotional connection.[104] Charlotte Smith's autobiographical sonnets and prefaces—those "everlasting lamentables" of which Seward was so critical—reject the proper limits of familiarity that, according to eighteenth-century thinkers, prompt sympathy. As one reviewer noted, Smith's "plaintive strain, though interesting when lightly touched, is too monotonous to be long dwelt upon, though by the most skillful finger."[105] In other words, Smith became an eolian harp with a single, sorrowful string, and one perhaps playing too loudly.

In some ways, Smith's decision to reveal more autobiographical information is in keeping with Adam Smith's claim that sympathy requires specificity: "General lamentations, which express nothing but the anguish of the sufferer, create rather a curiosity to enquire into his situation," but in such circumstances, "our fellow-feeling is not very considerable."[106] Information about Charlotte Smith's life offered necessary circumstantial evidence to contextualize the "general lamentations" in her sonnets. However, it was one thing to provide context for emotional anguish and quite another to turn exhibitionist. As the early nineteenth-century writer and lexicographer George Crabb cautioned, "The unlicensed freedom which commonly attends *familiarity* affords but too ample scope for the indulgence of the selfish and unamiable passions."[107] Smith was in a difficult position of needing to indulge her readers' curiosity without seeming to overindulge her own sorrow.

The various editions of *Elegiac Sonnets*, especially the prefaces, struggle to achieve this balance. The preface to the first volume of the sixth edition explains that Smith would be embarrassed were she "compelled to detail" the causes of her sorrow "more at length." She goes on, "I am well aware that for a woman—'The

Post of Honour is a Private Station.'"[108] Smith presents an implicit binary between sharing a secret as with a friend and being forced into public statements as if on trial. However, the intimate details that Smith provides complicate distinctions between choice and compulsion. Smith's prefaces attempt to convince her audience that her repetitive sad sonnets reveal sincere, autobiographical sentiments, and she does so by doubling down on the circumstantial evidence about her hard life. Often Smith's prefatory remarks attempt to pre-emptively share personal information that she knew might be weaponized against her. As a skillful attorney tries to shape a narrative around potentially unflattering information that may come up in cross-examination, Smith shares personal information to control the story around her and to suggest that her choice to share that information is, in fact, no real choice at all.

In 1797, Smith defended herself against charges that she had "an intention to impose on public generosity" and her paying subscribers.[109] She explains in the preface to volume 2 of *Elegiac Sonnets*, "[S]o much has been said . . . of the *delay* of this publication, that it becomes in some measure a matter of self-defence, to account for that delay." Smith then claims she is now "compelled to complain" about those who wronged her.[110] Smith uses the gossip surrounding the delayed edition of *Elegiac Sonnets* to justify providing more circumstantial information than might otherwise seem inappropriate. Indeed, the new preface describes the exact scenario that Smith claimed she feared in 1792: "*I shall be sorry*, if on some future occasion, I should feel compelled to detail its [her sorrow's] causes more at length."[111] Smith offers herself as a reluctant witness exploited by legal and literary systems of power. She asserts that any breaches in familiarity's proper limits arise from critics' ill will and lawyers' greed, and not from her desire to be indecorously forthright: "Let not the censors of literary productions, or the fastidious in private life, again reprove me for bringing forward 'with querulous egotism,' the mention of myself, and the sorrows, of which the men, who have withheld my family property, have been the occasion. Had they never so unjustly possessed, and so shamelessly exercised the power of reducing me to pecuniary distress, I should never, perhaps, have had occasion to ask the consideration of the *reader*, or to deprecate the severity of the *critic*."[112] The phrase "the fastidious in private life" flags Smith's awareness that her openness may initially seem improper, and she directly addresses those willing to read beyond fastidious literary and social limits. She also appeals to readers rather than critics as the proper judges of her sorrows and her decision to share them.

Elegiac Sonnets divides readers into two categories: the sympathetic public and the antagonistic, probing "censors of literary productions."[113] Smith attracts readers' sympathy by allowing them to read in direct opposition to her unfeeling critics.[114] She aligns "the public" with her "particular friends" in the preface to the third and fourth editions, thus conflating general readers with her circle of friends. As she writes in her first preface, only those "few, who, to sensibility of heart, join simplicity of taste" shall appreciate *Elegiac Sonnets* as Smith's real friends did.[115] The publication by subscription of both the fifth edition of *Elegiac Sonnets* in 1789 and the second volume in 1797 heightened Smith's blurring of friends, readers, and patrons—those whom she believes will judge her testimonial work correctly. The preface to the third and fourth editions reinforces her connections with the public through references to the positive "reception given by the public, as well as my particular friends."[116] As we saw earlier with sonnets like "To Mrs. ****," the prefaces frame *Elegiac Sonnets* as a private collection, and throughout subsequent editions, Smith expands the category of "friend" outward to embrace her growing audience of dedicated readers. Like Labbe, I believe that Smith's appeal to friends in the prefaces "effectively enrolls her readers as new 'friends.'"[117] Smith invites readers to partake in the imagined exclusivity of poems supposedly intended for her friends. Demarcating her audiences, Smith ultimately places the burden of proof on readers who are responsible for recognizing the authenticity and sensibility of her often repetitive sonnets. In short, according to Smith, bad readers and untrusting critics projected their own false sensibility and insincerity onto her texts.

SMITH'S AND WORDSWORTH'S "MONOTONOUS LANGUAGE"

Smith's invectives against her unfeeling critics put present-day readers in a difficult position, for, as Stuart Curran admits, "Smith's reiterated sorrows are somewhat numbing."[118] If we take seriously Smith's criticisms of bad readers, then does failing to feel fully her repetitive sonnets implicate us? If so, it is worth considering how Smith's apparent derivativeness may arise not from the sonnets themselves but rather from a gendered Romantic inheritance—an inheritance seeded in a period hesitant of and even actively hostile toward women writers' claims to sincerity and authority. In this last section, I attempt to counteract Smith's "somewhat numbing" effect by outlining affinities between Smith's and Wordsworth's views about repetition and familiarity. Recognizing how Wordsworth's theoretical ideas about repetition largely repeat Smith's own reveals the complexity of her work on language more clearly than if we read her in isolation. In other words, to lift "the film of familiarity" from Smith's repetition and to recognize her novelty, it helps to see how her ideas are echoed in Wordsworth's work.[119]

Like Smith before him, Wordsworth transfers the responsibility of sincerity from author to audience, and in "Essay, Supplementary to the Preface" he distinguishes between "judicious Reader[s]" who appreciate his poetry and critics whose "incompetence" as readers is even "more flagrant than their malice."[120] Wordsworth's note to "The Thorn" from the 1800 edition of *Lyrical Ballads* also follows Smith's earlier criticisms of incompetent readers and celebrates repetition's emotive power: "There is a numerous class of readers who imagine that the same words cannot be repeated without tautology: this is a great error . . . There are also various reasons why repetition and apparent tautology are frequently beauties of the highest kind."[121] For Wordsworth, tautology arises from "great error[s]" in reading rather than failures of repetitive expression. Importantly, Wordsworth identifies the comforting qualities of repetition; that which is familiar predisposes the mind to "fondness, exultation, and gratitude" so that "the mind luxuriates in the repetition of words which appear successfully to communicate its feelings."[122] At issue is the ease with which readers might mistake affecting repetition for banal unoriginality. In *Biographia Literaria* Coleridge revisits this tension. Drawing on Wordsworth's note to "The Thorn," Coleridge contrasts two types of repetition: "Unmeaning repetitions, habitual phrases, and other blank counters" arising from an "unfurnished or confused understanding" and "*apparent* tautologies of intense and turbulent feeling, in which the passion is greater and of longer endurance, than to be exhausted or satisfied by a single representation of the image or incident exciting it."[123] Coleridge's and Wordsworth's emphases on apparent tautologies evoke Smith's defense of her "apparent despondence, which, when it is observed for a long series of years, may look like affectation"; Smith's authorial defenses point to the enduring nature of her suffering which has, in turn, led to a style both sincere and repetitive.[124] However, as Smith, Wordsworth, and Coleridge also acknowledge, "beauties of the highest kind" may, to the untrained eye, convey tautology and affectation.[125]

Wordsworth returns to questions of sincerity and repetition in "Essays Upon Epitaphs." In the first essay, published in *The Friend* in 1810, Wordsworth explains that an epitaph should employ "the general language of humanity" because this "general language may be uttered so strikingly as to entitle an epitaph to high praise."[126] In the second essay, he expands on the value of general language, arguing that it would be "obviously unjustifiable" to "slight the uniform language" of many epitaphs.[127] Though epitaphs are repetitive, and though their tropes are familiar, according to Wordsworth, they remain affecting. His example of similar epitaphs found in a coastal churchyard places emotional responsibility on the reader rather than on the text: "[T]hese [epitaphs] are uniformly in the same strain; but surely we ought not thence to infer that these words are used of course, without any heart-fêlt sense of their propriety. . . . An experienced and well-regulated mind will not, therefore, be insensible to this monotonous language of sorrow and affectionate admiration; but will find under that veil a substance of individual truth."[128] A good reader, Wordsworth believes, will see beyond banal, familiar language and will feel a sympathetic connection with a text, its author, and its subject. Later in the essay Wordsworth argues that sincere intentions can efface linguistic and stylistic problems altogether: "[T]here are no errors in style or manner for which it [sincerity] will not be, in some degree, a recompence."[129] The problem becomes how to assess sincere intent if original language and style are not reliable indicators. As Angela Esterhammer observes, "The only evidence for the writer's feeling *is* the external signs or words."[130]

Wordsworth, like Smith, partly addresses the problem of sincerity by attacking his readers: "If those primary sensations upon which I have dwelt so much be not stifled in the heart of the Reader, they [the epitaphs] will be read with pleasure; otherwise neither these nor more exalted strains can by him be truly interpreted."[131] In "Essay, Supplementary to the Preface" Wordsworth even claims that the faults his critics see in his poetry arise from "phantoms of their own brain."[132] Vapid readers, he claims, make texts vapid. Reminiscent of Smith's prefatory defenses in *Elegiac Sonnets*, Wordsworth challenges his audience: if they are not affected, the problem is with their reading rather than with his evidence. Smith and Wordsworth become witnesses who see problems not with their own testimony but rather with those who misinterpret it.

Wordsworth attempts to limit misinterpretations by training readers' responses to familiar, repetitive language. Across his works, Wordsworth describes situations in which the vulgar and the miseducated could misread repetition and sincerity, and he celebrates his own ability to recognize value in the familiar. A notable example is Wordsworth's description of his interpretive triumphs on the public road in book 12 of *The Prelude*:

> When I began to inquire,
> To watch and question those I met, and held
> Familiar talk with them, the lonely roads
> Were schools to me in which I daily read
> With most delight the passions of mankind,
> There saw into the depth of human souls—
> Souls that appear to have no depth at all
> To vulgar eyes. (12.161–168)

Here Wordsworth equates vulgarity with the misreading of true feelings. His willingness to converse familiarly with strangers gives him insight into the depths of humanity. The interplay between *familiar* and *vulgar* points to Wordsworth's rejection of traditional limits of familiarity. The people Wordsworth meets are, for the most part, those from vulgar, common life—exactly the sort of strangers with whom it would be improper for a man of Wordsworth's stature to communicate on familiar terms. However, ignoring the elements of class that organized Romantic-era interpersonal familiarity, Wordsworth connects with them on terms of openness and equality.[133] As with Smith's criticism of "the fastidious in private life" who may look askance at the private information she shares in *Elegiac Sonnets*, here Wordsworth claims that the class-inflected gatekeeping of familiarity is itself vulgar—a gesture that points to familiarity's radical potential. Thus, for Wordsworth, familiarity cultivates social connection as well as fertilizes the growth of the poet's mind. Wordsworth sees beyond the potentially common, negative aspects of familiarity and reaps the benefits. By extension, Wordsworth implies that a good reader can make the banal revelatory by shifting familiarity's focus. From this viewpoint, repetitiveness, familiarity, and common language do not indicate false emotions. Similarly, singularity does not signify authenticity. The onus for interpretation is divided between author and reader, but ultimate responsibility lies with readers. They must read beyond linguistic noise—a large number of gravestones, a sea of London advertisements, a series of similar sonnets—to recognize intention and "beauties of the highest kind."[134]

Elsewhere in *The Prelude* Wordsworth attempts to educate his audience by reflecting on his own exemplary reading habits. Describing the spectacles of London in book 7, Wordsworth meditates on familiarity and the ease with which novelty can become unsettling banality. "Thus have I looked," he writes,

> Until the shapes before my eyes became
> A second-sight procession . . .
> And all the ballast of familiar life—
> The present, and the past, hope, fear, all stays,
> All laws of acting, thinking, speaking man—
> Went from me, neither knowing me, nor known. (7.599–607)

The anchoring aspects of "familiar life" no longer offer Wordsworth the mooring for his identity or sense of community; he is lost in the city's sea of difference. Here, familiarity is not a negative to overcome, but a necessary quality to promote connection with oneself and with society. Here familiarity fulfills its function as a social tie and a balm—the "spirit of fondness" associated with familiarity that he identifies in the note to "The Thorn."[135] Later in the frenzied atmosphere of St. Bartholomew's Fair, Wordsworth describes how the plethora of people and objects are "melted and reduced / To one identity by difference" (7.703–704). The overproduction of difference creates sameness. Only the observant mind can see through both difference and sameness, and for the poet of nature or perhaps a sympathetic reader, these sites reveal familiarity's connective potential. From Jack the Giant-killer with "the word / INVISIBLE flame[d] forth upon his chest" (7.309–310) to the blind beggar "Wearing a written paper, to explain / The story of the man, and who he was" (7.614–615) to the London "Advertisements of giant size" (7.210) to the generalized chaos of the city, the literal and figurative texts that Wordsworth reads are not the important part. Rather, the importance rests in how his reading is ultimately connective, producing what he calls "a feeling of the whole" (7.713). Familiarity—with people, with customs, with seemingly ordinary or repetitive language—offers a sociable, comforting form of transcendence. This is not familiarity as banality but rather familiarity that, if seen correctly, brims with emotional potential.

Smith's and Wordsworth's respective claims about the power of common, repetitive language to establish a positive sense of familiarity demonstrate just how important perspective is in reading sincerity. The focus on audience in both their work gestures toward shifting understandings of sincerity, repetition, and evidence in the Romantic era. Smith and Wordsworth attempt to promote this new understanding through didactic examples of generous readings of their own writing—writing which may initially seem too common or too derivative. In the end, both Smith and Wordsworth suggest that it is our responsibility as readers to see the sincerity behind the "monotonous language of sorrow"; they ask us to read the circumstantial evidence around poetic composition with a sympathetic eye.[136]

Like *The Prelude*'s blind beggar, whose sign, according to Wordsworth, serves as both a "label" and "a type / Or emblem" for humanity (7.618–619), Smith metaphorically labels herself as a sentimental heroine by drawing on established literary tropes in her poetry, prefaces, and novels. And, like Wordsworth's figure, she tells her story to gain sympathetic as well as monetary support from the public. But, unlike with Wordsworth and the people and epitaphs he encounters, Smith's use of quotation becomes a form of literary labeling that, through repeated use (many sonnets instead of a single beggar's sign), runs the risk of seeming insincere; quotation becomes quotidian. Though Smith's theory and practice of familiarity and repetition prefigure Wordsworth's, she was condemned by critics. Wordsworth's ability to transcend "apparent tautology," then, may be less an artistic achievement than a triumph of gendered double standards.[137] Practices made familiar by Charlotte Smith were subsumed into a narrative of literary history that privileges Wordsworth's supposed originality. While both Smith and Wordsworth make it the reader's decision which sense of *familiar* to apply, this chapter has suggested that Romantic readers were conditioned to apply familiarity's limits differently to men and women writers.

2

"THOUGH A STRANGER TO YOU"

Byron's Poetics of Familiarity and Readerly Attachment

Indeed it is the real romance of that person's life, immeasurably more than the fabled one of his pen, which the public expects to find in his pages, and which not so much engages its sympathy, as piques its curiosity, and feeds thought and conversation.

—Review of *Childe Harold's Pilgrimage*, Canto III*

WHEN THE THIRD CANTO OF *Childe Harold's Pilgrimage* appeared in 1816 few could ignore Lord Byron's dominance in the literary marketplace and the public imagination. Like the social lives of today's celebrities, Byron's friendships, lovers, and even clothes became fodder for "thought and conversation," and his works, as many contemporaries and later scholars have noted, seemed to encourage his readers' interest in "the real romance of that person's life." Byron's autobiographical hide and seek in *Childe Harold* I and II had made him a literary and cultural sensation starting in 1812.[1] As with Charlotte Smith, whose literary profitability and productivity, I argued in chapter 1, gave some readers pause, Byron's poetic output and notorious personal life also provoked criticism. In an 1816 review of Byron's *Hebrew Melodies*, one critic, sounding much like those who attacked Smith some twenty years earlier, claimed, "The truth is, that an individual who publishes so much and so repeatedly, ought to have a larger stock of true poetical feeling than is possessed by the author of these melodies."[2] At issue, too, was that Byron's poetry seemed inseparable from his life. Clara Tuite observes that in the years following Byron's self-exile from England in 1816 there is a "sense that these high-souled villains [in Byron's poetry] are authorial self-projections, hence particularly intriguing, wearying."[3] Byron's seeming autobiographical projections charmed many readers but also risked numbing them. As a result, Byron's years of fame were troubled by conflicting pressures to innovate, on the one hand, and, on the other, to give his fans more of what they had come to expect from his autobiographically charged poetry.[4] Throughout his career, Byron often pointed to his life in his works—sometimes obliquely and sometimes directly. In doing so, Byron focused the prismatic elements of familiarity on its associations with intimacy and sociability.

The previous chapter argued that Charlotte Smith contended with familiarity as forms of unaffecting repetition and autobiographical revelation, both of which were coded by the period's gendered expectations of propriety and authorship. This chapter focuses on familiarity as a mode of social behavior and literary address inflected by gender and, especially, class. Analyzing Byron's poetics of familiarity, readers' responses in their letters to him, and contemporary reviews, this chapter examines the relationship between sympathy and familiarity, particularly how their limits were informed by class-inflected social etiquette. The familiar relationships with readers that Byron's poetry encouraged challenged empiricist philosophies about familiarity's ability to either prompt or stifle sympathy. For Byron's contemporaries, his frenzied fans raised concerns about how sympathy might function differently across mediums (in person versus on the page) and across social classes in a world unsettled by the Napoleonic Wars and their wake. Transgressing boundaries, Byron's poetry offered readers a type of familiarity with him that not only inflamed their curiosity but also, for many, encouraged a sympathetic attachment that one would expect of a familiar friend. As Walter Scott wrote of the fourth canto of *Childe Harold*, readers felt "novelty and pride" in "being called as it were into familiarity with a mind so powerful."[5] Throughout his career Byron teased, tested, and, at times, transgressed the period's acceptable bounds of familiarity. However, as a male aristocratic author in the Regency period, Byron's dance of familiarity carried different risks than Charlotte Smith's did at the end of the eighteenth century.

Unlike other chapters in this book, which focus primarily on authors who seemingly got the balance between familiarity and overfamiliarity wrong, this chapter explores how, especially before 1816, Byron's readers related to him with intense feelings of familiarity. The strength of these feelings was, as we shall see, one reason why Byron's influence alarmed some commentators. One critic in 1822 advised that Byron should "not be astonished . . . if disgust should at length be excited by such frequent exhibitions of himself."[6] That Byron's "frequent exhibitions of himself" prompted emotional attachment from so many readers suggested to his contemporaries that earlier eighteenth-century understandings of moderated passions—a touchstone of Adam Smith's ideas about sympathy—may not map onto the rapidly changing media, social, and political landscape of the nineteenth century.

It was these very shifts that helped Byron become what one reviewer termed a "remarkable phenomenon of the time."[7] Concerns about "the phenomenon" of

Byron partly sprung from anxieties about the shifting standards of sociability and sympathy arising from the expansions of print culture and the public sphere. Overwrought sympathy with authors and others created worrying possibilities of emotional contagion among the unruly crowd.[8] Even more alarming, Byron's celebrity and his fans' passion suggested dangerous enthusiasm—a quality that in the period, according to Jon Mee, "comes to name the tendency within the population to be swept by crazes."[9] Throughout the years of fame, Byron embodied just such a craze, and Ghislaine McDayter reminds us that Byron and his most popular works were "originally seen as a thoroughly political and potentially subversive social force."[10]

As historians of celebrity have noted, the emotional attachment that readers felt for Byron marks a shift in author-reader relations, foreshadowing elements of fan culture today. Tom Mole, building on Jerome Christensen's analysis of "the literary system named 'Byron,'" explains that Byron's celebrity was the collaborative result of his poetry ("an individual"), publicity ("an industry"), and readers ("an audience").[11] Mole's book historical methodology, including his careful attention to the nontextual ways in which "Byron" circulated, informs my own ideas about how Byron's celebrity is both unique to him but also embedded in Romanticism's larger, politicized media landscape. Tuite's more recent *Lord Byron and Scandalous Celebrity* shows how Byron and others mobilized notoriety. More so than Mole, Tuite focuses on standards of sociability that informed Byron's straddling of "two modes of celebrity sighting: one is small-scale and intimate, involving communing with known readers, while the other occurs with the anonymous reading public, initiating the new form of readerly relations between consumer and producer that emerges within a fully industrialized commodity culture."[12] Building on this previous work, this chapter places Byron's poetry and the standards of sociability that shaped his celebrity directly into conversation with archival evidence of his readers. Surviving fan mail that readers wrote to Byron provides concrete evidence of how what Mole terms Byron's "hermeneutic of intimacy" and what Tuite terms Byron's "scandalous celebrity" manifested in readers' reactions to his poetry.

My attention to Byron's fan mail extends related work by McDayter and Corin Throsby. McDayter's *Byromania and the Birth of Celebrity Culture* is especially important because it rejects narratives from the Romantic period to today that see Byromania "as an extraliterary event" outside more traditional scholarly concerns.[13] However, whereas McDayter and Throsby both focus on female fans and their flirtatious and even sexual interest in Byron, I consider the diversity of the extant fan mail in terms of gender and class.[14] Recognizing the variety of readers who wrote to Byron makes the letters' similarities striking. The fan mail reveals that Byron's poetry encouraged not only readers' feelings of interpersonal connection but also the specific forms of familiar address that they deployed in their letters to him. Assessing common rhetorical tropes in the fan mail, I outline how his fans responded to and mimicked Byron's poetics of familiarity and, in doing so, rejected established epistolary modes of the familiar letter and their associations with class-based decorum.

Throughout, I ask three central questions. First, what strategies did Byron use to encourage his readers' feelings of familiarity? From autobiographical denials that actually foreground the personal elements of his poetry to tropes of isolation and observation, Byron prompted Romantic readers to search for him in his works. Second, how did Byron's readers respond to his poetics of familiarity? To answer this question, I draw on the substantial collection of Byron's fan mail, much of it now held at the John Murray Archive in the National Library of Scotland. Readers who wrote to Byron repeat the refrain of the stranger made familiar, and their letters subvert social conventions surrounding the genre of the familiar letter. Finally, I ask why Byron's ability to encourage his readers to feel so much was met with both excitement and fear. I suggest that fears about Byron's hold on readers were not, as other scholars have posited, a general response to the growth of celebrity culture. Rather, they were a reaction to how Byron's work destabilized theories of emotional connection and moderation, and particularly how emotions worked across mediums. Byromania demonstrated that medium matters for establishing sympathy and familiarity, and his reception history reveals that what might seem overfamiliar and off-putting in person may prompt sympathy in print.[15]

Throughout Byron's career, the social, political, and literary game was changing, though the new rules were still being contested, not only on the floor of Parliament but also in the pages of poetry. These changes intensified in the wake of the age of revolutions characterized by what Andrew Franta describes as "an emerging, but not yet realized, transformation of politics and sociability."[16] The presumption of familiarity both on Byron's part and on that of his readers prompted concerns about sociability and the literary marketplace. Fears about Byron's public influence grew after his self-exile and, later, his role in the "Satanic school" of poets. Anxieties about social hierarchy and traditional sociability became even more pressing in the post-Napoleonic era, when Byron was firmly established as both a celebrity and a radical; the re-establishment of both peace and the European monarchies after Waterloo also bolstered traditional class- and gender-based models of decorum and respectability. Byron's popularity across diverse readerships and his readers' eagerness to write to him harbingered the shifting sands of sociability that threatened to destabilize the hierarchies on which polite society depended.

BYRON'S POETICS OF FAMILIARITY

Byron's strategies of autobiographical display and retreat appear most explicitly in *Childe Harold's Pilgrimage*, a poem that Nicholas Mason accurately describes as "the most consciously autobiographical 'nonautobiographical' poem of the nineteenth century."[17] When John Murray published the third canto of *Childe Harold* in 1816, the *Edinburgh Review* observed that "it seem[ed] no longer possible to ascribe" Harold's sentiments "to any other than the author himself."[18] The general consensus, according to Walter Scott, was that it was "impossible . . . to divide Lord Byron from his poetry."[19] Readers pushed biographical connections as far as they might go in *Childe Harold* and in Byron's other poems that, at least on the surface, seemed further from the poet's own life. One enthusiastic fan, referring to the pirate Conrad from Byron's *The Corsair*, asked, "Has his lines any[, even] the most distant allusion to himself"?[20]

However, early in his career Byron repeatedly denied the autobiographical elements of his work. The preface to *Childe Harold* I and II offers a preemptive strike against biographical readings: "It has been suggested to me by friends, on whose opinions I set a high value, that in this fictitious character, "Childe Harold," I may incur the suspicion of having intended some real personage: this I beg leave, once for all, to disclaim—Harold is the child of imagination, for the purpose I have stated. In some very trivial particulars, and those merely local, there might be grounds for such a notion; but in the main points, I should hope, none whatever."[21] Byron's admission of similarities in minor details calls attention to possible similarities in the main points. As Gérard Genette argues, prefatory denials of autobiographical resemblances have "always had the double function of protecting the author from the potential 'applications' and, inevitably, of setting readers in search of them."[22] Almost two hundred years before Genette's instrumental work on paratext, the reviewer for the conservative *Christian Observer* identified this same issue: "In fact, the disclaimer, already noticed in the Preface, seems merely like one of those veils worn to draw attention to the face rather than to baffle it."[23] Byron (and as we shall see in the following chapter, Lady Caroline Lamb) explicitly rejected accusations of autobiographical referentiality. However, such denials invited readers in by the back way and sent them searching for hidden information.

The preface's playful links between locality and identity highlight connections between poem, place, and poet. Harold's "merely local" autobiographical elements reinforce Byron's assertion that such elements are precise and limited. But "local" also gestures back to the preface's opening paragraph, which emphasizes the veracity of the poem's descriptions of landscapes, locations, and local people. Byron explains that the poem was "composed from the author's observations in those countries" that Harold also visits (3). As Stephen Cheeke remarks, "Byron's entire poetic career is shaped by the claims for authority he stakes upon the authenticity of historical places."[24] The authenticity of Byron's geographic localities informs the autobiographical, local details in the poem. That is, the preface's reference to the "local"—in this sense, minor—aspects of Harold that are not "the child of imagination" recall the initial references to place and the poet's travels. Together, they plant a seed that encourages readers to cultivate other potential connections between poem and poet. The flexibility of *local* as location and as limitation counters Byron's claims about "merely local" autobiographical elements of the poem, suggesting that cartographies of place and inner poet overlap.

Byron similarly foregrounds location and autobiography in his dedication to John Cam Hobhouse in Canto IV of *Childe Harold*: "[P]erhaps it may be pardonable vanity which induces me to reflect with complacency on a composition which in some degree connects me with the spot where it was produced" (121). Nostalgia for writing the poem, for the places where it was written, and for the friend who shared his journey, frames the dedication's later claim that Byron has "become weary of drawing a line [dividing himself and Harold] which every one seemed determined not to perceive" (122). This line and its disappearance map onto the locations that Byron and Harold both visit. Just as the shorter lyrics like "Written in Passing the Ambracian Gulph, November 14, 1809" and "Written After Swimming from Sestos to Abydos" published in Cantos I and II inject autobiography back into the longer poem preceding them, Byron's acquiescence to biographical readings of Harold in Canto IV encourages similar interpretations of the earlier cantos. The autobiographical and place-focused dedication in Canto IV, then, widens outward and backward to the rest of the poem.

The trope of the local in *Childe Harold* and its notes offers readers a treasure map of sorts to locate Byron behind his works. Take the relationship between poem and note in Canto I's descriptions of Sierra "Morena's dusky height" surrounded by evidence of armament and "the ball-pil'd pyramid" (I.531, 539). The accompanying note reads, "All who have seen a battery will recollect the pyramidal form in which shot and shells are piled. The Sierra Morena was fortified in every defile through which I passed on my way to Seville" (188). The "I" in Byron's notes gestures back to a potential autobiographical "I" in the poem proper. The frequency with which Byron refers to his own experiences, observations, and emotions in the notes—including referencing his mother's death in the final note in Canto I—conflates Harold's experiences with Byron's. The material organization of the volume, too, intensifies these autobiographical connections. The preface at the front and the lyrics and notes at the back bookend *Childe Harold*, surrounding it with explicitly autobiographical content.

Throughout *Childe Harold* and his other works, Byron plays with incompleteness and inference—such as the mutable meanings of "local" in the preface to the first two cantos. Mole notes that Byron's autobiographical revelations were "never stable or complete," so part of his appeal arose from beliefs that his interior self "was hidden from the view of the undiscerning, but was also continually making itself legible, expressing itself in poems where its secrets could be read by the discerning few."[25] The notion of the "discerning few" directly connects Byron's literary strategies to the dynamics of familiarity. One way to avoid accusations of indecorousness was, according to one eighteenth-century moralist, to limit familiarity to "none but such as are eminent for some commendable Qualifications."[26] Byron made readers feel as though they had commendable qualifications to recognize his hidden self behind his characters, creating what David Brewer describes as "a virtual community modeled not on the commons but the coterie."[27] Resisting the biographical fixity that Brewer associates with genres like romans à clef, Byron's appeals to discerning readers and the uncertain links between himself and his poetic characters gave readers room to imagine, to expand, and, in some ways, to possess him through characters like Childe Harold. As in the eighteenth-century fictional works that Brewer studies, in Byron's poetry "there is no apparent way to confirm or refute the 'truth' of imaginative expansion."[28] This resistance to truth invited Byron's readers to feel uniquely equipped to uncover autobiographical hints in his characters.

The first two cantos of *Childe Harold* encourage readers to identify as Byron's friends. The preface's reference to "friends, on whose opinions I set a high value"—the same friends who believed that Byron "may incur the suspicion of having intended some real personage" in Harold—suggests that readers with similar suspicions think like Byron's friends (4). Praising his friends' value and drawing connections between their suspicions and his readers', Byron effectively projects onto unknown readers the "commendable Qualifications" that were necessary to decorous familiarity. Moreover, the poems published along with *Childe Harold*, particularly "Written in an Album" and "To * * *," contribute to the collection's familiarity and its associations with friendship. Similar to poems in Charlotte Smith's *Elegiac Sonnets* like "To Mrs. ****" and "To Miss C—on being desired to attempt writing a comedy"—and, as we shall see, similar to album verses in literary annuals examined in my final chapter—Byron's lyrics invite readers to insert themselves into the volume and into the poet's familiar circle.[29] Because manuscript albums were records of sociability, the album lyrics in *Childe Harold* contribute to an ethos of familiarity that extends back into the longer poem.

The dedication to Hobhouse continues this link between readers and Byron's familiar friends: "In parting with an old friend [Childe Harold] it is not extraordinary that I should recur to one still older and better,—to one who has beheld the birth and death of the other, and to whom I am far more indebted for the social advantages of enlightened friendship, than—though not ungrateful—I can, or could be, to Childe Harold, for any public favour reflected through the poem on the poet" (120). Hobhouse was not the only one who had followed Byron and his poem between 1812 and 1818. Some readers, like those who sent him fan mail, imagined themselves not as the "public" who reflected favor on poem and poet but rather as members of the elite few who, like Hobhouse, "knew" the poet. This is a strategy that we have already encountered in *Elegiac Sonnets* in which Smith's differentiates cruel critics from her "few friends."[30]

The idea that careful readers could access Byron's intimate thoughts appears in the poem itself. Byron describes the hiddenness of Harold's emotions, and, in doing so, he alludes to the evocatively hidden nature of his own feelings. For example, Byron identifies the ease with which Harold hides the "Strange pangs" and passions that "lurk'd below" the surface:

> But this none knew, nor haply car'd to know;
> For his was not that open, artless soul
> That feels relief by bidding sorrow flow,
> Nor sought he friend to counsel or condole,
> Whate'er his grief mote be, which he could not control. (I.68–72)

The illegibility of Harold's emotions and the vague cause of his unhappiness seem to represent Byron's own closed emotional nature, which perceptive readers might open. Byron places readers in the role of "friend[s] to counsel or condole," which Harold lacks. These lines suggest that those in closest physical proximity to Harold (and, by extension, Byron) may be less apt to recognize his hidden feelings and offer comfort than a distanced print-mediated public. Counterintuitively—and counter to Romantic-era philosophies about sympathy—it is the absence and not presence of "proximity [that] becomes the occasion for awareness of relational possibilities," as Nancy Yousef has explained.[31] Byron and his characters are not solitary, but rather alone in a sociable world. Opportunities for connection and sociability arise from physical absence and print mediation—a topic explored more fully in this chapter's final section.

The autobiographical connections that Byron simultaneously stoked and stifled—or perhaps stoked by stifling—are most often noted in *Childe Harold*, yet similar techniques also appear in his Turkish Tales. We can see this in *The Corsair*'s descriptions of Conrad, whose hidden emotions are darker than Harold's: "Slight are the outward signs of evil thought, / . . . and to judge their mien, / He, who would see, must be himself unseen" (1.227–234). As in *Childe Harold*, distanced observers and strangers are best positioned to penetrate the innermost thoughts of Byron's characters and, by extension, the poet himself. *The Corsair* continues to thematize the stranger's unique emotional access:

> Then—with each feature working from the heart,
> With feelings loosed to strengthen—not depart;
> That rise—convulse—contend—that freeze, or glow,
> Flush in the cheek, or damp upon the brow;
> Then—Stranger! if thou canst, and tremblest not,
> Behold his soul—the rest that soothes his lot! (1.239–244)

Such passages encourage the stranger to interpret Conrad, and Byron promotes a type of facial reading. (Recall that Edmund Kean's famous facial expressions hit Drury Lane by storm in 1814—the same year that *The Corsair* appeared. Like Byron, Kean attracted fans and was "reputed to send female audience members into hysterics."[32]) But beyond the physical, these descriptions of Conrad present a more general trope of recognizing small details that others neglect. It is possible to decipher Conrad's passions, but not everyone is capable of doing so. In the Turkish Tales, Byron emphasizes the (il)legibility of body and psyche.[33] This air of exclusivity—of making emotional access seem difficult but not impossible—helped temper charges that Byron was overfamiliar with the public.

Lara reveals a similar preoccupation with emotional opaqueness. To some, these themes seemed to reflect Byron's own experiences of celebrity's isolating effects. Like Conrad, Lara keeps his inner feelings outwardly suppressed: "Nor common gazers could discern the growth / Of thoughts that mortal lips must leave half told; / They choak the feeble words that would unfold" (1.286–288). But if there are common gazers, there must be, by extension, uncommon ones. Byron's poetics of familiarity, then, arises in part from his depictions of inadequate audiences: friends who fail to see Harold's private distress or "common gazers" unable to discern Lara's mind. If readers can better interpret Byron's heroes than the fictional crowds in his poems, then they might also be better able to understand him than the friends mentioned in his paratexts. Drawing anonymous mass readers into an "exclusive" group, Byron subverts one of the touchstones of modern celebrity carefully explored by Sharon Marcus. "While celebrities cannot exist without fans," Marcus explains, "celebrity culture is nonetheless fundamentally hierarchical, based as it is on the differences between the anonymous many and the celebrated few."[34] Byron disrupts this hierarchy with the suggestion that "the anonymous many" have more perceptive power than "the celebrated few."

As *Lara* continues, the descriptions of the hero's celebrity intensify, becoming sinister:

> You could not penetrate his soul, but found,
> Despite your wonder, to your own he wound;
> His presence haunted still; and from the breast
> He forced an all unwilling interest;
> Vain was the struggle in that mental net,
> His spirit seemed to dare you to forget! (1.377–382)

Byron presents Lara as irresistible. Negatively charged diction frames the indescribable connection between Lara and those around him, making his appeal less a choice than a disease. As I argue in the following sections, the disturbing elements of Lara's infectious magnetism also appear in the letters that fans wrote to Byron and in critics' fears about Byromania's consequences. Strong feelings, like those that onlookers have for Lara, appear throughout the fan letters, demonstrating that Byron "entwined / Himself perforce around the [reader's] mind" (*Lara*, 1.371–372).

"BREAKING THE BOUNDS OF CUSTOM": BYRON'S FAMILIAR FANS

The previous section outlined Byron's strategies for evoking familiarity. This section traces how his readers responded: flirtatiously, longingly, disapprovingly, lovingly. To the unconverted, the hold that Byron had over his readers seemed a plague—and one that spread quickly. One apocalyptic reviewer bemoaned "a moral disease abroad contagious and pretty prevalent that may be termed the *Byromania* . . . At the very idea of it, I feel as when I see a heavy black cloud gathering between us and the Sun, and darkening the face of universal nature."[35] One thing that made Byron and those infected with "the *Byromania*" so dangerous was their departure from customary limits of sociability.

To track Byron's reception and fears about its moral and social consequences, I turn to his fan mail. Reception and reading histories are notoriously difficult to study, and they often rely on exceptional cases to infer more general readerly habits. In Byron's case, his readers' fan letters offer a rare resource, and the fan archive's robustness is more akin to what might be expected of later celebrity writers.[36] The readers who sent letters to Byron are, in many ways, uncharacteristic. Yet, as H. J. Jackson notes of annotated books, "Special cases can lead us to seek a better understanding of ordinary practice."[37] And while writing a fan letter is an act even more exceptional than annotating one's books, these letters still reflect a more generalized cultural preoccupation with Byron. We might, then, read Byron's fan letters as an important, though imperfect, sample of, in the words of one reader, the "thousands, to whom [Byron] exist[ed]—as a Power a Wonder—an agent of Pleasure or Pain."[38]

Here I want to pause to reflect on the archive of Byron's fan mail as an important but highly mediated artifact of Byron's celebrity from the Regency onward. That is, Byron's fan mail is a product of his poetry, the particular media moment that enabled his celebrity, and the preservation practices that led to the letters' survival. Because his poetics of familiarity attracted readers in particular ways, Byron likely received more fan mail than his contemporaries, but other eighteenth- and nineteenth-century authors also received readers' impassioned letters. One calls to mind the letters that pleased (and perhaps plagued) Samuel Richardson following the appearance of *Pamela*, or the "huge bundle" of fan letters written to Rousseau that express "an overwhelming to desire to make contact with the lives behind the printed page."[39] However, few Romantic authors benefited from dedicated attempts to amass such a collection as that now preserved in the John Murray Archive, and the survival of Byron's fan mail owes much to the poet's own hubris as well as to Murray's interest in gathering material related to his most lucrative poet. Together, Murray and Byron curated and culled the collection. Notably, while some of the mail politely admonishes Byron for his characters' (and his own) immorality, I have seen no surviving examples of what could be considered hate mail.[40] James Smith Allen's observations about the fan mail sent to francophone writers held in French archives holds true for the mail sent to Byron: "Besides the self-selecting nature of the correspondents, these letters express the selective retention of the recipients, the heirs to the authors' papers, and the libraries that acquired them."[41] The extant archive, then, evidences not only readers' responses to the poet but also Byron's, Murray's, and others' impulses to save particular kinds of letters.

The majority of the surviving letters were written between 1812 and 1820. Of course, dating undated letters only provides a likely window. A letter mentioning *Lara*, for instance, could not have been written in 1812. However, a letter addressing the first two cantos of *Childe Harold* was not necessarily written in 1812. Many letters allude to—and quote from—favorite works, with *Childe Harold*, *The Giaour*, and *Lara* being frequently cited and other later works, like *Manfred* and *Don Juan*, only sparingly so. That many of these letters appear to be from Byron's earlier career may partly result from the postal practicalities of his self-exile on the continent. A more likely influence on the archive was a shift in his poetry and reputation after 1816. His departure from England was colored by his separation from Annabella Milbanke, rumors of incest with his half sister Augusta Leigh, and the resurgence of his earlier scandalous affair with Lady Caroline Lamb after the publication of her autobiographical novel *Glenarvon* (1816). In particular, his infamously vituperative poem "Fare Thee Well," about his separation from Milbanke, disgusted many readers for being, in the words of one critic, "wholly unfit to meet the public eye" and "cruel and disgraceful."[42] Later works like *Manfred*, *Cain*, and *The Vision of Judgement* shocked even dedicated fans. In the last few years of his life, perhaps fewer fan letters were written, fewer reached him on his travels, or fewer found their way back to Murray for preservation, especially after Byron's break with the publisher over the final cantos of *Don Juan*.[43]

Of the surviving letters, many were written by readers who never knew or would never meet Byron. Unlike either Rousseau or Richardson before him, Byron's status as both an author and an aristocrat amplified the presumption of the unknown readers who wrote to him. Even so, Byron's fans express the freedom (and in some instances, a compulsion) they feel to address him in familiar terms. For instance, young Eliza Horatia Sommerset breathlessly begins, "I can resist no longer, how I could have remained so long silent, after reading your poetry astonishes me."[44] With an apologetic tone more reminiscent of a belated birthday greeting rather than a letter sent to a stranger, Miss Sommerset offers excuses for her previous silence: "Had you my Lord been . . . not surrounded by fortune, my pen would have told you how much I admired your writing . . . I thought that the admiration of a young enthusiast could add no leaf to the wreath which adorns your brow."[45] Her letter identifies a socioeconomic disparity between them that makes a letter like hers inappropriate, but she also indicates that writing to Byron was almost involuntary. In writing emotive personal letters to Byron, readers like Miss Sommerset claimed a familiarity with him that went beyond the period's understandings of epistolary decorum. As a popular letter-writing manual noted: "A different style is often necessary on the same topics, to old people and to young; to men and to women; to rich and to poor; to great personages and to little people; to scholars and to the illiterate; to strangers and to familiar companions."[46] Countering this advice, fans' letters to Byron address an author and peer as though they were familiar companions, and the letters run the gamut from admiration to love to almost stalker-like sentiments. "You cannot retire to any part of the civilized globe," wrote one fan in 1819, "where you will not be followed by the echoes of the world[']s applause."[47] Byron's fans and their powerful reactions to his poetry did follow him, and the moving, shocking, and even funny elements of readers' reactions to Byron share key rhetorical similarities that push the bounds of class- and gender-based sociability.

Much of Byron's existing fan mail repeats tropes about emotional and social closeness, which respond to and adapt Byron's own poetics of familiarity. Fans typically identify the emotiveness of Byron's poetry as providing almost a carte blanche to address him familiarly. Byron made his large audience feel, in the words of the *Edinburgh Review*, "as if chosen out from a crowd of lovers."[48] The fan mail reveals this dynamic, and readers acknowledge that they are anonymous strangers who still feel they know him. These letters support William Hazlitt's claims about class, familiarity, and poetry from his essay "On the Aristocracy of Letters." "If the poet lends a grace to the nobleman," Hazlitt explains, "the nobleman pays it back to the poet with interest . . . His name so accompanied becomes the mouth well: it is repeated thousands of times, instead of hundreds, because the reader in being *familiar* with the Poet's works seems to claim acquaintance with the Lord."[49] The slip from stranger to friend, from familiarity with literary works to familiarity with the man behind them, defines many of these letters and the critical anxiety around Byron's celebrity.

Penned by fellow aristocrats, aspiring poets, governesses, men with Werther-worthy ennui, would-be valets, tradesmen, teenaged admirers, and a number of unknown anonymous writers, many of the letters make requests. They swing from concrete appeals for autographs, personalized poems, literary endorsements, locks of hair, and even sex to more abstract pleas for, among other things, Byron's return to a Christian path or clarification about which of Byron's poems apply to himself. Though the genre of fan mail was well established by the later nineteenth century, the common elements of Byron's Romantic-era fan mail reveal an epistolary genre in the midst of becoming. Courtney Alice Bates, one of the few scholars to theorize literary fan mail as a genre, explains its characteristic elements: "A reader usually makes clear that he or she is an unknown person addressing the author, yet at the same time, they often excuse their presumption by describing the reason behind their urgent need to write the author."[50] Later in the nineteenth and twentieth centuries—the periods which Bates studies—these apologies seem a rhetorical nicety. However, the need to apologize to an English lord for the presumption of randomly writing him in the early 1800s was a genuine necessity. Though there were specific rules for epistolary petitions to peers—letter-writing manuals of the period include extensive examples of how to make requests for money or legal intervention—dashing off a letter without official purpose to an unknown celebrity aristocrat departed significantly from established forms of polite communication. Bates observes that many fans "may worry over a mistaken sense of familiarity, based on the true-but-false sense of knowing the author after reading a book."[51] Notably, the worry of not knowing Byron is absent from his surviving fan mail; rather, as Throsby notes, many fans "seem to feel that they understand the workings of Byron's mind completely."[52] Readers who wrote to Byron felt as though his poetry provided them with the prior acquaintance needed to justify their familiar forms of address.

A tone of forward familiarity characterizes much of Byron's fan mail. For instance, the Irish writer John Stewart unabashedly asked for Byron's endorsement of "a New Work" he had "just completed," and the letter points to the power of Byron's name: "The celebrity of your name, my Lord, assumes a distinction more imperishable than mere wealth or tiles could confer;—I mean, as it is identified with refined Taste, classical celebrity, and critical acumen."[53] Another request came from a Miss Pipper, who, though she admits not knowing Byron, is audaciously specific in her demands for "a verse of four or eight lines" to accompany "a painting collection of flowers" that she was making. She even "takes the liberty of writing a few names of flowers—that his Lordship may select which he pleases."[54]

Like Miss Pipper, some of Byron's most extravagant fans were women. Henrietta d'Ussières wrote a series of letters beginning in 1814 to ask for Byron's autograph. Referencing John Bellingham, who assassinated Prime Minister Spencer Perceval in 1812, she warns: "Meanwhile, do you remember my threats? They are never-failing threats—far worse than those of a Bellingham. He killed his man at once, & I'll tire you to death by degrees."[55] Another fan, "Rosalie," wrote Byron two letters in 1814 requesting, rather specifically, that he write her a few secret lines in the *Sunday Observer* "bearing the signature of Antonio."[56] Other letters by women suggest a desire for carnal familiarity with Byron. One pseudonymous letter appears to offer a sexual liaison: "Should curiosity prompt you, and should you not be afraid of gratifying it, by trusting yourself <u>alone</u> in the Green Park at seven o'clock this even you will see <u>Echo</u>. . . . Be on that side of the Green Park that has the gate opening into Piccadilly, and leave the rest to Echo."[57] Such salacious letters from female readers have focused much of the foundational work on Byron's fans.[58] Though intriguing, women like Miss Pipper, Henrietta d'Ussières, "Rosalie," and "Echo" are only part of the story. Fan mail from self-identified male readers shows that Byron attracted men and women, and I am more hesitant than previous scholars to presume that unsigned letters primarily came from female readers.

Much of Byron's fan mail, irrespective of the gender of the writer, points to the impropriety of addressing a lord who was not even an acquaintance. One admirer, John Joseph Stockdale, wondered if Byron might "not [be] pleased to receive this letter, unceremoniously, from a Stranger & that stranger a mere tradesman" before concluding, "I cannot persuade myself that you will be offended."[59] An anonymous letter sent in 1814 signed "your unknown <u>Friend</u>" more directly explains the problems of class: "The person who addresses you is a stranger to yourself, and to your family. She never has had, and probably never will have even the honor of an acquaintance. She is therefore impelled by no motive of interest in thus breaking the bounds of custom, and addressing one who is unknown, except by his writings. Those writings must be her excuse, as it is the strong interest they have excited that causes her to take this Liberty."[60] The underscoring of "Friend" at the letter's conclusion, combined with its opening emphasis on the writer's choice to break "the bounds of custom," encapsulate the conundrum facing readers who wrote to Byron. The feeling of interpersonal familiarity is there, but so is the knowledge that such feelings from those without "even the honor of an acquaintance" were, by standards of the day, indecorous and risked provoking disdain. Letters like those written by fans signing themselves "A Stranger" or "your unknown Friend" point to the boundaries that they break, thus demonstrating how socially engrained such boundaries were. Some writers identify and excuse their forwardness almost in the same epistolary breath: "Though a stranger to you . . . even this [letter] may be a comfort to a mind as desolate as yours."[61] Some readers felt that Byron's poetry invited them to write to him in the familiar style that they saw in his work. As Throsby observes, "Although many of the women [who wrote to Byron] apologise for the presumptuousness of writing to someone whom they have never met, they continually emphasize that they 'know' Byron through his poetry."[62] Throsby's astute assertion also applies to the men who sent letters. Indeed, perhaps part of the scandal of these letters was the fact that both women and men wrote to Byron in highly familiar and even romantic ways.

Not known for its modesty, Byron's poetry lacks the apologetic thread of the fan letters. Readers point to and sometimes explicitly blame Byron's poetic style for motivating their familiar letters. Take William Edmund Romedy, an Irish eighteen-year-old, who begs Byron's forgiveness for the "obtrusion of a stranger upon your Lordship's private feelings, and the apparent extravagance of his sentiments and requests." Like others, Romedy immediately voices his hope that Byron will forgive such boldness, implicitly suggesting that Byron is above the pettiness of performative politeness. His request, Romedy admits, "might by the many be termed impertinence or imposition but he who writes this, thinks too meanly of the world, and too proudly of Lord Byron; to be deterred."[63] Identifying Byron as one of the discerning few, Romedy's letter replicates the trope of exclusivity central to Byron's poetics of familiarity. Romedy aligns himself and Byron with the poet's solitary characters who exist beyond typical codes of sociability.

Like Romedy, the Quaker poet Bernard Barton was equally undeterred by rules governing familiarity and the impertinence of its misapplication. Barton wrote several adoring and rather flustered letters to Byron beginning in 1812.[64] One opens with an acknowledgement of his stranger status: "I hope your Lordship will forgive an obscure and nameless stranger for thus presuming to you his interest, his warmest thank you for the pleasure delivered from the perusal of your 'Childe Harold' . . . [W]ithout allowing myself to reflect on our respective situations in Society, which might deter me from any attempt to express my admiration and gratitude, I hasten to return my acknowledgments for the delight you have afforded me."[65] The four-page letter, somewhat longer than others Byron received, points directly to Byron's poems, particularly "To Thyrza," as justification for "the freedom of this address." Barton identifies his admiration for the lyrics in *Childe Harold*, many of which imply an autobiographical speaker and origins in the manuscript albums of Byron's inner circle. Barton claims it is the intimacy of these lyrics which drew him to Byron and led him to believe the poet would feel for him: "[T]he benevolence of heart exemplified in some of the smaller pieces of the Volume [*Childe Harold*] before me now, encourage me to hope for your indulgence."[66] Barton was one of a handful of fans who received Byron's indulgence. Responding to a fellow published author, Byron's succinct reply to Barton is cordial though does not explicitly encourage further correspondence.[67]

Other letter writers acknowledge more boldly how social class delineates familiarity's boundaries and how their fan mail pushes propriety. One anonymous writer wonders how Byron will interpret a stranger having the audacity to address a member of the peerage: "Your Lordship may perhaps smile, and with a smile not wholly free from satire, that one to whom you are personally entirely unknown should take the liberty of addressing you—But he who is known through the medium of his works, cannot be uninteresting even to a stranger."[68] Similarly, another fan points to Byron's nature—gleaned only from his poetry—as an excuse for overstepping the limits of propriety: "That gentleness of nature which I conceive your Lordship possesses, will incline you to forgive what you may probably consider as a presumptuous freedom; and you are also requested to destroy these lines as soon as you have thrown a glance [over] them."[69] This request to destroy the letter places the writer in a position of perceived power; they demand that Byron dispose of their correspondence with the same forcefulness that one may expect of a correspondent whom one actually knows.

Like Byron's poetry, the fan letters sent to him wrestle with genre conventions—in this case, the genre of the familiar letter. And, like his poetry, they resist and reshape genre conventions as well as the models of sociability that they represent. The familiar letter formed a key part of social life, and its role increased throughout the eighteenth and nineteenth centuries as the developing "postal system meant that the mail, which previously had been restricted to government agents and private couriers, was now theoretically open to anyone willing to pay the price of admission." As a result, according to Rachael Scarborough King, letters "filter[ed] through the social spectrum."[70] Pressures to maintain social distinctions increased alongside technological and postal advances that democratized letter writing, and eighteenth- and nineteenth-century didactic manuals reveal the importance of proper epistolary conduct with one's familiars and with strangers. In her work on the role of letters in eighteenth-century sociability and family structures, Sarah M. S. Pearsall explains, "Writing sensible familiar letters in this period was one way to signal and even to reinforce status, wealth, and authority."[71] Familiar letters bolstered social connections rather than created them; though epistolary "cold calling" was not unheard of, it would not have been standard. Occasionally, eighteenth- and nineteenth-century letter-writing manuals offer examples of how one might attempt to begin a familiar correspondence with a stranger. David Fordyce's *The New and Complete British Letter-Writer* includes templates for letters "From a young Man of respectable character to a lady, with whom he became enamoured at a place of public resort" and "From a young Man who had failed in business to a Gentleman of fortune."[72] The tone of these exemplars is notably more restrained than the gushing forwardness of Byron's fan letters. Typically, such warmth in familiar letters implied trust and prior attachment, and the genre conventions of the familiar letter served a key purpose. As Pearsall observes, they "carved out a particular social space, one in which certain freedoms were permitted. They were allowed only to certain people, though, and this meant that familiarity excluded as much and as many as it included."[73] The emotive and social value of familiar letters depended on the difference between the crowd and the chosen few—the same dynamic central to *Childe Harold* and the Turkish Tales.

Familiar letters written to Byron by his regular correspondents reveal difficulties of negotiating familiarity's aspects of inclusion and exclusion, especially when class was involved. Murray's letters to Byron, for example, often acknowledge the social disparity between them while reminding Byron of their financial—but also friendly—relationship. These letters show Murray navigating an increasingly familiar relationship with a social superior who was also his most lucrative poet. Take the apologetic letter addressing Murray's deletion of *Manfred*'s final line: "I sometimes feel a deep regret that in our pretty long intercourse I appear to have failed to shew, that a man in my situation, may <be> possess the feelings & principles of a Gentleman—most certainly I do think that from personal attachment, I could venture as much in any shape for your service as any of those who have the good fortune to be ranked amongst your Lordships friends."[74] Murray politely chides Byron for not giving him the benefit of the doubt about the deleted line; Byron should know him better than that. But in claiming to know Byron and be attached to him, Murray also expresses a clear awareness of their social positions—Murray a publisher, Byron a lord. Murray offers a skilled example of an appropriate familiar letter, especially one that traverses class: it points to the history of their relationship, it bridges and supports their existing social connection, and it does so in decorous language appropriate to the sender's and receiver's respective social roles. By contrast, most of the letters that fans sent to Byron claim a social connection that did not previously exist, and many excuse their familiar language in order to bridge boundaries between classes and between friend and stranger. Epistolary forwardness from unknown readers, then, challenged normative expectations governing familiarity's associations with exclusivity and emotional attachment. Familiarity was typically only recognized as a social virtue in moderation; there was an element of unseemliness when droves of readers imagined familiar connections with Byron.

I would like to turn again to Bernard Barton, who first wrote to Byron in 1812 and whose letters intensified in subsequent years. He wrote two pleading letters to Byron in two days in April 1814. While the tone of Barton's letters is informed by the fact that Byron responded to his initial letter in 1812, it seems the two did not have a sustained correspondence. Like Murray, who pointed to his willingness to be at Byron's service as a sign of their friendship, Barton identifies his desire to serve the poet as an excuse for his epistolary familiarity. In one of his 1814 letters, Barton offers to be Byron's valet and perhaps something more: "Although in my last [letter] which as I before observed was hastily written, I express'd my wish to be allow'd in one capacity or other, to serve your Lordship . . . the Services of one who is warmly attach'd to you, perhaps romantically, for I know nothing of your Lordship but by your writing, might be acceptable."[75] The reference to Barton's romantic desire for Byron is notable for its simultaneous charges of platonic idealization and perhaps sexualized infatuation. Byron's sexuality, certainly considered radical in the period, was not well known beyond his close circle, though gossip grew following his separation from his wife in 1816. Even if not intended in a sexualized way, Barton's letter, coming two years earlier, reveals a rhetoric of longing that has been more often associated with Byron's female fans.

As we have seen in other readers' letters to Byron, Barton balances his self-described "presumption" and "impertinence" with claims that Byron's poetry invites such treatment.[76] Barton acknowledges Byron's rank only to claim that both men are somehow above it: "I esteem you my Lord not merely for your Rank, still less for your personal qualities, the former I respect as I ought, of the latter I know nothing; but I feel something more than mere respect for your genius and your talents, & from your past conduct towards myself I cannot be insensible to your kindness. For these reasons, my Lord I acted as I have done; I therefore told you that I considered you no common Character."[77] Here Barton plays with rank and commonness. Barton's sense of *common* implies that Byron's qualities—qualities Barton repeatedly admits he has little knowledge of, apart from what he gleans from Byron's poetry—place the poet outside the formalities of rank. This is not unlike Charlotte Smith's earlier appeals in *Elegiac Sonnets* to sympathetic readers who can see beyond the "fastidious" limits of familiarity.[78] While Barton had previously received a letter from Byron, it is his knowledge of Byron's poetry that drives his decision to test the bounds of decorum and write repeatedly on familiar terms.[79]

The desired leap from stranger to servant to (perhaps) lover indicates significant slippages in traditional standards of sociability, sympathy, and affection. Similar slippages between the public and Byron's friends appear in a letter from Eliza Horatia Sommerset, whose overture to Byron I quoted above. She writes, "[I]n a note at the end of the Bride of Abydos, you say you possess poems never published . . . [I] entreat you not to keep such a treasure from the Public from your Friends, from your admirers."[80] The letter's list conflates the different groups mentioned, and the final group of "admirers" presumably contains members of the public and Byron's friends. Other letters, too, offer familiar friendship, such as one urging Byron to embrace religion signed "your unknown Friend," or another whose writer acknowledges she is "unknown" to Byron but hopes that it might give him "satisfaction to know there is a heart that considers with deep interest every change in your life and feels for your happiness and misery as its own."[81] Though prefiguring recognizable modes of fan culture today, in the early nineteenth century, such letters represented rather radical class crossing: recall that Miss Sommerset's letter to Byron also points to the social disparity between herself and the poet as the reason for not writing him earlier. Questions of whom one should bring into familiarity intensified later in the period as distinctions between classes increasingly blurred. At the turn of the century shifts in textile and clothing production narrowed visual cues of class; the upwardly mobile merchant classes rubbed elbows with socially respectable—but often economically strained—landed gentry; and, as I explore in more detail in chapter 4, the explosion of cheap editions of classics from Milton to Shakespeare to Pope made the cultural capital of literary knowledge more widely available. As a result, conservatives held more steadfastly to social norms that reinforced class distinctions such as the conventions surrounding familiar letters—the very conventions that Byron's fans almost relished breaking.

The fan mail reveals that fears about the "moral disease" of "the *Byromania*" were not entirely unwarranted.[82] As Byron's popularity spread, it dangerously seemed to encourage readers to cross class-based boundaries of sociability and authority. Byron's reception history evidences "the motif of poisonous or otherwise dangerous reading" that Patrick Brantlinger associates with the rise of the novel.[83] Writing of *Childe Harold* III and *The Prisoner of Chillon*, Walter Scott noted that elites no longer had much influence on their inferiors' responses to Byron: "Reading is indeed so general among all ranks and classes, that the impulse received by the public mind on such occasions is instantaneous through all but the very lowest classes of society, instead of being slowly communicated from one set of readers to another, as was the case in the days of our fathers."[84] Without the mitigating effects of class in Scott's idealized recollections of "the days of our fathers," the Byron disease infected indiscriminately. Byron and his reception, then, signaled not only familiarity run rampant but also emotions gone wild.

Consider the anonymous fan letter that demands that Byron burn it. Before its instructions for destruction, the letter flatters Byron by comparing him to his fellow celebrity author Walter Scott. The letter reveals the inflamed emotions that Byron's poetry stoked: "[A]ssuredly the muse of Walter Scott can never raise those transports of mournful delight, which Lord Byron has the powerful (and I believe exclusive) ability of exciting whenever he pleases."[85] It was exactly this power that caused concern, and the letter's rhetoric recalls Byron's descriptions of Lara's celebrity power. Even more extreme, the abovementioned Irish teenager William Edmund Romedy imagines Byron's poetry as a zombie-like infection consuming his mind: "I thought I was alone upon earth but I was deceived. In Harold, in the Giaour and in Lara, have I,—and proudly! recognized the workings of a kindred spirit. The moulding of the forms is gigantic, but in features and in figure, they are the same—By some mysterious agency they have clouded my mind,—they increasingly work upon my fancy—they eat into the very core of my thought, and sleeping or waking they are before me!"[86] Critics also feared that Byromania was eating into the core of the literary marketplace and, more shockingly, the literary and moral values of the day. Francis Jeffrey noted that by the 1820s "the great body of the English nation—the religious, the moral, and the candid part of it—consider the tendency of his [Byron's] writings to be immoral and pernicious."[87] Though neither Byron's critics nor the period's moralists had access to the letters examined here, it was no secret that many readers adored him. Byron boasted, joked, and complained about the letters he received, and a handful of fans later became lovers—Lady Caroline Lamb being the most famous among them. The seductive elements of Byron's verse—particularly its dark references to immorality—made Byromania a pressing part of Regency-era culture, and it colored his poetry's reception with concerns about moral contagion more often associated with gothic novels and Jacobin political tracts.

THE POLITICS OF BYRON'S FAMILIARITY

As Byromania spread across the Romantic world, the poet's authorized works, excerpts, and piracies reached readers everywhere, from Birmingham to Boston to Bengal. In 1821, Byron bragged about reports of his cultural prominence:

"Moore wrote to me from Paris months ago that 'the French had caught the contagion of Byronism to the highest pitch.'"[88] Significantly, Byron's rhetoric of disease mirrors Romedy's earlier frantic claim that Byron's poetry ate "into the very core" of his mind.[89] As both a poet and a phenomenon, "Byron" became a politicized literary disease. The momentum of Byromania converges with one of the two periods—1789–1796 and 1815–1819—during which, according to Andrew Stauffer, "English debates over revolution and reform" attained a fever pitch, with texts, readers, "and most often, 'the people' as a potentially insurrectionary aggregate . . . described as being 'inflamed.'"[90] Byron's celebrity and his fans' responses played out against the backdrop of the Napoleonic Wars, the aftermath of Waterloo, and growing unrest about reform. There were fears that Byron's mob of readers might relish not just him but also the increasing radicalism of his poetry.

According to Jon Mee, the expanding reading public in the Romantic period was seen as potentially "infectious in such a way as to make it a dangerous enthusiasm."[91] Byron was a particularly virulent strain of this problem because of what critics saw as his pandering to, in the words of one reviewer, "the lowest and vulgarest classes" in "very condescending and un-aristocratic" ways.[92] Byron's association with inflamed readers connected his poetry's popularity to Romantic-era suspicions of novel-reading women. Female (novel) readers were, Deidre Lynch aruges, colored "with the kind of consumption, sponsored by the circulating library, that turns books into fungible merchandise."[93] Later in his career, Byron's interest in his copyrights as valuable commodities suggested a rather unaristocratic, merchandising impulse. The conservative periodical *John Bull* quipped, "LORD BYRON is a hireling—a hireling of MR. JOHN MURRAY'S," while another sarcastically noted the low cost of *Don Juan*: "[H]e has very judiciously accommodated the price of his poetry to the purses of his readers. If every one cannot contrive to muster a shilling, at least two or three can club their pence, and so compass the purchase of a copy of Don Juan."[94] Negative responses to Byron's later work typically accuse Byron of immorality, aesthetically poor poetry, and pandering to a paying public. While sometimes social and political concerns bubble explicitly to the surface in Byron's critical reception, more often their presence appears obliquely behind dismissals of the poet's works and his readers. McDayter observes that "like Byron's romances," Byromania "was quickly dismissed as vacuous 'pap' suitable only for women and adolescents."[95] The problem, then, was not Byron's poetry but its readers, particularly what they implied about the instability of literary and social value.

The historical context of Byron's celebrity touched on charged political wires connected to earlier anti-Jacobin fears of the unruly public, "of mass literacy, of empowering the wrong people to read and write, and therefore to begin questioning and attempting to rewrite the forms of traditional authority."[96] Byron attracted a large, and as we have seen, passionate following, and his fans' own letters gesture toward the unruliness of Byron's effect on them. Recall Romedy, who blamed "some mysterious agency" in Byron's poetry for infecting his mind, or Eliza Horatia Sommerset, who claimed she could "resist no longer" her overwhelming desire to write to Byron.[97] According to John Wilson's review of the fourth canto of *Childe Harold*, readers had "formed a kind of strange, wild and disturbed friendship" with the poet.[98] Indeed, the wildness of readers' perceived friendship with Byron was disturbing to many because it fed fears about unruly enthusiasm, the rapidly expanding literary marketplace, and the celebrity culture that they enabled.

Byron's infectious presence in the public imagination forced a re-evaluation of the dynamics between authors and readers and between literature and moral philosophy. Romantic-era dismissals of popular culture and disparaging comments about Byron's readers, then, reveal larger concerns about the subversive nature of the strong emotions that writers like Byron evoked. Marcus explains, "Celebrity culture is always a debate about whom and what we value."[99] Celebrity, then, is also a debate about how to assess both aesthetic and moral values. As with Elizabeth Gunning in this book's introduction, and as we shall see in the next chapter with Lady Caroline Lamb, some believed that it was primarily Byron's name and the scandal surrounding him that sold his later works: "Any production issued under the name of a writer so distinguished not only by talent, but by *questionable* extensive celebrity as Lord Byron, cannot fail to excite considerable attention and inquiry."[100] Byron's familiar style and readers' enthusiastic responses upended Romantic-era philosophies about how familiarity and sympathy functioned. In their resistance to class-inflected interaction and moderated emotional display, Byron and his readers challenged how aesthetic valuations and sympathetic connections were made.

The affective relationships between Byron, readers, and the public resist theories of sociability and sympathy proposed by thinkers from Edmund Burke to Joanna Baillie to Adam Smith. All three grapple with relationships between curiosity and sympathy, between revelation and emotional regulation. At the heart of these relationships is the problem of familiarity—in some circumstances it prompts closeness and sympathy, but in others it heightens distance and disdain. Burke and Baillie each suggest that mystery and incompleteness increase interest and sympathy. Burke writes, "In reality a great clearness helps but little towards affecting the passions, as it is in some sort an enemy to all enthusiasms whatsoever."[101] Like the boundaries between familiarity and overfamiliarity, the difference between clarity and too much clarity determines if and how much sympathy we feel for another person. Burke admits the difficulty of this balance: "Some degree of novelty must be one of the materials in every instrument which works upon the mind; and curiosity blends itself more or less with all our passions."[102] While important for jump-starting sympathy, curiosity alone cannot sustain it because, according to Burke, "curiosity is the most superficial of all the affections; it changes its object perpetually"; once curiosity is satisfied, sympathy wanes.[103]

Reviews of Byron's work bear a striking resemblance to Burke's ideas and rhetoric. The review of *Childe Harold* quoted in this chapter's epigraph mirrors Burke's sentiments about full disclosure and its negative consequences for sympathy: "As the reader will have expected, the third canto of Childe Harold is still more replete than the two preceding ones with allusions, and even direct passages, which belong to the personal circumstances of the author . . . which not so much engages its sympathy, as piques its curiosity."[104] For the reviewer, as for Burke, sympathy and curiosity differ in kind as well as in degree. The review suggests a downward trajectory from sympathy in the first two cantos of *Childe Harold* to mere curiosity in the third, which readers believed offered more fulsome autobiographical details. From this perspective, Byron's later poetry veers toward overfamiliarity by revealing many personal details to a wide audience. The reviewer's diction—"engages" versus "piques"—also points to Burke's assertions that curiosity is more superficial than sympathy.

Similar to Burke and the reviewer above, Adam Smith identifies clarity as a potential problem, and concerns about clarity and curiosity in moral philosophy align with debates about familiarity's limits. In both cases the line between too much and too little proved notoriously difficult to navigate. Too much clarity repulses—a type of overfamiliarity that, today, would be associated with the vulgarity of TMI (too much information). However, according to Smith, a lack of clarity can also provoke superficial curiosity: "This passion to discover the real sentiments of others is naturally so strong, that it often degenerates into a troublesome and impertinent curiosity."[105] Some believed that Byron catered to this impertinent curiosity. John Wilson's review of the final canto of *Childe Harold* draws parallels between Rousseau and Byron, and Wilson accuses the former of "seizing upon all his most hidden thoughts . . . and flinging them out into the open air, that they might feed the curiosity of that eager, idle, frivolous world."[106] Like throwing meat to a pack of wolves, Rousseau and Byron, Wilson suggests, share autobiographical information to create a feeding frenzy predicated on familiarity. This frenzy speaks to Smith's concerns that sympathy, like familiarity, could transition into something vulgar if overexcited. As with understanding the genre expectations of the familiar letter, negotiating dynamics between curiosity and self-exposure and between familiarity and overfamiliarity proved equally fraught.

Preoccupations with these boundaries also arise in Baillie's *Plays on the Passions.* Like Smith and Burke before her, she privileges the emotional power of hidden passions; unlike them, she withholds judgment about potentially negative consequences of curiosity. Baillie suggests that just as all people inevitably harbor within them passions that are "concealed from the world's eye," they naturally wish to discover these secret emotions in others. If it were possible, she claims, we would follow someone "into his lonely haunt, into his closet, into the midnight silence of his chamber."[107] The image of the private closet secretly observed carries a sense of transgression. Baillie's invisible observer would have access to the imagined man's authentic, concealed passions by crossing the boundary between public identity and private space.

Baillie's perspective provides a foil for Smith and Burke, but all three writers' views about sympathy and curiosity point to the period's preoccupation with sociability and the moral values it either upheld or challenged. The spatial imagery found in Baillie and Smith suggests not only potential movements between sympathy and curiosity but also, implicitly, movement across class. While Smith's domestic metaphors for sympathy avoid the uneasy—and presumably nonconsensual—surveillance found in Baillie's theories, the possibility that sympathy, if unchecked, could degrade into curiosity haunts his theories of emotion. Rather than a secret spy observing a man in his closet, Smith imagines a cordial invitation; the man "who invites us into his heart, who as it were, sets open the gates of his breast to us, seems to exercise a species of hospitality more delightful than any other."[108] Echoing Smith, Scott claimed readers relished being "invited to witness and partake" in Byron's emotions when, in *Childe Harold*, "the noble pilgrim thus exposed the sanctuary of his bosom."[109] Again, the central focus of Byron's reviewers mirrors the preoccupations of moral philosophers.

A key question for moral philosophers as well as for Byron's critics was who belonged in the category of Smith's imagined "us." That is, if the gate to the sanctuary of one's bosom is open to anyone, does gaining admission still have emotive, sociable value? In her *British Synonymy; or, An Attempt Regulating the Choice of Words in Familiar Conversation*, Hester Lynch Piozzi begins to answer this question. She points to a hierarchy where "one may be of Easy Intercourse with all, Familiar to many; yet Friendly to a few."[110] Readers' imagined relationships with Byron challenged this hierarchical distinction between all, the many, and the few. Byron was open with many and, in turn, his readers claimed a familiarity (both epistolary and emotional) to which they, as strangers, were not entitled. Typically, eighteenth- and nineteenth-century assessments about the propriety of more lenient, cross-class understandings of familiarity's limits divide along conservative and more radical lines. In Byron's case, though, reviewers across the political spectrum expressed concerns about his pull over the public, his courtship of their emotions, and conjectures about how readers might react. In the *Eclectic Review*, for instance, Josiah Conder notes that "his Lordship has made the public his confidant"—something antithetical to theories of sympathy proposed by Baillie, Burke, Smith, and Piozzi that claim privilege should be extended only to the chosen few.[111] Conder observes, "He seems willing to receive from the impersonal multitude that homage of sympathy, which perhaps we would be too proud to accept from an individual who could answer or gaze upon the speaker."[112] Distance is key, and Conder's descriptions of the multitude's "gaze" emphasizes visuality, much like Baillie's reference to "the world's eye." For Conder, the public's inability to gaze upon Byron makes the poet seek their sympathy and divulge autobiographical details.

Conder's claims also gesture toward and implicitly dispute Smith's idea of the impartial spectator whose imagined judgments of one's sentiments regulate the expression of those sentiments. "In solitude," Smith writes, "we are apt to feel too strongly whatever relates to ourselves." The anodyne for feeling "too strongly" is sociability, real or imagined: "The conversation of a friend brings us better, that of a stranger to a still better temper. The man within the breast, the abstract and ideal spectator of our sentiments and conduct, requires often to be awakened and put in mind of his duty, by the presence of the real spectator: and it is always from that spectator, from whom we can expect the least sympathy and indulgence, that we are likely to learn the most complete lesson of self-command."[113] Byron, Conder claims, does the opposite; the poet relaxes his self-command before the public. Like Byron's heroes who are best understood by strangers, Byron claims the most sympathetic indulgence from his anonymous audience of strangers—the very strangers who wrote fan letters to him. From this perspective, Byron's familiarity and emotional exposure flies in the face of prominent eighteenth-century theories of sympathy. His emotions are disregulated before strangers. However, judging from his extant fan mail, Byron still managed to encourage sympathy and not just curiosity. It is as if he used the absence "of the real [physical] spectator" to let loose. Counter to Smith's ideas about how sympathy and self-command work, Byron allows himself and his readers "to feel too strongly"—yet with sympathetic effect.

Conder strikes a similar tone in his largely positive review of *The Corsair*. Describing the "mingled feelings of admiration, pity, abhorrence, and sympathy" which Byron's poetry evokes, Conder suggests that this "interest in the minds of his [Byron's] readers" may be "more soothing to the sullenness of intellectual pride, than the familiar caresses of affection."[114] Byron's unknown readers surpass physical familiarity; they offer Byron a sympathetic balm predicated on the absence of bodily proximity. Physical distance between writer and readers, Conder suggests, increases sympathetic connection, which raises the question of how sympathy and familiarity might function differently across various mediums. Byron's era was a time when the technologies for communication, including a rapidly improving mail system and faster modes of printing, were changing the media landscape. In this context, medium mattered in more pressing ways than before.

Though typically implicit rather than explicit, this anxiety about medium—unresolved by eighteenth-century thinkers—underlies assessments of Byron's ability to stoke readers' familiarity, curiosity, and sympathy.[115] Byron's poetry and its reception suggest that interpersonal familiarity in print is stronger than flesh and blood sociability. This possibility counters Hume's claim that sympathy arises from physical proximity rather than ties of kinship. Nancy Yousef summarizes: "As a mere perception or apprehension of another, sympathy has everything to do with proximity, with near exposure. . . . In the immediate presence of another, sympathy makes no distinction between the beloved and the stranger."[116] The precondition of immediate presence, important for Hume, is absent between Byron and his readers. While some readers like "Echo" and Lady Caroline Lamb sought physical connection with Byron, by the Regency period literature had largely shifted toward a mediated model of authorship, with distance between authors and readers growing. Though contact between Byron and his fans would have been, in most cases, a fantasy of an improbable kind, particularly after his departure from England in 1816, they still wrote to and felt for him. This raises questions about how print and the literary field could recreate—in worrying ways—the sympathy that moral philosophers associated with physical interaction. Byron's isolated heroes and his inflamed fans, then, embody but also challenge these Romantic-era beliefs about sympathy that Yousef has so thoughtfully explored. For Byron and his publics, it is in print rather than in person that the "communities of mutually transparent, open-hearted confidants and citizens," like those presented by Rousseau, "render sympathetic identification a matter of indubitable fact as well as irresistible feeling."[117] Byromania brought troubling questions about the medium of communication to the fore because everything from his heroes to his fan mail are, at their core, material and textual phenomena.

Wilson addresses the issue of medium in his review of the fourth canto of *Childe Harold* and, unlike Conder, excuses Byron for the social customs his autobiographical poetry disregards: "But there are other reasons why we read with complacency writings which, by the most public declaration of most secret feelings, ought, it might seem, to shock and revolt our sympathies. A great poet may address the whole world in the language of intensest passion, concerning objects which, rather than speak, face to face, with any one human being on earth, he would perish in misery."[118] Like Byron's fan mail, which acknowledges decorous limits of familiar address only to break them, Wilson accepts that Byron's declarations of his "most secret feelings" might provoke revulsion. Also like Byron's fans, Wilson attempts to dismiss breaches of decorum, and he does so by citing the medium of communication as a factor: print versus speech. Wilson offers the same nonapology for Byron's impassioned, seemingly improper emotions that fans did when they wrote Byron familiar letters. For Wilson, for Conder, and for Byron's fans, physical distance and the medium of communication together shifted the boundaries governing familiarity, emotional regulation, and sympathy.

In bucking established expectations for autobiographical revelations—revelations that, in the words of one reviewer, left readers "dismayed to find a man frankly avowing the most disgraceful vices"—Byron's familiarity with his mass audience implicitly rejected the moral philosophy of the time.[119] Byron refused to moderate his emotions in the ways those like Burke and Smith thought necessary for sympathy. Instead, according to Francis Jeffery, Byron "unbosomed his griefs a great deal too freely to his readers."[120] Ultimately, Byron's ability to leverage seeming overfamiliarity into readers' sympathetic familiarity presented his contemporaries with a disconcerting possibility: that the foundational philosophies of sociability and morality framing eighteenth-century thought begin to buckle under the rapidly changing social, technological, and political conditions of the Romantic period. It was as if his own seemingly unhealthy relationship with familiarity's traditional boundaries infected readers, igniting their passions and their compulsion to write him familiar letters. The poet and his publics, then, rejected the most basic rule of familiarity: that it should be limited, measured. Byron partly got away with personal disclosures to a mass public by coupling familiarity with physical distance and forwarding the idea of the stranger as confident—strategies that his readers mimicked in their letters. As we shall see in the following two chapters, on Lady Caroline Lamb—socialite turned Byron fangirl turned author turned social outcast—and William Hazlitt, other writers similarly embraced these strategies. Like Byron's, Lamb's and Hazlitt's familiarity reveals itself in autobiographical allusions which they (superficially) declaim. However, unlike Byron, their most autobiographical works were met with resounding vitriol from critics and lay readers alike.

3

LADY CAROLINE LAMB'S FEMALE FOLLIES AND THE DANGERS OF FAMILIARITY

Why should I hide men's follies, whilst my own
Blaze like gas along this talking town?
—Lady Caroline Lamb, "Lines to Harriet Wilson"*

CONCERNS ABOUT BYRON'S POETRY, the last chapter argued, partly arose from Byromania's influence on the public imagination. To some of his contemporaries, the frenzied, familiar feelings that readers felt for Byron signaled both the power of his poetry and its ability to destabilize Romantic-era norms of sociability and sympathy. For Regency readers as well as for scholars of Romanticism, Byron's most famous fan turned lover, Lady Caroline Lamb, seemed to offer an extreme example of the poet's magnetism and its potentially disastrous consequences. Lamb and Byron's explosive affair in the spring of 1812 and its aftermath—especially the publication of Lamb's semi-autobiographical novel *Glenarvon* in 1816—rocked London with a force not seen since the Elizabeth Gunning scandal in the 1790s with which this book began. Like Gunning, Lamb's reputation took on a life of its own in magazines, newspapers, poems, novels, memoirs, music, and even portraits.

Two portraits in particular irked Lamb. In November 1813, visitors to Thomas Phillips's studio would have seen two paintings hanging side by side. In one sits an attractive man wearing a black robe and a white shirt; his distinctive hairline and cleft chin made him immediately recognizable as Byron. In the other stands Lamb dressed as a pageboy with cropped curly hair; a black dog looks longingly at the platter of fruit she offers someone beyond the canvas. While Lamb's picture eventually retreated into relative obscurity, Phillips's "cloak portrait" would become one of the most recognizable and reproduced images of Byron for decades. Considered separately, the portraits would have been fairly innocuous to their original viewers. Displayed together, however, they immediately recalled Lamb and Byron's tumultuous relationship.

Gossip about Lamb had not died down in 1813, and she claimed that Phillips intentionally fueled it to bolster traffic in his semi-public studio. She wrote a frustrated letter to her friend and frequent correspondent (and Byron's publisher) John Murray: "I was asked whether I was painted at Phillips as a Page Holding a plate of Fruit to Lord Byron as [a] friar! Will you tell Phillips to put my picture out of sight . . . [E]very one going in sees us two together."[1] In Phillips's studio, their affair was on display for "every one" to see, and Byron's presence in the adjacent canvas reframed Lamb's portrait. Offering Byron fruit, she becomes subservient—a role that Lamb sometimes accepted willingly; she alluded to herself in one of her commonplace books as a "Bitch whom Lord Byron took a fancy for."[2] Still, her angry response to misreadings of her portrait should make us question whether more recent understandings of Lamb's life and career may, like her portrait's placement in Phillips's studio, mistakenly privilege Byron. Examining Lamb's life and work primarily in terms of Byron leaves us with, if not a completely wrong picture of Lamb, then at least an incomplete one.

This chapter sees Lamb's works in relation to Byron but not as primarily dependent on him, and it examines the picture of Lamb's authorship in the wider literary and social context of Regency England. Throughout, I counter prominent scholarly views that Byron provides the "unifying principle" of Lamb's authorship and that she "envied and certainly wanted to ape" his works in her own.[3] Over the past few decades, Lamb has received increasing scholarly attention but often through Byronic lenses. James Soderholm's *Fantasy, Forgery, and the Byron Legend*, for instance, explores Lamb's, Lady Blessington's, and Teresa Guiccioli's influences on Byron's image.[4] Relatedly, Duncan Wu, Nicola Watson, Paul Douglass, Rosemary March, and Clara Tuite have argued that Lamb's literary works seek to control Byron's public reputation.[5] However, Lamb's authorial career and the extensive archival record surrounding her reveal an author less concerned with Byron per se and more concerned with the larger cultural field that her literary works entered and the hypocritical, gendered standards by which they were judged. As a famous and wealthy aristocrat, commercially successful author, friend of the prince regent, prominent member of the Whig circle, and wife of future prime minister William Lamb (later Lord Melbourne), Caroline Lamb lived at the center of Romanticism's cultural, political, and literary life. As such, she was uniquely positioned to interrogate it. "When Lamb and her works are read against the context of her milieu," Leigh Wetherall Dickson observes, "her critique of the moral and political bankruptcy of her sphere of her existence, in which she includes herself, becomes clear."[6] While Byron was an important figure in that sphere, Lamb's life and works move well beyond him to challenge the gendered organization of Regency-era life and its rules for acceptable sociability.

Lamb lived much of her life in flagrant defiance of the period's standards of decorous familiarity. Even taking into account the more liberal Whig circle in which she was a mainstay, Lamb embodied the "Ease and forwardness of address, and excessive familiarity" that Romantic-era moralists worried were becoming all too fashionable among women.[7] Lamb's own familiar fan letter to Byron in 1812 led to carnal familiarity with the poet, and soon she shared the details of their affair in *Glenarvon* with such "excessive familiarity" with readers that her in-laws threatened to institutionalize her. According to one family member, *Glenarvon* "made a great noise in London" but was "more blamed than admired."[8] Rather than portray Lamb as a Byron-obsessed celebrity embarrassment (a description which, admittedly, conveys some measure of truth), this chapter highlights how her novels criticize the social and moral systems that put women on a track to ruin and that also made it difficult for them to change course.

Years before and after her entanglement with Byron, Lamb conducted a PR campaign both within and beyond her immediate circle. While not always successful, her attempts to excuse and reframe her behavior show her complex engagement with the decorous expectations that shaped female reputation in the period. This chapter argues that concerns about familiarity are central to this shaping. It shows that contemporary interpretations of Lamb's behavior, her first novel, and her subsequent literary works return to the importance of familiarity's boundaries and the disastrous consequences of crossing them. Lamb's case demonstrates how familiarity's limits were differently imposed on men and women, on different social classes, and on different literary genres, and I detail Lamb's keen awareness of the gender dynamics that disadvantaged her. Lamb prefigures the type of celebrity train wrecks often seen today, whose spiraling, shocking lives audiences feel compelled to watch, but with schadenfreude rather than sympathy, and this chapter seeks to understand what made Byron's references to his personal life compelling and Lamb's allusions to hers embarrassing.[9] As Lamb asked, "Why should I hide men's follies, whilst my own / Blaze like gas along this talking town?"[10] This chapter explores her question.

I begin with an overview of Lamb's scandalous life prior to *Glenarvon*, before turning to the novel and readers' reactions to it. Lamb's use of an autobiographical style similar to Byron's provoked largely negative responses and the type of superficial curiosity that, according to the moral philosophers explored in the previous chapter, subverted sympathy. Exposing details about Lamb's life, *Glenarvon* also attacks the social rules that delineated decorous familiarity. Her reception—recorded in her family's letters, manuscript books, marginalia, contemporary reviews, and satiric novels—reveals that Lamb's contemporaries thought her novel a failure of judgment, though not necessarily one of narrative craft. Byron's and Lamb's strikingly divergent reception histories point beyond aesthetic valuations toward larger issues of symbolic production, which, as Bourdieu asserts, are synonymous with "the production of the value of the work."[11] Lamb's case demonstrates how the nineteenth-century literary field was positioned to assess the works of an autobiographical, aristocratic female novelist very differently from those of a male poet of the peerage.

The chapter then turns to Lamb's later career and the attempts that she made to recuperate her image among both her inner circle and the public. Like *Glenarvon*, Lamb's second novel *Graham Hamilton* (1822) indicts aristocratic values that mask immorality and subjugate women, but it decidedly moves beyond her first novel's autobiographical focus. This shift demonstrates Lamb grappling with her negative public reputation as well as the larger social mechanisms that circulated and structured it. *Graham Hamilton*, more than *Glenarvon*, reveals how familiar customs create public morality but propagate private depravity, and her work engages prominent writers, including Mary Wollstonecraft, Jane Austen, and Frances Burney. The chapter concludes with a brief consideration of Lamb's other literary works across genres and mediums: her lyrics set to music, her poetry in literary annuals, and her name and art in children's literature. Lamb's later works sought to lift "the film of familiarity" that had settled over her and to encourage the public to see and feel for her in new ways.[12] Throughout her life, Lamb hoped that she might be judged, if not more kindly, then at least more fairly. She confided her wish to her friend and fellow novelist Lady Morgan: "[M]ay those who so well know & speak of my errors & follies pardon some of them . . . when they hear & see the strange circumstances into which I have been placed."[13] Here I attempt to interrogate the strange circumstances into which Lamb's female celebrity placed her and to read her works and reactions to them within that gendered context.

"WHEN ONE BRAVES THE OPINION OF THE WORLD"

Even before Lamb met Byron, she had courted single men and bad press. Her extramarital affair in 1810 with the popular gallant Sir Godfrey Vassal Webster anticipated her later indiscretions, and her family was appalled by the public nature of her relationship with the young soldier. After Lamb had been particularly imprudent at a party, her mother-in-law, Lady Melbourne, wrote angrily, "Yr behavior last night was so disgraceful in its appearances and so disgusting in its motives that it is quite impossible it should ever be effaced from my mind. When one braves the opinion of the World, sooner or later [they] will feel the consequences of it."[14] Lamb replied with histrionic letters, and her correspondence about Webster flirts with contrition and blame as her later letters about Byron would. On the one hand, she admits, "I can most truly & painfully feel for your reproof & the grief & infamy I am bringing on myself & family." On the other, she accuses her husband William Lamb of corrupting her morals: "William himself taught me to regard without horror all the forms & restraints I had laid so much stress on."[15] Rarely do her own letters or her family's reproofs point to the immorality of her affairs; rather, they focus on her growing public infamy and the damage it did to her Whig circle's reputation.[16]

To the mortification of Lamb's family and the delight of those who followed Regency gossip, her behavior reached new extremes when she met Byron. From conspicuously waiting outside balls for him during their affair to cutting herself at a ball and burning him in effigy after it ended, Lamb knew how to make a scene and had few qualms about doing so.[17] In the scolding words of her mother's personal maid: "[A]las you have exposed yourself to all of London you are the talk of every Groom and Footman about Town."[18] Notably, Mrs. Peterson's comments highlight not Lamb's behavior but its public consequences, particularly among nonaristocrats. A lady's reputation in the eighteenth and nineteenth centuries depended more on "the public recognition of her virtue" than her life behind closed doors, and affairs were tacitly accepted if quietly conducted.[19] For instance, the fashion and political icon Georgiana Cavendish, Duchess of Devonshire (Lamb's aunt) lived for many years with her husband and Elizabeth Foster—her friend and the Duke's mistress. The eyebrow-raising living arrangements at Devonshire House were no secret, but public gossip never quite reached the salacious fever pitch of that surrounding Lamb and her affair with Byron. The outward respectability of women like Lamb's aunt, mother (Countess of Bessborough), and mother-in-law (Lady Melbourne)—all of whom had affairs—depended on keeping trysts within a circumscribed group bound by ties of familiarity. As Mrs. Peterson's letter above suggests, Lamb's biggest sin was not adultery but rather her unwillingness or inability to be discreet.

Published articles intensified gossip, and throughout Lamb's life, notices about her appeared in popular venues, including *Bon Ton Magazine*, the *Morning Post*, and the *Morning Herald*. More than Byron's, Lamb's treatment in the press foreshadows today's paparazzi-fueled gossip magazines and their inflammatory, gendered coverage of female celebrities. The most famous example of this published gossip depicted an incident at Lady Heathcote's ball on July 5, 1813. After a tense encounter with Byron at the ball, Lamb cut herself. Rumors quickly circulated that she had stabbed herself and perhaps had attempted suicide. Shortly after, Byron reported having heard "a strange story of C[aroline]'s scratching herself with glass . . . of all this I was ignorant till this Evening."[20] Lamb later complained that the incident "was in all the papers & put not truly."[21] A few days after the ball, she wrote urgently to John Murray, "[D]o tell me if you read in the Morning Herald & some other papers this cruel account about a Lady In High life &ct and if you did[,] do you not think it ought to be contained?"[22] The *Satirist*, for example, covered the incident in hyperbolic detail. It claimed that Lamb "in a paroxysm of jealousy . . . took up a dessert-knife and stabbed herself. . . . The desperate Lady was carried out of the room, and the affair endeavoured to be hushed up."[23] These endeavors were unsuccessful; very few of her affairs—romantic or otherwise—remained contained and out of the press. Private calamities attracted public attention (and ridicule), and periodicals invasively noted less scandalous events: the birth and death of her infant daughter was reported in *Bell's Weekly Messenger* just six days after it occurred.[24] The degree to which all facets of Lamb's life were exposed—both with and without her permission—offers a troubling precursor to the exploitative elements of current celebrity culture.

The publication of *Glenarvon* on May 9, 1816 made matters worse. Her circle thought the novel crossed lines that should divide private life and public gossip, separate high and low classes, and demarcate familiarity and overfamiliarity. Lady Melbourne wrote of her "abhorrence & detestation of the book."[25] Byron's half sister, Augusta Leigh, was similarly incensed, writing to Byron's friend John Cam Hobhouse, "What I hear of Glenarvon is really enough to rouse every feeling of indignation—it has revived all the sad business, indeed I have not time by this post to say all I have to say about it."[26] *Glenarvon* revived talk of Byron's torrid affair with Lamb, and it contributed to the flurry of gossip surrounding the poet after his legal separation from his wife Annabella Milbanke and his subsequent self-imposed exile from England.[27]

Glenarvon rather confusingly tracks the life and death of Lady Calantha, whom many saw as a stand-in for Lamb. Calantha's marriage to the respectable but increasingly distanced Lord Avondale collapses after her public affair with the charismatic, politically rebellious Lord Glenarvon. Under various disguises, Glenarvon lures multiple women into immorality, causing their social and, in some cases, physical destruction; he also colludes with Calantha's aunt to orchestrate the (feigned) murder of an infant to ensure her own son's inheritance of the family's Irish estate. Despite *Glenarvon*'s setting during the Irish Rebellion of 1798 and its commentary on Anglo-Irish relations, contemporary readers seemed primarily interested in the sordid, sad business it supposedly revealed about Lamb and her circle.[28] Readers mapped the novel—a love marriage turned sour, a seductive lord with poetic and political proclivities, a brief but explosive affair, a woman socially ostracized, and a man empowered—directly onto Lamb's life, the details of which were already common knowledge. The novel's title character was instantly recognized as Byron. Milbanke's correspondent Robert Wilmot-Horton (Byron's cousin) assured her that "nobody doubts the correctness of Glenarvon's character."[29] The absence in 1816 of any biographies of Byron enabled biographical interpretations of the novel, and, according to Peter Graham, Regency readers "would have had no reason not to accept Lady Caroline's portrait [of Byron] as an accurate one."[30] There were other portraits in the novel, too: Lord Avondale as William Lamb, Sir and Lady Mowbray as Lord and Lady Melbourne, the pale poet Tremore as Samuel Rogers, Princess Madagascar as Lady Holland, Lady Mandeville as Lady Oxford, and William Buchanan as Sir Godfrey Webster.

Readers made keys identifying the real people portrayed in *Glenarvon*. For instance, a copy now held at the British Library contains a manuscript key inserted after the title page of the first volume (see figure 3.1).[31] The back flyleaf of another copy, once owned (and perhaps annotated) by Alexander Dyce, identifies Princess Madagascar as Lady Holland, Bombay House as Holland House, and the "poet of an emaciated and sallow complexion" as Samuel Rogers. Comments in the rear endpapers of the second volume attest to the accuracy of Lamb's unflattering descriptions: "P. 158 'besides a cook,' etc. It is quite true that Lady Holland (the Princess Madagascar) used to travel with such a train."[32] Similarly, a copy of the fourth edition of *Glenarvon* inscribed to the physician George Hamilton Roe "from the author" contains a manuscript key on one of the flyleaves of the first volume, though it is not in Lamb's hand.[33] Keys were also exchanged in letters. For instance, Wilmot-Horton wrote to Milbanke explaining, "Of course Lady C[aroline] & W[illiam] L[amb] you will easily recognise. . . . Lady Mandeville is Lady Oxford—P[rincess] Madagascar, Lady H[olland] . . . Some say that Buchanan is Sir G[odfrey] Webster, others that Lady Augusta is Lady Jersey, others that Lady Margaret is the present D[uchess] of D[evonshire]."[34] The prevalence of these key suggest that many readers, like the critic for the *British Lady's Magazine*, "expect[ed] allusions to existing characters; and, in truth, sent for these volumes with the idea of being entertained with all manner of fashionable scandal."[35]

Glenarvon's revelations about Regency elites not only kindled readers' curiosity but also solidified Lamb's celebrity status. The novel's original print run of 1,500 copies—1,000 more than the first run of *Childe Harold* I and II—sold out in a matter of weeks. Shortly after the novel's publication, Lamb informed her mother-in-law "that the 1500 copies are sold & a new Edition is wanted."[36] One can imagine how unenthused Lady Melbourne must have been. Knowing the novel was selling well, William Lamb wrote angrily to Lamb's publisher in May 1816, making clear his "determination that for the present at least there shall be published no second edition."[37] By June 1816 a revised second edition appeared, which

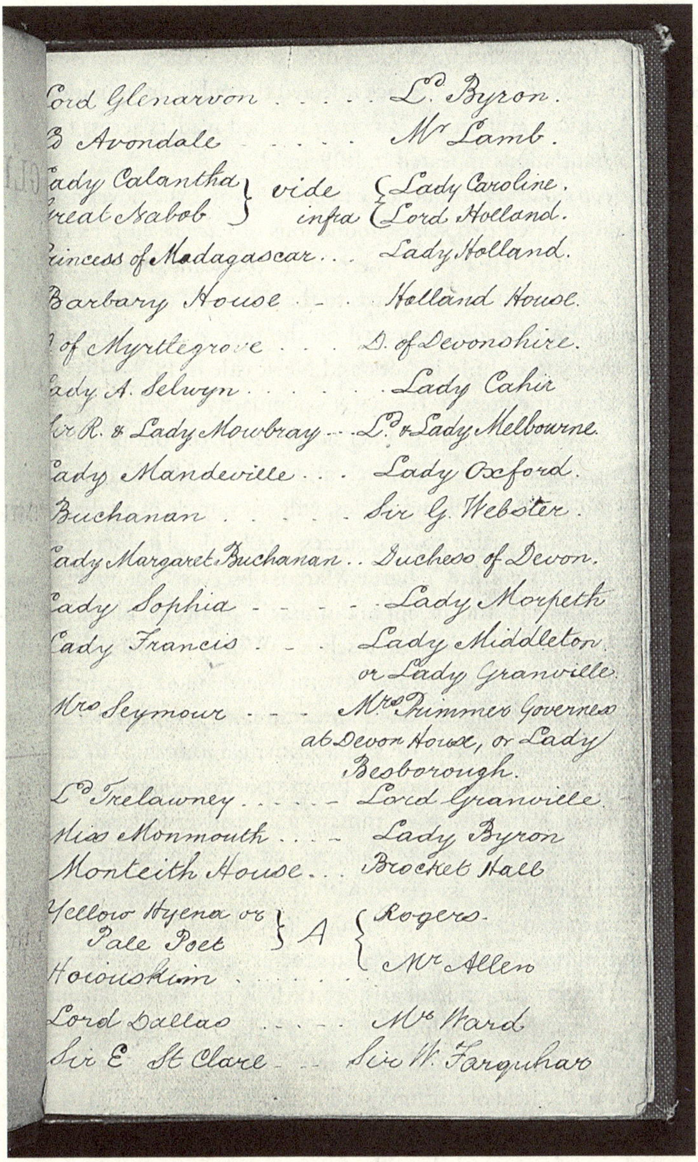

ord Glenarvon .... Ld Byron.
d Avondale .... Mr Lamb.
ady Calantha } vide { Lady Caroline.
reat Nabob } infra { Lord Holland.
rincess of Madagascar... Lady Holland.
Barbary House .. Holland House.
of Myrtlegrove ... D. of Devonshire.
ady A. Selwyn ..... Lady Cahir
ir R. & Lady Mowbray ... Ld & Lady Melbourne.
ady Mandeville .. Lady Oxford.
Buchanan .... Sir G. Webster.
ady Margaret Buchanan.. Duchess of Devon.
ady Sophia ---- Lady Morpeth
ady Francis --- Lady Middleton or Lady Granville.
Mrs Seymour --- Mrs Trimmer Governess at Devon House, or Lady Besborough.
Ld Trelawney .... Lord Granville
Miss Monmouth ... Lady Byron
Monteith House .. Brocket Hall
Yellow Hyena or Pale Poet } A { Rogers.
Hoiouskim ..... Mr Allen
Lord Dallas .... Mr Ward
Sir E St Clare .. Sir W. Farquhar

Figure 3.1 Manuscript key to *Glenarvon* (London: Colburn, 1816). © The British Library Board, N.1834–36 (vol. 1).

was soon reprinted; a fourth and further revised edition was released in 1817. Like Byron's popularity, which spread like a disease across the globe, news of Lamb's novel and her accompanying disgrace infected the public imagination around the world. An American edition of *Glenarvon* reached readers across the Atlantic in 1816. French translations appeared in 1819 and 1824.[38]

Glenarvon's cultural influence extended beyond the novel itself. Frederick Burwick has uncovered two stage productions of *Glenarvon* premiering in London in 1819 and 1821. He rightly asserts that "the scandals surrounding Byron" (and I would add Lamb) "drew crowds to the theatre."[39] In addition to theatrical productions, *Glenarvon* also appeared on the turf. A two-year-old colt named Glenarvon raced successfully in York and Newcastle in 1818—his winnings covered extensively in the press.[40] The novel's popularity as well as its theatrical and equine adaptations kept Lamb and her novel before the public. Her multimedia circulation made her name, her novel, and her scandalous life a familiar and, according to most of her contemporaries, vulgar example of a fallen woman.

Glenarvon's undeniable popular success undermined its literary clout. "Those dismayed by celebrity culture," Sharon Marcus observes, "are quick to associate it with low entertainment" and are apt to dismiss the merits of cultural products arising from celebrity and celebrities themselves.[41] While, as we shall see, many readers thought *Glenarvon* aesthetically accomplished, most also believed that its seemingly confessional content about an extramarital romance placed it beyond the bounds of acceptable literature and legitimate authorship. Its autobiographical elements adapt not only aspects of Byron's poetics of familiarity but also key elements found in secret histories, romans à clef, silver-fork novels, tête-à-têtes described in the pages of *Town and Country*, and salacious courtesans' memoirs—all "low" genres negatively associated with the vapid, voracious reading habits of female consumers and immoral (women) writers. Another issue was that the public's desire for stories about debauched aristocrats also blurred divisions between social classes. Lamb's depiction of aristocratic folly to nineteenth-century readers, then, represented a gross breach of familiarity's class- and gender-encoded limits.

Tensions between high and low literary culture remind us that the struggle for legitimacy in the field of cultural production—what Bourdieu describes as the struggle "to impose the dominant definition of the writer and therefore to delimit the population of those entitled to take part in the struggle to define the writer"—reflects other struggles for social and political legitimacy.[42] Lamb's decision to write such an unflattering novel about herself and her aristocratic circle was also an affront against the power and legitimacy of her own class. While other popular authors such as Mary Anne Clarke and Benjamin Disraeli wrote books that sometimes mocked the hypocrisy of the English aristocracy, they were not, like Lamb, born into the elite society their novels portrayed, and so their works drew less criticism and personal disdain. The popular conduct writer Vicesimus Knox explains the relation between familiarity and affective interest: "Beautiful minds, like beautiful bodies, appear graceful in an undress . . . we feel ourselves relieved when admitted to their familiarity."[43] For Knox, the vulnerability inherent in familiarity conveys privileged attachment and encourages emotional investment. However, Lamb's case demonstrates that assessments of one's familiarity and the dignified beauty of proverbial undress shift according to rank and gender—themes I also address in chapter 4, on Hazlitt. Critics took a Burkean view of Lamb because her first novel seemed to relish tearing away the "decent drapery" of traditional class-based sociability and its dependence on navigating familiarity's decorous limits. In many ways, *Glenarvon* embraced the same untoward, indiscriminate familiarity with the mass public that concerned some of Byron's critics. Yet, unlike Byron, she unmasked her familiar circle in addition to herself, thus betraying the trust and confidence on which ties of sociable familiarity depended.[44]

"IF RESEMBLANCES THEY BE"

Despite *Glenarvon*'s flagrant autobiographical elements, Lamb claimed the novel was, to borrow from Byron's preface to *Childe Harold*, "the child of imagination."[45] *Childe Harold* offered Lamb a precedent for *Glenarvon*'s autobiographical resonances as well as her denials of them, and like Byron, Lamb invites the autobiographical readings she purports to discount. The second and third editions of *Glenarvon* include a preface rejecting "resemblances [to real life], if resemblances they be, which have been recognized, admitted, claimed with so much eagerness, and then condemned with so much asperity."[46] The new edition contained numerous revisions, some of which tempered unflattering depictions of her contemporaries and slightly obscured links between her fictional characters and her family.[47] The preface, for instance, explains that the Miss Seymours and Lady Dartford may be loosely correlated with many people, before noting, "Miss St.-Clare and Lady Margaret Buchanan are more entirely fictitious" (355). Lamb's emphasis on elements that are "more" fictitious begs the question: What characters are the least fictitious? Conspicuously absent from Lamb's list are Calantha, Lord Avondale, Glenarvon, and Princess Madagascar, the characters contemporaries thought closest to their real-life counterparts. The preface's implicit suggestion that some characters may share traits with real people—a movement similar to Byron's acknowledgment that "In some very trivial particulars . . . there might be grounds" for autobiographical readings of Harold—sent Lamb's readers searching for connections.[48]

Lamb's claims that *Glenarvon* had "no foundation in fact" and that the "crimes related in these volumes are evidently imaginary; the situations fictitious" perform the same function as Byron's prefaces to *Childe Harold* (353). Her "evidently imaginary" recalls Byron's qualified rejections of his autobiographical style, which I explored in the previous chapter. Employing techniques of autobiographical denial similar to those Byron uses, Lamb reflects back on the boundaries that Byron established between himself and Harold as well as the literary tactics that he used to cross those very boundaries. For instance, Lamb's preface to *Glenarvon* meditates on the similarities between art and authorship, evoking Byron's dedication to Thomas More in *The Corsair*. Byron writes, "[I]f I have deviated into the gloomy vanity of 'drawing from self', the pictures are probably like, since they are unfavourable."[49] Lamb echoes Byron's sentiment: "[T]he painter well knows, that, when he is sketching the personages of history, or the creatures of his imagination, the lineaments, with which he is most familiar, will sometimes almost involuntarily rise beneath the touch of his pencil" (353). Lamb attempts to neutralize her novel's autobiographical elements; in doing so, she emphasizes the personal knowledge that informs her work. Moreover, while here "familiar" indicates habitual exposure and knowledge, it remains inflected with the word's social connotations. She is, Lamb reminds readers, personally familiar with aristocrats and literary leaders of her day, and it is the "lineaments" of her social landscape—peopled with her familiars—that "rise beneath the touch" of her authorial pencil. The preface's half-hearted denials did little to assuage Lamb's family and friends. "The real Princess," Lamb's cousin explained, "is very angry."[50] Lady Holland was not alone in her outrage. The family of the deceased doctor Sir Richard Croft was so incensed by allegations that he was one of the characters in *Glenarvon* that they took out corrective advertisements in the *Morning Post*.[51]

Moral philosophies of sympathy clarify the largely negative reactions to *Glenarvon*, and they point to a key difference between Lamb's work and Byron's: autobiographical explicitness. Of obscurity's role in "conveying the *affections*," Edmund Burke explains, "It is our ignorance of things that causes all our admiration, and chiefly excites our passions. Knowledge and acquaintance make the most striking causes affect but little."[52] Such a philosophy repeats the famous eighteenth-century axiom that too much familiarity led to contempt. The "great clearness" that Burke believes "helps but little towards affecting the passions" was exactly Lamb's problem.[53] Lamb had less room to flirt with ambiguous autobiographical details than Byron did because public gossip surrounding her had already made details of her life common knowledge years before *Glenarvon*. Byron's *Childe Harold* made him a celebrity; Lamb's *Glenarvon* appeared several years after she was already one of the Regency's most notorious socialites. Widespread gossip about Lamb's life predated her autobiographical work, which is significant because, as Patricia Meyer Spacks explains, gossip enacts "power by the illusion of mastery gained through taking imaginative possession of another's experience."[54] This imaginative possession can have a flattening effect, since the desire for a good story can overrule the accurate presentation of complex events—a reality that Lamb herself realized. "I have every fault," she admitted to Annabella Milbanke, "but you know them & yet it is strange people say things of me most false—and though perhaps not as bad as the truth always yet so utterly different that I scarce know how to defend myself."[55] *Glenarvon* and reactions to it enact this paradigm. Lamb commandeers her contemporaries' biographies and, thus, attempts to reverse the power dynamics of public gossip that had victimized her. *Glenarvon*'s strength arises from its self-conscious, thorough engagement with the blurry lines between reputation, public gossip, and rigid frameworks for judging female morality.

Felicity Nussbaum's work on seventeenth- and eighteenth-century autobiography applies here. Nussbaum notes that in dissenting women's spiritual autobiographies, an individual's complexities were often lost by "attempting to fit lived experience and subjectivity within the parameters of credible frameworks."[56] As we saw with Elizabeth Gunning and Charlotte Smith, Romantic authors and readers employed such frameworks and the stereotypes associated with them not only to read literary works but also to understand the authors behind them. Lamb's personality and actions were dramatic enough for fiction, and responses to her lived experiences and her literary works were informed by Romantic-era novelistic expectations. Frances Wilson has argued that Lamb's affair with Byron "conforms to the specific requirements of fictional melodrama in that it is reduced to the bare bones of a narrative structure alone. Melodramatic characters are drained of psychological depth."[57] Lamb, in other words, seemed a typical woman ruined by immoral love, and details of her life—circulated by her own works and through public gossip—were alternately exaggerated, overlooked, or reframed to align more closely with this well-established character type.

One compelling example of a reader fitting Lamb into an unflattering, familiar literary framework appears in unpublished character sketchbooks written over several years by Annabella Milbanke. (Milbanke was William Lamb's cousin and was related to Lamb by marriage; the two knew each other before Milbanke's marriage to Byron in early 1815.) Her largely disapproving character sketches may reveal more about Milbanke than those she describes, and few of her peers, especially women, were safe from her biting criticism. For example, she deems Maria

Edgeworth's gaiety self-serving and affected.[58] Her portrayals of Lamb—two of the longer, more detailed entries in her manuscript books—are particularly scathing: "[Her] coquetry is thoughtless and ungovernable imprudent to excess."[59] Milbanke's observations compare Lamb with "Lady Delacour in Miss Edgeworth's Belinda."[60] The seven passages from *Belinda* that Milbanke quotes are all confessions of folly and guilt, and she uses Lady Delacour's speeches to reinforce her opinions about Lamb. In one instance, Milbanke has transcribed a passage in which Lady Delacour admits, "A coquet I have lived, & a coquet I shall die."[61] At the beginning of the character sketch she similarly draws on *Belinda* to describe Lamb's shamelessness: "[S]he dares not lose its [the world's] notice & its wonder, by descending from the conspicuous heights of Folly to the humble path of Reason. She has the pride of a spoiled child; glorying in stubbornness and ashamed of concession—It is thus that 'false shame makes her act as if she had no shame.'"[62] The passage incorporates a sentence from *Belinda* that Milbanke then expands at the end of her entry on Lamb. "Quoting" Lamb through Lady Delacour, Milbanke writes, "False shame made me act as if I had no shame. You would not suspect me of knowing any thing of false shame, but depend upon it, many who appear to have as much assurance as I have are secretly its slaves."[63] Milbanke envisions Lamb's follies ventriloquized through Lady Delacour. Lady Delacour's speeches serve as imagined confessions from Lamb, blurring novelistic tropes with the traits of someone in Milbanke's familiar circle. This is a darker version of the same tendency to novelize women's lives that, as I argued in chapter 1, influenced Charlotte Smith's reception as a sentimental heroine.

While there is no evidence that Lamb read Milbanke's character sketches, her correspondence indicates a keen awareness that the public as well as her friends and family interpreted her life within novelistic frameworks. Shortly after the Byron affair ended, Lamb wrote, "When I am unhappy I cannot appear otherwise—however do not say I am so—let me not be thought a love sick deserted Lady that is all I request."[64] Her request to Lady Melbourne shows a frustration with and resistance to being read as a predictable stereotype.

Despite such private protestations, most female characters in *Glenarvon* embody the type of "love sick deserted Lady" that Lamb's letter rejects. Several of Glenarvon's romantic conquests behave in ways that are typical of fallen sentimental heroines of the period—including in Calantha's dramatic death from a broken heart and guilty conscience.[65] By incorporating recognizable character types from fiction, *Glenarvon*, like the spiritual autobiographies that Nussbaum studies, partly embraces the flattening frameworks that empty women of their complexity. Lamb typecast herself and was also typecast by those around her, including, as we shall see, by fellow novelists. Lamb's use of tired tropes as well as their associations with popular genres contributed to overwhelmingly negative assessments of her novel.

"THE SPITEFUL & CURIOUS": PUBLIC FAMILIARITY AND INAPPROPRIATE AUDIENCE

There is some truth to claims that *Glenarvon* is a bad novel. It has a complicated, confusing plot. It draws idiosyncratically on several genres: secret history, historical novel, novel of manners, sentimental novel, bildungsroman, and gothic novel. For example, *Glenarvon*'s supernatural gothic elements remain largely unincorporated into the rest of the plot. Belfont Abbey, where Calantha meets Glenarvon, appears to be inhabited by spirits, which do not appear again. At the novel's abrupt conclusion, Glenarvon suddenly dies while being pursued by a ghost ship. Also, for much of the novel, Glenarvon inexplicably masquerades as a character named Viviani without raising anyone's suspicions that they are the same man. The novel's contemporary reception, however, rarely identifies *Glenarvon*'s supposed literary limits and, instead, largely focuses on Lamb's overfamiliarity with the reading public. In fact, many Romantic readers thought *Glenarvon* well written. The *Theatrical Inquisitor* praised the novel for its "animated style, brilliance of imagery, and the skilful delineation of gloomy and mysterious character."[66] Lamb's cousin Caroline George Lamb criticized "the indecency of the moral" in *Glenarvon* but also appreciated "the cleverness of many parts."[67] Annabella Milbanke's father enjoyed both its biographical and stylistic elements; Judith Noel Milbanke wrote to her daughter, "Dad is reading Glenarvon—and teases me to tell him the Characters, which I cannot do entirely—he likes some parts very much."[68] That Sir Ralph was reading the novel at all perhaps seems strange. That he was enjoying it—despite what it revealed about his daughter's estranged husband and his nephew William Lamb—is even more intriguing and suggests that the current tendency to discount *Glenarvon*'s quality does not accurately reflect the tastes of Regency readers.[69] Indeed, according to Percy Shelley, the painter James Northcote "had recommended Godwin to read Glenarvon, affirming that many parts of it exhibited extraordinary talent."[70] Edward Bulwer was also struck by *Glenarvon* when he read it as a boy: "[It] made on me a deeper impression than any romance I remember."[71]

However, for many readers, and especially those in Lamb's immediate circle, *Glenarvon*'s literary strengths could not outweigh its overfamiliarity with a wide audience. Caroline George Lamb wrote to her friend Annabella Milbanke, "I cannot forgive her, for the ridicule that she showers on William [Lamb], by publishing all their private secrets."[72] Lady Emily Cowper thought Lamb (her sister-in-law) had a narcissistic "wish to show off which never can be quietted [*sic*]," even though that wish harmed her family.[73] A common criticism was that *Glenarvon* gratified Lamb's desire for attention without regard for decorum or the public reputations of her circle; such assessments about the novel echo Milbanke's earlier indictments of Lamb in her character sketches. Yet it was not just that Lamb indiscriminately shared secrets, but that these secrets reached readers beyond—and below—Lamb's class.

Lamb's aristocratic status became a rallying point for criticism. According to Lady Cowper, *Glenarvon*'s appeal to a mass middle-class audience was one of its most objectionable features. In a long letter to Lamb, Cowper explains that she had returned to town in 1816 to find *Glenarvon* "upon every Table and the subject of general conversations & animated discussion to the Great distress of your Friends."[74] The tables that Cowper encountered would have presumably been aristocratic, though she angrily goes on to detail the worrying reach of *Glenarvon*'s readership: "[T]here are none but bad feelings that could dictate such a course to sit down calmly & write for public inspection all that is malicious & without an object but to offend and to hold up to ridicule those who have been your Friends."[75] Intentionally sharing personal details to incite the public's curiosity, Lamb seemed to preclude her readers' sympathy as well as betray the trust bestowed on her by her familiar circle. If, according to Adam Smith, "Nothing is so mortifying as to be obliged to expose our distress to the view of the public," then Lamb's willingness to expose herself and others directly defied expectations for sympathy and sociability.[76] For Smith, motivations arising from revenge are particularly offensive: "[T]he disposition to anger, hatred, envy, malice, revenge; is . . . much more apt to offend by its excess than by its defect. The excess renders a man . . . the object of hatred, and sometimes even horror, to other people."[77] Smith's claims suggest why Lamb's novel and, as chapter 4 argues, Hazlitt's, were so distasteful. Lamb was seen as sharing and feeling too much—especially too much malice. The perception of vindictiveness stood out to one reviewer, who claimed that Lamb's "delineations of certain individuals in exalted life, are more remarkable for their malignity than their correctness."[78] Lamb caused a stir, then, not just because what she wrote harmed her, but because she seemed to relish the harm it might do to those around her.

Smith's theories of sociability clarify Cowper's anger at her sister-in-law: Lamb used her familiarity with friends and family—their closeness, their confidences—against them in a direct subversion of sociability. In short, Lamb broke the reciprocal trust on which interpersonal familiarity depended. Cowper was palpably irate, and the repetitiveness of her letter shows the seriousness of Lamb's betrayal. Cowper reminds Lamb of "the shame you bring upon your Family & Friends." *Glenarvon,* she angrily writes, had given "the spiteful & curious part of society . . . an opportunity . . . of ridiculing those they feel above them by reviewing their whole lives and endeavouring to find some traces of resemblances between them and even the most abandoned Characters you have drawn."[79] That Lamb exposed herself was bad enough. That *Glenarvon* also exposed the folly of her family and her peers to those beneath them was simply too much. The latter issue was more serious, for Lamb risked destabilizing class hierarchies by giving a mass readership damning information about the inner (amoral) workings of aristocratic society. This cross-class exposure particularly concerned those around Lamb, for it granted the "the spiteful & curious" access to information that previously remained exclusive within the Regency elite. Recall that moral philosophers distinguished between sympathy and curiosity—the latter evoking interest though not necessarily affection. According to Smith's *Theory of Moral Sentiments,* pretensions to greatness and sympathy "are supported by high rank and great power, when they have often been successfully exerted, and are, upon that account, attended by the loud acclamations of the multitude; even the man of sober judgment abandons himself to the general admiration."[80] *Glenarvon* inverted this dynamic. Lamb's high rank exacerbated the follies of her overfamiliarity, and those of sober judgment both within and below the aristocracy loudly derided her.

Lambasting Lamb's inappropriate revelations about herself and others, Cowper also criticizes *Glenarvon*'s similarities to vulgar popular genres associated with middle- and lower-class authors and audiences. She could not fathom Lamb's choice "to disclose to the world (to all the Chamber maids and Footmen) a Story which most people would have given their fortune to buy up, if any scribbler had threatened to write of them."[81] Another one of Lamb's sins, then, was writing like a low-class scribbler or a blackmailing hack who pandered to the vulgar tastes of the serving classes. Cowper rejects Lamb's claims to legitimate authorship; *Glenarvon* here is not a novel but a mere "Story" written for unsympathetic readers.

Cowper was likely not alone in seeing connections between *Glenarvon* and other degraded forms of popular writing associated with hacks rather than respected authors. Connections between *Glenarvon*'s characters and their real-life counterparts tie it to the subgenre of the secret history. Drawing from popular chronique scandaleuses based on the French court, secret histories were known for revealing personal details, often sexual in nature, about the social and political elite; however, they were typically not written by aristocrats but rather by the sorts of parasitic scribblers that Cowper references in her angry letters.[82] Though Ina Ferris suggests that secret histories slowly began to have more of a "scholarly inflection" during the Romantic period, she notes that the genre was generally "banished from serious literary consideration."[83]

Lamb's choice to publish with Henry Colburn strengthened *Glenarvon*'s associations with scurrilous fiction and undiscerning readers. Colburn was known for "recruiting authors with aristocratic blood or connections and printing puffing reviews and advertisements strongly suggesting that his novels were *romans à clef*."[84] Throughout the 1810s and 1820s Colburn made a name for himself by publishing scandalous, semi-autobiographical novels, particularly silver-fork novels, which developed from the secret history. *Glenarvon*'s publication in 1816 predates by more than a decade foundational works of the silver-fork genre, like Benjamin Disraeli's *Vivian Grey* (1827) and Edward Bulwer Lytton's *Pelham* (1828), and it is an influential transitional novel that points from secret history toward the emerging genre of the silver-fork novel. The genre was so low "within the generic hierarchy . . . that Benjamin Disraeli, one of Colburn's authors, figured Colburn as a brothel madam, referring to him as 'Mother Colburn' and to himself as a 'literary prostitute.'"[85] The disjunction between Lamb's elevated social position and the debased genres that Colburn's name and *Glenarvon*'s autobiographical content evoked demonstrate powerful genre divisions within Romanticism's literary field.

Lamb's seeming autobiographical admissions of guilt and repentance in *Glenarvon*—her doppelganger Calantha dies in disgrace, after all—mirror eighteenth-century confessional memoirs by factual and fictional courtesans, actresses, and other fallen women. Lamb's participation in a memoirist tradition associated with whores and hacks further lowered *Glenarvon* and her reputation. One reviewer even compared *Glenarvon* to "those infamous productions" of John Cleland's pornographic *Memoirs of a Woman of Pleasure*.[86] According to Felicity Nussbaum, popular autobiographical works by courtesans such as Constantia Phillips, Ann Sheldon, Elizabeth Gooch, and Margaret Leeson simultaneously "celebrate and apologize for their behaviour," and their general lack of contrition implicates others so much so that "writing finds its genesis in an accusation."[87] It is the trope of "sorry, not sorry" that made Lamb's work popular but also unforgiveable and unsympathetic. It provoked from most readers a sort of shocked, disgusted interest, rather than sympathy.

Even before *Gleanrvon* appeared, Milbanke had already criticized Lamb's confessional tendencies, which, she believed, were disingenuous and performative. She thought Lamb, like the unsavory women who wrote scandalous memoirs, was motivated not by guilt or contrition but rather by a desire to justify and excuse herself: "[She] tries to disarm the condemnation of her friends, by unreserved confession of her errors, and our generosity may at first be touched . . . But its frequent repetition destroys all esteem for the <u>motive</u>. An avowal of this kind is easy &

degrading, often the sense of humiliation, which made it a virtuous effort, is worn out. Her confidence is also diminished by perceiving a delicate attempt at self-justification, through the apparent candour of self-reproach."[88] Lamb's self-serving confessions, according to Milbanke, lost their power through repetition. Milbanke believed that Lamb's intention in publishing *Glenarvon* was no better; the goal "however disguised to herself ~~appears to be~~ is to create a sensation."[89] Striking out her initial qualified reaction to the novel and underscoring her disapproval, Milbanke condemns Lamb's indecorous desire for public attention. Her critique of the novel slips between referring to Lamb, to Calantha, and to Lamb as Calantha. Readers, Milbanke claims, "must look upon her throughout as a very weak woman having no existence but in the opinion of others—Philosophers have said 'I think—therefore I am'—but Calantha's metaphysical creed is—'I am thought of—therefore I am'—She [Lamb] perhaps endeavours to fix the identity of this being by the present work [*Glenarvon*]—and as Natural History would inform her that the butterfly only lives one Summer, she may seek to prolong her ephemeral existence . . . exempt from the common laws of her tribe."[90] The initial "her" ambiguously may apply to Lamb, Calantha, or both, though the end of the passage clearly ridicules Lamb's clamoring for public notice. Milbanke portrays Lamb as attempting to subvert the natural order by courting public interest. Rejecting the common laws of sociability that govern behavior is, Milbanke suggests, as foolhardy as the butterfly's desire to live longer. Milbanke's assessment resembles more recent conceptions of celebrity as "flaunting its performance and trying desperately to keep our attention."[91]

One thing that disgusted Milbanke and intrigued Lamb's contemporaries was her overt sexual freedom and her willingness to allude to it in her novel. Lamb's experiences as well as those of Calantha display the gendered rules of decorum that governed carnal familiarity in the period—*familiarity* was used as a euphemism for sex—and Milbanke's comments show the consequences of Adam Smith's unforgiving assessment of female chastity: "Breach of chastity dishonours irretrievably. No circumstances, no solicitation can excuse it; no sorrow, no repentance atone for it."[92] Byron himself echoed this idea in his poem "To Lady Caroline Lamb": "[T]he woman once fallen forever must fall."[93] Her circle's outrage was cemented by the period's expectations for female decorum and theories about how breaching it subverted sympathy.

Beyond Lamb's circle, *Glenarvon* was widely ridiculed for both its unfeminine openness and its ability to corrupt readers. Similar to Milbanke, the *British Critic* criticized Lamb's lack of shame: "She speaks not in the language of a repentant sinner; she appears to glory in her guilt, even though she represents herself as writing under its punishment . . . Every great and good mind must stand appalled at the crimes, which now no longer are veiled in secrecy, but openly defy public decency."[94] The *Monthly Review* called the work "of the *doubtful gender*, though a feminine production."[95] Lamb's shocking choice to share her indiscretions compounded the indecency of her original crimes. Lamb's authorship, then, was a monstrous public display of folly, which betrayed not just her family and her class but also her gender.

The most sustained public attack came from Elizabeth Thomas's parodic novel *Purity of Heart . . . Addressed to the Author of "Glenarvon"* (1816). Thomas's introduction decries *Glenarvon*'s "horrible tendency, its dangerous perverting sophistry; its abominable indecency and profaneness."[96] To combat *Glenarvon*'s corrupting influence, *Purity of Heart* traces the virtuous Camilla's reconciliation with her husband. While Camilla is the model of decorum, her acquaintance Lady Calantha Limb is not. Thomas makes clear that the "speeches of Lady Calantha Limb, are many of them copied from Glenarvon," thus connecting her novel to Lamb's and, implicitly, to Lamb's life.[97] Of Limb, Thomas writes, "[T]here was a sort of masculine daring in her air and manner; which terrified and alarmed; and she was so totally dissimilar from all other women . . . Lady Calantha possessed not the timidity of feminine feeling . . . she needed not supporters when she mounted her horse; but vaulting gaily into her saddle, she rode forth upon every public occasion, to see, and to be seen."[98] Limb rejects normative expectations of feminine passivity, and she becomes transgressive and terrifying. Thomas's criticism of Calantha's unfeminine equestrian independence is particularly biting; Lamb was known as an avid horsewoman.[99] For those around her, everything from Limb's confidence to her equestrian skills speaks to her supposed desire to be seen—and to be seen rejecting the gendered rules of sociable behavior.

Purity of Heart also offers explicit criticisms of Lamb's scandalous authorship. Limb publishes a book about her affair with the Byronic poet De Lyra. The moral, matronly Mrs. Merton berates Limb for "writ[ing] a book . . . which others must blush to read, and which will stand up to outraged posterity, as the work of a woman of quality; had it been written by a man I should have burnt and forgotten it, now I shall never hear it named without a blush."[100] Mrs. Merton, sounding remarkably similar to Lamb's angry relatives, indicates that standards for female conduct differed from those for male conduct. Mrs. Merton's comments recall Adam Smith's claims that a fallen woman can never recover. Additionally, Mrs. Merton emphasizes the disjunction between Limb's aristocratic status—her position as "a woman of quality"—and her tell-all novel. As a lady, she should know better. And Mrs. Merton makes clear that, for a lady, the rules of decorous sociability are less forgiving. The reception of Limb's novel and of Lamb's own demonstrate that a Romantic-era woman's elevated social position intensified responses to her scandalous amours and authorship.

Lamb's personal experiences bear witness to the accuracy of Mrs. Merton's words. Her circle was reluctant to trust her after *Glenarvon* appeared, and her family encouraged William Lamb to separate from her. Lamb lamented, "[H]alf of my friends cut me [and] all my acquaintances are offended," and she admitted, "I am already nearly ruined by my own imprudence . . . my novel may have made me many foes."[101] Uncharacteristically for Lamb, her description is not exaggerated. For example, Milbanke described the social ostracism that followed *Glenarvon*: "Lady C. Lamb was at Anglesea house the other night, and nobody spoke to her."[102] Others saw the situation in more dire terms: "[Lamb] has ruined herself . . . in public opinion by her imprudence," wrote Caroline George Lamb.[103] Both the public and Lamb's private circle turned against her.

The delight that readers—both within Lamb's familiar circle and beyond it—took in admonishing Lamb's missteps makes her the archetype for the socialite turned scandalous celebrity with which we are familiar today. Romantic-era "scandalous celebrity," Tuite has argued, has the ability to translate "bad fame—or infamy and notoriety—into good fame."[104] However, Lamb's case shows the difficulty that women faced in capitalizing on bad press, even if they had written it themselves. As Tuite explains, Lamb offers a "comparative failure of translation from *succès de scandale* to redemptive posterity."[105] I have been arguing that Lamb failed in part because she started from a different point than Byron did. Many more autobiographical details about her circulated before she published. And while she did, like Byron, engage in a type of authorial hide and seek, she had less room to hide. Lamb's authorial reception—both private and public—demonstrates the difficulty of writing oneself out of vulgar overfamiliarity.

"SOME DAY OR OTHER": RECOUPING REPUTATION

Prior to and directly following *Glenarvon*, Lamb was familiar to her contemporaries as a notorious woman with a sharp tongue and a bold pen. To the horror of Lamb's family, *Glenarvon* was "upon every Table," despite the fact that, according to one reviewer, its "scenes of depravity . . . should exclude it from the parlour of every virtuous family."[106] Lamb's second novel, *Graham Hamilton* (1822), also found its way to many parlors, though, as a novel of manners with few autobiographical resonances, its place in virtuous family homes was less controversial. Lamb's later authorial endeavors presented more socially acceptable versions of "Lady Caroline Lamb," and this chapter's final section analyzes Lamb's continued presence in the public imagination years after *Glenarvon*—years during which she attempted to rewrite the familiar characterizations of herself as the Regency's most notorious fallen woman turned scandalous author. *Graham Hamilton* and her contributions to other more acceptable, traditional genres represent an important shift in her career. While her work decidedly moved beyond Byron, Lamb remained an astute critic of the hypocritical standards of female morality that left her with a reputation in need of recuperation. In her later publications, from a novel of manners and pianoforte music to poems in literary annuals and contributions to schoolbooks, Lamb attempted to reinvent her reputation through the use of decorous genres as well as by associations with the respectable people who contributed to and consumed them. These later works show Lamb trying to distance herself from her earlier reputation for unfeminine, unaristocratic overfamiliarity.

Perhaps hoping that more conservative literary pursuits might rehabilitate Lamb's associations with vulgar familiarity, her husband embraced *Graham Hamilton*. William Lamb worked closely on the page proofs of *Graham Hamilton* before its publication by Colburn in 1822, and Lamb's correspondence notes her husband's willingness to edit it: "Mr Lamb in kindness to me says that if he can have the whole of Graham Hamilton a MS in Mr Colburns hands he will now until the meeting of Parliament devote his time to correcting it[.] I should be pleased therefore if this could be done as he seemed to like the manner in which it was written."[107] The manner of *Graham Hamilton* departs significantly from that of *Glenarvon*. Its lack of autobiographical content foregrounds Lamb's more general indictments of the construction and destruction of female reputation and the stringent, yet confusing boundaries of familiarity that stack the deck against women. Though clearly a novel of manners, *Graham Hamilton* questions the typical marriage plots of other Romantic-era novels and the ideals they represent.

Unlike *Glenarvon*, *Graham Hamilton* aligns with the period's genre conventions, and it has fewer characters and follows a straightforward plot. Graham Hamilton's wealthy uncle, Sir Malcolm, adopts him in his youth. Made into a gentleman and heir, Graham enters London society, where he meets the beautiful socialite Lady Orville, whose outward gaiety hides a miserable marriage and extravagant debt. Their friendship remains chaste, yet their public familiarity prompts gossip that destroys Lady Orville's reputation; she is forced into obscurity in the country. Through Lady Orville's downfall—despite no actual wrongdoing on her part—Lamb criticizes a society that made it easy for women to fail socially, morally, and economically.

The strength of the novel and its clear narrative is a testament to the sociable literary context in which it was written—a far cry from her husband's frustration that Lamb published *Glenarvon* "without any consultation with her friends."[108] In one of several letters about *Graham Hamilton* that Lamb sent to William Godwin (her long-standing correspondent) she explains that the novel's more traditional plot arose from a suggestion from her friend the Italian novelist Ugo Foscolo to "try if you like to write—to take one simple plot [and] describe one character."[109] She explains that she strove "to write a simple and proper story within certain bounds & rules."[110] With her typical assertiveness, she also wrote to Thomas Malthus seeking his editorial advice.[111] The supportive literary community that gave rise to *Graham Hamilton* is perhaps why it is her best work, exhibiting, in the words of the *Monthly Review*, "a style and execution [that] would not reflect discredit on names much more known in this department of literature."[112] The *Morning Post* declared it "a most pleasing Novel," noting that "the characters are touched with delicacy and feeling"; unlike responses to *Glenarvon*, the review concludes that the "moral of the work is also good."[113] *Blackwood's Edinburgh Magazine* agreed, praising the novel for remaining "within the bounds of good taste" and "belong[ing] to the class of proper and good novels."[114] The novel's reception was generally warm, and it appears to have sold well enough to warrant a second edition in 1823.[115]

Despite the praise *Graham Hamilton* would receive, Lamb was anxious about its reception: "I feel very nervous that it should not be liked—after all publishing has more pain with it than pleasure suppose it be reckoned stupid—bad—How can <u>I bear it?</u>"[116] Her minute instructions about everything from the look of the epigraph to the novel's punctuation suggest a new authorial seriousness. "I beg you," she wrote to Colburn, "also to remember that I must see each proof from the beginning."[117] Lamb's concerns for her work's reception are connected with her insistence on anonymity, despite the knowledge that her scandalous name would have undoubtedly bolstered sales.[118] In her later career she remained conflicted about her anonymity: "It was my wish to put my name . . . I had rather stand by what I write however bad."[119] When her third novel, *Ada Reis*, published by John Murray in 1823, neared completion, she claimed it "need never be known to be mine," yet she later asked Murray "to remember and put my name."[120] She wanted to have it both ways, yet she feared that her bad reputation from *Glenarvon* would stain the reception of her subsequent works. Her letters to Colburn frequently warn him about leaking her identity. She implores him to "perform yr promise and by no suggestion allow Graham Hamilton to be thought mine . . . pray be guarded in this & in other respects and let it steal quietly out & not make a noise like Glenarvon."[121] In another letter she reminds him, "[R]emember yr promise <u>this year</u> of inviolable secrecy . . . remember yr promise & to let it come out quite quietly."[122] William Lamb also pressed the issue: "I particularly request that in publishing G. H., there be no mention whatever of Glenarvon, nor any connection with it in advertisement or otherwise."[123]

Predictably, these attempts at anonymity failed at a time when readers sought to uncover the authors behind literary works. *Blackwood's Edinburgh Magazine* helped narrow the authorial suspects, attributing "GRAHAM HAMILTON to a lady of noble birth and high fashion."[124] The *Monthly Review* was more explicit: "A singular kind of novel appeared a few years ago, intitled Glenarvon . . . It was generally understood to be the production of Lady Caroline Lamb; whose rank and connections render her well known in circles of fashion, and to whom her talents and a certain degree of excentricity have also given a place not only in the annals of literature but in the general range of public cognizance. According to the report, the volumes now before us proceed from the same source."[125] The *Analytical Review* also connected her to *Graham Hamilton*, and she complained to Colburn, "they ought not to put my name."[126] Concerns about her second novel's reception indicate Lamb's recognition of the difficulties of moving beyond her notoriety. She understood just how engrained her negative reputation was in the "public cognizance"—even a decade after her affair with Byron ended.

Attempting to combat scandalous associations with her own name, Lamb foregrounds other names in *Graham Hamilton*. In a letter about an early draft of *Graham Hamilton* she explains, "[S]ince the Fashion is to call every thing in the manner of Pride & Prejudice, sense & sensibility, I have named mine Principle & passion."[127] While the novel's title changed, Lamb's reference to Austen shows her interest in conforming to contemporary novelistic trends, and it is clear that Lamb saw *Graham Hamilton* in conversation with the novel of manners rather than low genres like the secret history.[128] She deflects readers' familiarity with her notoriety by presenting them with familiar elements from fiction. Lamb's decision to name her central female character "Lady Orville" clearly establishes *Graham Hamilton*'s connection to Frances Burney's *Evelina*.[129] The *Monthly Review* claimed the novel could not "fail to remind the reader of Miss Burney's *Evelina*."[130] Substituting the notoriety of her name with the respectability of Burney and her characters, Lamb reshapes her authorship within a non-Byronic and more decorous literary tradition. In doing so, she pushes beyond her first novel's shocking rejection of familiarity's limits.

Even while working within the bounds of a more conservative genre, Lamb adapts the conventions of the Burney school to critique aristocratic society's control over women's reputations. Indeed, if *Evelina* is about what it takes to make a place and gain a name for oneself in the world, then *Graham Hamilton* is about what it takes to retain that name. Picking up where Burney left off, Lamb's novel begins after Lady Orville's marriage, when she has become a bored, neglected wife and mother. Lady Orville's introduction to Graham offers a welcome distraction, though his entrance into the fashionable world is entwined with her disastrous exit from it. Lamb skillfully adapts the trope of the novice, which Stephanie Insley Hershinow identifies as a key component of early realist fiction. Lady Orville herself is no novice, and Graham's inexperience fails to embody "the potential of futurity . . . without any of the messy negotiating of the future's terms and conditions" that Hershinow sees as a defining aspect of fiction in the long eighteenth century.[131] Instead, Lamb evokes themes of futurity central to the novel of manners in order to undermine the genre's optimism. Something follows marriage, and *Graham Hamilton* suggests that for women, society's conditions often turn that "something" into a downfall or, at the very least, the drudgery of an unhappy marriage. *Graham Hamilton* suggests that women fall easily and permanently, and the novel fictionalizes similar assertions in Lamb's private letters where she writes of the "difficulties playing ever on the verge of a precipice & everyone almost wishing you in it."[132] Using the vehicle of the novel of manners, Lamb offers her own theories about notorious celebrity and public female folly.

The most poignant suggestion that *Graham Hamilton* makes is that female identity has little substance beyond its public forms, and the novel illustrates that identity is always mediated. Just as women in Lamb's final novel, *Ada Reis*, are punished not for "any actual misconduct" but "for having fallen under the suspicion of errors," Lady Orville is ostracized not for real immorality but for the public's mistaken perception of it (*Ada Reis*, 178). After newspapers publish rumors that Graham and Lady Orville are lovers, he laments that "no inquiry would be made by the multitude whether the report were true or false" (94). Lady Orville's selfhood depends on the public circulation of her name—whether that circulation be true or false, flattering or unflattering. Early in the novel Graham explains, "Lady Orville's name was the most frequent in the public papers; her house was the most splendid; her extravagance was said to have exceeded that of any other lady, whether in dress, magnificence, or donations to the distressed" (31). Yet, public recognition empties Lady Orville of her personal value; she becomes a recognizable figure, but one without substance. As Leigh Wetherall Dickson notes, Lady Orville is "paralysed by the fear of losing her identity"—so much so that her "existence is only validated in the gaze of others."[133] Even with the danger of a separation from her husband looming, Lady Orville initially refuses to retrench and live in the country. She will lose herself, she explains, if she ceases to be admired publicly: "[T]he friends who now consider me as their first object—my parties . . . my suppers, at which politics are debated, and where statesmen settle their measures—all these will be lost for ever, and the world will seek some other general place of union, if I give up my present place in society, and retire into the country" (66). Important here is not the idea that dinners and debates will cease without her, but rather that such events will no longer orbit *around* her—a concern that, according to Lamb's circle, she shared: "[She] delights in braving the world's opinion—But though she should defy its censure she dares not lose its notice & wonder."[134]

While *Glenarvon* employs autobiographical elements in an aggressive attempt to set the record straight, *Graham Hamilton* criticizes the social system that shapes and circulates those records. *Graham Hamilton* exposes the flawed gendered framework within which a woman's public reputation is made, managed, and destroyed. Lamb's own case also suggests how a woman's reputation might be partially repaired. As a novel of manners, *Graham Hamilton* did not cause a stir, which may have been part of the point. *Graham Hamilton* and her other literary endeavors apart from *Glenarvon* aligned her with more respectable genres and publication venues, and they partially recontextualized her public reputation within more traditional literary and moral limits.

Take her poetry, which was performed on public stages and in private homes throughout the nineteenth century. When it was originally published, *Glenarvon* contained fourteen lyrics by Lamb, accompanied by sheet music composed by Isaac Nathan, who had also composed the music for Byron's *Hebrew Melodies* (1815). Nathan's compositions and other adaptations of *Glenarvon*'s songs remained popular well after the novel's initial publication, and Lamb's songs were still being printed and performed at the end of the century.[135] On the pages of sheet music and in the physical spaces of concert halls and homes, Lamb's name appeared alongside those of her respectable contemporaries throughout the late 1810s and 1820s. For example, the prominent London composer George Kiallmark published at least two different musical settings of Lamb's lyric "Waters of the Elle" from *Glenarvon*. One of Kiallmark's compositions names the poem and Lamb, but does not include lyrics, suggesting that this poem was so familiar to audiences that the words need not be printed.[136] Other composers also wrote music for Lamb's poetry, including B. Hime, G. A. Hodson, and Francis Joseph Klose, one of the period's foremost pianoforte instructors.[137] Klose's arrangement of "And Canst Thou Bid My Heart Forget" from *Glenarvon* went into at least four editions.[138] According to the sheet music itself, Klose's score was performed to "Enthusiastic Applause at the London & Bath Concerts."[139] The continued popularity of music inspired by her work suggests that Lamb's poetry and songs became partially uncoupled from *Glenarvon*'s scandalous overfamiliarity.

In the 1820s, Lamb's name and work also appeared with other well-respected Romantic authors in literary annuals, to which I turn again in chapter 5 of this book. In *The Bijou* for 1828, for instance, Lamb's poem "To a Friend" was published alongside works by Walter Scott, Felicia Hemans, and Mary Russell Mitford, whose public reputations were more respectable than her own.[140] Moreover, the genre itself was imbued with respectability and domesticity. Literary annuals were marketed as polite Christmas gifts for women and children. Displayed in drawing rooms, they signaled one's participation in the decorous and fashionable consumption of material books. The sanitizing effect of the annual allowed Lamb's literary work and her public reputation to circulate in spaces from which she was largely excluded.

Beyond polite drawing rooms, Lamb also found a place in schoolrooms, through Frances Arabella Rowden's didactic books *A Biographical Sketch of the Most Distinguished Writers of Ancient and Modern Time Intended for the Use of Schools and Private Education* (1820) and *A Christian Wreath for the Pagan Deities: Or an Introduction to the Greek and Roman Mythology* (1820). Rowden is most famous for attending, and later teaching at, the school that Jane and Cassandra Austen also attended. The publication of both volumes coincided with Rowden's opening of a new school in Paris and seems to have been a way to puff her reputation as an educator. *A Biographical Sketch* contains a preliminary address, "To Parents and Guardians," which advertises her school. Rowden outlines the "useful attainment[s]" and "moral conduct" that will be "particularly impressed on the minds of . . . Pupils," and she emphasizes the school's Anglican affiliation.[141] Lamb's name and works were embedded in this Christian, moral context. In addition to Lamb's name appearing in the subscription list for *A Biographical Sketch*, her name and art appear in both *A Biographical Sketch* and *A Christian Wreath*. The volumes feature signed frontispieces based on Lamb's drawings of cherubic figures, and the religiously inspired frontispieces mirror Rowden's Christian messaging. *A Christian Wreath*, for example, depicts "Superstition" being "directed by the Angel of Light to behold the manifestation of the Gospel, which is symbolised by the Cross of Christ."[142] Lamb's appearance in these didactic volumes used to support Rowden's school suggests that, by the 1820s, Lamb's reputation was perhaps rebounding.[143]

Together, Lamb's later authorial endeavors and their surrounding socio-literary field suggest that her largely unsuccessful attempts to establish sympathetic familiarity with readers early in her career may have more to do with Romantic-era ideologies of gender, authorship, and propriety than with the presumed aesthetic weakness of her work. Her struggles to move beyond her overly familiar, scandalous reputation as well as her associations with negative female archetypes and low genres reflect a cultural landscape that enabled women to fail easily and frequently. It is this culture of female failure that Lamb depicts with biting accuracy in *Graham Hamilton*. Lamb remained confident that at some point her indecorous behavior would be partially vindicated. After her affair with Byron, she aggressively assured Lady Melbourne that "some day or other facts & not vile words shall be judg'd of."[144] Perhaps the time has come for us to consider the historical, archival facts surrounding the judgments Lamb received in her day and in ours, for they bring into focus not only gendered standards of Romantic-era morality, sympathy, and literary reception but also an author with a keen critical pen that challenged the limits of all three.

4

"THE WHOLE CURSED STORY"

William Hazlitt's Familiar Style

If the unreserved communication of feeling or opinion leads to offensive familiarity, it is not well.
—William Hazlitt, "On Coffee-House Politicians"*

IN THE UNCERTAIN SOCIOPOLITICAL TERRAIN of the 1810s and 1820s, familiarity's literary and social limits remained as crucial as they were difficult to define. Familiarity preoccupied authors, critics, politicians, and readers in a cultural climate that, especially after Waterloo, saw renewed calls for parliamentary reform, violent government backlashes against it, and an expanding periodical print culture that informed and mobilized diverse readerships.[1] The growth of an increasingly literate and upwardly aspirational (if not exactly mobile) middle class began to erode assumed connections between rank, education, and political influence that had long stratified British society. As a key figure in the period's radical politics and periodical publishing, William Hazlitt was also one of Romanticism's most explicit theorists of familiarity. However, surprisingly little work has been done to contextualize Hazlitt, the famous familiar essayist, within the debates about familiarity that, this book has been arguing, shaped the Romantic period. Much of Hazlitt's work centers on questions of familiarity: how to write in a familiar style, how to read familiar literary texts, how to cultivate interpersonal familiarity between classes, and how to decide if, in Hazlitt's words, "constant intercourse and familiarity breed weariness and contempt," and "[i]f we are repelled after a while by familiarity."[2] Like his contemporaries, Hazlitt recognized familiarity's conflicting tendencies to either "prop up and reinforce our fondness" or "breed an indifference for those objects we are most conversant with."[3]

For Hazlitt, familiarity comes into focus primarily in two ways: first, as a mode enabling sociability that could either reinforce or challenge class hierarchies, depending on to whom familiarity extended; and second, as a literary style that Marcus Tomalin describes "as a particular linguistic register the use of which in literature was much debated in the early nineteenth century."[4] These two senses of familiarity often overlap in Hazlitt's work as well as in class-inflected critiques of it. Familiarity was a social issue in Hazlitt's personal life, a political focus of his essays, and a defining feature of his literary style. Hazlitt's career reveals that familiarity as a form of sociability and as a literary style was the third rail electrifying other elements of the Romantic cultural field, from debates about authorial oversharing and sympathy to concerns about the Cockney school and the vulgarization of literature.

Hazlitt's most significant entanglement with familiarity can be traced to his move in August 1820 to 9 Southampton Buildings in London, a lodging house owned by the tailor Micaiah Walker and his family. This is where he became familiar with and ardently attached to Sarah Walker, his landlord's nineteen-year-old daughter. Hazlitt believed that Walker's uneven response to his romantic advances arose not from the fact that he was more than twice her age, or acted erratically, or met with prostitutes in his rooms, but rather from the fact that he was married—a problem that he solved by traveling to Scotland in 1822 to divorce his wife, Sarah Stoddart Hazlitt.[5] Hazlitt returned to London in the summer of 1822, only to be rejected by the younger Sarah. She was in love with another man.[6]

The experience left Hazlitt with a broken heart and a loose tongue. His need to tell the tale of his failed romantic passion became Ancient Mariner–like in its pathology. Hazlitt himself seemed baffled by his uncontrollable desire to talk about it. "I could not help myself," he confessed, "It all came out; the whole cursed story. Afterwards I went to look at some lodgings at Pimlico. The landlady at one place, after some explanations as to rent, &c., said to me very kindly, 'I am afraid you are not well, Sir?' 'No, Ma'am,' said I, 'I am not well;' and on enquiring further, the devil take me if I did not let out the whole story from beginning to end."[7] In offering a landlady he had just met a minute account of his love life, Hazlitt certainly went beyond the period's standards of class-based interpersonal familiarity. This drive to share indiscriminately his heartache made Hazlitt an object of ridicule and downright confusion in the 1820s.

Even those in Hazlitt's circle were confounded by his behavior. The poet Barry Cornwall recalled how Hazlitt was "unable to think or talk of anything else . . . and fatigued every person whom he met by expressions of her [Sarah Walker's] love, of her deceit, and of his own vehement disappointment. . . . Upon one occasion I know that he told the story of his attachment to five different persons in the same day. And at each time entered into minute details of his love-story."[8] Less generously, Thomas De Quincey described how Hazlitt "went up and down London, raving about this girl. Nothing else he would talk of. 'Have you heard of

Miss—?' And, then, to the most indifferent stranger, he would hurry into a rapturous account of her beauty. For this he was abundantly laughed at."[9]

Hazlitt's decision to publish his autobiographical novel *Liber Amoris; Or, the New Pygmalion* in 1823 did little to quiet this laughter. It depicts Hazlitt's unsuccessful courtship of Walker in such detail that it makes Lady Caroline Lamb's revelations about her affair with Byron in *Glenarvon* look tame. *Liber Amoris* shares, among other things, that his unrequited love threw him into suicidal "dumb despair," and it describes a disturbing episode where he "shrieked curses" that were "so pitiful and so piercing" that others in the lodging house feared he was killing Sarah and himself.[10] Like *Glenarvon*, *Liber Amoris* appeared anonymously; however, it was quickly determined to be Hazlitt's work. The characters "H." and "S." (who is also called "Sarah" in the novel) were immediately identified as Hazlitt and Sarah Walker. The reviewer for *Blackwood's Edinburgh Magazine* put it simply: "[T]his work is not a novel, but a history."[11] Part I of *Liber Amoris* consists of dialogues between H. and S., and the general consensus since the novel's publication has been that they are based on real conversations. Hazlitt's famous memory for speech—the skill that made him a successful parliamentary reporter—lends weight to this theory. The epistolary correspondence in Parts II and III track H.'s divorce from his wife in Scotland and the realization that Sarah loves someone else; many of the letters printed in *Liber Amoris* are based on Hazlitt's actual letters.[12]

Much like Hazlitt's indiscriminate "raving about this girl" that had disturbed De Quincey and Cornwall, his novel about the same subject shocked readers.[13] *Liber Amoris* expands smaller references to Walker that appeared in *Table-Talk* (1821–1822) into a full exposé, enacting what was in effect a murder-suicide of Walker's public reputation and Hazlitt's own. As one of Hazlitt's late nineteenth-century editors noted, "a man could hardly have done a more deliberately stupid injury to his fame" than publish *Liber Amoris*.[14] Notwithstanding the vituperative criticism *Liber Amoris* received, it was reasonably successful and may have been issued as many as three times in 1823.[15] Similar to *Glenarvon*, *Liber Amoris* was a text that people enjoyed disliking. It is a Romantic-era precursor to contemporary culture's interest in hate-watching—consuming television "you think is awful purely for the joy of laughing at it."[16] Perhaps anticipating an audience of hate-readers, Hazlitt's publisher paid him the impressive sum of £100 for the copyright.[17]

Reviewers lampooned Hazlitt's amorous failure and his "indecent exhibition of himself as the modern Pygmalion."[18] The hyper-Tory *John Bull* believed that *Liber Amoris* revealed Hazlitt's "stupidity and folly," and *Blackwood's* declared,

"[N]othing so disgusting as this has ever fallen in our way."[19] More than just stupid or disgusting, *Liber Amoris* struck Romantic-era readers as morally repugnant. The reviewer for the *Literary Register* wrote, "It is really pitiable to see a man possessed of any thing like talent so utterly lost to every feeling of shame, as to be thus the bare-faced proclaimer of his own profligacy and disgrace."[20] The *Country Literary Chronicle and Weekly Review* proclaimed more forcefully that *Liber Amoris* insulted "public decency and public morals."[21] Hazlitt's former friend Henry Crabb Robinson recorded his equally offended reaction: "Finished early Hazlitt's disgusting *New Pygmalion* . . . such a story as this is nauseous and revolting."[22]

One goal of this chapter is to understand what made *Liber Amoris* "nauseous and revolting" to Romantic-era readers. Since its publication, readers have struggled with what to make of the novel, and, as John Whale has noted, "its difficulty and offensive strangeness to many contemporary critics" has made it challenging to connect *Liber Amoris* to the rest of Hazlitt's oeuvre.[23] Rather than see *Liber Amoris* as a departure from Hazlitt's other work, here I argue that it amplifies Hazlitt's self-described "familiar style" in his essays, many of which were written and published during his courtship of Walker and its disastrous aftermath. This chapter analyzes theorizations of familiarity in Hazlitt's essays and then reads these theories and *Liber Amoris* back into their contemporary social context. I suggest that, while readers found fault with the novel's egregious autobiographical detail, they were also startled by Hazlitt's romantic obsession with a lower-class woman and the highly literary way he described it. Like his better-known essays, *Liber Amoris* is strikingly intertextual, and reactions to the novel are tied to Hazlitt's modes of autobiographical writing in his familiar essays. Also like his essays, *Liber Amoris* combines elements of high and low culture—an aspect of his familiar style and, more generally, the Cockney school that critics had previously attacked. Because some of the most virulent critics of the Cockneys were not themselves of high rank, as Gregory Dart has noted, the question was less about upper class versus middling class and more about "where the dividing line of cultural legitimacy lay."[24] In short, debates about Cockney writers like Hazlitt were about who got to draw the ladder of cultural legitimacy up behind them, leaving those below as decidedly vulgar. Hazlitt's familiar style in his essays and in *Liber Amoris*, then, is embroiled in debates about who and how one can earn familiarity with people from different classes and with high culture.

I open by outlining Hazlitt's struggle to interpret Sarah Walker's familiarity with him and others. I then contextualize H.'s familiarity with Sarah in *Liber Amoris* alongside Hazlitt's exploration of familiarity in his essays, especially those collected in *Table-Talk* (1821–1822) and *The Plain Speaker* (1826). Reading the novel alongside the essays clarifies how *Liber Amoris* pushes the limits of familiarity on multiple fronts. First, *Liber Amoris* engages in the type of confessional overfamiliarity that I have explored in other chapters in this book. Second, the spiteful anger of Hazlitt's emotional revelations undermined his ability to evoke sympathetic familiarity, both from readers and from Walker. Third, Hazlitt's familiar style applied elevated cultural tropes to a love that his contemporaries thought degrading. Hazlitt's literary and social familiarity is intertwined with discourses about sympathy, and I detail links between Hazlitt's theories of familiarity and theories of sympathy and passion by Adam Smith and Joanna Baillie. While both moral philosophy and class have been threads throughout the earlier chapters of this book, here they become more central, especially in relation to the propriety of one's passions, their cause, and their decorous (literary) presentation.

I end by analyzing how Hazlitt deploys literary allusions to different effect in his familiar essays than he does in *Liber Amoris*. While in his essays, quotations forge connections with readers, in *Liber Amoris* they reflect a frenzied narcissism. Critics found Hazlitt's literary allusions affected, ill placed, and pompous. Hazlitt's use of literary references to describe his seemingly vulgar attachment to Walker pointed to familiarity's dangerously unmarked terrain in Romanticism's changing cultural and literary landscape. If etiquette is an invisible boundary dividing groups of people, those boundaries became both more important and unsteady as the period progressed, and the cultural value of familiarity became a free-market anxiety intensifying within Britain's expanding capitalist and imperialist project.

INTERPRETING "SUCH FAMILIARITIES"

Liber Amoris and Hazlitt's essays frequently focus on problems of interpreting interpersonal familiarity. In the novel, familiarity alternately demonstrates Walker's love or her vulgarity. For instance, H. justifies his frightening outburst of shrieking by pointing to Sarah's frequent familiarity with him: "I did not see how it was in human nature for any one who was not rendered callous to such familiarities by bestowing them indiscriminately on every one, to grant the extreme and continued indulgences she had done to me, without either liking the man at first, or coming to like him in the end, in spite of herself" (59). Hazlitt, his contemporaries, and more recent critics have partially defended his interactions with Walker and his choice to publish *Liber Amoris* by pointing to her indulgent familiarities. In this line of thinking, Hazlitt's disturbing choices arise from Walker's manipulative familiarity with him and "every one"—a narrative that problematically normalizes and justifies Hazlitt's misogyny.

I want to pause to consider Walker's social position as a tradesman's daughter in a lodging house, because that positioning informed Hazlitt's relationship with her and contemporary reactions to *Liber Amoris*. It also continues to influence scholarly debate. Because the Walkers owned the lodging house, she was not technically a servant. Yet Walker performed some servants' duties; she brought Hazlitt his prostitutes and his tea.[25] Her liminal role—servant but not quite—likely emboldened Hazlitt's behavior. In his work on *Liber Amoris*, Dart suggests that in the Romantic-era cultural imaginary "the London servant girl" was at times "considered as only one step up from a prostitute because of her singleness, sexual availability and subservience," yet she "could also be seen in Pamela-like terms, as a gentlewoman in embryo, a veritable lady-in-waiting."[26] In either view, the specter of sexual violence looms; after all, Samuel Richardson's Pamela is repeatedly sexually assaulted and must fend off Mr. B.'s attempts to rape her before their eventual marriage and her social elevation. The threat of violence and sexual coercion was so pervasive that conduct manuals advised female servants how best to avoid the advances of male masters. Eliza Haywood's popular *A Present for a Servant-Maid*, originally published in 1743 and reprinted numerous times, includes a section on "*Temptations from your Master.*" Haywood warns against "Importunities" of lustful employers, "which it must be confessed are not easy to surmount."[27] Summarizing conduct literature from the long eighteenth century, Kristina Straub observes "an overwhelmingly clear consensus: any female domestic servant is a walking sexual target."[28] Given widespread connections between service and sex in the period, Walker's behavior toward Hazlitt and other male lodgers is more complicated than it may initially seem. This is not to say that Walker had no agency; she may have expressed interest in Hazlitt, sexual or otherwise. However, their relationship crossed class lines and was founded on inequality, making her ultimate rejection of him particularly ego bruising.

While certainly not universal in Romantic studies, there remains a worrying trend to accept Sarah Walker at Hazlitt's word. My own assessment of *Liber Amoris* and the relationship between Walker and Hazlitt on which it is based aligns with feminist scholarship by Catherine Burroughs and Sonia Hofkosh; both have identified the inherent power disparity between Walker and Hazlitt.[29] Connecting *Liber Amoris* to an episode in 1803 when Hazlitt accosted (and likely assaulted) a local girl in Keswick, Hofkosh highlights the tenuous social positions that women held in the period and that are replicated in more recent scholarship, so that literary history's tendency to privilege male perspectives like Hazlitt's "perpetuat[es] the masculine narrative of the romantic tradition."[30] Despite feminist work on *Liber Amoris* begun in the 1990s, Hofkosh's assessment remains relevant.[31] Moreover, reading *Liber Amoris* today against the backdrop of movements like #MeToo makes H.'s unrelenting pursuit of Sarah as well as more recent defenses of Hazlitt especially startling.

In the first part of the novel, there emerges an unsettling narrative of a woman's repeated "no" meaning, if not "yes," then at least "maybe." "I have always been consistent from the first," S. says in the opening pages of *Liber Amoris*, "I told you my regard could amount to no more than friendship" (15). Yet H. refuses to listen, and his romantic optimism transforms into an aggressive refusal to be rejected by a woman whom he describes as "a kissing convenience" (14). Hazlitt's unwillingness to listen to Walker culminated in his vindictive publication of *Liber Amoris*. Duncan Wu explains, "If he could not possess Sarah Walker, the publication of *Liber Amoris* would at least be their joint undoing. . . . His uncompromising portrayal of his own sexual appetite would leave his reputation—and that of the woman he loved—in ruins."[32] Contemporary accounts confirm the very real ruin Hazlitt caused. Even before *Liber Amoris* appeared, Sarah Stoddart Hazlitt's journal recounts how Walker's "character began to be blown" through Hazlitt's repeated references to her in print.[33] Stoddart Hazlitt chided him for references to Walker in essays published in periodicals and reprinted in *Table-Talk*: "I told him he had done a most injudicious thing in publishing what he did in the [*New Monthly*] Magazine about Sarah Walker . . . and that every body in London had thought it a most improper thing . . . it had hurt the girl too, and done her an injury."[34] *Liber Amoris* exacerbated these earlier reputational injuries. The novel, then, seems less "an act of open defiance" against Hazlitt's critics, as Wu has claimed, or, "an act of willed reputational suicide born of despair, both personal and political, like a Roman republican falling on his sword," as Lucasta Miller has suggested, and far more like the Romantic-era equivalent of revenge porn.[35]

My focus here is not simply to highlight the obvious misogyny of *Liber Amoris* or of Hazlitt's sense of entitlement to Walker's body and her affections. Instead, I want to emphasize the elements of class and propriety informing Hazlitt's relationship with Walker, his novel, and reactions to both. Hazlitt's (mis)interpretation of Walker's familiar behavior points to the insidious ways that the limits of familiarity were used to police social and literary decorum. Walker's familiarity, not unlike criticisms of Hazlitt's "vulgar" familiar style, was deployed against her to prove that she was not, as he once believed, a "glorious girl" who "would ennoble any family," but rather a low woman (19). Hazlitt's struggles to read Walker's familiarity reveal a tension in his ideas about sociability and hierarchies of class, evidencing both the high stakes of familiarity and the increasing instability of its boundaries as the nineteenth century progressed. Like his contemporaries, Hazlitt grappled with familiarity's dueling potential as something that could bind or bore, connect or disgust. He claimed, "If the unreserved communication of feeling or opinion leads to offensive familiarity, it is not well." He also acknowledged that "no good society" could exist "without perfect freedom from affectation and constraint."[36] Hazlitt, however, seemed undecided about who should be included in "good society." Though Hazlitt's political beliefs led him to criticize what he saw as arbitrary distinctions between elevated and common life, he also described the difficulty of achieving authentic, familiar relations between classes.

Concerns about interpreting familiarity are heightened in *Liber Amoris*, but they also appear in his essays. Hazlitt's *Table-Talk* essay "On Vulgarity and Affectation" attacks superficial social hierarchies; however, it also shows how familiarity between classes can signal vulgarity. The essay criticizes a stereotypical "fashionable Miss" who scorns an unfashionable bonnet worn by "a country-girl who comes to be hired by her Mamma as a servant." Hazlitt postulates that this same Miss "would herself the next day be delighted with the very same bonnet if brought her by a French milliner and told it was all the fashion, and in a week's time will become quite familiar with the maid, and chatter with her (upon equal terms)."[37] The girl's superficial (and nationalized) class consciousness depends on what Hazlitt calls the "glittering varnish of pretended refinement and conventional politeness."[38] Critical of the girl's vapidity, Hazlitt also reproaches her familiar relationship with her maid. Because "servants occupied an important role in defining class attitudes," overfamiliar relations between domestics and their employers undermined social hierarchy.[39] Rather than retain a polite, yet unidirectional, condescension, Hazlitt's "fashionable Miss" lowers herself to the level of her servant. The maid's and the Miss's familiar conversation—not entirely unlike Hazlitt's own relationship with Walker—enacts the type of "*levelling Scheme*" resulting from "convers[ing] so familiarly with our domestics" that eighteenth- and nineteenth-century moralists found so worrisome.[40]

In other essays, Hazlitt's discomfort with cross-class familiarity is more apparent, and his elitism chaffs against his more radical ideals. "On the Knowledge of Character" alludes to Walker and specifically attacks the lower middle classes, a group to which she belonged: "Persons of liberal knowledge or sentiments have no kind of chance in this sort of mixed intercourse with these barbarians of civilised life."[41] He ties a reference to Walker with examples of misreading familiarity: "After a familiar conversation with a waiter at a tavern, you overhear him calling you by some provoking nickname. If you make a present to the daughter of the house where you lodge, the mother is sure to recollect some addition to her bill . . . So little is there in common between the different classes of society, and so impossible is it ever to unite the diversities of custom and knowledge which separate them."[42] Hazlitt presents the dangers of mistaking familiarity for authentic connection—hence his indignation that a waiter might feign goodwill as part of his job or that a family "of the house where you lodge" might use an infatuation with their daughter to turn additional profits. Hazlitt recognizes that familiar intercourse might mask commercial relationships in the garb of personal ones. In theory familiarity should connect people of "different classes of society," but Hazlitt suggests that in practice authentic connections proved difficult.

Another factor complicating Hazlitt's views about familiarity was his belief that it blunted one's powers of discernment. "Familiarity," he explains, "confounds all traits of distinction: interest and prejudice take away the power of judging."[43] According to Hazlitt, familiarity brings people together, but emotional, social, and spatial proximity also potentially inhibit judgments of character and conduct. Hazlitt's criticisms of Walker in *Liber Amoris* center on the fact that she offered her familiarity freely without distinction or judgment. Hazlitt's concerns about what Walker's familiarity might reveal about her vulgarity exemplify how the scope of one's audience influenced the interpretation of interpersonal familiarity. If S.'s familiarity went beyond H., then it signaled her "want of both common propriety, and I might say, of natural feeling" (60). Or, as Hazlitt put it more bluntly in his private correspondence: without love, Walker's familiarities showed her to be a "bitch [who] wants a *stallion*."[44]

Hazlitt's struggle to assess Walker's familiarity came to a head on his return to London after his divorce. In the novelized version of events, H. reports his painful realization that Sarah "had gone on in the most forward and familiar way with both [him and another lodger] at once" (71). His discovery substantiates his earlier fears that she was "a common lodging-house decoy" and that her "lips were as common as the stairs" (14). H. connects Sarah's supposed loose sexuality and emotional manipulation to the house in which they live. In a lodging house, the stairs were typically shared. More generally, lodging houses like that owned by the Walkers were liminal spaces where different classes mixed and where boundaries of social, personal, and economic relationships blurred. Accusations of Sarah's commonness, then, engage three interrelated definitions of *common* from Johnson's *Dictionary*: "vulgar," "Publick" or "serving the use of all," and without "rank."[45] According to Hazlitt's radical principles, Walker's lack of rank did not, in and of itself, signify, yet it was another matter if she "serv[ed] the use of all" the male lodgers. The problem, though, was knowing which definition to apply to Walker. Hazlitt ultimately concluded that, like a tavern waiter who uses false familiarity to foster a profitable "personal" connection, Walker's familiarity demonstrated inauthentic, exploitative sociability. Coming to see Walker's familiarity as a sign of vulgarity rather than innocent affection, Hazlitt's narrative speaks directly to contemporary questions about "the servant problem" and, in particular, sexual relationships between employers and domestics. Indeed, though neither Richardson's

Pamela nor Henry Fielding's *Shamela* are directly referenced in *Liber Amoris*, its narrative arc tracks H.'s "realization" that Sarah is less an innocent Pamela waiting to be raised above her station and more a conniving Shamela exploiting her sexuality for personal gain. Hazlitt cast himself as the dupe of her supposed wantonness, but in doing so, he also risked making himself ridiculous rather than sympathetic. The novel awkwardly depicts H. as both sexual rake and broken-hearted victim.

SYMPATHIZING WITH HAZLITT

In many ways, Hazlitt's attacks on Walker's vulgar familiarities implicate his decision to publish *Liber Amoris.* The appearance of *Liber Amoris* demonstrates Hazlitt's willingness to bestow autobiographical details "indiscriminately on every one" who could buy or borrow the book (71). His undiscerning familiarity with both Walker and readers points to Adam Smith's theories of decorous passion. Smith suggests that the propriety of one's passions and their ability to evoke sympathy depend on the relationship between emotional expression and audience—not unlike how familiarity's decorousness depends on one's relationship with the people to whom it is directed. Complicating this relationship between displays of passion and its audience was the connection between passion and its cause. Smith explains that "two different relations" must be considered when evaluating the propriety of passions: "[F]irst, in relation to the cause which excites it, or the motive which gives occasion to it; and secondly, in relation to the end which it proposes, or the effect which it tends to produce."[46] Many nineteenth-century readers thought that the cause—unrequited love of a lower-class woman—was disproportionate to Hazlitt's passion. As a result, according to the *Times*'s notice about *Liber Amoris*, Hazlitt evoked readers' "pain and disgust, instead of producing respect and admiration."[47]

De Quincey identified Hazlitt's seeming disregard for readers' pain, disgust, respect, or admiration in *Liber Amoris.* "It was an explosion of frenzy," De Quincey wrote. "He threw out his clamorous anguish to the clouds, and to the winds, and to the air; caring not *who* might listen, *who* might sympathise, or *who* might sneer. Pity was no demand of his; laughter was no wrong."[48] De Quincey's description evokes Smith's observation: "We are disgusted with that clamorous grief, which, without delicacy, calls upon our compassion with sighs and tears and importunate lamentations."[49] Moral conduct, Smith argues, is moderated conduct. With practice, regulating the passions and their outward display with the impartial spectator in mind "become[s] perfectly familiar."[50] In *Liber Amoris*, Hazlitt refused to calibrate his feelings "according to those of this awful and respectable judge."[51] Instead, Hazlitt's novel offered what readers saw as unseemly emotional exhibitionism; Hazlitt's primary concern became, according to De Quincey, his own "overburdened spirit."[52]

The propriety of one's passions also depended on the particular passion in question. Smith and, later, Joanna Baillie cautioned against anger. Both conclude that anger and concomitant passions, like revenge and resentment, are largely unsympathetic. "There are some passions," Smith writes, "of which the expressions excite no sort of sympathy . . . The furious behaviour of an angry man is more likely to exasperate us against himself than against his enemies."[53] Smith returns to this point later in *The Theory of Moral Sentiments*, noting that "hatred and resentment" are passions that "must always be brought down to a pitch much lower than that to which undisciplined nature would raise them."[54] This is a far cry from *Liber Amoris*'s "explosion of frenzy."[55] While ostensibly a "book of love," *Liber Amoris* is also a book of resentment, spite, and anger. Andrew Stauffer has convincingly shown that in the Romantic period, which saw a marked interest "in the causes and consequences of anger, just indignation is firmly separated from anger per se, which is made equivalent with irrational rage."[56] Ideas about sympathy and anger took on new urgency in the changing market and political economy of the post-Waterloo era that coincided with Hazlitt's work. Given Hazlitt's association with the Cockney school and radical politics, his ill-fated passion for a lower-class woman in *Liber Amoris* was depicted by the Tory press as irrational, improper love turned into vulgar rage.

In her "Introductory Discourse" to *Plays on the Passions*, Baillie similarly identifies anger as a special case: "Anger is a passion that attracts less sympathy than any other, yet the unpleasing and distorted features of an angry man will be more eagerly gazed upon, by those who are no wise concerned with his fury or the objects of it, than the most amiable placid countenance in the world."[57] For Baillie, anger attracts curiosity though not necessarily sympathy—an important distinction that, as I outlined in chapters 2 and 3, also influenced Byron's and Lamb's reception histories. While autobiographical hiddenness, I argued, brought Byron's readers into familiarity with him, Hazlitt's *Liber Amoris*, much like *Glenarvon*, has few autobiographical gaps and even less emotional delicacy regarding his resentment toward Walker. While "[e]very eye is directed" toward an angry man, and while onlookers will "gaze after him more eagerly than the gaudiest equipage," curiosity, Baillie claims, is a superficial passion that passes quickly, like a carriage in the street.[58]

Hazlitt's own theories of sympathy and familiarity take their lead from the era's moral philosophy, and Hazlitt's ideas about familiarity identify curiosity's superficiality. For instance, in his 1826 essay "On Novelty and Familiarity," Hazlitt explains, "There is a craving after information, as there is after food; and it is in supplying the void, in satisfying the appetite, that the pleasure in both cases chiefly consists. When the uneasy want is removed, both the pleasure and the pain cease."[59] He goes on to observe that the absence "of novelty, of curiosity, and of mystery" effect "an end also of our transport, our wonder, and our delight."[60] According to the standards of familiarity outlined in the essay, *Liber Amoris* glutted readers with detail, satiating their curiosity but not necessarily soliciting their sympathy. As the essay continues, Hazlitt asks, "[D]oes not our familiarity . . . breed an indifference for those objects we are most conversant with and most masters of? I am afraid the answer, if an honest one, must be on the unfavourable side."[61] Applied to his own novel, Hazlitt's ideas about familiarity suggest that once he told his tale about what the *Times* called "one of the most baneful and disgusting frailties of our nature," his readers would lose interest.[62] Though compelling in its raw details, *Liber Amoris*, according to reviewers, deserved "the castigation and contempt it most universally received."[63]

Within a Smithian framework of emotional decorum, Hazlitt's book about failed love made him particularly vulnerable to contempt. Smith argues that passions related to love require extra care if one desires sympathy, for observers are prone to question the appeal of one's lover and the intensity of one's heartbreak: "The merit of his favourite, we say, is not so great, his misfortune is not so dreadful, his provocation is not so extraordinary, as to justify so violent a passion. We should have indulged, we say; perhaps, have approved of the violence of his emotion, had the cause been in any respect proportioned to it."[64] Smith's hypothetical situation anticipates Hazlitt's experience. Barry Cornwall, for instance, disapproved of the violence of Hazlitt's love and its cause, and he was especially focused on Walker's class status: "I used to see this girl, Sarah Walker, at his lodgings, and could not account for the extravagant passion of her admirer. She was the daughter of the lodging-house-keeper."[65] The painter Benjamin Robert Haydon similarly thought his friend's emotions overwrought and misplaced: "He has fallen in love with a lodging-house hussy . . . His imagination clothed her with that virtue which her affected modesty induced him to believe in, and he is really downright in love with an ideal perfection, which has no existence but in his own head!"[66] That Hazlitt would make so much fuss over a near servant and would assume his pain interested others represented multiple layers of misapplied familiarity. Wanting to bed Walker would have been one thing, but wanting to marry her seemed quite another. *Liber Amoris* reveals—in detail—how he failed on both fronts. Friends and conservative critics alike attacked not only Hazlitt's romantic failure but also his decision to write about it in a style that tried to elevate Walker and himself.

"THE GREAT SLANG-WHANGER'S MANNER AND MODE"

Attacks on *Liber Amoris*, Hazlitt's essays, and the Cockney school at large disapproved of a style that intermingled high culture with vulgarity—a style that *Blackwood's* believed "talks indelicately like a tea-sipping milliner girl" while having misplaced pretentions to greatness.[67] Readers identified this dynamic in, for example, Hazlitt's Latin title and allusion to the Pygmalion myth in his book about his unsuccessful courtship of a lodging house woman. Notably, charges against Hazlitt's style echo Smith's theories about narcissistic presumption in *The Theory of Moral Sentiments*: "Why should the man, whom nobody thinks it worth while to look at, be very anxious about the manner in which he holds up his head, or disposes of his arms while he walks through a room? He is occupied surely with a very superfluous attention, and with an attention too that marks a sense of his own importance, which no other mortal can go along with."[68] Smith focuses on pretentious physical self-presentation; however, a similar theme appears in criticisms of Hazlitt's prose, which, according to his Tory critics, was vulgarly self-important. Critics refused to go along with what they saw as Hazlitt's "superfluous attention" to himself and to common subjects.

In "Hazlitt Cross-Questioned," published in *Blackwood's* in 1818, John Wilson accuses Hazlitt of giving himself airs that neither he nor his prose deserve. He even questions whether Hazlitt belongs to the category of author, and, instead, calls him "a mere quack . . . and a mere bookmaker; one of the sort that lounge in third-rate bookshops, and write third-rate books."[69] According to Wilson, Hazlitt was not a respectable literary man but a lowly "bookmaker" catering to an uneducated mass readership who frequented unprestigious bookshops. Reviewers like Wilson also criticized the incongruity between Hazlitt's alleged third-rate prose and his books' first-rate costs and physical format. Five years after Wilson's critique, *John Bull* attacked both the content and price of *Liber Amoris*. Sarcastically imitating Hazlitt's own disregard for class-informed propriety, the reviewer declares his intention to rescue Walker from Hazlitt's ungentlemanly portrayal of her: "[N]ever, perhaps, was a poor, honest, *sublime* little girl in SALLY's station made the subject of a seven shilling and sixpenny book—as it is, we have done our duty—rank to us signifies nothing, and we will not submit to have beastliness and folly stuffed down the public throat, or a virtuous female calumniated groundlessly, though her libeller be a cockney lecturer on Shakespeare, and she no better than '*a tradesman's daughter*.'"[70] The sarcastic references to Walker's sublimity reinforce her common class status and Hazlitt's hyperbolic praise of her. The review bathetically borrows from Hazlitt's more radical ideas on rank that appeared in *Table-Talk*—a collection that also included references to Walker. (The allusions were so obvious that one review of *Table-Talk* warned, "Let us have no more of his landlord's daughter in italics.")[71] Under the guise of rank-blind chivalry, *John Bull* lampoons Hazlitt's misplaced passion for a lower-class woman and his overpriced book about it. That *Liber Amoris* featured an elegant engraved title page with a portrait of a girl also struck Hazlitt's detractors as presumptuous and déclassé.

This was not the first time Hazlitt had been attacked for the format and relatively high price of his books. In 1822, a *Blackwood's* review of *Table-Talk* mocked the cost of the two volumes: "Eight and twenty shillings for Hazlitt's Table-Talk! Good heavens! . . . It is truly wonderful, that even a Cockney should have thought people would give eight-and-twenty shillings merely to hear in what horrible dudgeon a single unfortunate author has taken the ill-treatment of *the critics* and of *the public*."[72] By comparison, octavo editions of Byron's *The Giaour*, *The Corsair*, and *Childe Harold's Pilgrimage, Canto the Third* sold for five and a half shillings each. De Quincey's *Confessions of an English Opium Eater* (1822) could be purchased for five shillings.[73] *John Bull* and *Blackwood's* contrast the high price of Hazlitt's volumes with the Cockney origins of their author. They acknowledged that readers might be willing to read Hazlitt's essays as they originally appeared in periodicals like the *New Monthly Magazine*, but his decision to sell them in a volume for twenty-eight shillings signified that Hazlitt understood his place neither in the literary nor in the social pecking order.

By lecturing on great writers such as Shakespeare and charging a high price for his printed works, Hazlitt attempted to align himself with respectable notions of reception—what Jon Klancher has described as "the symbolic giving and receiving of texts between great writers and singular, sensitive readers."[74] This symbolic giving seeks to distance authorship from the market economy associated with mass readerships. Distance from the market economy was often predicated on high prices because expensive volumes excluded a common readership through their unaffordability. A high price, then, could legitimize the cultural capital associated with a commodity.[75] Sensitive readers, Hazlitt's antagonistic reviewers argued, would not be fooled so easily. If one aspect of familiarity is its insistence of grouping like with like as a way to police relationships—recall that Romantic-era conduct literature advised limiting familiarity to one's socioeconomic group—then indecorous familiarity reveals itself in refusals to acknowledge one's place within a particular group. This is part of the problem of Hazlitt's essays and *Liber Amoris*, which for some readers seemed the literary equivalent of the maid dressing up like the mistress and having the audacity to think no one will notice.

The discourse about *Liber Amoris*'s vulgar presumption—the same "superfluous attention" to one's importance that Adam Smith cautioned against—is an inheritance of earlier debates about Hazlitt's familiar style and the Cockney school.

A year before *Liber Amoris* appeared, the *Quarterly Review* attacked Hazlitt "the great Slang-whanger's manner and mode."[76] The epithet points toward the decorous manners and polite modes of sociability that Hazlitt's familiar style challenged. Critiques about Hazlitt's writing, then, reflect fears about eroding distinctions between literary and cultural hierarchies—distinctions vigorously defended by Tory critics who attacked Hazlitt and the Cockney school. Indeed, it was the combination of high literary material with common diction and everyday topics that led one reviewer to conclude that Hazlitt "too often appears familiar or affected," so that his familiar style "might be defined, on the whole, as that of making slight and trivial things the object of serious discussion, rather than of the easy and familiar explication of great subjects."[77]

Hazlitt himself noted the difficulty of writing in a conversational style that avoided the vulgarity of lowness and the vulgarity of affectation and "unmeaning pomp."[78] Hazlitt opened his essay "On Familiar Style" by admitting, "It is not easy to write a familiar style."[79] Debates about class made Hazlitt's familiar style even harder to pull off. In Hazlitt's case, class and politeness come to a head in the seeming incongruences between high and low elements that characterize Hazlitt's familiar essays—essays that mix autobiographical content with commentary about everything from politics and playgoing to metaphysics and mail coaches. In doing so, Hazlitt's style, according to Robert Ready, "challenges eighteenth-century essay decorum by running the risk of being too familiar."[80] For instance, "The Fight" applies the precision of literary criticism to the then-illegal blood sport of boxing, and Hazlitt uses slang alongside allusions to Shakespeare and Rousseau. The most personal essays in *Table-Talk* situate Hazlitt's cultural criticism alongside his stomachache before eating partridge and his heartache after courting Sarah Walker.[81] Conservative readers were appalled by this combinatory style. Hence, the *Quarterly Review*'s assertion that Hazlitt was a "Slang-whanger" who "deals his blows indiscriminately among all ranks of people."[82] From this perspective, Hazlitt knew neither proper English nor his place in polite society.

Hazlitt's essays challenge the validity of traditional markers of politeness and rank that, he believed, arbitrarily delineated English social and literary hierarchies. In "On Vulgarity and Affectation," Hazlitt attacks surface-level distinctions on which accusations of lowness and vulgarity often depended: "It is prejudging things in the lump, by names and places and classes, instead of judging of them by what they are in themselves, by their real qualities and shades of distinction. . . . It is a vapid assumption of superiority. It is exceeding impertinence. It is rank coxcombry."[83] Hazlitt plays with the flexibility of "rank coxcombry": stinking, extreme foolishness as well as the foolishness of social rank. Hazlitt attacks an older social order where birth and class were synonymous with quality and authority.

Maintaining these boundaries is itself, Hazlitt claims, a sign of vulgarity, and he asks readers to take a more critical and, by extension, egalitarian approach. What Dart terms Leigh Hunt's "aesthetics of familiarity" applies here. For Hazlitt, the aesthetics of familiarity not only created "a relationship of warmth and candour and shared common feelings" with readers. It also "position[ed] oneself in relation to politics and high culture" and, by extension, claimed familiarity with a cultural inheritance that had previously remained the purview of the elite.[84]

Hazlitt's style and his reception are embedded in a changing sociopolitical landscape. Class lines increasingly blurred, and calls for parliamentary reform (though not actualized until the Reform Act of 1832) sought to flatten distinctions within England's socioeconomic hierarchy. Increased print production and the expansion of cheap reading material produced a growing population of British autodidacts and upwardly mobile classes. Mary Fairclough notes that Hazlitt's "writings constitute a pernicious example of just the kind of broadening of the intellectual franchise" that worried both his conservative critics as well as, at times, Hazlitt himself.[85] Criticisms of Cockney school writers including Hazlitt, Leigh Hunt, and John Keats often pointed to their social inferiority—an inferiority that, critics argued, displayed itself in the Cockneys' want of birth, education, and taste. In one invective against the Cockney school, "Z." (John Gibson Lockhart) made much of Hunt's imperfect classical education: "He knows absolutely nothing of Greek, almost nothing of Latin, and his knowledge of Italian literature is confined to a few of the most popular of Petrarch's sonnets and an imperfect acquaintance with Ariosto, through the medium of Mr. Hoole."[86] Pointing to Hunt's lack of languages, just as he would in his later review of Keats's *Endymion* in 1818, "Z." makes the common education of the Cockney writers a symbol of vulgar morality and vulgar manners.

Blackwood's similarly accused Hazlitt of vulgarity and of feigning education and cultural capital. The review of *Table-Talk* ridicules Hazlitt's travels in "On Going a Journey": "Now, the object of the above passage is to puff Mr Hazlitt as a travelled man. He has, it appears, (we really never suspected it before,) made the grand tour of Oxford and Blenheim, and also lounged in the long gallery of the Louvre. . . . What a fine thing to be in FRANCE, understanding, as it appears, only English."[87] The reviewer mockingly compares Hazlitt's travels in Oxfordshire and London with the European Grand Tour. Since the eighteenth century such tours of Europe were a marker of (masculine) cultural experience, especially for those with money and gentle birth, neither of which Hazlitt had. Implicitly, too, the review criticizes the circumstances under which Hazlitt traveled to Paris in 1802 shortly after the Treaty of Amiens was signed. Unlike the slew of aristocratic leisure travelers from England who went to Paris in the summer of 1802, Hazlitt was paid to go. Mr. Railton from Liverpool had commissioned him to copy paintings from the Louvre. Hazlitt as an employee rather than as an independent art connoisseur is a pointed distinction. Hazlitt may travel from one place to another, the review implies, but his social place remained fixed.

Along with his references to travel, Hazlitt was also criticized for his quotational, intertextual style. At times, his allusion-laden prose seems designed to counter accusations that he was uncultured. As I argued in chapter 1 on Charlotte Smith, here also I contend that Hazlitt's literary references provide what John Hollander calls a "set of credentials" that connects his work to authors such as Chaucer, Spenser, Shakespeare, Milton, Rousseau, Wordsworth, Coleridge, and Byron.[88] Some censorious critics saw Hazlitt's literary credentials as forged documents. William Gifford, for instance, charged Hazlitt with quoting inelegantly from Shakespeare. Hazlitt's "*constant stitching in of these patches*" of quotations, Gifford claimed, produced a stylistic "*deformity*."[89] Like Victor Frankenstein sewing together body parts to make his creature, Hazlitt stitches together quotations that, while beautiful in their original context, combine into something reviewers found monstrous. De Quincey also criticized "a vice in Mr. Hazlitt's mode of composition, viz., the habit of trite quotation." Hazlitt's intertextual style "places the reader at the mercy of a man's tritest remembrances from his most school-boy reading. To have the verbal memory infested with tags of verse and 'cues' of rhyme is in itself an infirmity as vulgar and morbid as the stable-boys habit of whistling slang airs."[90] For De Quincey, Hazlitt's quotations mirror mindlessly repetitive school exercises, and, therefore, signal vulgarity rather than refinement.[91] De Quincey's assertions recall a central criticism of members of the Cockney school—that their writing displayed a common "stock knowledge."[92]

Hazlitt himself was deeply concerned about class tensions and his uneasy relationship with the reading public. His "On Reading Old Books" criticizes a superficial (and feminized) style of reading that contrasts with his own (re)reading. By rereading great works, he remembers not only past reading experiences but also his past self: "Standard productions of this kind are links in the chain of our conscious being. They bind together the different scattered divisions of our personal identity."[93] These "standard productions" affect and affirm by making a reader familiar with both literary content and one's self. By extension, Hazlitt's "cultivation of an intimacy with such works, and to have familiarly relished such names" also cultivates his audience's intimacy with him.[94] Put differently, the quotations and heightened intertextuality of Hazlitt's prose extend his familiarity with the "standard" authors into a familiarity with his readers. If, as Graham Good contends, "connections between thoughts in the essay are often made through things, rather than being linked directly in a continuous argument," then in

Hazlitt's familiar essays quotations are these "things."[95] Hazlitt's prose creates an imagined community of good readers who are familiar with him and with each other through their shared knowledge of standard texts.

In his familiar essays, Hazlitt often employs quotations transitionally to shift from his personal observations to his more theoretical assertions, linking personal experiences to abstract, universal thinking as well as linking his own experiences with his readers'. Many of Hazlitt's quotations, as De Quincey noted, would have been recognizable to his audience, particularly male readers who may have undertaken similar "school-boy reading."[96] These literary references create an "in crowd" for those able to identify them—something that the *Edinburgh Magazine* praised: "[Hazlitt's] object is to excite others to think for themselves, or, by the exhibition of agreeable imagery, and the use of smart allusion, to make them pleased with the labour of thinking."[97] Hazlitt's familiar style gives readers the satisfaction of solving a literary puzzle and of joining a club of shared literary knowledge. However, Hazlitt's entitlement to the literary club was something his critics questioned. The jarring elements of Hazlitt's intertextuality seemed to reveal his literary illegitimacy.

"GROSS FAMILIARITIES" IN THE LANGUAGE OF "STANDARD PRODUCTIONS"

Liber Amoris amplifies the intertextuality central to his familiar essays. Marilyn Butler has called it "the most continuously literary of love affairs," and Robert Ready has identified its "almost hyper-literary sensibility."[98] For instance, *Liber Amoris* uses literary characters, including Lovelace, Hamlet, Sardanapalus, Saint-Preux, Othello, and Werther, to frame H. and S.'s behavior. Similar to how Charlotte Smith aligned herself with sentimental archetypes in *Elegiac Sonnets*, Hazlitt offers his autobiographical character H. as an embodiment of established male roles of both sentimentality and, also, villainy. According to Butler, "Fictionalizing the story is a device for objectifying it, above all for setting up a distance and some measure of control between the author and H—."[99] The fictionalized and highly literary presentation of Hazlitt's relationship with Walker in *Liber Amoris* enacts possession over her and over his experiences. In *Liber Amoris,* references to what Hazlitt called "standard productions" reflect inward toward his own experiences rather than outward toward readers, and the novel's narcissism makes its literary allusions work against sympathetic familiarity.[100] If our sense of our own subjectivity is, as Hofkosh suggests, "our familiarity to ourselves," then I posit that Hazlitt uses these standard authors to help make his experiences with Walker familiar and interpretable to himself.[101] Though literary references in *Liber Amoris* mediate selfhood and may make Hazlitt familiar to himself, they did not necessarily precipitate readers' sympathy. Many found Hazlitt's representation of what he termed H.'s "gross familiarities" with S. in intertextual, literary language distasteful (41). Crabb Robinson wrote in his diary: "One can tolerate the passion of a St. Preux or a Werther as it is set off by the eloquence of Rousseau or Goethe, but such a story as this is nauseous and revolting."[102]

Joanna Baillie's thoughts about the negative effects of florid language in drama suggest why readers like Crabb Robinson found Hazlitt's intertextual literariness offensive in the context of a book about Walker. Florid language, Baillie claims, flattens the power of passions, and this flattening is "very greatly aggravated by embellishing . . . the speeches of passion with the ingenious conceits, and compleat similies of premeditated thought." For Baillie, "This, perhaps, more than any thing else has injured the higher scenes of tragedy. For having made such free use of bold hyperbolical language in the inferior parts, the poet when he arrives at the highly impassioned sinks into total inability: or if he will force himself to rise still higher on the wing, he flies beyond nature altogether, into the regions of bombast and nonsense."[103] Overembellishment desensitizes and even vulgarizes. Even worse, it undermines the seeming authenticity of the passions and their effect on an audience.

The type of embellishment that Baillie believed undermined emotional power was, as we have seen, a touchstone of Hazlitt's style. Even Leigh Hunt's positive review of *Lectures on the English Comic Poets* (1819) admits that Hazlitt "is too uniformly emphatic and dazzling, and fatigues us by placing all objects in the strongest lights, without any space for shade or repose."[104] *Liber Amoris* takes the emphatic elements of Hazlitt's prose even further; it interweaves expressions of passion with quotations and literary expressions that Baillie claims deaden emotion. Even putting aside class-based objections to Hazlitt's love for Walker, the heightened tenor of *Liber Amoris* reveals a frantic literariness that seemed affected, bombastic, and unsympathetic to many readers. The end of Part I of *Liber Amoris* exemplifies Hazlitt's layered literariness and its potential pitfalls. The section includes lines "Written in a blank leaf of Endymion," referencing Keats's *Endymion*, published in 1818. The appearance of *Endymion* in *Liber Amoris* aligns Hazlitt with Keats's most negatively reviewed poem and solidifies the novel's associations with the Cockney school. From a Tory perspective, Hazlitt had bad taste both in women and in poetry, and he willingly paraded both in *Liber Amoris*. Hazlitt's novel mimics the heightened sentimentality of Keats's volume in which H. writes his note about Sarah: "But by her dove's eyes and serpent-shape, I think she does not hate me; by her smooth forehead and her crested hair, I own I love her; by her soft looks and queen-like grace (which men might fall down and worship) I swear to live and die for her!" (22). Ready suggests that the note's inscription "in a blank leaf of *Endymion* allies H with the prototype of a man who falls in love with an ideal woman"—a prototype emphasized in *Liber Amoris*'s subtitle: *Or, The New Pygmalion*.[105] In hindsight, the irony of Hazlitt's comparison of H. with Endymion and Pygmalion becomes clear; Sarah, it turns out, is not the ideal goddess he originally imagines. She resolutely refuses to conform to his hopes, leaving him angry and disillusioned. Yet even in Part I, before Sarah's supposed betrayal, Hazlitt's heightened language and his classical and contemporary allusions risked becoming bathetic when applied to a woman who was effectively a servant.

Hazlitt's earlier allusion to Byron's *Sardanapalus* similarly displays tensions between the source text and its context in *Liber Amoris*. In a letter to Sarah, H. writes,

> [I] keep repeating over and over to myself two lines of Lord Byron's Tragedy—
> So shalt thou find me ever at thy side
> Here and hereafter, if the last may be—
> Applying them to thee, my love, and thinking whether I shall ever see thee again. (20)

Wu remarks that Hazlitt "found himself drawn irresistibly into this play" because "it portrayed a dilemma Hazlitt recognised as comparable with his own."[106] Wu, though, bypasses the significance of H.'s quotation of Myrrha rather than Sardanapalus and the feminization it entails. Given Byron's popularity, the quotation acts as a reference to "standard productions" that Hazlitt previously celebrated in his essays. Yet the lines from act 4 quote Myrrha's speech to Sardanapalus and, thus, align Hazlitt (via H.) with a female concubine who immolates herself with her master. The letter's conclusion reinforces H.'s feminization and the theme of his enslavement: "Ah! if you can never be mine, still let me be your proud and happy slave" (21). Hazlitt's quotation chafes in its new context, carrying charges that undermine the sympathetic appeal of H.'s situation.

Often *Liber Amoris* clusters literary references together. The frantic effect of this intertextuality veers dangerously close to Baillie's dreaded "regions of bombast and nonsense."[107] Consider the numerous allusions in H.'s final realization that Sarah had supposedly duped him:

> With the morning's light, conviction glared in upon me that I had not only lost her for ever—but every feeling I had ever had towards her—respect, tenderness, pity—all but my fatal passion, was gone. The whole was a mockery, a frightful illusion. I had embraced the false Florimel

> [*sic*] instead of the true; or was like the man in the Arabian Nights who had married a *goul*. How different was the idea I once had of her! Was this she,
>
> Who had been beguiled—she who was made
> Within a gentle bosom to be laid—
> To bless and to be blessed—to be heart-bare
> To one who found his bettered likeness there—
> To think for ever with him, like a bride—
> To haunt his eye, like taste personified—
> To double his delight, to share his sorrow,
> And like a morning beam, wake to him every morrow?
>
> I saw her pale, cold form glide silent by me, dead to shame as to pity. (70, emphasis Hazlitt's)

The passage evokes multiple sources in quick succession—sources likely familiar to Hazlitt's readers. The associations between Sarah and "false Florimel" recall book 3 of Spenser's *The Faerie Queene*. Perhaps realizing that Sarah's "deceptions" are ill fitted to a Spenserian framework, Hazlitt shifts in the same sentence to a reference to "The History of Sidi-Nouman" in the *Arabian Nights*. Sidi-Nouman unwittingly married an evil corpse-consuming witch who turned him into a dog and beat him—a rather different situation than that in which H. finds himself. While the thrust of the reference—deception—may apply, the fact that H. has failed to marry Sarah in the first place lends irony to the passage. Hazlitt then quotes Leigh Hunt's *The Story of Rimini* (itself an adaptation of the Paolo and Francesca episode in fifth canto of Dante's *Inferno*) to contrast the deceitful "true" Sarah with the ideal lover H. imagined. Rapid transitions between literary references reveal the inadequacy of each allusion to capture Hazlitt's situation, and the allusions to Spenser and Hunt are especially loaded.

Hazlitt's allusion to the false Florimell from *The Faerie Queene* refers specifically to the witch's deception of her son, who lusts after the chaste, beautiful Florimell. Taking refuge with the witch and her son, Florimell "grew familiare" with them. Her familiarity causes the witch's son to conceive of "affection bace, / And cast to loue her in his brutish mind; / No louve, but brutish lust, that was so beastly tind."[108] His wicked desire for Florimell causes her to flee, leaving him in a lovesick frenzy. In order to "heale her sonne, whose senses were decayd," the witch fools him by creating a false Florimell who looks exactly like the original (3.8.4). The more one untangles Hazlitt's allusion, the more its application to H.'s love for Sarah appears clumsy and implicitly damns his own actions. Indeed, Spenser's Florimells, both original and false, are persecuted figures. Like Walker, they are subject to relentless, unwanted male attention and patriarchal control. Repeatedly almost victims of rape, these Florimells depict female virtue under assault. True, in addition to deceiving the witch's son, the false Florimell also fools Tromparts and Braggadochio and seems to change her affections easily. Yet she is consistently portrayed as an object of abject male lust. While she may not be as virtuous as the true Florimell, Spenser demonstrates that those she betrays are no less culpable. To them she is nothing more than beautiful "spoyle," prized for her appearance not her virtue (3.8.13). Even the initial passion for the true Florimell arises from "brutish lust," complicating the idea that the men in *The Faerie Queene* and *Liber Amoris* have been hoodwinked by duplicitous women. The men's own vulgarity aids their deception.

Beyond Spenser, few readers would have missed the scandalous undertones of Hazlitt's quotation from Hunt's *The Story of Rimini* (1816), a poem that Kim Wheatley has described as "set[ing] forth the poetics as well as the values of Cockneyism, [and] deliberately challenging both the Augustan tastes and the conservative ideologies of the reviewers."[109] Hunt was at the center of the Cockney school, and *Rimini* featured in the notorious review articles "On The Cockney School of Poetry" published in *Blackwood's*; the poem was widely condemned by other outlets as well.[110] *Rimini* was censured for its immorality; its strained combination of couplets, literary language, and what the *Monthly Review* termed "*quaintness* and *familiarity*"; and the overfamiliar tone of its dedication to "My dear Byron."[111] With its lengthy reference to Hunt's poem, Hazlitt's conclusion to *Liber Amoris* implicitly draws attention to the dynamics of class and presumption for which he and Hunt had already been attacked.

Critical consensus was that *Rimini*'s portrayal of adultery was shockingly inappropriate. According to *Blackwood's*, Hunt's "mind seems absolutely to gloat over all the details of adultery and incest."[112] In *Rimini*, then, the damnation was in Hunt's detailed, sympathetic portrayal of Paolo and Francesca's adulterous love—details to which Hazlitt alludes in *Liber Amoris*. The passage Hazlitt quotes comes from the third canto of Hunt's poem, when Francesca's marital fidelity fades. Thus, H.'s lament about what he had thought Sarah was—his ideal woman—explicitly compares her to an adulteress in a poem that "No woman who has not either lost her chastity, or is desirous of losing it, ever read."[113] The wealth of detail makes both *Rimini* and *Liber Amoris* indecorous and, because Hazlitt's novel was read biographically, overly familiar. Descriptions of H.'s physical intimacy with Sarah offer the same type of details for which Hunt's text was criticized. For example, H. writes to C. P—in Part II, "I have *lipped her*, God knows how often, and oh! is it even possible that she is chaste, and that she has bestowed her loved 'endearments' on me?" (29; emphasis Hazlitt's). H. relates his "gross familiarities" with Sarah with, in the words of one reader, "soul-harrowing fullness of detail" (41).[114] Divulging details about a failed adulterous romance in *Liber Amoris* and then framing them with familiar quotations from contemporary works that had been accused of immorality strengthened associations between Hazlitt's work and both low literature and vulgar overreaching.

The amount of autobiographical detail in *Liber Amoris* was not without precedent, and Hazlitt's compulsive confessions have a Rousseauian lineage. However, the fact that Hazlitt attempted to elevate his experiences by novelizing them drew criticism; *Liber Amoris* is not so much a confession of Hazlitt's weaknesses as it is a complaint against Walker's supposed duplicity. The novel's most explicit references to Rousseau's *Confessions* are entangled with failure—H. admits that his own heightened language hindered rather than helped his courtship. H. compares his courtship to Rousseau's love for Sophie d'Houdetot in *Confessions*: "I don't believe that any woman was ever courted more passionately than she has been by me. As Rousseau said of Madame d'Houptot [*sic*] (forgive the allusion) my heart has found a tongue in speaking to her, and I have talked to her the divine language of love. Yet she says, she is insensible to it" (29). This passage simultaneously calls attention to and apologizes for its reference to Rousseau. While women in both texts are the objects of unrequited love, the similarities stop there. "Rousseau's words," Dart explains, "were addressed to an elegant young aristocrat and framed by a beautiful pastoral landscape." Conversely, Hazlitt's were aimed at a tailor's daughter, and thus his Rousseauian evocations were "'cribb'd, cabin'd and confin'd' by their Cockney setting."[115] Sarah's insensibility to H.'s "divine language of love" also highlights her lower social status (29). H.'s familiar language of love is not familiar to her, and H.'s request for forgiveness for his allusion to Rousseau highlights its uneasy application to his situation.

The disjunction between Hazlitt's literary language and the woman to whom it is applied shocked nineteenth-century readers: "To think of Hazlitt gravely lavishing his choice Elizabethan quotations on the hussey."[116] While "sexual encounters with servants seemed 'natural' and were 'socially acceptable'—at least to the upper class," obsessive emotional attachment to a servant girl was quite another matter.[117] Critics thought his attachment to Walker was nothing more than "a degrading infatuation."[118] Admittedly, she seems to have been a far cry from Richardson's articulate, letter-writing Pamela whose character implicitly informs Hazlitt's initial perception of Walker as a diamond in the rough and his later novelization of her in *Liber Amoris*.[119] The (biased) accounts left by Hazlitt and his circle reveal that even those closest to him were confused by his feelings for Walker, who was reportedly plain in appearance and limited in education.[120] Sarah Stoddart Hazlitt, for example, recorded that her acquaintance Mr. Bell, who helped with the divorce proceedings, "said he had seen some passages of her [Sarah Walker's] letters, and they were such low vulgar milliner's or servant wench's sentimentality, that he wondered Mr. Hazlitt could endure such stuff."[121] The reception of *Liber Amoris* shows that the public would not endure such sentimental stuff from Hazlitt prompted by a woman like Walker.

Liber Amoris attempts to frame Hazlitt's failed courtship in terms of familiar literary tropes, yet the variety of his references only calls attention to their inapplicability. The frequency with which Hazlitt changes his literary frame of reference—moving, as we have seen, from Spenser to the *Arabian Nights* to Leigh Hunt to Rousseau—demonstrates the difficulty of relating his experiences with Walker to the literary tradition of "standard productions" central to his familiar essays. It is as if he were trying on different hats until finding one that fits, yet the overall effect is of bathetic, vulgar fancy dress. Hazlitt struggles to find a literary trope that fits his situation and his love's social station. According to Hofkosh, quotation "always signals that something has been broken," so that *Liber Amoris* "presents itself as a layered transcription, a palimpsest that is also always in some sense under pressure."[122] I agree, but would push the brokenness of Hazlitt's quotation further. The fractures between H.'s situation and the quotation- and allusion-infused descriptions of it demonstrate what we might describe as Hazlitt's familiar style broken. Connections between Hazlitt's source texts and his experiences break down and, as a result, so too does his ability to bring his readers into familiarity with him. *Liber Amoris* recreates on a stylistic level the problems that his contemporaries saw with his decision to write about his failed courtship of a lower-class woman. If, as Deidre Lynch has argued, the love of literature is a "steadying influence" in the Romantic period, then Hazlitt's *Liber Amoris* demonstrates his perversion of standard, steadying authors.[123] Hazlitt's text combines so many different literary allusions while embedding itself problematically in the genre of the secret history. Hazlitt's mash-up of genres ultimately seems to suggest that his faculties have been so deranged by his passion that the problem is not simply his inability to interpret Walker's familiarities but also that he cannot distinguish low from high literature, nor can he distinguish what is appropriate to tell "round the fireside" versus "to the public."[124] As Hazlitt himself said, "familiarity breed[s] weariness and contempt."[125] Hazlitt's indiscriminate familiarity with both Walker and his audience seems to prove that assertion.

As I have argued, one problem that critics saw with Hazlitt's (overly) familiar style was its combination of high and low markers of both literature and class. From depicting a "lodging-house wench" in Shakespearean and Rousseauian terms to charging what some saw as an inflated price for a volume of vulgar romantic gossip about himself, Hazlitt shocked conservative readers with his Cockney overreaching. Similar issues of class informed the production and reception of

British literary annuals, which I consider in the following chapter. These mass-produced volumes allowed middle-class readers to participate in a simulacrum of the coterie culture of manuscript albums. With lavish bindings and elaborate steel-plate engravings, annuals were objects of conspicuous consumption that were used to establish and reinforce sociable ties of friendship, love, and familiarity. Like Hazlitt's familiar style, too, they combined elements of elevated and common culture that pushed the limits of familiarity in the late Romantic period.

5

MEDIATING A MANUSCRIPT ETHOS

Familiarity in Albums and Literary Annuals

> The ideas that seemed at first so delightful are grown common,
> by passing through the familiarizing process
> of writing, printing and correcting.
> —Letitia Elizabeth Landon, introduction to
> *Fisher's Drawing Room Scrap-book**

WITH AUTHORIAL FAME AND AN ENTHUSIASTIC fan base that rivaled Byron's, Letitia Elizabeth Landon was certainly no stranger to "the familiarizing process of writing, printing and correcting" that she describes in her introduction to the 1832 edition of *Fisher's Drawing Room Scrap-book.* As a prominent contributor to popular literary annuals like *The Keepsake, The Literary Souvenir, Forget Me Not, Friendship's Offering,* and *Fisher's Drawing Room Scrap-book,* Landon had extensive experience transforming "ideas that seemed at first so delightful" into tangible, commercial texts.[1] Literary annuals like those for which Landon wrote "dominated the market for poetry from 1825 to 1835" at a time when it was shifting away from poetry to prose.[2] Rudolf Ackermann published the first annual, *Forget Me Not,* in the autumn of 1822, and by 1828, "100,000 copies of fifteen separate annuals earned an aggregate retail value of over £70,000."[3] These figures become even more impressive when one remembers that throughout the first half of the nineteenth century "most books were published in editions of somewhere between 500 and 1,500 copies."[4]

Landon's comments introduced a new title to a crowded field of competing literary annuals, and *Fisher's Drawing Room Scrap-book* amplifies the characteristics of annuals that had been solidifying for a decade: a combination of poems and short prose pieces by prominent Romantic-era writers and socialites, numerous detailed steel-plate engravings, and an elaborate publisher's binding.[5] Even more than other successful annuals like *The Keepsake* or *Friendship's Offering,* Landon's volume exuded luxury. Priced at twenty-one shillings and produced as a quarto, it was both more expensive and larger than other annuals that sold for around twelve shillings and were octavos or duodecimos. The size of *Fisher's Drawing Room Scrap-book* showcases its embossed binding and the illustrations within, and Landon's introduction acknowledges the open secret that the literary content in annuals was written to illustrate the engravings. "It is not an easy thing to write illustrations to prints," she admitted to her readers.[6]

Earlier annuals published in the 1820s certainly promoted their impressive illustrations and lavish appearances, but they also gestured toward manuscript albums, pocketbook diaries, and almanacs—genres that encouraged readers to write. In early literary annuals, riddles and charades called for written answers (figure 5.1); inscription plates asked for names and messages of endearment (figure 5.2); and diary pages invited musings and records of daily life (figure 5.3).

Yet, by the time *Fisher's Drawing Room Scrap-book* for 1832 appeared, most annuals left little room for users' marginalia. Annuals became more akin to today's coffee-table books, which few would consider annotating. Though the title of Landon's volume explicitly points to a manuscript tradition—a tradition in which, during the Romantic period, the terms *scrapbook* and *album* were interchangeable—the bibliographic codes of her annual and others like it discouraged readers from writing in them.[7]

In the context of the literary marketplace in which Landon and her annuals were a driving force, her comments about the "familiarizing process" of writing are notable for their emphasis on the material conditions facing Romantic authorship. Landon explicitly identifies the "terrible realit[ies]"—like correcting page proofs—that mediate her thoughts into "common," familiar commercial products.[8] Landon's preoccupation with familiarity, commonness, and poetic production reflects widespread anxieties about the industrialized and commercialized literary marketplace. While, as my previous chapters have suggested, concerns about the expanding literary marketplace and diverse readerships extend back to the eighteenth century, they reached a fever pitch in the 1820s and 1830s when the shift from the hand-press to the machine-press period was in full swing. In 1829—the same year that saw the publication of the literary annual *The Keepsake* in its famous crimson watered silk binding—Thomas Carlyle went so far as to decry "the Mechanical Age" in which he lived. "[B]ooks," he observed, "are not only printed but in a great measure, written and sold, by machinery."[9] Advances like the increased use of lithography, steel-plate engravings, wove paper, and the rise of publishers' bindings made a growing amount of printed materials available to unprecedented numbers of readers. These technological shifts as well as general fears about commercialism and the democratization of high culture directly coincide with the heyday of literary annuals. The reception history of annuals hums with technological anxieties, concerns about class stratification and destabilization, and

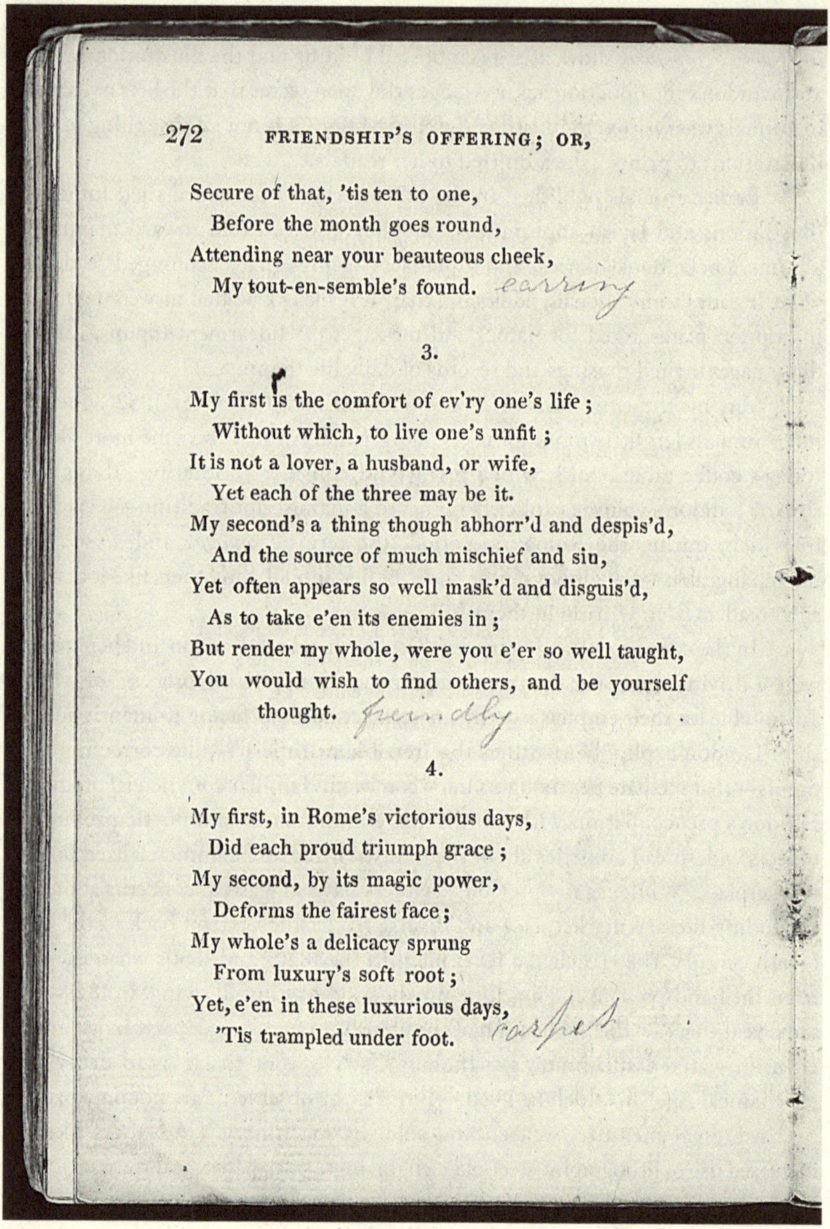

272 FRIENDSHIP'S OFFERING; OR,

Secure of that, 'tis ten to one,
  Before the month goes round,
Attending near your beauteous cheek,
  My tout-en-semble's found. earring

3.

My first is the comfort of ev'ry one's life;
  Without which, to live one's unfit;
It is not a lover, a husband, or wife,
  Yet each of the three may be it.
My second's a thing though abhorr'd and despis'd,
  And the source of much mischief and sin,
Yet often appears so well mask'd and disguis'd,
  As to take e'en its enemies in;
But render my whole, were you e'er so well taught,
You would wish to find others, and be yourself
    thought. friendly

4.

My first, in Rome's victorious days,
  Did each proud triumph grace;
My second, by its magic power,
  Deforms the fairest face;
My whole's a delicacy sprung
  From luxury's soft root;
Yet, e'en in these luxurious days,
  'Tis trampled under foot. carpet

Figure 5.1 Annotated riddle page in *Friendship's Offering; Or, the Annual Remembrancer: A Christmas Present or New Year's Gift for 1825* (London: Relfe, 1825). McLean Collection, D 0418, Copy 2. Courtesy of the Robertson Davies Library at Massey College in the University of Toronto.

Figure 5.2 Annotated inscription plate in *Forget Me Not; A Christmas and New Year's Present for 1825* (London: R. Ackermann, 1825). Author's private collection.

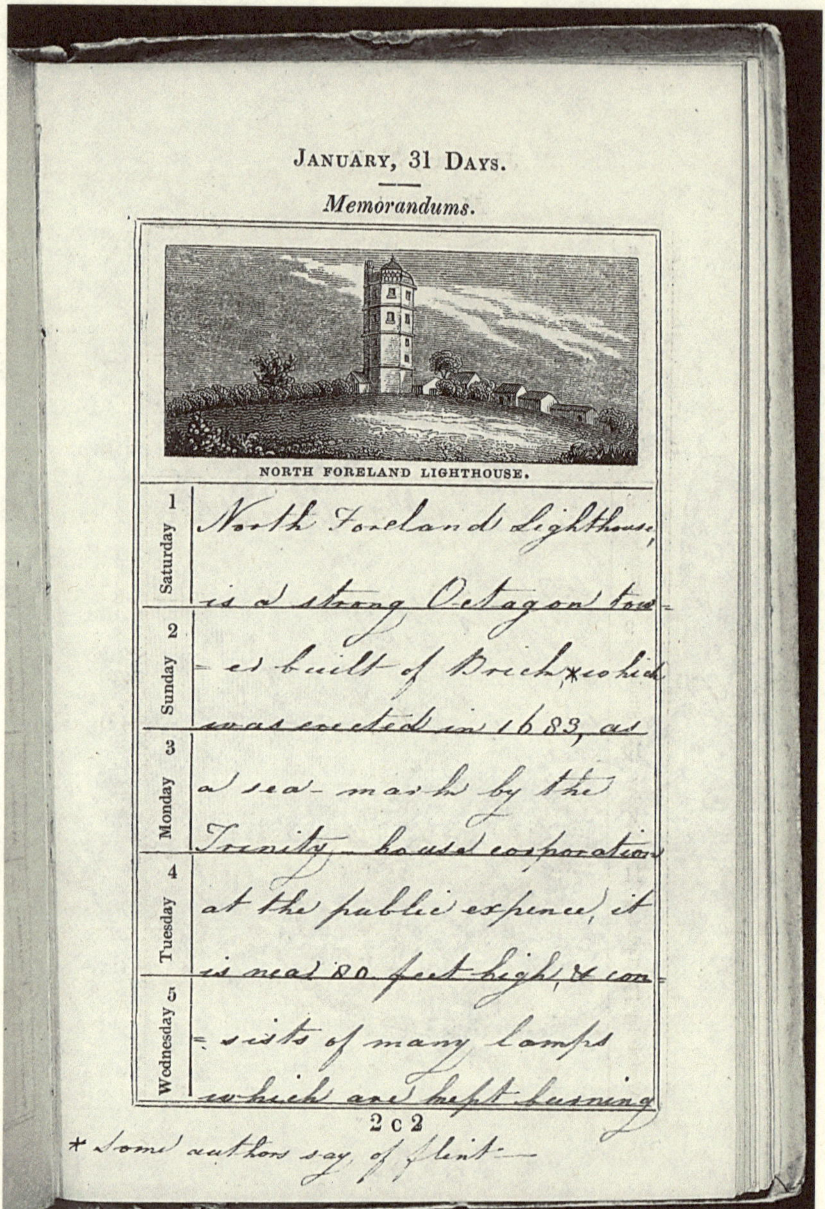

Figure 5.3 Annotated diary page in *Friendship's Offering; Or, the Annual Remembrancer: A Christmas Present or New Year's Gift for 1825* (London: Relfe, 1825). McLean Collection, D 0418, Copy 1. Courtesy of the Robertson Davies Library at Massey College in the University of Toronto.

fears about the (in)ability of commercial texts to bring people together on familiar terms.

Though derided by many nineteenth-century critics and, until relatively recently, often overlooked by scholars of Romanticism, literary annuals were important objects whose circulation manifests how nineteenth-century evocations of literary familiarity engaged the complex dynamics of the growing middle and upper-middle classes. As affordable luxury items, annuals were regularly exchanged as gifts, and they brokered real familiar relationships between friends, lovers, and family members. So central were the medium's associations with love that one reviewer suggested that if the annual *The Literary Souvenir* were used as a tool of courtship, the odds are "a hundred to one that you are a married man in six weeks or two months; nay if it be a 'large paper copy' one flesh will ye be before the new moon."[10]

The social role of annuals was partly modeled on the communal production and exchange of manuscript albums. Romantic-era manuscript albums usually began as volumes of bound blank pages that users would collaboratively fill with literary and pictorial content. Annuals provided readers with a printed "album" experience that evoked manuscript traditions and the affective connotations of familiarity that those traditions promoted. Not only did literary annuals sometimes publish content that originated in manuscript albums—shifting text from one medium to another—but they also remediated the social arrangements central to albums and the cultural value of manuscript exchange.[11] Sonia Hofkosh has argued that, in purchasing annuals, "the middle-class reader bought the privileges of ownership, [and] a bourgeois semblance of aristocratic (self) possession."[12] Literary annuals offered expanding audiences of middle-class readers a remediated, printed version of literary manuscript culture.

Similar to the silver-fork novels addressed in chapter 3, annuals spoke to a bourgeois social reaching. However, whereas readers of Lady Caroline Lamb's *Glenarvon* read *about* the habits of the aristocratic elite, those buying annuals were able to *participate* in a similar cultural practice. For twelve shillings, one could buy a volume filled with a variety of literary content, including "album" poetry by famous writers and aristocrats. Literary annuals and their ties to earlier manuscript traditions appealed to readers hankering to get close to literary elites and supposedly elite cultural codes of sociability. "Supposedly" is important here: when literary annuals were on the rise in the 1820s, manuscript albums inhabited an uncertain position in the cultural hierarchy. With strangers' requests for album poems plaguing Romantic authors from Wordsworth and Coleridge to Byron and Walter Scott, the (feminized) process of creating and circulating manuscript albums was, itself, charged with presumptuous overfamiliarity. By the 1810s and

1820s, manuscript albums had, to borrow again from Landon, "grown common." Their associations with "fashionable elite social circles, elegant accomplishments, and a surplus of leisure time" diminished as the practice of making albums and soliciting poems for them spread among the middling classes, reaching a literary crisis that Samantha Matthews terms "albo-mania."[13] Literary annuals drew on a culture of manuscript albums at a time when albums were becoming kitsch.

This chapter explores how literary annuals, much like Landon's description of her own ideas in *Fisher's Drawing Room Scrap-book*, were initially seen as "delightful," only to be later colored with negative connotations of banal familiarity. William Makepeace Thackeray, who published in annuals while also deriding them, went so far as to describe the annuals as "a sea-pie, made up of scraps that have been served at many tables before."[14] Thackeray also complained that writing for annuals had made Landon an authorial prostitute who was "made over to the highest bidder" and "pawned for so many pounds per sheet."[15] From such a perspective, the annuals' unoriginal, commercialized elements undermined their pretensions as artifacts of high culture, and arbiters of taste returned to the potentially dangerous consequences of both albums' and annuals' ability to flatten literary and cultural prestige. The gatekeeping anxieties underpinning negative responses to the explosive popularity of manuscript albums and literary annuals mirror the class-inflected responses to Hazlitt's familiar style, which I explored in the previous chapter. Discourses surrounding albums and annuals reveal that Romantic-era fears about class hierarchies, the depersonalization of social interaction, and a mass reading public shaped both print and manuscript production.

Analyzing the shifting cultural valences of manuscript albums and literary annuals' indebtedness to them, I suggest that the annuals' development and eventual decline are tied to their (in)ability to evoke in print the interpersonal closeness of manuscript albums. I focus on strategies that annuals employed to convey what I term a "manuscript ethos," and my work bridges the fields of material bibliography and formalist analysis in order to capture how, to borrow from Jerome McGann, "meaning is transmitted through bibliographical as well as linguistic codes."[16] At its core, this chapter models a methodology of book historical poetics—a methodology that reads "form" as both literary and bibliographic. In doing so, it explores how material and literary form in the annuals informed readers' affective responses to each other, to their books, and to the authors who wrote them. As Celeste Langan and Maureen McLane assert, "We find in this period a sustained effort to reimagine poetry not as a genre—a literary kind among kinds—but as a medium."[17] Here I highlight annuals' and albums' preoccupation not only with medium but also with (re)mediation. I pay particular attention to the cultural importance of the largely overlooked subgenre of lyric, album verse—poems "that represent themselves as 'lines written in' or 'on a blank leaf.'"[18] These poems, whether handwritten in albums or reprinted in annuals, engage the desire for seemingly authentic traces of the hand amid an explosion of print. By printing album verses, facsimile signatures, and diary pages, literary annuals forwarded a manuscript ethos imbued with interpersonal familiarity.

Editors used this manuscript ethos to highlight their annuals' potential as tokens of love and friendship while attempting "to downplay the frankly commercial nature of their undertakings."[19] What Judith Pascoe has termed the annuals' "souvenir ethos" alludes to two developing senses of the word *souvenir* in the Romantic period: an older notion of the word "as a remembrance, a memory" and a later sense as a material object, "something (usually a small article of some value bestowed as a gift) which reminds one of some person, place or event."[20] However, the annuals' printed content supports not only a souvenir ethos but also a manuscript ethos, and my work attempts to refocus the tensions that Pascoe identifies between the affective, commemorative aspects of the annuals and their commodified marketability. These tensions reveal that the noncommercial value of the annuals largely depended not on their gift exchangeability in general but on the way their material form and literary forms attempted to emulate the type of personal exchange fostered by the culture surrounding manuscript albums—a culture associated, albeit unevenly, with literary and aristocratic circles. Annuals attempted to accomplish a counterintuitive goal: commodifying elite cultural practices associated with manuscript production by making them common to a growing audience while also making these commodified objects vehicles of interpersonal familiarity.

Though other chapters of this book have focused on case studies of individual authors, here I examine a medium—a medium in which, it should be noted, works by Byron, Lady Caroline Lamb, and William Hazlitt all appeared. This shift in my approach mirrors the changing literary marketplace and the annuals' role within it. Considering the annuals more widely, I resist the trend of author-focused work on literary annuals, which implicitly suggests that their primary importance rests in what they may reveal about the canonical authors who appeared in them.[21] Readers' imagined interpersonal familiarity with annual-authors like Landon represents only one way that familiarity informs the medium's reception. The role of familiarity in annuals also arose from their status as objects of sociability in an increasingly industrialized, bookish world. The complex codes that divided print from manuscript, public from private life, and reader from author—like the equivocal concept of familiarity—shifted constantly in the period. Editors of annuals tried to sell high culture and previously elite cultural practices to a wide audience, and they were able to do this by playing on fluid boundaries that defined both the media ecology of the Romantic period and the cultural value of familiarity. As I have argued in previous chapters, it was difficult for authors to maintain familiarity's more positive connotations—its ability to encourage sympathy, polite sociability, and connection. The development of the literary annuals in the 1820s alongside the uneven cultural associations of manuscript albums seems to prove on the scale of genre and medium the famous adage that too much familiarity could breed weariness and contempt.

FROM ALBUM TO ANNUAL

I am not the first to note connections between annuals and Romantic-era manuscript practices. Paula Feldman and Andrew Piper have both drawn attention to how readers' gift inscriptions in annuals gave value to these mass-produced objects, and Michelle Levy has described "the sociability that the annuals sought to initiate but, on a structural level, could not reproduce."[22] Recognizing literary and social links between albums and annuals, Samantha Matthews has observed the annuals' "commercial exploitation of manuscript culture."[23] Relatedly, Katherine D. Harris has suggested that "blank pages offered in the 1823 and 1824 literary annuals were used as 'albums' with owners creating notations, writing poems, and requesting autographs to fill the space."[24] My arguments extend this scholarship, and I mark fluid connections between manuscripts and commercial print. In doing so, I resist dichotomizing representations of print versus manuscript culture.[25] While helpful for considering some modes of literary production, such binaries map uneasily onto literary annuals and manuscript albums—two mediums that imitated each other. The overlapping histories of manuscript album and literary annual demonstrate that social aspects of familiarity were predicated on literary works and cultural practices that traversed media. To recover how a manuscript ethos appears in printed annuals, it is first important to understand the social context of Romantic-era albums as well as the terminology used to describe them.

Taking off in the 1780s, manuscript albums predate literary annuals by four decades; however, the popularity of manuscript albums "reached its peak in the late 1820s, in conjunction with a comparable printed manifestation of feminine taste, the literary annual."[26] As collaborative volumes produced over years and even decades, Romantic-era manuscript albums displace notions of print's perceived finality and challenge the notion of "book" as a linear, unified form. Albums, in Deidre Lynch's vivid description, "thwart the order of books and behave badly."[27] This partly explains the difficulties that they still present for classification, cataloguing, and analysis. Throughout this chapter I refer to "albums," though the sources that I address are not uniformly catalogued as such. Cataloguing practices frequently collapse albums and commonplace books under the same subject heading or label manuscript albums with unspecific terms like "family papers" or "untitled MSS."[28] Classification of these items is far from straightforward, and my goal here is not to criticize cataloguers. However, distinctions matter if one wants to accurately place Romantic-era albums in relation to other manuscript mediums.

"Commonplace book" implies a more personal, systematic handwritten volume, perhaps organized using one of the indexing systems forwarded by empiricist thinkers like John Locke. Commonplace books inhabit a rather different social and literary space than albums. Though produced by a variety of people for a variety of purposes, they had utilitarian, even masculine associations, and, unlike albums that often contain illustrations, commonplace books typically privilege text. For example, Felicia Hemans's commonplace book seems to have functioned as a notebook of sorts, perhaps along the lines of Coleridge's famous fly-catchers. It contains miscellaneous notes from Thomas Moore's *Lalla Rookh* and passages from Samuel Richardson's *Pamela* as well as Hemans's personal observations about landscapes.[29] Commonplace books like Hemans's were more likely than albums to be the production of a single hand.

Conversely, Romantic-era albums tended to be social productions, and they point outward to an audience beyond the individual owner of the volume. Manuscript albums included a variety of material contributed by different people in one's circle: handwritten literary entries and notes, autographs, drawings and paintings either pasted into the volume or drawn directly onto its pages, and clippings from printed sources. While diverse content was a touchstone of manuscript albums, the conceptual unit was the blank page intended for writing. In this way, they differ from other adjacent genres that may include handwriting but are primarily organized around print—either text or image. Albums, then, overlap with but are distinct from the type of extra-illustrated books or the volumes of ephemera, called collectanea, which Gillian Russell's recent work has brought into focus.[30] While men contributed to albums and while some curated and kept them, late eighteenth- and early nineteenth-century manuscript albums were more closely associated with women. Samantha Matthews, whose foundational work on albums is central to my own, observes that by the early nineteenth century "albums were strongly identified with the intellectual, artistic and affective culture of middle- and upper-class younger women."[31] In the Romantic period, then, album keeping was seen as a respectable pastime for women who were privileged enough to have ample leisure time that needed passing. Though press coverage of prominent aristocrats, including Queen Victoria, being presented with albums associated the medium with privileged people and practices, commentators also complained that albums had become a middle-class craze for the upwardly aspirational.[32]

Since the contents of manuscript albums were written by different contributors, albums recorded an owner's literary tastes and social connections. Thus, the creation of albums depended on a culture of collaboration and familiarity. Stephen Colclough has examined the public nature of these seemingly private volumes. "The majority of 'albums,'" he explains, "were group or family productions. It was common for visitors and friends to be asked to contribute to an album that was put on display as a public document. Adding to the manuscript was seen as an important ritual of friendship."[33] Similarly, Lynch notes that manuscript albums bring "into being a space whose allure lies in its balancing between exclusivity and sharing, concealment and display," and so they challenge easy distinctions between public and private writing.[34] For instance, Lady Caroline Lamb's manuscript albums were written for and by her friends and family. Her green album, now held at the John Murray Archive, contains occasional poems by the Duchess of Devonshire (her aunt), a poem by her husband William Lamb, and pieces by Lamb herself commemorating the deaths of those close to her.[35]

One might connect the social practice of contributing to an album with the notes written in American school yearbooks in our own time. The notes are personal and directed to the individual who owns the yearbook. However, annotations also point outward because contributors know their entries will be read by others. The specificity of a note in a yearbook, much like occasional album verses, displays a social closeness that is very different from the dreaded, unspecific "Have a great summer!" Yet, as those who have written in yearbooks may have felt, it can be difficult to know what to write when put on the spot, and rather bland contributions frequently appear in albums. Even "intimate" album poems were often far more mechanical and distanced than they may appear. For instance, Thomas Colley Grattan, who met Wordsworth and Coleridge in 1828, was skeptical of their impromptu contributions to the album of Mrs. Pryce Gordon: "Both pieces seemed to have been kept 'ready cut and dried' for such an occasion, and they might possibly have previously done similar service in the same way, for they were contributed at the very first asking and in the room with a dozen people."[36] That Romantic authors had strategies to cope with mounting requests for album verses is unsurprising. Though being asked "to write or draw in an album seems to have been part of a common culture of politeness and exchange," in practice, Patrizia Di Bello notes, it was "also to be imposed on with an obligation to produce something on demand."[37]

Later in the period such obligations were widespread and often unwelcome. Requests for album contributions that vexed many Romantic authors mirror the familiar letters from fans that Byron received. In many instances they smack of the same impertinent pretension. (Recall the letter from Miss Pipper, who asked Byron for "a verse of four or eight lines," and who also took "the liberty of writing a few names of flowers—that his Lordship may select which he pleases.")[38] Indeed, one way to gauge the cultural prominence of manuscript albums is the frequency with which authors complained about them. Inundated with requests, Robert Southey teased that he and William Wordsworth should "institute a society for the suppression of albums."[39] Southey seems to have been particularly startled by the audacity of strangers asking him for verses: "A lady here, whom we never saw, nor ever heard of, sent her album for Wordsworth and myself to write in, with no preliminaries than desiring the physician here, Dr. Jaques, to ask leave for her!"[40] Southey emphasizes the lady's status as a stranger; neither Dr. Jaques nor the unnamed lady seems to have been entitled to the familiarity with Southey that the request presumes.

Like Southey, Coleridge also grumbled about albums in an 1827 letter to his friend J. H. Green:

> A portly Dame would fain have something in the Ottigraph way, from me in the splendid Book which by a somewhat italinized mode of pronunciation she calls her Olbum or Awlbum—Would this do?
> Parry seeks the Polar Ridge:
> But rhymes seeks S. T. Coleridge
> Fit for Mrs Smudger's Olbum
> Or to wipe her Baby's small bum.[41]

With its reference to butts, Coleridge's poem is certainly an outlier when it comes to album verse. Yet his invective against Mrs. Smudger's implied inability to discriminate between high poetry and, as his joke suggests, shitty poetry indicates how album culture was often negatively feminized in the period. In Coleridge's and Southey's eyes, women like Mrs. Smudger who avidly acquired verses for albums were akin to the supposedly vapid female consumers blamed for popularizing literary annuals and the trite, sentimental poems in them.

Lynch's incisive work on scrapbooks and albums reveals that the tensions of class, which, I argue in more detail below, informed the reception and eventual decline of literary annuals, were already latent in the manuscript albums: "[T]hose who used their books to preserve poems from published authors or who hunted those authors down for autograph contributions appear frequently to have presented themselves, in a kind of cross-class masquerade, as poor petitioners. Scrapbooks per se came into existence as a consequence of such petitions: they were understood to have been assembled from the odds and ends that could be spared to the poor by those who had plenty."[42] While playing on the dynamics of poor versus plenty was a largely performative stance when albums were circulated among those within an established social circle, overtones of begging and cross-class impertinence intensified as contributions for one's album were sought further afield. Albums and the cultural practices that supported them contended with associations with a parvenu public that pestered authors for contributions. In certain contexts, manuscript albums were seen as plebeian and presumptuous; without interpersonal familiarity, the process of creating albums seemed audaciously forward, as was the case with Coleridge's Mrs. Smudger and Southey's unnamed lady.

Presenting albums much more positively, Charles Lamb's poetry collection *Album Verses, with a Few Others* (1830) exemplifies how manuscript albums and the poetry in them influenced print publications. Lamb's volume also demonstrates that the genre conventions of album verse were widely known to Romantic readers, as were the social motivations for possessing albums. Lamb's poem "In the Album of a Clergyman's Lady" explains:

> An Album is a Garden, not for show
> Planted, but use; where wholesome herbs should grow.
> A Cabinet of curious porcelain, where
> No fancy enters, but what's rich or rare.
> A Chapel, where mere ornamental things
> Are pure as crowns of saints, or angels' wings.
> A List of living friends[.][43]

Lamb makes clear that part of an album's use value also depends on its display value as an object circulated among friends. As Pierre Bourdieu reminds us, social relations are objectified in material objects, and both albums and literary annuals cultivated spaces for showing these social relations.[44] Yet these spaces shifted, even for the same poem: album verses were recopied from one manuscript volume into another; published poems were transcribed into (and adapted for) personal albums; and annuals sometimes reprinted album verses originally published elsewhere. Traveling album verses demonstrate the fluidity of Romantic-era manuscript and print cultures and the accompanying networked systems of literary and social value attached to them. Recall that album verses both evidenced and evoked familiar attachments, but, as we shall see, the genre's affective power was not necessarily attached to the medium of a manuscript album itself. Lamb's *Album Verses* manifests the common (re)mediations of manuscript albums. The titles of many of the poems in Lamb's collection point to their original status as personal verses in manuscript albums. Some of the poems also appeared in literary annuals like *The Bijou* and *The Gem* before being republished in *Album Verses*.[45]

One typical example of the kind of manuscript album that Lamb's printed poetry evokes is the volume kept by Anna Birkbeck, second wife of George Birkbeck who founded Birkbeck College (now one of the colleges constituting the University of London). The album, begun in 1825 and continued for more than twenty years, is a multimedia manifestation of the couple's familiar circle. In addition to illustrations and autographs, it includes original entries from powerful politicians and prominent writers. Among the contributors are Landon, Amelia Opie, and Eliza Emmerson, who also published work in literary annuals.[46] Handwritten verses celebrating Birkbeck's beauty and feminine grace, praising her husband's professional and charitable activities, or commenting on the volume's other literary and pictorial entries all contribute to the album's role in creating, solidifying, and displaying the couple's influential role in society. Not unlike virtual communities today, Birkbeck's album functions "as both subject and object of the process of remediation; it remediates the notion of community."[47] That is, albums like that owned by Mrs. Birkbeck remediated in manuscript form the social communities surrounding them, and entries in these volumes demonstrate a hyperawareness of their status as collaborative, social, and material objects.

Consider the ambassador of the Empire of the Sultan, whose entry observes that his name in Birkbeck's album appears alongside "those of so many persons, distinguished by rank, or superior acquirements, by the services they have rendered to their country, or by the relief and enjoyments they have procured for their fellow men."[48] The emphasis on rank is significant, for albums proclaimed and performed one's place in society. A problem was that some owners—like Coleridge's derided Mrs. Smudger—gauchely used their albums to obtain evidence of (tenuous) connections with respected literary, social, and political figures. However, when created organically by well-placed individuals like Mrs. Birkbeck, manuscript albums developed social communities shaping the Romantic public sphere by, in the words of another contributor, "becom[ing] a repository for the most endearing sentiments of friendship, & affection."[49]

Often in albums these "endearing sentiments" focus on the act of writing as a tangible sign of "friendship, & affection." The genre of album verse is characterized by tropes of handwriting wherein the somatic acts of writing, reading, and circulating poetry both focus lyric's textual content and provide its value. In other words, the value of interpersonal familiarity central to albums and the album verses in them arises as much from the material modes of production and circulation as from the content of the text itself. The affective weight of handwriting and its manuscript ethos points to what might be thought of as the romance of the written preoccupying albums, literary annuals, and Romanticism more generally.[50]

Take the entries in an album compiled in the 1820s through the 1840s by a member of the Wordsworth circle—a volume that, like Birkbeck's album, is contiguous with literary annuals' peak popularity.[51] Like many album verses from the period, the poems in this volume establish connections between poetic form and the album's material form. One such poem is by Owen Lloyd, curate of Ambleside and third son of the poet Charles Lloyd. His poem, signed "Rydal M[oun]t 1 Oct 1839 | Written in the dark," foregrounds the conditions of its composition, locating it in time (both date and time of day) as well as place. The poem further emphasizes place—calling attention to its placement in the album itself:

> They who light & good things write,
> Choose the pages clear & white,
> On such bestow their valued labour
> W. W. and Frederic Faber
> . . .
> And I whose thoughts are dark & blue,
> Will choose this dusky page for you
> And you'll accept this greeting droll
> As coming from your dear friend OLL.[52]

The poem appears in one opening of the volume, taking advantage of the "clear & white" verso and "this dusky" recto, framing the poem's content solidly in its material context (figure 5.4). The underlining in the opening lines underscores the relationship between poetic content and physical form, not only in this specific album verse but also in others written in the same album. In fact, the lighthearted album verses by William Wordsworth and Faber that Lloyd references do appear on "pages clear & white" elsewhere in the volume rather than on the blue pages that intermittently interleave the album. Lloyd's formal decision to divide his poem's two sections at the page break highlights the album's material form, encouraging a reader's interaction with the physical page. Lloyd's poem and one's interpretation of it depend on bibliographic codes—the differently colored pages—to shape the meaning of linguistic codes—"this greeting droll."

I want to pause to consider "this greeting," "the pages," and "this dusky page" in Lloyd's poem and in album verse more generally. As other scholars have noted, deixis is crucial to lyric. Deictics like *it*, *here*, *this*, and *you*, which depend on context to have referential meaning, establish and collapse notions of lyric time, creating what Jonathan Culler has referred to as "lyric temporality."[53] Culler suggests

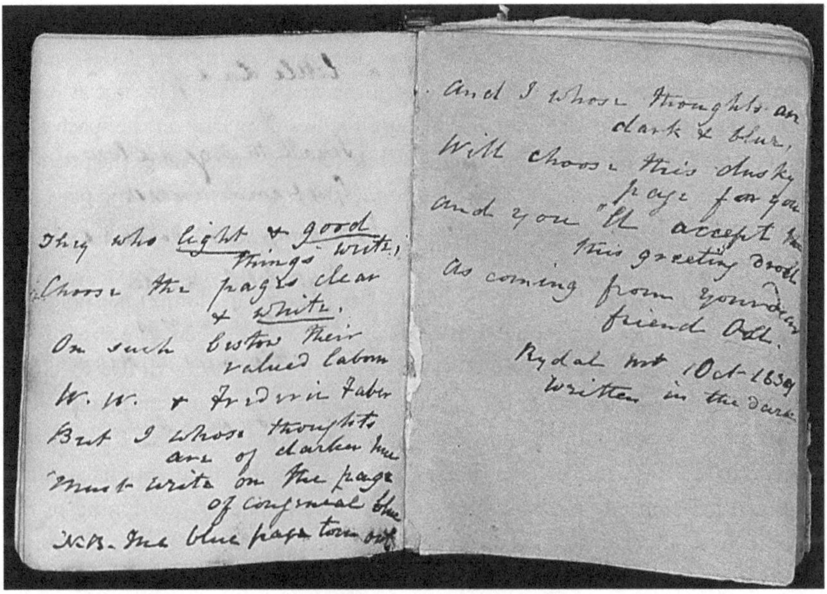
They who light & good
things write,
Choose the pages clear
& white.
On such bestow their
valued labour
W. W. & Frederic Faber
But I whose thoughts
are of darker hue
Must write on the page
of congenial blue
N.B. The blue page torn out

And I whose thoughts are
dark & blue,
Will choose this dusky
page for you
And you'll accept the
this greeting droll
As coming from your dear
friend Oll.
Rydal Mt 10 Oct 1839
Written in the dark

Figure 5.4 O[wen] Ll[oyd], untitled poem, in MS Autograph Album (unknown compiler). Jerwood Center, DCMS181. Courtesy of the Wordsworth Trust, Grasmere.

that apostrophe—the *you* central to so many lyrics—"accentuate[s] the paradox of poetry, that evokes immediacy while adopting a temporality of deferral, as it repeats itself for readers in a future not even imagined."[54] Put differently, the now of the poet writing on the dusky page, the now of our reading it, and the now of both past and future readers are different but are connected through the practice of (re)reading. Lyric temporality, then, is immediate as well as constantly deferred. I agree that deixis in lyric draws attention to the temporal complexities of reading that simultaneously distance and connect readers and writers. However, I want to push the importance of deixis towards lyric spatiality, something fewer scholars have attended to.[55] In Lloyd's poem the deictic *this* in "this dusky page" prioritizes the place of the album page rather than the time of its writing. The emphasis on personal, bibliographic context and medium in album verse promotes associations between albums and interpersonal familiarity.

In manuscript album verses like Lloyd's and in printed poems in annuals that draw on the tradition of album verse, the emphasis on materiality complicates the loco-descriptive characteristics of the greater Romantic lyric outlined by M. H. Abrams. As he has shown, poems such as Coleridge's "The Eolian Harp, Composed at Clevedon, Somersetshire" and Wordsworth's "Lines Composed a

Few Miles Above Tintern Abbey, on Revisiting the Banks of the Wye During a Tour, July 13, 1798" extend eighteenth-century loco-descriptive poetics, making the landscapes they describe "localized, in place, and sometimes in time as well."[56] However, the lyric spatiality in album verse focuses primarily on the space of the book rather than on geographic locale. While Lloyd's verse situates the poem in a specific landscape, its content privileges connections between poem and page, thus shifting these lyrics from loco-descriptive poetry to what might be called biblio-descriptive poetry.

The simultaneous specificity and fluidity of deixis in album verse holds particular significance in a changing media landscape where poems traversed books and mediums in newly intensified ways. Despite the biblio-descriptive specificity characteristic of album verses like Lloyd's, the contents of albums migrated. Verses moved from one album to another or into printed books, as was the case with poems in Charles Lamb's *Album Verses*. This remediation calls attention to a potential gap between one *this* and another while also implicitly positioning printed album verses in relation to the affective possibilities of an original manuscript context. If, as Andrew Piper has suggested, the Romantic period is the age of the "bibliographic imagination," then it is also an age in which both real and imagined familiar relationships play out on physical pages as well as in the gaps and tensions between one manuscript (or printed) page and another.[57]

Like Lloyd's poem, Martha Noble's contribution to Birkbeck's album emphasizes its status as a handwritten manuscript in an album:

My pen, and pencil willingly I lend,
And enter in this hallowed book my name;
Though all unskill'd the mimic lines to blend,
Nor yet ambitious of a poet's fame;
For higher honor waiteth her whose hand
Is free to write on these love-hallowed leaves
Midst genius, merit, rank, she takes her stand,
From <u>Thee</u> the title of a friend received.[58]

Evident are multiple references to hand, writing, and writing implements; Noble pledges both her pen and pencil, though the poem itself is written only in ink. Such references highlight the idea of hand as a sign of sincerity and poetic value. Album verses like Noble's often acknowledge the tired, familiar sentiments that they employ. Playing with ideas of familiarity as interpersonal closeness and of familiarity as common and stale, album verse substitutes traditional aesthetic value for affective value—affective value that in many cases arises from the repetition of familiar, banal tropes about writing album verses. Again and again, album verse alludes to the hand behind the poetic lines and the physical album in which they are written that, together, should compensate for an apparent lack of literary freshness. As albums physically manifested Romantic readers' familiar circles, so too do the poems within them privilege embodiment, making the embodied practice of reading and (hand)writing a crucial part of albums' affective, social potential.

One more example of how handwriting's seeming authenticity might overcome poetic banality appears in Eliza Emmerson's contribution to Birkbeck's album:

> Lady! I can't a garland twine
> Of high, and choice imaginings—
> These, these alas! can ne'er be mine;—
> This simple tribute only brings
> Before thy kind indulgent eye,
> Feeling, and truth, and sympathy—
> And these, I offer at thy shrine![59]

Emmerson's repetition of "these" shifts from abstract "choice imaginings" to material signs of good intention. By the final line, "these" signals not only "Feeling, and truth, and sympathy" but also "This simple tribute" handwritten on the page. "This" refers both to the poem as a literary work and to the poem as a commemorative manuscript artifact. It could be that Emmerson's muse was fickle that day, but it seems more likely that her poem was written to conform to the common rhetoric of album verse—a rhetoric that foregrounds the act of writing and the interpersonal familiarity that a true friend and adept reader will recognize even behind predictable poetry. Matthews observes, "No matter how conventional or derivative the contribution [to an album], it retained the capacity for affective and symbolic significance through this mediation by the hand."[60] Matthews is right about how the autographical qualities of albums created value for readers, though I would go further to suggest that the repetitiveness of such contributions in fact *adds* to their affective potential. The familiar language of album verse—language and tropes that are on the surface common and even hackneyed—evokes interpersonal familiarity through the embodied act of handwriting and the somatic act of reading that writing.

Album verse's focus on the power of seemingly banal, predictable poetry aligns with debates in the period about repetitive, common language and sincerity that I have explored in my other chapters. For instance, one might recall chapter 1's exploration of Charlotte Smith's repetitiveness as a sign of her sincerity in *Elegiac Sonnets*—a collection, remember, that also contained album verses. Either printed or handwritten, album verses asked readers to see beyond, to borrow from

Wordsworth, "monotonous language" and to recognize the affective value behind a particular album verse and its original context—even if a poem is remediated.[61] Whereas the act of handwriting might make bland and even bad poetry endearing in albums, in printed annuals those same album verses were more vulnerable to familiarity's negative associations with unaffecting banality.

HAND, PRINT

Album verses in annuals convey a manuscript ethos and emphasize the commemorative aspects of handwriting. Poems with titles such as "Written in An Album," "Impromptu On Being Desired by a Young Lady to Write Some Lines in Her Album," and "Written in a Lady's Album" not infrequently appeared in annuals.[62] These printed album verses convey what Meredith McGill describes as "the phantom presence of handwritten forms in print."[63] Some who wrote for annuals conjure these phantom presences explicitly. In references to the somatic process of writing, album verses in annuals evoke the supposed authenticity and interpersonal value of handwriting, even when those traces of script have been translated into print, and the "this" of an album's manuscript page has become the "this" of an annual's printed page.

John Malcolm's poem "Written in a Lady's Album" from *The Literary Souvenir* for 1827 exemplifies the type of album verse appearing in annuals. Sentimental and rather unremarkable, the poem attempts to eschew its commercial context and printed form:

> I ask not for the meed of fame,
> The wreath about my rest to twine,—
> Enough for me to leave my name
> Within this hallowed shrine;—
> To think that o'er these lines thine eye
> May wander in some future year,
> And Memory breathe a passing sigh
> For him who traced them here.[64]

Malcolm highlights his poem's original manuscript context, therefore establishing a connection between manuscript and print, between album and annual, and between sociable codes of manuscript production and the commercialized literary marketplace. In his poem, the "hallowed shrine" is no longer a personal album, the "thine" no longer a known, individual reader, and the lines are no longer traced in script but in typography. The deictic "here" at the stanza's close connects Malcolm's tracing hand with the page on which he writes as well as his reader's future interaction with the page. As with Lloyd's poem above, Malcolm's allusion to handwriting in the "here" of an album forwards a lyric spatiality and biblio-descriptiveness that invites readers to imaginatively transcend the physical space that binds their reading to print.[65] Importantly, it is not simply their printed form that album verses in literary annuals resist but also the impersonal, commercial apparatus surrounding the printed volumes in which they are published. Allusions to handwriting suggest editors' and contributors' attempts to align annuals with the seeming authenticity of handwritten manuscripts.

Given the prevalence of album-like material in annuals, it seems likely that editors sought such contributions to enhance the manuscript ethos of their printed annuals. This possibility complicates both historical and current dismissals of the annuals' aesthetic value. Contemporary reviewers attacked the annuals' weak literary contributions; subsequent scholars often have either struggled to locate quality texts in the annuals or have overlooked their content, focusing instead on the annuals' influence on the nineteenth-century literary marketplace. I come at the question of literary value from a different perspective. I posit that annuals' literary and social value arose partly from the repetitive album verses that they contained and, by extension, the specific strategies of lyric reading used to interpret repetitiveness and predictability as a virtue. The seeming aesthetic weakness of printed album verses in annuals trades on the very elements of repetition and familiarity embraced by writers who contributed to manuscript albums. Put differently, the familiar tropes of album verse might in some ways counter what Landon called "the familiarizing process" of print and commercialization in the annuals. Annuals remediate the genre expectations of album verse—expectations rooted in the sociability and intimacy of handwriting—into mass-produced print commodities. If, as Michelle Levy contends, "manuscript writing produces genres unique to it, often indicative of an expected intimacy between writer and reader," then the seemingly trite tropes that characterize the genre of album verses cannot be disentangled from the intimacy of handwriting, even when album verses appear in print.[66]

One striking example of a weak printed poem presenting itself as a valuable personal manuscript can be found in Martin Archer Shee's poem "An Impromptu, Addressed to a Lady who required a Specimen of the Author's Hand-writing," published in *The Literary Souvenir* for 1827:

As I write the pen shakes in my hand, when I think
I'm depicting myself in a permanent ink;—
How, by carelessly cutting my letters, my name
I myself may scratch out from the records of Fame.
But your will is the law—I obey the decree;—

> There's a chance of escape still for scribblers like me:
> Such writing my character cannot declare,
> For 'tis plain there's no legible character there.[67]

Shee's references to the supposed sloppiness of his scribbles repeat the illegibility trope commonly found in manuscript albums, and he plays with the multiple meanings of *character* as both letterforms and the poet's nature.[68] What precludes analysis of Shee's character, though, is not that that "there's no legible character there" but instead the fact there is no "dash of the pen" to decipher, only the typographical text. Despite this tension, the poem contributes to the manuscript ethos of the volume through its explicit evocation of its status as a written object.

Annuals also forwarded a manuscript ethos in their mise-en-page. "Written in an Album" by W. A. (William Alexander), published in *The Literary Souvenir* for 1826, references the blank album into which it has been transcribed. The writer wonders if it is wise to "disturb the virgin white" of the page—a familiar trope in album verse.[69] More interesting than the poem's content is its presentation: W. A.'s initials appear beneath the poem. The page replicates how contributions usually appeared in manuscript albums, with names following a writer's entry as with Owen Lloyd's poem signed "OLL." W. A.'s initials record not just the author of the poem but also a manuscript signature translated into print. As the hand stands for the self, these allusions to hand in annuals stand in for the type of interpersonal familiarity facilitated by manuscript albums. The contents of annuals and albums anticipate their own reading and social circulation, and they dramatize the remediation and materiality that make reading possible.

The content and mise-en-page of poems like "Written in a Lady's Album," "An Impromptu, Addressed to a Lady who required a Specimen of the Author's Hand-writing," and "Written in an Album" present an alternative way of reading album lyrics as "written" rather than "overheard." John Stuart Mill famously forwarded the idea that lyric is overheard—an understanding of lyric which continues to inform how scholars discuss and analyze poetry. Barbara Johnson, drawing on Paul de Man, claims, "However much a poem may be written or read *in fact* on the page, common wisdom says the 'real' poem is spoken."[70] In annuals, however, poems like Shee's and W. A.'s are less about a speaking voice than they are about a writing hand. Readers of album poems are not in the position of overhearing the poet "speak"; rather, they sit alongside the poet, coveting the authenticity of the imagined orthographic process.

Printed album poems, stripped of their "original" intimate writtenness, perform one half of a manuscript exchange, leaving conceptual space for the reader to inhabit the role of the unspecified receiver of the poem. Much of the album verse that appeared in annuals encourages readers to imagine themselves as the original poetic recipient, further eliding annuals' roots in an expanding, lucrative commercial marketplace. While sometimes a recipient is specified, as in Charles Lamb's "Verses Written in Lady Barton's Album," more often than not the addressee is left either blank in album verses printed in annuals, as in Captain William Elliot's "For ———'s Album," or unspecified, as in "Lines Written in the First Page of a Young Lady's Album" by Mrs. Cockle and "Verses Written for a Lady's Album" by J. A. St. John.[71] Ambiguously addressed album verses in literary annuals offer sights of imagined address between authors and readers; annuals, to adapt Charles Lamb's description of albums, offered readers a printed list of imagined literary friends.[72] By publishing album verses and, as I argue in the next section, facsimile signatures, annuals offer a self-conscious meditation on mediation in Romanticism's changing literary and cultural landscape.

SIGNING AND SELLING FAMILIARITY IN THE ANNUALS

Beyond printing album verses, literary annuals also forwarded a manuscript ethos by including facsimile signatures and pages for users' annotations. *The Literary Souvenir* for 1825, edited by Alaric A. Watts, was the first annual to print autographs. In addition to ten steel-plate engravings, the volume contained three pages of lithograph signatures from leading literary figures, among them Landon, Charles Lamb, Wordsworth, and Southey (figure 5.5).

As Sara Lodge explains, *The Literary Souvenir* was "strikingly preoccupied by signatures," which signals its "conceptual indebtedness to the private, handwritten 'album.'"[73] While I would emphasize that albums were not typically private, Lodge is right to identify the importance of handwriting in early annuals. As with the album verses that appeared in annuals, the value of these signatures was not in their "writtenness" alone, but in their evocation of a wider culture of signatory exchange predicated on sociable familiarity. The signature plates offer a facsimile of autographs as well as a facsimile of manuscript practices and the social interactions supporting (and supported by) them. The plates' mise-en-page, like the layout of W. A.'s poem, mirrors the pages found in contemporary manuscript albums (figure 5.6).

The signatures in *The Literary Souvenir* for 1825 must have been received well, for autographs also appeared in the 1826 edition. The trend spread to other annuals. *The Amulet; or Christian and Literary Remembrancer* for 1827 also

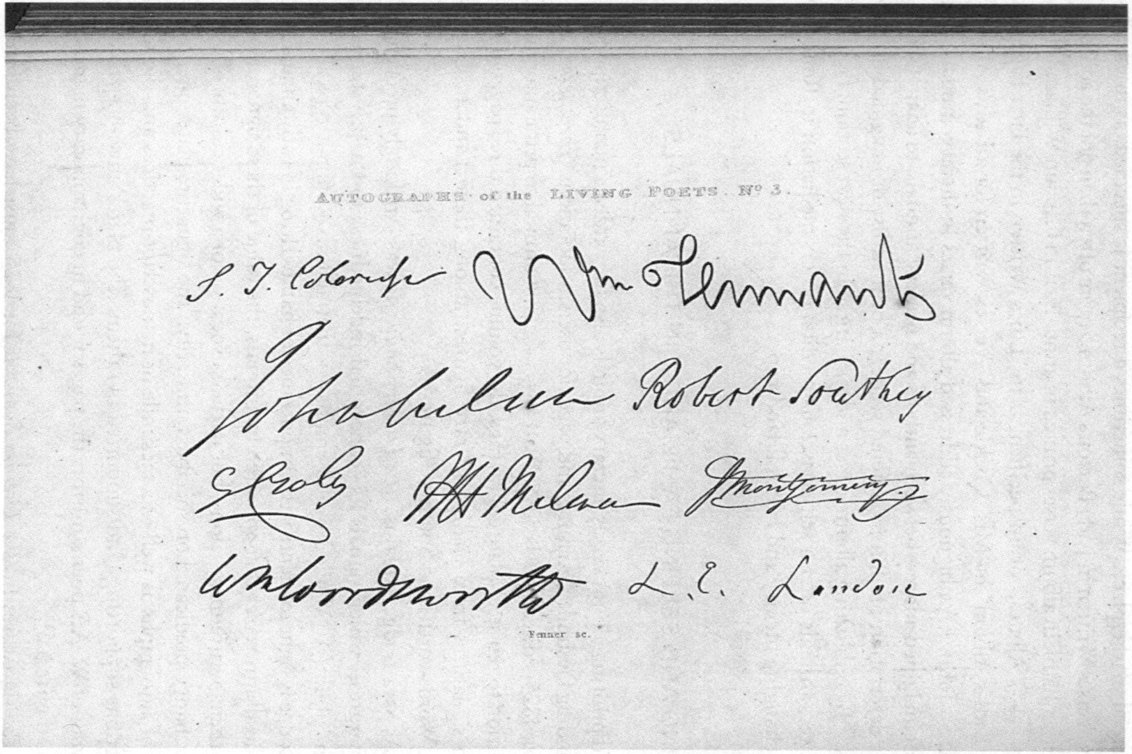

Figure 5.5 "Autographs of the Living Poets No. 3," in *The Literary Souvenir; Or, Cabinet of Poetry and Romance* [for 1825] (London: Hurst, Robinson, 1825). Courtesy of Victoria University Library (Toronto).

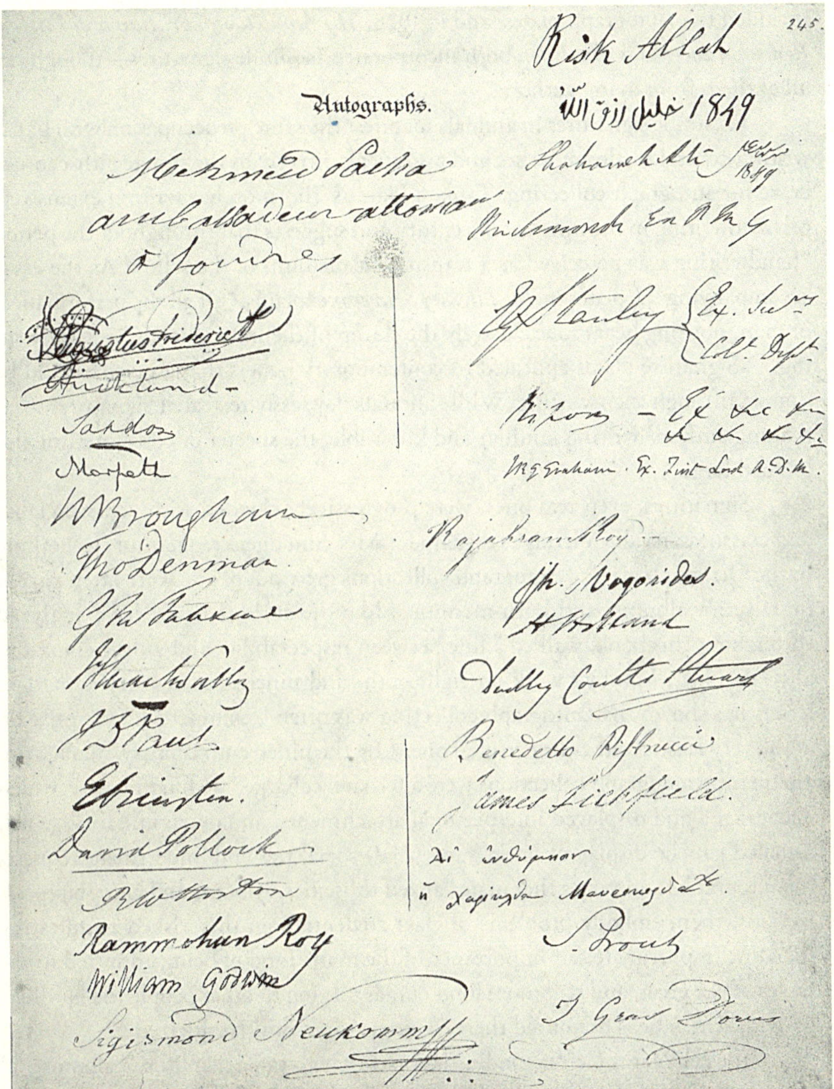

Figure 5.6 Autograph page in the Album of Mrs. Birkbeck. Courtesy of The Birkbeck College, London.

included two autograph plates, and in 1828, *The Amulet; or Christian and Literary Remembrancer* and *The Bijou* both incorporated facsimile signatures—though not all of them from living authors.

Facsimile signatures in annuals manifest the same preoccupation with handwriting central to album verses and also speak directly to the nineteenth-century craze for autograph collecting. Tamara Plakins Thornton has written extensively on handwriting in the nineteenth century and suggests that throughout the period "handwriting was perceived as a transparent medium of the self."[74] As the essay accompanying the plates in *The Literary Souvenir* explains: "Of all the performances of man, nothing bears so exclusively the stamp of the individual as his handwriting."[75] Signature plates appealed to contemporary beliefs that a person could be known through their writing. While annuals flawlessly recreated signatures, thus making authors' writing familiar and knowable, the specter of consumerism also loomed large.

Signatures, even real ones, were progressively clouded with commerciality and crassness; recall Coleridge's disdain for Mrs. Smudger's request for "something in the Ottigraph way."[76] Autograph collections grew out of and were often part of manuscript albums, and both mediums, like the authors that I have analyzed throughout this book, walked a line between respectability and vulgar commonality. A. N. L. Munby's work on eighteenth- and nineteenth-century autograph letters has shown that autograph collecting was often a commercial enterprise or, at the very least, a rather impersonal one.[77] By the nineteenth century, manuscript albums and autograph collections were alternately charged with familiarity, which encouraged and displayed interpersonal attachments, and overfamiliarity, which signaled gauche display of one's (superficial) social ties and impertinent requests for autographs and verses that materialized those ties. Albums and autograph collections, then, embody problems of class credentialing; they risked manifesting the same importunate self-importance of the man "fond of being admitted to the tables of the great, and still more fond of magnifying to other people the familiarity with which he is honoured there," whom Adam Smith criticized.[78]

The challenges facing middle-class users who created manuscript albums and autograph collections mirror the difficulties faced by editors of annuals who sought to associate their volumes with a particular type of manuscript practice that, by the 1820s and 1830s, was increasingly imbued with the vulgar social reaching characteristic of overfamiliarity. One potential solution was to encourage readers' imagined familiarity with the writers whose signatures appeared in the annuals, as well as to encourage readers of annuals to write in them, often via dedicated inscription plates. Handwritten inscriptions at the front of an annual implicitly engage in a dialogue with the lithographed signatures, allowing readers to participate vicariously in coterie manuscript practices.[79] As a result, manuscript inscriptions give personal weight to the mass-produced signatures in literary annuals—an act not unlike signing a Hallmark card. Carrying more affective weight than autographs, readers' inscriptions, according to Piper, "functioned as a crucial counterpoint to the romantic fascination with the autograph. The inscriptions captured the fundamental sharedness of writing."[80] In annuals, users' inscriptions and marginalia shifted the facsimile autographs into the realm of "sharedness," gift exchange, and interpersonal familiarity.

Early annuals also contained blank diary pages that further heightened the medium's manuscript ethos. Editors positioned their annuals alongside print genres like pocketbooks and almanacs, which promoted the interaction between printed text and users' manuscript additions. For example, the preface to *Friendship's Offering* for 1824 explains the annual's relationship to pocketbooks: "[I]t is hoped that the mere Pocket-book of the year (the purposes of which it [*Friendship's Offering*] is particularly intended to supply) will be elevated in character, and rendered more generally useful and interesting than hitherto."[81] Replicating this trend, the annual *Remember Me!* for 1825 contains a calendar and twenty-four album pages; the calendar recreates the formatting typically found in published pocketbooks, with two months per page separated by a vignette wood engraving.[82] Like *Remember Me!*, the 1825 edition of *Friendship's Offering* provided readers with substantial space to write. Its sixty-page diary section, twenty-five charades, and twenty-two riddles all invite annotation.

The presence of riddles and charades in some annuals enhances connections between print and the sociable elements of manuscript production. We need only recall Emma Woodhouse and Harriet Smith's project of "collecting and transcribing all the riddles of every sort . . . into a thin quarto of hot-pressed paper" in Jane Austen's *Emma* as evidence of the popularity and social import of charades and riddles. Indeed, the inclusion of Mr. Elton's "friend's" gallant riddle in Emma and Harriet's volume—an honor which Mr. Elton claims his "friend" would consider "the proudest moment of his life"—demonstrates how manuscript contributions were used to solidify familiar relationships and, in some cases, further romantic intentions.[83] Early editions of *Friendship's Offering* included riddles and charades, and copies that I have encountered include handwritten answers. For instance, in a copy now held at the Robertson Davies Library at Massey College in the University of Toronto, someone has written, "Each has its corps," below the riddle "Why is a basket of apples like an army of volunteers?"[84] Another copy records the answer "carpet" written in response to a charade poem which ends: "Yet, e'en in these luxurious days, / 'Tis trampled under foot" (see figure 5.1).[85] Readers also wrote notes in other places, including flyleaves.[86] The pages of the early annuals promoted the permeable boundary between printed text and readers' handwritten additions.

Editors invited readers not only to write in their annuals but also to write for them. Printed notes often found in the front of annuals instructed readers to submit their work for consideration in the following year's annual. Similar to the way in which Walter Benjamin believes "letters to the editor" function, the annuals blur "the distinction between author and public."[87] By encouraging amateur contributions that would appear alongside those of Landon, Wordsworth, or Scott, editors sought to efface distinctions between professional and amateur and between consumerism and collaborative, communal exchange.[88] In the early annuals, readers became both real and imagined co-contributors to the ready-made volumes they read. Editors aggressively marketed the personalizable elements of their volumes. *The Keepsake* for 1828 featured an essay championing the value of inscriptions. In "Pocket-Books and Keepsakes," Leigh Hunt claims that "one precious name, or little inscription at the beginning of the volume, where the hand that wrote it is known to be generous in its wishes, if not in its means, is worth all the binding in St. James's."[89] Hunt is clear: personalization adds far more value to a volume than gold block, gilt-edged paper, or detailed engravings, and his comments recall tropes emphasizing handwriting that so often appear in album verses. However, Hunt's essay appeared when the annuals were changing in significant ways.

FAILING TO INSCRIBE AND EDIT FAMILIARITY

By the late 1820s the value of individual annuals became recursively tied to the perceived social value of the medium as a whole. Just as one may desire a birthday card more for the idea of receiving one than for what the card actually says, purchasers and receivers of literary annuals came to view the volumes as necessary—though also somewhat empty—gifts. Editors engaged conflicting discourses of value and value making by asserting that their volumes were desirable for two reasons. First, they were expensive to make and so had value based on economic considerations alone. Second, their value could be further increased by personal manuscript additions like those explicitly encouraged by Hunt's essay. The development of the annuals reveals a shift between these two reasons, with the annuals' value being increasingly dependent not on their evocation of a manuscript ethos but on their value as annuals in and of themselves. As Paula Feldman has argued, for a young lady not to receive an annual was an embarrassment, so much so that what "otherwise might have been a discretionary purchase became for some young women an essential item for the drawing room table."[90] Editors, then, came to rely on the status of literary annuals as essential social artifacts. As the annuals' popularity grew and as the volumes removed dedicated spaces for readers' annotations, it was difficult for contributors, publishers, and editors to position their annuals as part of a sociable, participatory culture akin to manuscript exchange. The positive aspects of familiarity that the annuals evoked early in the 1820s began to fade as later annuals increasingly left little space, both materially and ideologically, which individuals could use to personalize them. According to William St Clair, later annuals "left nothing for the owner to write except her name," and some annuals did away with inscription plates altogether.[91]

As the annuals developed distinct qualities that set them apart from manuscript albums and pocketbooks, they became more akin to art books rather than volumes that encouraged interactions between manuscript and print. Annual-editors faced pressure to remain on the cutting edge of visual and technological display. Inscription plates from *Forget Me Not* and *The Gem* published in the late 1820s and early 1830s used cameo embossing and dual-color printing techniques that had only recently been invented. While presentation plates produced with new technologies would not necessarily have precluded readerly personalization, their elaborateness shifted them closer to the realm of art. The trend toward visual innovation also appeared in the annuals' bindings and illustrations. Printed paper-board bindings were replaced by elegant watered silk, fly-embossed leather, and gold-blocked covers. In later annuals, illustrations were sometimes larger than the text blocks, signaling a "shift away from the annual's literary contents towards its visual contents."[92] These shifts fundamentally influenced how readers perceived their annuals. As H. J. Jackson has observed, "the better produced and the more beautiful the book is, the less hospitable it is likely to be to manuscript additions."[93] Feldman's study of 354 literary annuals from 1824 to 1859 seems to support this theory, with only 40 percent of the volumes having personal inscriptions.[94] This turn toward beauty and its implicit discouragement of readers' annotations distanced later annuals from the manuscript traditions out of which they arose. These changes shifted the focus of familiarity that drove early annuals' popularity. Rather than encourage interpersonal familiarity between readers as well as imagined familiarity between readers and authors, the genre became too familiar in the sense of predictable and unaffecting.

Even as they removed spaces for annotations, editors sought ways to combat their volumes' commercial and increasingly familiar qualities. Poems in annuals not infrequently identify themselves as being from the albums of either aristocrats or those with social ties to the aristocracy. For instance, in his preface to *Friendship's Offering* for 1826, the editor Thomas K. Hervey claimed that Byron's

"Stanzas. To her who best can understand them" was "extracted . . . from the Album of CAPTAIN MEDWIN." In his preface to the volume Hervey also thanks "LADY CAROLINE LAMB, for the verses at page 230; taken from the note-book of her Ladyship, and addressed to her, by Lord Byron, sixteen years ago."[95] Prefaces like Hervey's portray editing literary annuals as analogous to creating a manuscript album with the help of one's friends, and editors often eschewed the vast payments that prominent authors received.[96] Lodge explains that "contributors frequently also conveyed the sense that their work in the annual had originated in a private context of unpaid literary exchange."[97] This trend appears in the preface to *The Literary Souvenir* for 1825, where Alaric Watts notes his annual's roots in personal albums: "[T]he beautiful Poem from the pen of Mr. [Thomas] Campbell, which will be found at page 149 [titled "Lines on Leaving a Scene in Bavaria"], was not contributed by that gentleman, but transcribed from the album of a mutual friend."[98] Watts's comment frames his annual within a culture of familiar friendship enabled by manuscript albums. Just as the "mutual friend" shared his album poem from Campbell with Watts, Watts shares his authorial friends with his (purchasing) public friends.

Once women like Landon and Countess Blessington began editing annuals such as *Fisher's Drawing Room Scrap-book* and *Heath's Book of Beauty*, invitations to buy their volumes were more obviously invitations to imagine one's participation in their familiar circle—circles that in Blessington's case were explicitly aristocratic. The seemingly autobiographical nature of many of Landon's and Blessington's poems in annuals further enhanced the understanding that annuals offered readers' access to an author's personal and social life. Several of the poems in the 1839 edition of *Fisher's Drawing Room Scrap-book* (the last that Landon would edit before her marriage to George Maclean and her mysterious death in Cape Coast) focus on departure and love. "The Farewell," for example, is told from the perspective of someone leaving on a voyage.[99] Referencing her own looming departure in the volume's preface, Landon encourages her audience to read autobiographical elements of her work, even when there are clear distinctions between Landon and her poetic speakers. Such poems played on the public's desire to feel as though they knew her personally. Additionally, like the contributions in manuscript albums, poems in *Fisher's Drawing Room Scrap-book* commemorate friends, as Landon does in "To Marguerite, Countess of Blessington."[100] Other poems like "To L.E.L.—After Meeting Her for the First Time" gave readers the impression that they read a printed version of Landon's own album.[101] Thus, while later annuals removed features that encouraged readers to write in them, the volumes still pointed to sociable practices of exchanging manuscript albums and writing personal poems for one's circle.

Ultimately, the relationship between annuals and the manuscript albums kept by privileged (often female) members of society exposes a new type of what William St Clair terms "tranching down."[102] In *The Reading Nation in the Romantic Period*, St Clair identifies a trend to sell works at successively lower price points and smaller material formats. Once a market for a certain work at a certain price was saturated, publishers would produce it in less expensive formats—say, a title moving from quarto to octavo to duodecimo. The annuals, however, do not represent a tranching down of a particular title. Instead, the annuals enacted a tranching down of a cultural practice through a shift from manuscript to print—print that evoked semi-elite practices of creating albums like that owned by Mrs. Birkbeck.[103] Interestingly, the tranching down of this cultural practice involved a tranching up of the material formats of later annuals; subsequent editions of many titles increased in format from small duodecimos to octavos to quartos. In an attempt to make annuals seem like exclusive luxury items, they were published in larger formats with more lavish-looking case bindings. However, economies of scale and new production methods allowed even large annuals to be sold at prices similar to those of some small duodecimos from the 1820s.

Because annuals attempted to commercialize a culture of coterie manuscript production that, by the time the annuals rose to prominence, was itself becoming associated with untoward social reaching, they struggled to maintain cultural legitimacy. By the late 1830s, annuals had become familiar in the most boring sense of the word: banal, common, and predictable. The "familiarizing process" of commercial production that Landon lamented in the introduction to *Fisher's Drawing Room Scrap-book* changed the nature of annuals and their ability to evoke lingering senses of elitism that even manuscript albums, with their growing popularity among the middling classes, struggled to retain throughout the nineteenth century.[104] Distinctions between different annuals such as *The Keepsake* or *The Literary Souvenir* became less clear, and explicit allusions to manuscript culture disappeared. Even contributors began to confuse the very annuals to which they contributed. James Hogg wrote to Thomas Pringle, editor of *Friendship's Offering*: "But so perfectly am I confounded by the number of annuals that . . . at this moment I do not know which is your's and which I have wrote for and which not!"[105] Literary annuals faltered as volumes flooded the market with their sameness and with pages that discouraged personalization and marginal markings, and even album verses printed in them struggled to uphold the manuscript ethos and its associations with sociable familiarity. As a result, literary annuals became utterly familiar and un(re)markable.

CODA
Lifting "the film of familiarity"

Poetry . . . purges from our inward sight the film of familiarity which obscures from us the wonder of our being.
—Percy Bysshe Shelley, "A Defence of Poetry"*

I WANT TO CONCLUDE BY RETURNING briefly to the scandal surrounding Elizabeth Gunning in the 1790s, with which this book began. Gunning's case illustrates the difficulties facing Romantic-era authors who attempted to evoke feelings of familiarity in their readers. As I have argued throughout the preceding chapters, conjuring familiarity was certainly not the same thing as controlling it—something that Gunning discovered when her attempted seduction of the Marquis of Blandford caused a popular backlash that destroyed her reputation.

James Gillray's caricatures about the scandal from March 1791 underscore this loss of control. The scandal offered Gillray ample material, and his depictions of Gunning recall the intricate, multimedia factors shaping public perceptions of familiarity. His first print, which I examined in the introduction, features Gunning falling off of an exploding cannon while a barrage of feces—presumably emitting from Blandford's own aristocratic rear end—repels her (see figure I.1). A few weeks later, Gillray produced another image about what Horace Walpole termed "The Gunninghiad," which similarly emphasizes volatility and manipulation.[1] The caricature features Gunning, her family, a demon, and a groom willing to "ride, or swear, or anything" on his way to Blandford's family residence, Blenheim Palace (figure C.1).

Characteristic of Gillray, the image is complex, and it remains unclear who, if anyone, controls the situation. Gunning and her father sit at the table, and under them the demon of forgery menacingly aids their plot. "I swear that I never wish'd or tried directly or indirectly to get a Coronet," Gunning's speech bubble reads—a denial of the widespread belief that she pursued Blandford for his aristocratic title.

Figure C.1 James Gillray, "Betty Canning Revived: or a Peep at the Conjuration of Mary Squires, & the Gypsey Family" (London: S. W. Fores, March 25, 1791). Courtesy of the Yale Center for British Art, Paul Mellon Collection.

But her flushed cheeks, as well as the demon's hand up her dress, suggest that Gunning may have lost control of the situation as well as her virtue.

Other figures vie for the viewer's attention and exert control over Gunning and the "truth" that she swears. Her mother Susannah and aunt Margaret ("Nauntee Peg"), the novel-writing Minifie sisters, "cook up the Coronets" at the side of the room. The two women make soup from melting coronets, literalizing the complexities of class, taste, and consumption that the Gunning scandal evoked. Susannah fans the flame beneath the cauldron with a book turned bellows entitled "Letter to the D—of A." This is not just any book, but *A Letter from Mrs Gunning, Addressed to His Grace the Duke of Argyll*, Susannah's pamphlet about the scandal published in 1791. Recall that the pamphlet, reprinted several times to meet high demand, proclaimed her daughter's innocence and courted public sympathy in the hyperbolic style reminiscent of Susannah's novels.

The image of Susannah puffing the fire with her book-as-bellows reminds us how personal details like those included in her pamphlet inflamed Romantic readers' desire for information about public figures' private lives. Gillray also suggests just how difficult it was to manipulate public perception in practice; the figures are surrounded by different items of print plastered to the walls: music, affidavits, and title pages of novels. Moreover, the title of the caricature, "Betty Canning Revived," casts the Gunning family as characters from the earlier sensational mystery of Elizabeth Canning, a servant girl who disappeared for several weeks in 1753. Canning accused Mary Squires, a gypsy, of abducting her and attempting to turn her into a prostitute. Squires was jailed, but soon a counterattack was launched, and Canning was convicted of perjury and transported to New England. Much like Gunning, Canning captured the public's imagination and prompted an extensive pamphlet war about feminine innocence, deception, and carnal familiarity.[2] Gillray's direct reference to Canning, along with the print artifacts decorating the room, demonstrate the extent to which the Gunning scandal was read through existing narrative lenses. The image exemplifies the interconnected media environment in which details about Gunning's relationship with Blandford became gossip not just for her familiar circle but also for the country at large.

Though Gillray's scheming figures appear calm, the large flame billowing smoke that Susannah tends and the demon arising from the fiery floor threaten to ignite them all. Much like the increasingly personal prefaces to Charlotte Smith's *Elegiac Sonnets* or Hazlitt's autobiographical forthrightness in *Liber Amoris*, Susannah's revelations about her daughter in *A Letter from Mrs Gunning* had an uneven effect on readers. Susannah and Elizabeth Gunning were ridiculed both for the marriage scandal that engulfed them and for their choice to write about it in works like Susannah's pamphlet and Gunning's novel *The Packet*. Indeed, if Gunning and the case studies explored throughout this book demonstrate anything, it is that trying to evoke familiarity in the Romantic public sphere was akin to playing with fire.

In many ways, the conditions of Romantic authorship were a tinderbox and familiarity the kindling. My research has explored familiarity's volatile associations with sympathy and closeness as well as with banality and vulgarity. I have tried to demonstrate how familiarity's limits shifted as it interacted with the equally unstable dynamics of gender and class in a period characterized by technological, literary, and political revolution. In Romanticism's changing literary marketplace some authors sought to connect with growing numbers of anonymous readers by penning increasingly self-revelatory works. Readers used these imaginative works to form bonds with each other and with writers like Byron whom they would likely never meet.

On a stylistic level, these bonds were often cultivated through familiar, seemingly repetitive or even banal language. Authors like Charlotte Smith, Wordsworth, Hazlitt, and those who wrote for manuscript albums and literary annuals explicitly embraced the power of familiar literary language to convey sincerity. Just as familiar social intercourse could promote affection, familiar language could forge strong connections between authors and their audiences, and this style of literary familiarity privileged the power of discerning and sympathetic readers. Yet, critics viewed this style as dependent on trite tropes and common language that signaled vulgarity, unoriginality, or inauthenticity—this is perhaps closer to the undesirable "film of familiarity" that Percy Shelley sought to lift.[3]

The forcefulness with which prominent Romantic authors either courted or rejected familiarity signals its widespread importance in the period, and a central argument here has been that familiarity haunts Romanticism. For instance, in "A Defence of Poetry," Shelley praises poetry by attacking familiarity. "Poetry," he writes, "lifts the veil from the hidden beauty of the world, and makes familiar objects be as if they were not familiar."[4] Indeed, familiarity is an overlooked element of Shelley's philosophy, one to which he notably returns several times in his essay. Near its conclusion he reiterates poetry's potential as an antidote to familiarity; poetry, he asserts, "purges from our inward sight the film of familiarity which obscures from us the wonder of our being."[5] For Shelley as well as for Coleridge, whose ideas about "the film of familiarity" in *Biographia Literaria* the younger poet borrows, familiarity blunts human sight, intellect, and soul.[6] For them, familiarity is more than banal; it hobbles human interaction and obscures both political and literary vision. In this view, familiarity is something to avoid, to fix, and to overcome.

The urgency of Shelley's and Coleridge's denunciations of familiarity suggest the need for a reconsideration of familiarity's governing role in the eighteenth and nineteenth centuries, and *The Limits of Familiarity* has tried to begin this reconsideration. Readers of the twenty-first century might themselves be most immediately familiar with these negative Romantic-era assessments of familiarity. However, this book's case studies have shown not only the pervasiveness of concerns about familiar sociability and familiar literary style but also how these discourses were charged in intricate, conflicting ways. As a trait whose decorous limits governed social interactions, familiarity, in theory, insulated different groups from each other—say, a lodging-house girl from a (predatory) paying lodger and author. In some instances, the problem was not that familiarity "obscures," as Shelley claimed, but rather that too much familiarity exposes. That is, overfamiliarity brought people too clearly into focus before too many people, resulting in what conservatives thought was a vulgar effacement between public and private life as well as between different classed and gendered groups. From this perspective, the "film of familiarity" and its structuring of everything from social interaction to politics to literature was not necessarily a barrier but rather a balm that eased sociability.

As my case studies demonstrate, deploying familiarity in the literary sphere was particularly difficult. The works examined here were market successes, yet they were also seen by many critics and readers as failures of judgment, decorum, and taste. It was often context, rather than a text itself, that determined what type of familiarity people saw. Hence, Byron's status as a male aristocratic poet and Lady Caroline Lamb's status as a female aristocratic novelist struck readers very differently. Exploring these distinctions, the attacks leveled at Romantic-era works, and authors' (pre-emptive) responses to them has been the project of this book. I have tried, with more rigor than the Gunnings, to conjure the shadows of familiarity in the Romantic era. In the process, I hope that I have not only shed light on the contours of Romanticism but also offered a historical perspective on our current moment.

While this book is decidedly not about media in the twenty-first century, the history of familiarity and fan culture in the Romantic period are direct precursors to today's celebrity culture of tell-all exposure, reality TV, and pervasive fandoms. Romantic-era authors and publishers attempted to capitalize on a system of audience adoration, curiosity, and disgust that simultaneously supported and exploited authors' lives and literary careers. These dynamics anticipate today's media monster that celebrities alternately feed, criticize, and manipulate. Concerns about familiarity and overfamiliarity, about sharing and oversharing, about closeness and distance, about authenticity and inauthenticity that shaped Romantic authorship remain germane today. A stronger understanding of the subtleties of familiarity in the eighteenth and nineteenth centuries clarifies how our Romantic inheritance has shaped the darker sides of current culture, including what Eva Wiseman in the *Guardian* has called our aggressive desire to "hate-watch" programs and destroy the celebrities in them.[7] By attempting to lift the "film of familiarity" from Romanticism—a film composed of issues like sincerity and sympathy that have long interested scholars of the period—I have argued for the importance that familiarity had, and continues to have, as a cultural and literary value.

NOTES

INTRODUCTION

* Walter Scott, "Memoir of the Early Life of Sir Walter Scott, Written by Himself," in *Memoirs of the Life of Sir Walter Scott* by John Gibson Lockhart (Edinburgh: Robert Cadell; London: John Murray, 1837), 1:1.

1. Blandford was the same individual who on June 17, 1812, paid £2,260 for a first edition of Boccaccio's *Decameron* at the famous Roxburghe sale.
2. A Knight of Chivalry, *A Friendly Letter to the Marquis of Lorn, on the Subject of Mrs. Gunning's Pamphlet* (London: J. Ridgway, 1791), 86.
3. Horace Walpole to Mary Berry, March 27, 1791, in *Horace Walpole's Correspondence with Mary and Agnes Berry and Barbara Cecilia Seton*, ed. W. S. Lewis and Dayle Wallace, vol. 11 of *The Yale Edition of Horace Walpole's Correspondence* (New Haven, CT: Yale University Press, 1944), 229.
4. At least nine caricatures about the Gunnings appeared over the next year, including several by Isaac Cruikshank and William Dent. For a description of these images, see Mary Dorothy George, *Catalogue of Political and Personal Satires Preserved in the Department of Prints and Drawings in the British Museum*, vol. 6, *1784–1792* (London: British Museum, 1938), 839, 848–853, and 955–956.
5. Lawrence E. Klein, "Gender and the Public/Private Distinction in the Eighteenth Century: Some Questions about Evidence and Analytic Procedure," *Eighteenth-Century Studies* 29, no. 1 (1995): 99.
6. Samuel Johnson, *A Dictionary of the English Language*, 2nd ed., s.vv. "familiarity" and "familiar" (London: J. and P. Knapton, T. and T. Longman, C. Hitch and L. Hawes, A. Millar, and R. and J. Dodsley, 1755–1756).
7. George Crabb, *English Synonymes Explained*, 2nd ed., s.v. "acquaintance" (London: Baldwin, Cradock, and Joy, and T. Boosey, 1818), emphasis in the original.
8. Crabb, s.v. "free," 497, emphasis in the original.
9. Samuel Taylor Coleridge, *Biographia Literaria, or Biographical Sketches of My Literary Life and Opinions*, ed. James Engell and W. Jackson Bate, in *The Collected Works of Samuel Taylor Coleridge*, ed. Kathleen Coburn (Princeton, NJ: Princeton University Press, 1983), 7.2:17.
10. Edmund Burke, *Reflections on the Revolution in France*, ed. Conor Cruise O'Brien (New York: Penguin, 2004), 171.
11. Walpole to Mary Berry, July 29, 1790, *Walpole's Correspondence*, 104.
12. [John Gunning], *An Apology for the Life of Major General G*[unning], *Written by Himself* (London: J. Ridgway, 1792), 78.
13. See, for instance, "London," *London Chronicle*, February 19–22, 1791.
14. *Walpole's Correspondence*, 225n; Susannah Gunning, *A Letter from Mrs. Gunning, Addressed to His Grace the Duke of Argyll*, 2nd ed. (London: printed for the author, 1791).
15. For more on Susannah Gunning's authorial career and its relation to the scandal, see Betty A. Schellenberg, *The Professionalization of Women Writers in Eighteenth-Century*

Britain (Cambridge University Press, 2005), 120–140; Thomas O. Beebee, "Publicity, Privacy, and the Power of Fiction in the Gunning Letters," *Eighteenth-Century Fiction* 20, no. 1 (2007): 61–88; and Kurt Edward Milberger, "'The First Impression, You, Yourself, Will Buy': The Gunninghiad, *Virginius and Virginia* and the Art of Scandal at the Minerva Press," *Romantic Textualities: Literature and Print Culture, 1780–1840*, no. 23 (2020): 39–59.

16. *A Narrative of the Incidents which Form the Mystery, in the Family of General Gunning* (London: Taylor, 1791), 5.
17. Walpole to Mary Berry, February 18, 1791, *Walpole's Correspondence*, 205.
18. "The Marquis of Blandford's Marriage," *Times*, September 14, 1791, Gale Document Number CS50990382, *The Times* Digital Archive. For more on the novelistic elements of the scandal, see Beebee, "Publicity, Privacy"; and Pam Perkins, "The Fictional Identities of Elizabeth Gunning," *Tulsa Studies in Women's Literature* 15, no. 1 (1996): 83–98.
19. Crabb, *English Synonymes Explained*, 28.
20. A Knight of Chivalry, *Friendly Letter*, 65. The author's pseudonym as well as the pamphlet's celebration of female innocence point directly to Burke's descriptions of Marie Antoinette in *Reflections on the Revolution in France*, which appeared less than a year earlier.
21. Felicity Nussbaum has described the shift from object to agent that occurs when a woman with a scandalous past turns to authorship: "Once a 'fallen woman' speaks a textual 'self,' she becomes a subject—the perceiver instead of the perceived." Nussbaum, *The Autobiographical Subject: Gender and Ideology in Eighteenth-Century England* (Baltimore: Johns Hopkins University Press, 1989), 185. Relatedly, Milberger argues that Susannah Gunning's publications with the Minerva Press following the scandal were an attempt "to wrest control of the public narrative of the Gunninghiad back from the critics and satirists." Milberger, "First Impression," 43.
22. Gunning also published five translations from French, two plays, and a children's book.
23. Johnson, *Dictionary*, s.v. "familiar."
24. Perkins, "Fictional Identities," 85.
25. Elizabeth Gunning, *The Packet: A Novel* (London: J. Bell, 1794), 1:2, emphasis in the original.
26. Gunning, *Packet*, 3:7.
27. Julian North, *The Domestication of Genius: Biography and the Romantic Poet* (Oxford: Oxford University Press, 2009), 29.
28. Paul Keen has similarly suggested that in the 1790s producers of literature began to share importance with the products that they produced. Paul Keen, *The Crisis of Literature in the 1790s: Print Culture and the Public Sphere* (Cambridge: Cambridge University Press, 1999), 8. John Brewer also addresses the blurring of the public and private spheres in "This, That and the Other: Public, Social and Private in the Seventeenth and Eighteenth Centuries," in *Shifting the Boundaries: Transformation of the Languages of Public and Private in the Eighteenth Century*, ed. Dario Castiglione and Lesley Sharpe (Exeter: University of Exeter Press, 1995), 1–21.

    North, *Domestication of Genius*, 29.
29. Philip Dormer Stanhope, *The Art of Pleasing; or, Instructions for Youth in the First Stage of Life, in a Series of Letters to the Present Earl of Chesterfield, by the Late Philip Earl of Chesterfield* (London: G. Kearsley, 1783), 83–84.
30. Tom Mole, *Byron's Romantic Celebrity: Industrial Culture and the Hermeneutic of Intimacy* (New York: Palgrave, 2007), 22. See also Ghislaine McDayter, *Byromania and the Birth of Celebrity Culture* (Albany: State University of New York Press, 2009); Eric Eisner, *Nineteenth-Century Poetry and Literary Celebrity* (New York: Palgrave Macmil-

lan, 2009); and Corin Throsby, "Byron, Commonplacing and Early Fan Culture," in Mole, *Romanticism and Celebrity Culture, 1750–1850*, ed. Tom Mole (Cambridge: Cambridge University Press, 2009), 227–244.

31. Clara Tuite, *Lord Byron and Scandalous Celebrity* (Cambridge: Cambridge University Press, 2015). My research also seeks to extend the type of historical work found in Mole's edited collection, *Romanticism and Celebrity Culture, 1750–1850*, in which contributors' essays on figures like George "Beau" Brummell, Sarah Siddons, and Mary Robinson present Romantic-era celebrity as a cultural development beyond Byron.
32. I have in mind G. J. Barker-Benfield, *The Culture of Sensibility: Sex and Society in Eighteenth-Century Britain* (Chicago: University of Chicago Press, 1992); Chris Jones, *Radical Sensibility: Literature and Ideas in the 1790s* (New York: Routledge, 1993); John Barrell, *The Spirit of Despotism: Invasions of Privacy in the 1790s* (Oxford: Oxford University Press, 2006); and Tim Milnes and Kerry Sinanan, eds., *Romanticism, Sincerity and Authenticity* (Basingstoke, UK: Palgrave Macmillan, 2010).
33. Pierre Bourdieu, *The Field of Cultural Production: Essays on Art and Literature*, ed. Randal Johnson (New York: Columbia University Press, 1993), 32.
34. The most extensive examples of using readers' annotations to gauge historical reading are H. J. Jackson's *Romantic Readers: The Evidence of Marginalia* (New Haven, CT: Yale University Press, 2005); and H. J. Jackson, *Marginalia: Readers Writing in Books* (New Haven, CT: Yale University Press, 2001). For a more recent consideration of marginalia and other evidence left by nineteenth-century readers, see Andrew M. Stauffer, *Book Traces: Nineteenth-Century Readers and the Future of the Library* (Philadelphia: University of Pennsylvania Press, 2021).
35. Jon Klancher, "Configuring Romanticism and Print History: A Retrospective," *European Romantic Review* 23, no. 3 (2012): 375. Klancher's article reflects on his earlier work in *The Making of English Reading Audiences, 1790–1832* (Madison: University of Wisconsin Press, 1987).
36. Andrew Franta, *Romanticism and the Rise of the Mass Public* (Cambridge: Cambridge University Press, 2007).
37. The term *Byromania* appeared publicly in a review of *Manfred* published in *Knight Errant; A Literary Miscellany, consisting of Original Prose and Verse, with Occasional Notices of New Books Drama, etc.* (July 1817), in *Romantics Reviewed*, part B: *Byron and Regency Society Poets*, ed. Donald H. Reiman (New York: Garland, 1972), 3:1223. Subsequent references to reviews reprinted in *Romantics Reviewed* (hereafter *RR*) cite the review's original publication venue, month, and year, followed by the relevant part in *RR*, volume, and page number.
38. Adela Pinch, *Strange Fits of Passion: Epistemologies of Emotion, Hume to Austen* (Stanford, CA: Stanford University Press, 1996).
39. Andrew M. Stauffer, *Anger, Revolution, and Romanticism* (Cambridge: Cambridge University, 2005); Nancy Yousef, *Romantic Intimacy* (Stanford, CA: Stanford University Press, 2013); Melissa Sodeman, *Sentimental Memorials: Women and the Novel in Literary History* (Stanford, CA: Stanford University Press, 2014); and Deidre Shauna Lynch, *Loving Literature: A Cultural History* (Chicago: University of Chicago Press, 2015).
40. Pinch, *Strange Fits of Passion*, 4.
41. Coleridge, *Biographia Literaria*, 1:59.
42. Walter Scott, review of *Childe Harold's Pilgrimage*, Canto IV, by Lord Byron, *Quarterly Review* (April 1818), in *RR*, part B, 5:2049.
43. William Wordsworth, *A Letter to a Friend of Robert Burns: Occasioned by an Intended Republication of the Account of the Life of Burns, by Dr. Currie* (London: Longman, 1816), 19–20.

44. Isaac D'Israeli, *A Dissertation on Anecdotes* (1793; facsimile, New York: Garland, 1972), 14 and 51.
45. Eisner, *Nineteenth-Century Poetry and Literary Celebrity*, 1.
46. Scott, "Memoir," 1.
47. D'Israeli, *Dissertation on Anecdotes*, 73.
48. Wordsworth, *Letter to a Friend*, 16.
49. Lynch, *Loving Literature*, 248.
50. Review of *The Packet*, *Critical Review* 11 (May 1794): 181, emphasis in the original; and Crabb, *English Synonymes Explained*, 28.
51. Review of *Poems*, by Lord Byron, *Farrago* (June 1816), in *RR*, part B, 3:1046.
52. Percy Bysshe Shelley, "A Defence of Poetry," in *Shelley's Poetry and Prose*, ed. Donald H. Reiman and Neil Fraistat (New York: Norton, 2002), 517.
53. Coleridge, *Biographia Literaria*, 1:8.
54. Coleridge, 2:7.
55. Joanna Baillie, *Plays on the Passions*, ed. Peter Buthie (Peterborough, ON: Broadview Press, 2001), 69 and 78.
56. Adam Smith, *The Theory of Moral Sentiments*, ed. D. D. Raphael and A. L. Macfie (Indianapolis: Liberty Fund, 1982), 29.
57. Johnson, *Dictionary of the English Language*, s.v. "familiarity."
58. Smith, *Theory of Moral Sentiments*, 306.
59. J. M., *The agreeable variety . . . Containing . . . discourses, characters, and poems, relating to the most useful subjects* (London: printed for the author, 1717), 218.
60. Hester Lynch Piozzi, *British Synonymy; or, An Attempt at Regulating the Choice of Words in Familiar Conversation* (London: G. G. and J. Robinson, 1794), 1:17, HathiTrust, https://hdl.handle.net/2027/nyp.33433069256968 (accessed May 30, 2021).
61. Jonas Hanway quoted in Bridget Hill, *Servants: English Domestics in the Eighteenth Century* (Oxford: Oxford University Press, 1996), 110, emphasis in the original.
62. Samuel Adams and Sarah Adams, *The Complete Servant; Being a Practical Guide to the Peculiar Duties and Business of All Descriptions of Servants* (London: Knight and Lacey, 1825), 10, HathiTrust, https://hdl.handle.net/2027/pst.000005795819 (accessed May 30, 2021). I owe my awareness of this source to Kristina Straub, *Domestic Affairs: Intimacy, Eroticism, and Violence Between Servants and Masters in Eighteenth-Century Britain* (Baltimore: Johns Hopkins University Press, 2009).
63. For more on the "servant problem," see Straub, *Domestic Affairs.*
64. John Styles, "Involuntary Consumers? Servants and Their Clothes in Eighteenth-Century England," *Textile History* 33, no. 1 (2002): 9.
65. William Hazlitt, "On Vulgarity and Affectation," in *The Selected Writings of William Hazlitt* (hereafter *SWWH*), ed. Duncan Wu (London: Pickering and Chatto, 1998), 6:139.
66. Mary Wollstonecraft, *A Vindication of the Rights of Woman and a Vindication of the Rights of Men*, ed. Janet M. Todd (Oxford: Oxford University Press, 2008), 205.
67. For more on the role of familiarity in Dissenting thought and pedagogy, see Anne Janowitz, "Amiable and Radical Sociability: Anna Barbauld's 'Free Familiar Conversation,'" in *Romantic Sociability: Social Networks and Literary Culture in Britain, 1770–1840*, ed. Gillian Russell and Clara Tuite (Cambridge: Cambridge University Press, 2002), 62–81. As Janowitz notes, William Turner used the phrase "free and familiar conversation" to describe John Aikin's pedagogy.
68. Michèle Cohen, "'Familiar Conversation': The Role of the 'Familiar Format' in Education in Eighteenth- and Nineteenth-Century England,' in *Educating the Child in Enlightenment Britain: Beliefs, Cultures, Practices*, ed. Mary Hilton and Jill Shefrin (Burlington, VT: Ashgate, 2009), 112 and 110.

69. Rachael Scarborough King, *Writing to the World: Letters and the Origins of Modern Print Genres* (Baltimore: Johns Hopkins University Press, 2018), 5.
70. For more on eighteenth-century letter-writing manuals and familiarity, see Sarah M. S. Pearsall, *Atlantic Families: Lives and Letters in the Later Eighteenth Century* (Oxford: Oxford University Press, 2008), especially 67–79. For an earlier but still valuable overview of the familiar letter's literary and social importance, see Howard Anderson, Philip B. Daghlian, and Irvin Ehrenpreis, eds., *The Familiar Letter in the Eighteenth Century* (Lawrence: University Press of Kansas, 1968). Michelle Levy and Betty A. Schellenberg offer three helpful case studies of eighteenth-century familiar correspondences. Levy and Schellenberg, *How and Why to Do Things with Eighteenth-Century Manuscripts* (Cambridge: Cambridge University Press, 2021), 30–49,
71. Konstantin Dierks, "The Familiar Letter and Social Refinement in America, 1750–1800," in *Letter Writing as a Social Practice*, ed. David Barton and Nigel Hall (Philadelphia: John Benjamins, 1999), 34.
72. Clifford H. Siskin, *The Historicity of Romantic Discourse* (Oxford: Oxford University Press, 1988), 93.
73. Jane Austen, *Emma*, ed. Kristin Flieger Samuelian (Peterborough, ON: Broadview Press, 2004), 256.
74. Jane Austen, *Mansfield Park*, ed. James Kinsley (Oxford: Oxford University Press, 2008), 121, emphasis in the original.
75. Jane Austen, *Pride and Prejudice*, ed. Robert P. Irvine (Peterborough, ON: Broadview Press, 2002), 203.
76. William Godwin, *Caleb Williams*, ed. Gary Handwerk and A. A. Markley (Peterborough, ON: Broadview Press, 2000), 182.
77. Godwin, 76.
78. *Donaldson v. Beckett* in 1774 reaffirmed the earlier 1710 Act of Queen Anne, which rejected the principle of perpetual copyright. The case shortened the term of copyright for new works and allowed numerous older texts to enter the public domain. For work on *Donaldson v. Beckett*'s importance in the expansion of the British reading public, see Mark Rose, *Authors and Owners: The Invention of Copyright* (Cambridge, MA: Harvard University Press, 1993); William St Clair, *The Reading Nation in the Romantic Period* (Cambridge: Cambridge University Press, 2004), especially 43–65 and 103–121; and James Raven, *The Business of Books: Booksellers and the English Book Trade 1450–1850* (New Haven, CT: Yale University Press, 2007), especially 230–238. For an alternative view, see J. E. Elliott, "The Cost of Reading in Eighteenth-Century Britain: Auction Sale Catalogues and the Cheap Literature Hypothesis," *ELH* 77, no. 2 (2010): 353–384.
79. Stereotype technology was available in the eighteenth century, but it only began to be used on a wider scale in the early nineteenth century.
80. According to Raven, "In 1782 the Post Office annually dispatched some three million London newspapers to the rest of the country. Ten years later, the volume had doubled, and by 1796 the annual postal distribution of London newspapers stood at 8.6 million copies." Raven, *Business of Books*, 258–259.
81. Jackson, *Romantic Readers*, 1–59; Deidre Shauna Lynch, *The Economy of Character: Novels, Market Culture, and the Business of Inner Meaning* (Chicago: Chicago University Press, 1998), especially 129–131 and 220–221; Patrick Brantlinger, *The Reading Lesson: The Threat of Mass Literacy in Nineteenth-Century British Fiction* (Bloomington: University of Indiana Press, 1998); and St Clair, *Reading Nation*, 103–121. Though Jon Klancher suggests, "No mass audiences would clearly appear in England before the 1820s," he acknowledges the massive growth of periodicals from the 1790s onward and a corresponding growth of different groups and classes of readers. Klancher, *Making of English Reading*

Audiences, 43. An answer to Klancher might be in historical perceptions of mass reading versus hard evidence of it. Ina Ferris observes that "whatever empirical data on literacy (and they are notoriously problematic), the *perception* in the [contemporary] reviews was of a huge, recent increase in readers." Ferris, *The Achievement of Literary Authority: Gender, History, and the Waverly Novels* (Ithaca, NY: Cornell University Press, 1991), 22.

82. [John Wilson], "Monologue or Soliloquy on the Annuals," *Blackwood's Edinburgh Magazine* 29, no. 160 (December 1829): 950.
83. Elliott, "Cost of Reading," 376.
84. David Allan, *A Nation of Readers: The Lending Library in Georgian England* (London: British Library, 2008), 122–124.
85. Ina Ferris, *Book-Men, Book Clubs and the Romantic Literary Sphere* (New York: Palgrave Macmillan, 2015), 101–154.
86. For more on salacious content in *Town and Country* and other eighteenth-century periodicals, see John Brewer, "Personal Scandal and Politics in Eighteenth-Century England: Secrecy, Intimacy, and the Interior Self in the Public Sphere," in *Media and Political Culture in the Eighteenth Century*, ed. Marie-Christine Skuncke (Stockholm: Kungl. Vitterhets Historie och Antikvitetsakademien, 2005), 84–106.
87. Coleridge, *Biographia Literaria*, 1:41n. Coleridge's note quotes his earlier essay from *The Friend*.
88. Robert Southey, quoted in Thomas Keymer, "Sterne and Romantic Autobiography," in *The Cambridge Companion to English Literature, 1750–1830*, ed. Thomas Keymer and Jon Mee (Cambridge: Cambridge University Press, 2004), 173.
89. [Thomas Colley Grattan], "The Confessions of an English Glutton," *Blackwood's Edinburgh Magazine* 13, no. 72 (January 1823): 86.
90. Jean-Jacques Rousseau, *The Confessions*, trans. J. M. Cohen (New York: Penguin, 1953), 65. For the scene involving Mme Clot's cooking pot, see 21–22.
91. Samuel Johnson, *The Lives of the Poets: A Selection*, ed. Roger Lonsdale (Oxford: Oxford University Press, 2006), 408.
92. William Wordsworth, Preface to *Lyrical Ballads*, in *Lyrical Ballads: 1798 and 1800*, by William Wordsworth and Samuel Taylor Coleridge, ed. Michael Gamer and Dahlia Porter (Peterborough, ON: Broadview Press, 2008), 177.
93. Lord Byron, *Don Juan*, vol. 5 of *Lord Byron: The Complete Poetical Works*, ed. Jerome McGann (Oxford: Clarendon, 1980–1993), 4.109. Further references to Byron's works are from this edition, hereafter *CPW*. Paula R. Feldman points to Southey's belief that the annuals caused declining sales of single-author poetry collections, in "Women, Literary Annuals, and the Evidence of Inscriptions," *Keats-Shelley Journal* 55 (2006): 54.
94. Coleridge, *Lay Sermons*, ed. R. J. White, in *Collected Works of Samuel Taylor Coleridge*, 6:169.
95. Coleridge, 171.
96. William Wordsworth, *The Prelude: 1799, 1805, 1850*, ed. Jonathan Wordsworth, M. H. Abrams, and Stephen Gill (New York: Norton, 1979), 7.117–120. All quotations are from the 1805 version of the poem.
97. Hazlitt, "On Londoners and Country People," in *SWWH*, 8:69.
98. Hazlitt, 8:70. Benedict Anderson, *Imagined Communities: Reflections on the Origin and Spread of Nationalism*, rev. ed. (New York: Verso, 2016).
99. Mole, *Byron's Romantic Celebrity*, 2.
100. Nicola Parsons, *Reading Gossip in Early Eighteenth-Century England* (Basingstoke, UK: Palgrave, 2009), 34.
101. Scott, review of *Childe Harold's Pilgrimage*, Canto IV, 5:2049.

102. David A. Brewer, *The Afterlife of Character, 1726–1825* (Philadelphia: University of Pennsylvania Press, 2005), 2.
103. Brewer, 17.
104. Brewer, 194. I want to be clear that I agree with Brewer that the changing political landscape in the Romantic period made it more difficult to imagine a unified readerly "public" than earlier in the eighteenth century. Indeed, Matthew Sangster's recent work on professional authorship notes that writers had to contend with "the conflicting ideologies of fissile and heterogeneous groups that reflected the divisions and uncertainties of an age of political, military and moral strife," and his observations reaffirm Brewer's earlier claims. Sangster, *Living as an Author in the Romantic Period* (Basingstoke, UK: Palgrave, 2021), 84. However, I suggest that if there was common ground to be had among readers—or at least subgroups of readers—then interest in authors' private lives offered an attractive prospect.
105. Lauren Berlant, "Intimacy: A Special Issue," in "Intimacy," edited by Lauren Berland, special issue, *Critical Inquiry* 24, no. 2 (1998): 281.
106. Lynch, *Economy of Character*, 135.
107. Patricia Meyer Spacks, *Privacy: Concealing the Eighteenth-Century Self* (Chicago: University of Chicago Press, 2003), 13.
108. Lynch, *Economy of Character*, 210.
109. Scott, review of *Childe Harold's Pilgrimage*, Canto IV, 5:2049.
110. Bourdieu, *Field of Cultural Production*, 34.
111. Charlotte Smith, "Preface to Volume II," in *Elegiac Sonnets*, in *The Poems of Charlotte Smith*, ed. Stuart Curran (Oxford: Oxford University Press, 1993), 11, emphasis in the original.
112. William Wordsworth, Advertisement, in *Lyrical Ballads*, 47.
113. Henry Crabb Robinson, quoted in P. P. Howe, *The Life of William Hazlitt* (London: Hamish Hamilton, 1947), 326.
114. Brian Glavey, "Lyric Wilt, or, The Here and Now of Queer Impotentiality," *New Literary History* 51, no. 3 (2020): 583.
115. Tony Bravo, "In the Oversharing Age, Why Some Parents Won't Post Photos of Their Kids," *San Francisco Chronicle Online*, April 18, 2019, https://www.sfchronicle.com/style/article/In-the-oversharing-age-why-some-parents-won-t-13776168.php (accessed May 30, 2021). For other examples of concerns about oversharing, see Kathy Caprino, "How Social Media Over-Sharing about Your Child Can Cause Irrevocable Harm," *Forbes*, April 12, 2019, https://www.forbes.com/sites/kathycaprino/2019/04/12/how-social-media-over-sharing-about-your-child-can-cause-irrevocable-harm (accessed May 30, 2021); and Gabrielle Parsons, "The Millennial Dating Struggle: Trying to Find Honesty in the Age of Oversharing," *Blavity*, June 13, 2018, https://blavity.com/the-millennial-dating-struggle-trying-to-find-honesty-in-the-age-of-oversharing?category1=community-submitted (accessed May 30, 2021).
116. "Memoir in the Age of T.M.I.," hosted by Amelia Lester and David Haglund, in *Out Loud* podcast, *New Yorker*, April 14, 2015, https://www.newyorker.com/podcast/out-loud/memoir-in-the-age-of-tmi (accessed May 30, 2021); Margot Kaminski, "Toward Defining Privacy Expectations in an Age of Oversharing," *The Economist*, August 16, 2018, https://www.economist.com/open-future/2018/08/16/toward-defining-privacy-expectations-in-an-age-of-oversharing (accessed May 30, 2021); and Andrea Brandt, "How to Set Boundaries in the Age of Oversharing," *Psychology Today* blog, December 2, 2019, https://www.psychologytoday.com/us/blog/mindful-anger/201912/how-set-boundaries-in-the-age-oversharing (accessed May 30, 2021).

CHAPTER 1 — CHARLOTTE SMITH, WILLIAM WORDSWORTH, AND THE PROBLEMS OF READING FAMILIARITY

* Charlotte Smith, "Preface to Volume II," in *Elegiac Sonnets*, in *The Poems of Charlotte Smith*, ed. Stuart Curran (Oxford: Oxford University Press, 1993), 11, emphasis in the original. Further references to Smith's poetry are from this edition; paratexts are cited by page, longer poems by book and line number, and sonnets by poem number, title, page, and line numbers.

1. Wordsworth, Advertisement, in *Lyrical Ballads*, 47.
2. Wordsworth, 47.
3. Wordsworth, "Essays Upon Epitaphs," in *The Prose Works of William Wordsworth*, ed. W.J.B. Owen and Jane Worthington Smyser (Oxford: Clarendon Press, 1974), 2:66.
4. Wordsworth, 70.
5. Wordsworth, 70.
6. Coleridge, *Biographia Literaria*, 2:17 and 2:7.
7. Samuel Taylor Coleridge, "Fears in Solitude. Written in April, 1798, During the Alarm of an Invasion," in *Samuel Taylor Coleridge: The Complete Poems*, ed. William Keach (New York: Penguin, 2004), lines 105–107.
8. Edmund Burke, *A Philosophical Enquiry into the Origin of Our Ideas of the Sublime and Beautiful*, ed. Adam Phillips (Oxford: Oxford University Press, 2008), 29.
9. Burke, 57.
10. For an alternative reading that argues for Wordsworth's Burkean conservatism, see James K. Chandler, *Wordsworth's Second Nature: A Study of the Poetry and Politics* (Chicago: University of Chicago Press, 1984).
11. Smith, "To William Cowper, Esq.," in *The Emigrants*, 132.
12. Wordsworth, "Essays Upon Epitaphs," 66.
13. Smith, *The Emigrants*, 2.353–354.
14. For Smith's role in the sonnet revival, see Stuart Curran, *Poetic Form and British Romanticism* (Oxford: Oxford University Press, 1986), 29–55. Bethan Roberts offers the most comprehensive recent assessment of Smith and the sonnet revival in *Charlotte Smith and the Sonnet: Form, Place, and Tradition in the Late Eighteenth Century* (Liverpool: Liverpool University Press, 2019).
15. Using G. Thomas Tanselle's definition of *edition*, it remains unclear how many editions of *Elegiac Sonnets* there were. Curran's textual notes to *The Poems of Charlotte Smith* refer to nine editions (313). However, Smith herself believed there were ten; in a letter in 1806 she told the publisher Joseph Johnson that "*the 1st volume* [of *Elegiac Sonnets*] *is in the 10th* [edition]." Smith to Joseph Johnson, July 12, 1806, in Judith Phillips Stanton, ed., *The Collected Letters of Charlotte Smith* (Bloomington: Indiana University Press, 2003), 742, emphasis in the original. In this chapter I do not use *edition* in the strict bibliographical sense. Instead, I refer to six editions of *Elegiac Sonnets*, this number being taken from Smith's prefaces to the collection, the latest of which is entitled "Preface to the Sixth Edition." For more information on thorny questions of edition, issue, and state, see G. Thomas Tanselle, "The Bibliographical Concepts of *Issue* and *State*," *Papers of the Bibliographic Society of America* 69, no. 1 (1975): 17–66.
16. Smith, "Preface to Volume II," 11, emphasis in the original.
17. Robert Bisset, "The History of Literature for 1799," in *The Historical, Biographical, Literary, and Scientific Magazine. The History of Europe, for the Year 1799* (London: G. Cawthorn, [1800?]), 1:70, ESTC Number N52538, Eighteenth Century Collections Online (hereafter ECCO). In ECCO this is listed as volume 2, but the title page of the volume indicates that is it volume 1.

18. Review of *Ethelinde, Biographical and Imperial Magazine* (January 1790), in *Romantic Women Writers Reviewed*, ed. Ann R. Hawkins (London: Pickering and Chatto, 2011–2013), 2:293. Subsequent references to reprinted reviews in *Romantic Women Writers Reviewed* (hereafter *RWWR*) include the review's original publication venue, month, and year, followed by the relevant volume and page number in *RWWR*.
19. Jacqueline Labbe, *Writing Romanticism: Charlotte Smith and William Wordsworth, 1784–1807* (New York: Palgrave, 2011), 23.
20. Mathew Arnold, "Memorial Verses," in *The Oxford Poetry Library: Matthew Arnold*, ed. Miriam Allot (Oxford: Oxford University Press, 1995), line 67; and Seward to Theophilus Swift, July 9, 1789, in *Letters of Anna Seward: Written between the Years 1784 and 1807* (Edinburgh and London: Constable, Longman, Hurst, Rees, Orme, and Brown, William Miller, and John Murray, 1811), 2:287.
21. Anna Laetitia Barbauld, "Mrs. Charlotte Smith," in *The Old Manor House* by Charlotte Smith, vol. 36 of *The British Novelists; with an Essay; and Prefaces, Biographical and Critical*, ed. Anna Laetitia Barbauld (London: Rivington, 1810), viii, HathiTrust, https://babel.hathitrust.org/cgi/pt?id=nyp.33433112069152 (accessed June 1, 2021).
22. Charlotte Smith, Preface to *The Banished Man. A Novel* (London: Cadell and Davies, 1794), 1:viii, ESTC Number T70700, ECCO.
23. Bisset, "History of Literature for 1799," 241 and 70–71.
24. Mary Wollstonecraft, *Analytical Review* (August 1791), quoted in Sodeman, *Sentimental Memorials*, 79.
25. Judith Pascoe, *Romantic Theatricality: Gender, Poetry and Spectatorship* (Ithaca, NY: Cornell University Press, 1997), 16. Sodeman similarly suggests that Smith's "tale of woe followed an established script that had already been played out many times before." Sodeman, *Sentimental Memorials*, 83.
26. Jacqueline M. Labbe, *Charlotte Smith: Romanticism, Poetry, and the Culture of Gender* (Manchester: Manchester University Press, 2003), 5. See also Jacqueline M. Labbe, "Selling One's Sorrows: Charlotte Smith, Mary Robinson, and the Marketing of Poetry," *Wordsworth Circle* 25, no. 3 (1994): 68–71.
27. Burke, *Philosophical Enquiry*, 29.
28. For Labbe the question is not whether sincerity animates Smith and Wordsworth's works "but whether the two poets are at the mercy of sincerity's inherent insincerity, or whether they play with this tension." Labbe, "Revisiting the Egotistical Sublime: Smith, Wordsworth, and the Dramatic Monologue," in *Fellow Romantics: Male and Female British Writers, 1790–1835*, ed. Beth Lau (Surrey, UK: Ashgate, 2009), 19.
29. Pinch, *Strange Fits of Passion*, 60.
30. There is a growing amount of work on Smith's speakers and ventriloquism, including Christopher Stokes, "Lorn Subjects: Haunting, Fracture and Ascesis in Charlotte Smith's *Elegiac Sonnets*," *Women's Writing* 16, no. 1 (2009): 143–160; Mary Anne Myers, "Unsexing Petrarch: Charlotte Smith's Lessons in the Sonnet as Social Medium," *Studies in Romanticism* 53, no. 2 (2014): 239–263; and Joy Currie, "'Mature Poets Steal': Charlotte Smith's Appropriations of Shakespeare," in *Shakespeare and the Culture of Romanticism*, ed. Joseph M. Ortiz, 2nd ed. (London: Routledge, 2016), 99–120. Labbe thoughtfully addresses the relationship between Smith's ventriloquism, sincerity, and dramatic monologue in *Writing Romanticism*, 106–119.
31. Curran, introduction to *Poems of Charlotte Smith*, xxvi.
32. Smith expanded the number of Werter-voiced sonnets from three to five in the third edition. For consistency, throughout the chapter I use Smith's spelling of "Werter" rather than "Werther."

33. John Hollander, *The Figure of Echo: A Mode of Allusion in Milton and After* (Berkeley: University of California Press, 1981), 72.
34. Judith Pascoe, "Female Botanists and the Poetry of Charlotte Smith," in *Re-visioning Romanticism: British Women Writers, 1776–1837*, ed. Carol Shiner Wilson and Joel Haefner (Philadelphia: University of Pennsylvania Press, 1994), 197. More recently, Ruth Knezevich has used distant reading techniques to make the related point that female poets' extensive notes "exercis[e] authority in the gendered sphere of literary genres." Knezevich, "Females and Footnotes: Excavating the Genre of Eighteenth-Century Women's Scholarly Verse," *ABO: Interactive Journal for Women in the Arts, 1640–1830* 6, no. 2 (2016): 1.
35. Michael Gamer, *Romanticism, Self-Canonization, and the Business of Poetry* (Cambridge: Cambridge University Press, 2017), 64.
36. Seward to Reverend Berwick, October 6, 1788, *Letters of Anna Seward*, 2:162.
37. Smith, "XXI. Supposed to be written by Werter," 26, lines 5–8.
38. Smith, "I. The partial Muse has from my earliest hours," 13, lines 13–14, emphasis in the original.
39. Smith, "I. The partial Muse has from my earliest hours," in *Elegiac Sonnets*, by Charlotte Smith, 4th ed., corrected (London: J. Dodsley, H. Gardner, and J. Bew, 1786), 2, lines 13–14. The third and subsequent editions of *Elegiac Sonnets* differ substantially from each other and from the first two editions. Smith added a significant number of poems, reordered them, and introduced endnotes and (in some editions) in-text indicators for endnotes. The bibliographic particularities of each edition are beyond the scope of my arguments here. Gamer discusses Smith's revisions and their importance in *Romanticism, Self-Canonization, and the Business of Poetry*, 54–90.
40. Smith changed how she signaled endnotes in different editions of *Elegiac Sonnets*. For instance, whereas in the third and fourth editions "*(a)*" flags the endnote to Pope's "Eloisa to Abelard," in the fifth edition the line remains italicized as before, and the endnote is present; however, no indicator of the note appears in the poem proper.
41. Smith, "XXIII. By the same. To the North Star," 28, line 2; and "IV. To the Moon," 15, line 7. Further references to these sonnets are parenthetical by line number.
42. Smith, "V. To the South Downs," 16, lines 13–14.
43. Smith, "Preface to Volume II," 10.
44. Smith, "Preface to the First and Second Editions," in *Elegiac Sonnets*, 3.
45. Susan B. Rosenbaum also addresses Smith's repetition in *Professing Sincerity: Modern Lyric Poetry, Commercial Culture, and the Crisis of Reading* (Charlottesville: University of Virginia Press, 2007), 113. For an alternative argument about the sequential nature of *Elegiac Sonnets*, see Gamer, *Romanticism, Self-Canonization*, 70–72.
46. Gamer, *Romanticism, Self-Canonization*, 68.
47. Paul Westover has shown how highly intertextual poems like "The Grave of the Poetess," though ostensibly about Mary Tighe, demonstrate Felicia Hemans's attempt to historicize her own future death to establish her canonicity. Westover, "Imaginary Pilgrimages: Felicia Hemans, Dead Poets, and Romantic Historiography," *Literature Compass* 2 (2005): 6–8. Recall, too, that Hemans's "Woman and Fame" borrows its epigraph from her earlier poem "Corinne at the Capitol." Relatedly, Sarah Anne Storti has analyzed Landon's practice of republishing her own works, effectively revising her own canon in the process. Storti, "Letitia Landon: Still a Problem," *Victorian Poetry* 57, no. 4 (2019): 533–556. In *Romanticism, Self-Canonization, and the Business of Poetry* Gamer also notes Smith's preoccupation with self-canonization, yet his work focuses on the level of "re-collection"—a new authorized edition or collection of a poet's work produced in their lifetime, of which later editions of *Elegiac Sonnets* are a prime example—rather than on the level of the poem.

48. Smith, "LXIII. The gossamer," 55, lines 5–6.
49. Roberts, *Charlotte Smith and the Sonnet,* 147; and Smith, "XLVIII. To Mrs. ****," 45, lines 6–8.
50. Smith, "LXIII. The gossamer," 55.
51. Review of *Elegiac Sonnets, Critical Review: or, Annals of Literature* 57 (June 1784): 472, Google Books, http://google.cat/books?id=lRQFAAAAYAAJ (accessed April 23, 2021).
52. "On Sonnets," *Lady's Magazine* (May 1789), in *RWWR,* 1:268.
53. Seward to Theophilus Swift, July 9, 1789, *Letters of Anna Seward,* 2:287.
54. According to Amy Garnai, the fact that "*Elegiac Sonnets I* (1789) had 817 subscribers, but *Elegiac Sonnets II* [in 1797] had only 283" suggests waning public interest and a backlash against Smith's supposed Jacobinism. Garnai, *Revolutionary Imaginings in the 1790s: Charlotte Smith, Mary Robinson, Elizabeth Inchbald* (Basingstoke, UK: Palgrave Macmillan, 2009), 46. However, despite a decreased number of subscribers, Smith's work remained profitable and popular.
55. "D.," "Sonnet To Mrs. Smith on Reading Her Sonnets Lately Published," *European Magazine* 9 (May 1786): 366, emphasis in the original.
56. Smith, "Preface to the First and Second Editions," 3.
57. "T. B.," "Elegiac Sonnet. To Charlotte Smith," *Biographical and Imperial Magazine* (March 1790), in *RWWR,* 2:294. For more on sonnets written to Smith by her readers, see Claire Knowles, *Sensibility and Female Poetic Tradition, 1780–1860: The Legacy of Charlotte Smith* (Surrey, UK: Ashgate, 2009), 57–67.
58. Smith, "Preface to the Sixth Edition," in *Elegiac Sonnets,* 6.
59. Smith, 5, emphasis in the original.
60. Smith, "XLVII. To fancy," 44, lines 1–5. Further references to this sonnet are parenthetical by line number.
61. Wordsworth, Preface to *Lyrical Ballads,* 178.
62. Smith, "XLVIII. To Mrs. ****," 45, line 3.
63. Smith, line 6.
64. Smith, "Preface to the First and Second Editions," 3. Michelle Levy notes that Smith's claims about the private manuscript origins of *Elegiac Sonnets* "became increasingly strained as the number of poems increased greatly, from sixteen in 1784 to ninety-two in 1800." Levy, *Literary Manuscript Culture in Romantic Britain* (Edinburgh: Edinburgh University Press, 2020), 41.
65. Smith, "XLVIII. To Mrs. ****," line 1. In a contrasting reading, Esther Schor argues that "Smith's sense of rhetorical failure is a displacement of her failure to move her well-placed friends to ameliorate her situation: the continuing oppression of enforced dependence on the husband whose livelihood, in fact, depended on her earnings." Schor, *Bearing the Dead: The British Culture of Mourning from the Enlightenment to Victoria* (Princeton, NJ: Princeton University Press, 1994), 64. Schor's connection between the failure of fancy in the poems and Smith's failure to overcome her financial and legal difficulties differs from my own emphasis on Smith's use of the rhetoric of failure to convey sincerity.
66. Burke, *Philosophical Enquiry,* 42.
67. "The Enquirer. No. IX, Question: Ought Sensibility to be Cherished, or Repressed?," *Monthly Magazine* 2, no. 9 (October 1796): 707, HathiTrust, https://hdl.handle.net/2027/chi.16684863 (accessed February 20, 2021).
68. Hannah More, "Sensibility: A Poetical Epistle to the Hon. Mrs. Boscawen," in *Sacred Dramas: Chiefly Intended for Young Persons: The Subjects Taken from the Bible. To Which Is Added, Sensibility, A Poem* (London: Cadell, 1782), 284–285.
69. Keen, *Crisis of Literature,* 8. Though Keen analyzes contrasting elements of classical republicanism and bourgeois liberalism, his recognition that the Romantic period

shifted from the literary to the authorial informs my own ideas about the growing importance of authors' private lives to literary reception.

70. Stanhope, *Art of Pleasing*, 84.
71. Review of the 5th edition of *Elegiac Sonnets*, *European Magazine* (October 1789), in *RWWR*, 1:192; and review of *Desmond*, *European Magazine* (July 1792), Women Writers in Review (Northeastern University Women Writers Project, 2016), https://www.wwp.northeastern.edu/review/reviews/smith.desmond.europeanmag.1 (accessed April 23, 2021). Subsequent references to reviews in Women Writers in Review (hereafter WWR) include the review's original publication venue, month, and year; the URL in WWR is given only in the first reference to a review.
72. "Art. V. [Review of] *The Young Philosopher*," *Anti-Jacobin Review and Magazine* 1 (August 1798): 187. HathiTrust, https://hdl.handle.net/2027/chi.16481211 (accessed April 23, 2021).
73. Smith's moves are documented in Elizabeth A. Dolan and Gillian Andrews, Charlotte Smith Story Map, 2018, https://arcg.is/08POqD (accessed April 23, 2021).
74. For a discussion of the will and its influence on Smith's life and work, see Loraine Fletcher, *Charlotte Smith: A Critical Biography* (New York: Palgrave, 1998), 4–58. So famous was Smith's lengthy legal battle that it may have been the inspiration for *Jarndyce v. Jarndyce* in Charles Dickens's *Bleak House.*
75. Smith to Thomas Cadell Sr., September 8, 1790, *Collected Letters of Charlotte Smith*, 29, emphasis in the original. Smith's complaints about the conditions under which she wrote reflect larger trends of Romantic-era professional authorship that Matthew Sangster has recently explored. Smith and many other professional authors "who needed money were often forced to work at an extremely high speed. Generally this impeded their quality of life, necessitating borrowing, thrift and writing for long periods in poor light and circumstances." Sangster, *Living as an Author*, 29.
76. For a detailed account of Smith's finances, see Judith Phillips Stanton, "Charlotte Smith's 'Literary Business': Income, Patronage, and Indigence," *Age of Johnson: A Scholarly Journal* 1 (1987): 375–401.
77. Review of *Ethelinde*, *Biographical and Imperial Magazine*, 2:293.
78. Barbauld, "Mrs. Charlotte Smith," vi.
79. Bourdieu, *Field of Cultural Production*, 40.
80. William Wordsworth to Joseph Cottle, [Summer?] 1799, in *The Letters of William and Dorothy Wordsworth*, vol. 1, *The Early Years 1787–1805*, ed. Ernest De Selincourt and Chester L. Shaver, 2nd ed. (Oxford: Clarendon Press, 1967), 267.
81. Smith, "Preface to Volume II," 8.
82. For information on coverage of the trial, see Daniel O'Quinn, *Staging Governance: Theatrical Imperialism in London, 1770–1800* (Baltimore: Johns Hopkins University Press, 2005), 165–221. The most thorough examination of fears of regicide in the 1790s and their ideological and political relevance is John Barrell, *Imagining the King's Death: Figurative Treason, Fantasies of Regicide 1793–1796* (Oxford: Oxford University Press, 2000).
83. Toby Ruth Benis, "'Likely Story': Charlotte Smith's Revolutionary Narratives," *European Romantic Review* 14, no. 3 (2003): 295.
84. Roberts, *Charlotte Smith and the Sonnet*, 103. Labbe notes that in *The Emigrants*, Smith "treads a dangerous line" and "comes perilously close to" imagining the death of the king and opening herself up to charges of sedition. Labbe, *Charlotte Smith*, 132–133.
85. Scholars have interrogated Smith's supposed retreat from her enthusiastic support of the French Revolution and have argued for more nuanced understandings of her politics. See, for instance, Antje Blank, "Things as They Were: The Gothic of Real Life in Charlotte Smith's *The Emigrants* and *The Banished Man*," *Women's Writing* 16, no. 1 (2009):

78–93; Garnai, *Revolutionary Imaginings in the 1790s*, especially 13–68; and Fuson Wang, "Cosmopolitanism and the Radical Politics of Exile in Charlotte Smith's *Desmond*," *Eighteenth-Century Fiction* 25, no. 1 (2012): 37–59. However, for many of Smith's contemporaries, her work after *Desmond* indicated a political about-face for which she was alternately praised and derided.

86. Alexander Welsh, *Strong Representations: Narrative and Circumstantial Evidence in England* (Baltimore: Johns Hopkins University Press, 1992), 8.
87. Annette Wheeler Cafarelli, *Prose in the Age of Poets: Romanticism and Biographical Narrative from Johnson to De Quincey* (Philadelphia: University of Pennsylvania Press, 1990), 23.
88. Smith, "Preface to Volume II," 11, emphasis in the original.
89. Samuel Whyte, "Lines, by Samuel Whyte, Esq. of Grafton-Street, In Answer to the Foregoing," in *The Protected Fugitives. A Collection of Miscellaneous Poems*, by Henrietta Battier (Dublin: James Porter, 1791), 204, ESTC Number T189070, ECCO.
90. Labbe, *Charlotte Smith*, 28.
91. Andrew Stauffer's comments about Byron's anger apply equally to Smith. A poet's angry outburst causes readers to question whether "the poet is either overacting (and thus insincere) or overreacting (and thus unsympathetic). In either case, the sincerity effect is disabled. . . . Such readerly detachment opens a gap into which rush hermeneutic suspicions and judgments." Stauffer, *Anger, Revolution, and Romanticism*, 137.
92. Kerry Sinanan and Tim Milnes, introduction to *Romanticism, Sincerity and Authenticity*, ed. Tim Milnes and Kerry Sinanan (Basingstoke, UK: Palgrave Macmillan, 2010), 15.
93. Sarah M. Zimmerman, "Varieties of Privacy in Charlotte Smith's Poetry," *European Romantic Review* 18, no. 4 (2007): 488. Other scholars also forward claims about the poetic ambiguity surrounding Smith's sorrow. Karen Weismen, for instance, identifies Smith's "vagueness about her life." Weisman, "Form and Loss in Charlotte Smith's *Elegiac Sonnets*," *Wordsworth Circle* 33, no. 1 (2002): 25. Similarly, Claire Knowles argues that Smith retained her propriety and her audience's interest by alluding to "her troubles in general terms." Knowles, *Sensibility and Female Poetic Tradition*, 50.
94. Stephen Behrendt, "Charlotte Smith, Women Poets, and the Culture of Celebrity," in *Charlotte Smith in British Romanticism*, ed. Jacqueline Labbe (London: Pickering and Chatto, 2008), 196.
95. Smith, "Preface to Volume II," 8.
96. Smith, "To the Goddess of Botany," 68n.
97. Smith, Preface to *Banished Man*, x, emphasis in the original.
98. Smith, Preface to *Desmond*, ed. Antje Blank and Janet Todd (Peterborough, ON: Broadview Press, 2001), 46, emphasis in the original; and Smith, Preface to *Banished Man*, vi.
99. Review of *The Emigrants, A Poem, In Two Books, Critical Review* (November 1793), WWR, https://www.wwp.northeastern.edu/review/reviews/smith.emigrants.criticalreview.1 (accessed April 23, 2021).
100. Review of *The Emigrants*.
101. Curran, introduction to *Poems of Charlotte Smith*, xxi.
102. Baillie, *Plays on the Passions*, 69.
103. Smith, *Theory of Moral Sentiments*, 24.
104. Smith, 24.
105. Review of *The Emigrants*.
106. Smith, *Theory of Moral Sentiments*, 11–12.
107. Crabb, *English Synonymes Explained*, 28.
108. Smith, "Preface to the Sixth Edition," 6.

109. Smith, "Preface to Volume II," 8.
110. Smith, 8–9, emphasis in the original.
111. Smith, "Preface to the Sixth Edition," 6, emphasis in the original.
112. Smith, "Preface to Volume II," 8, emphasis in the original. Smith's reference to her "querulous egotism" evokes Coleridge's defense of sonnets and monodies, which he admits "are not unfrequently condemned for the querulous egotism." Coleridge, Preface to *Poems on Various Subjects*, by S. T. Coleridge (London: G. G. and J. Robinsons; Bristol: J. Cottle, 1796), v. The anti-Jacobin writer Robert Bisset specifically criticized "the querulous egotism of Charlotte Smith." Bisset, "History of Literature for 1799," 24.
113. Smith, "Preface to Volume II," 8.
114. Brewer notes something similar at work in "the crazes which surrounded *Tristram Shandy* and *A Sentimental Journey*." Laurence Sterne invited readers into a virtual community whose membership and appeal "lay in its exclusion of all those who were not 'true feelers,' however the latter might be defined." Brewer, *Afterlife of Character*, 155.
115. Smith, "Preface to the First and Second Editions," 3.
116. Smith, "Preface to the Third and Fourth Editions," in *Elegiac Sonnets*, 3.
117. Labbe, *Charlotte Smith*, 27.
118. Curran, introduction to *Poems of Charlotte Smith*, xxv.
119. Coleridge, *Biographia Literaria*, 2:7.
120. Wordsworth, "Essay, Supplementary to the Preface," in *Prose Works of William Wordsworth*, 3:62.
121. Wordsworth, "Note to the Thorn," in *Lyrical Ballads: 1798 and 1800*, 288.
122. Wordsworth, 288.
123. Coleridge, *Biographia Literaria*, 2:57, emphasis in the original.
124. Smith, "Preface to the Sixth Edition," 6.
125. Wordsworth, "Note to the Thorn," 288.
126. Wordsworth, "Essays Upon Epitaphs," 57.
127. Wordsworth, 65.
128. Wordsworth, 65–66.
129. Wordsworth, 70.
130. Angela Esterhammer, "The Scandal of Sincerity: Wordsworth, Byron, Landon," in Milnes and Sinanan, *Romanticism, Sincerity and Authenticity*, 105, emphasis in the original.
131. Wordsworth, "Essays Upon Epitaphs," 92.
132. Wordsworth, "Essay, Supplementary," 62.
133. Chandler interprets "Wordsworth's claim to egalitarian sentiment" in *The Prelude* differently, suggesting it arises from a Burkean notion of "the ancient English tradition of equality . . . not the egalitarianism generated out of cosmopolitan discussion of the abstract rights of men." Chandler, *Wordsworth's Second Nature*, 51. However, I think that Wordsworth's descriptions of his interactions, his valuing of everyday life, and his willingness to socialize familiarly with strangers from different classes does gesture toward more egalitarian values.
134. Wordsworth, "Note to the Thorn," 288.
135. Wordsworth, 288.
136. Wordsworth, "Essays Upon Epitaphs," 66.
137. Wordsworth, "Note to the Thorn," 288.

CHAPTER 2 — "THOUGH A STRANGER TO YOU"

* Review of *Childe Harold*, Canto III, *Portfolio, Political and Literary* (November 1816), in *RR*, part B, 5:1966. Unless otherwise noted, subsequent references to contemporary

reviews of Byron are from *RR*; I provide the review's original publication venue, month, and year followed by the relevant volume, part, and page number in *RR*.

1. Nicholas Mason makes a strong case for Byron's fame arising from *English Bards and Scotch Reviewers* (1809). Mason, *Literary Advertising and the Shaping of British Romanticism* (Baltimore: Johns Hopkins University Press, 2013), 68–80. While the public was primed for Byron's celebrity before *Childe Harold*, given Byron's vitriolic treatment of his contemporaries in *English Bards* and the negative reviews it received, Byron and John Murray were both invested in reshaping his celebrity in 1812.
2. Review of *Hebrew Melodies*, *Critical Review* (April 1816), in *RR*, part B, 2:647.
3. Tuite, *Lord Byron and Scandalous Celebrity*, xv.
4. I borrow the phrase "years of fame" from Peter Quennell, though I extend the "years of fame" through the 1818 publication of *Childe Harold* IV. Quennell, *Byron: The Years of Fame* (Hamden, CT: Archon Books, 1967).
5. Scott, review of *Childe Harold's Pilgrimage*, Canto IV, *Quarterly Review* (April 1818), in *RR*, part B, 5:2049.
6. "Licentious Productions in High Life," *Investigator* (October 1822), in *RR*, part B, 5:1192.
7. Review of *Childe Harold*, Canto III, *Portfolio, Political and Literary*, 5:1966.
8. Mary Fairclough observes that fears about the "contagion" of sympathy feature in eighteen-century moral philosophy, particularly by David Hume. Fairclough, *The Romantic Crowd: Sympathy, Controversy, and Print Culture* (Cambridge: Cambridge University Press, 2013), 22–27. Such fears, she argues, intensified following the French Revolution. Amelia Dale's work on eighteenth-century print culture and female quixotism has relevance here; however, the critical rhetoric surrounding Byron's influence over his audience and the public focused less on the idea of impressionable readers and more the idea of diseased, contagious ones. Dale, *The Printed Reader: Gender, Quixotism, and Textual Bodies in Eighteenth-Century Britain* (Lewisburg, PA: Bucknell University Press, 2019).
9. Jon Mee, *Romanticism, Enthusiasm, and Regulation: Poetics and the Policing of Culture in the Romantic Period* (Oxford: Oxford University Press, 2003), 31. Mee's arguments about Romantic-era enthusiasm and Fairclough's examination of sympathy's ability to mobilize Romantic-era crowds identify widespread, intensifying concerns about contagious group behavior after the French Revolution. However, Fairclough argues that discourses around sympathy put less emphasis on pathology than do those surrounding enthusiasm. Fairclough, *Romantic Crowd*, 50–58.
10. McDayter, *Byromania*, 5.
11. Jerome Christensen, *Lord Byron's Strength: Romantic Writing and Commercial Society* (Baltimore: Johns Hopkins University Press, 1995), 92; and Mole, *Byron's Romantic Celebrity*, 1. Relatedly, Matthew Sangster, in his recent assessment of Byron as a professional poet, observes that Byron's "success was due principally to the ways in which he pioneered methods of approaching mass readerships through the powerful projection of poetic personality and through the newly realised powers of commerce activated on his behalf by John Murray." Sangster, *Living as an Author*, 312.
12. Tuite, *Lord Byron and Scandalous Celebrity*, 14.
13. McDayter, *Byromania*, 4.
14. See Corin Throsby, "Flirting with Fame: Byron's Anonymous Female Fans," *Byron Journal* 32, no. 2 (2004): 115–123; and Throsby, "Byron, Commonplacing and Early Fan Culture," 227–244. Throsby's work on commonplace books that quote Byron's poetry demonstrates the poet's cultural reach, particularly among women. However, a writer's gender is sometimes ambiguous, both in manuscript books and in Byron's fan letters. I

am more hesitant than Throsby or McDayter to assume that unsigned letters and other materials were written by female fans.

15. Accounts of print culture and sympathy in the Romantic period struggle to address how print's materiality might align with or depart from the bodily elements of sympathy that thinkers like Burke, Hume, and Smith imagine. Fairclough argues that sympathy was "a medium of communication" and, as such, was "associated with a range of material media and technologies of communication." She also notes that after Waterloo, there was a "shift from a focus on material collectives to virtual ones connected through the consumption of print," and here I wish analyze how even these "virtual" communities—like Byron's fans—are predicated on the material production, circulation, and consumption of physical texts. Fairclough, *Romantic Crowd*, 167 and 189.
16. Andrew Franta, "Godwin's Handshake," *PMLA* 122, no. 3 (2007): 698. Franta's comments are tied to the conditions of the 1790s that gave rise to *Caleb Williams*, yet his observations about the slipperiness of social gestures like the handshake and what they reveal about changing, unstable social relations also apply later in the Romantic period.
17. Mason, *Literary Advertising*, 80.
18. Francis Jeffrey, review of *Childe Harold's Pilgrimage, Canto the Third* and *The Prisoner of Chillon*, *Edinburgh Review* (December 1816), in *RR*, part B, 2:872.
19. Walter Scott, *Childe Harold's Pilgrimage*, Canto III, and *The Prisoner of Chillon*, *Quarterly Review* (October 1816), in *RR*, part B, 5:2030.
20. "Rosalie" to Byron, September 12, 1814, in "Correspondence, predominantly fan mail, sent to Lord Byron expressing love or requesting assistance," Edinburgh, National Library of Scotland, John Murray Archive (JMA), MS.43523. Most items in the JMA are unfoliated. Byron's fan mail, which I explore in detail in the chapter's following section, is cited by name of correspondent (if known), date (if known or can be estimated from information like postmark, watermark, or context), other identifying information (such as place), and call number.

    Until 2006, the Murray family owned what is now the basis of the JMA's more than 150,000 items, including Byron's fan mail. The collection has undergone recataloging. Thus, readers of this chapter will find references to some material from the JMA that has been cited differently by previous scholars working on Byron's fans, particularly George Paston and Peter Quennell, eds. *"To Lord Byron": Feminine Profiles Based upon Unpublished Letters, 1807–1824* (New York: Charles Scribner's Sons, 1939); Throsby "Flirting with Fame," 115–123; and McDayter, *Byromania*, especially 154–162. Since the materials have found a permanent home in the JMA at the National Library of Scotland and since I consulted the materials there, I cite the primary sources directly with their current call numbers. The John Murray Archive has recently been digitized, and access to it is now available to academic institutions (though not individuals) via Adams Matthew Digital's *Nineteenth Century Literary Society: The John Murray Publishing Archive*. The digital resource is certainly an exciting step in terms of preservation and access. Of course, that access is necessarily limited to institutions wealthy enough to afford it.
21. Byron, *Childe Harold's Pilgrimage*, in *CPW*, 2:5. All references to Byron's poetry are from *CPW*; paratexts are cited parenthetically by page number, and poetry is cited by canto number (where relevant) and line number.
22. Gérard Genette, *Paratexts: Thresholds of Interpretation*, trans. Jane E. Lewin (Cambridge: Cambridge University Press, 1997), 218.
23. Review of *Childe Harold* I–II (2nd ed., 1812), *Christian Observer* (June 1812), in *RR*, part B, 2:569.

24. Stephen Cheeke, "Being There: Byron and Hobhouse Seek the 'real' Parnassus," *Romanticism* 7, no. 2 (2001): 134. Christensen has also observed that the first two cantos present "the poem as the record of what Lord Byron saw during his travels." Christensen, *Lord Byron's Strength*, 66.
25. Mole, *Byron's Romantic Celebrity*, 24 and 25. Andrew Elfenbein makes the related point that the "central paradox of Byron's rhetoric was that he was taken to be at his most confessional when he was at his most abstract." Elfenbein, *Byron and the Victorians* (Cambridge: Cambridge University Press, 1995), 20.
26. J. M., *Agreeable variety*, 218.
27. Brewer, *Afterlife of Character*, 121–122. Brewer's example is the coterie public surrounding Richardson's *Pamela*.
28. Brewer, 28.
29. Samantha Matthews identifies Byron's "Written in an Album" from *Childe Harold* as "the highest-profile published album poem of the age." Matthews, *Album Verses and Romantic Literary Culture: Poetry, Manuscript, Print, 1780–1850* (Oxford: Oxford University Press, 2020), 129.
30. Smith, "Preface to Volume II," 11.
31. Yousef, *Romantic Intimacy*, 22.
32. Sharon Marcus, *The Drama of Celebrity* (Princeton, NJ: Princeton University Press, 2019), 53.
33. Mole makes a similar observation about the importance of Byron's "somatic inscription" which "offered readers by turns the pleasure of feeling especially perceptive or discerning." Mole, *Byron's Romantic Celebrity*, 70.
34. Marcus, *Drama of Celebrity*, 50.
35. Review of *Manfred* by Lord Byron, *Knight Errant: A Literary Miscellany* (July 1817) in *RR*, part B, 3:1223, emphasis in the original.
36. There are several notable collections of late nineteenth- and twentieth-century fan mail that have received scholarly attention. For instance, the Harry Ransom Humanities Research Center holds an 869-letter collection of Anne Sexton's fan mail. Janet E. Luedtke has written carefully about the collection, which seems rich enough to make one consider switching fields. The deep emotional connections (specifically, feelings of *knowing* the poet) that Sexton's twentieth-century readers express mirror the earlier effusions of Byron's fans, though many of the later letters carry an explicit political charge absent from Byron's fan mail. Luedtke, "'Something Special for Someone': Anne Sexton's Fan Letters from Women," in *Rossetti to Sexton: Six Women Poets at Texas*, ed. Dave Oliphant (Austin: Harry Ransom Humanities Research Center, University of Texas at Austin, 1992), 165–189. Over two hundred letters from readers to Virginia Woolf also survive, most of them at the University of Sussex. See Anna Snaith, "Wide Circles: The *Three Guineas* Letters," *Woolf Studies Annual* 6 (2000): 1–168; Melba Cuddy-Keane, "From Man-Mail to Readers' Letters: Locating John Farrelly," *Woolf Studies Annual* 11 (2005): 3–32; and Beth Rigel Daugherty, "'You Kind of Belong to Us, and What You Do Matters Enormously': Letters from Readers to Virginia Woolf," *Woolf Studies Annual* 12 (2006): 1–212. In the nineteenth and early twentieth centuries, Mark Twain received a huge amount of fan mail, much of it still preserved across multiple archives. For thoughtful work on Twain's fan mail, see Courtney Alice Bates, "Addressing Each Other: Reciprocal Relationships in American Fan Letters" (PhD diss., Washington University, Saint Louis, 2011), 64–124, ProQuest 3450716.
37. Jackson, *Marginalia*, 6.
38. "A Stranger" to Byron, April 17, 1819, JMA, MS.43523.

39. Robert Darnton, "Readers Respond to Rousseau: The Fabrication of Romantic Sensitivity," in *The Great Cat Massacre and Other Episodes in French Cultural History* (New York: Basic Books, 1984), 242 and 244. Darnton's chapter analyzes and quotes generously from fan letters to Rousseau.
40. That some readers sent castigating letters to Byron certainly seems possible if not likely. Later in the nineteenth century, the Byronic novelist and politician Benjamin Disraeli received—and kept—both fawning and inflammatory fan mail; see Bernard R. Jerman, "Disraeli's Fan Mail: A Curiosity Item," *Nineteenth-Century Fiction* 9, no. 1 (1954): 61–71.
41. James Smith Allen, *In the Public Eye: A History of Reading in Modern France, 1800–1940* (Princeton, NJ: Princeton University Press, 1991), 14.
42. Review of *Poems* by Lord Byron, *Farrago* (June 1816), in *RR*, part B, 3:1046. For a concise overview of the publication history of "Fare Thee Well" and its significance, see Gerald Egan, *Fashioning Authorship in the Long Eighteenth Century* (London: Palgrave Macmillan, 2016), 173–179. Despite the circulation of "Fare Thee Well," many of Byron's lyrics went unpublished in his life, which suggests his (and Murray's) understanding that they may have been too personal to print. For more on the shorter lyrics Byron wrote but did not publish, see Levy, *Literary Manuscript Culture*, 162–170.
43. Murray served as a conduit for some of Byron's fan mail. As early as September 1812, Byron was already receiving "some letters & verses (all but one) anonymous & complimentary" that Murray forwarded. Byron to Murray, September 14, 1812, in *The Letters of John Murray to Lord Byron*, ed. Andrew Nicholson (Liverpool: Liverpool University Press, 2007), 10.
44. Eliza Horatia Sommerset to Byron, [after 1813], JMA, MS.43523.
45. Sommerset to Byron, [after 1813], JMA, MS.43523.
46. [Vicesimus Knox], preface to *Elegant Epistles: Being a Copious Collection of Familiar and Amusing Letters, Selected for the Improvement of Young Persons, and for General Entertainment . . . A New Edition Improved and Enlarged* (London: T. Longman, 1794), vii, Google Books, https://books.google.com/books?id=Yc5bAAAAcAAJ (accessed May 1, 2021). New and revised versions of this popular work appeared throughout the later eighteenth century and into the first decades of the nineteenth century.
47. "A Stranger" to Byron, April 17, 1819, JMA, MS.43523.
48. John Wilson, review of *Childe Harold*, Canto IV, *Edinburgh Review* (June 1818), in *RR*, part B, 2:895.
49. Hazlitt, "On the Aristocracy of Letters," in *SWWH*, 6:187, emphasis mine.
50. Bates, "Addressing Each Other," 23–24.
51. Bates, 51.
52. Throsby, "Flirting with Fame," 117.
53. John Stewart to Byron, January 7, 1814, JMA, MS.43523.
54. Miss Pipper to Byron, February 28 [after 1812], JMA, MS.43523. The flowers she lists are: sweat pea, hyacinth, geranium, heliotrope, marigold, dwarf almond, iris, scarlet azalea, convolvulus, and amaryllis of the pink, heath, and jonquil varieties.
55. Henrietta d'Ussières to Byron, 1814, quoted in Paston and Quennell, *"To Lord Byron,"* 124. After several such letters, Byron eventually responded and assured her, "I promise not to make love to you unless you like it." Byron to Henrietta d'Ussières, June 8, 1814, in *Byron's Letters and Journals*, ed. Leslie Marchand (London: Murray, 1973–1994), 4:122. Hereafter cited as *BLJ*.
56. "Rosalie" to Byron, September 12, 1814, JMA, MS.43523. Both of Rosalie's letters to Byron are printed in full in Peter Cochran, "Byron's Fan Letters," in *The Burning of Byron's Memoirs: New and Unpublished Essays and Papers* (Newcastle upon Tyne, UK:

Cambridge Scholars, 2014), 85–88. Cochran's analysis of Rosalie's impertinence in addressing Byron is correct. However, his rejection of McDayter's assessment of the fan letters and his dismissive assertion that "[n]one of the other fan letters [in the John Murray Archive] give any more confidence than do Rosalie's that Byron's poems have been read, let alone understood" is an inaccurate portrayal of the collection. Cochran, "Byron's Fan Letters," 88.

57. "Echo" to Byron, [1813–1816], JMA, MS.43523. Byron certainly thought Echo's letter memorable. Years after receiving Echo's note, he wrote, "[D]o you remember *Constantia* and *Echo*—and *la Suissesse*—and all my other inamorate[?]" Byron to Augusta Leigh, November 7, 1822, in *BLJ*, 10:29. Marchand asserts that "*la Suissesse*" refers to Henrietta d'Ussières.
58. See, for instance, Paston and Quennell, *"To Lord Byron"*; and Throsby, "Flirting with Fame," 115–123.
59. John Joseph Stockdale to Byron, June 1, 1821, in "Letters to Byron from various correspondents," JMA, MS.43508.
60. "Friend" to Byron, March 20, 1814, JMA, MS.43523. This is one of the more moralizing, religious letters in the collection, telling Byron that he "should repent" and do so "before it is too late."
61. Anonymous letter to Byron, postmarked 1814, day and month obscured, JMA, MS.43523.
62. Throsby, "Flirting with Fame," 117.
63. William Edmund Romedy to Byron, July 21, 1819, JMA, MS.43523.
64. A poet himself, Barton was also a serial fan of sorts. He also wrote celebratory poems to Letitia Elizabeth Landon and begged Robert Southey to secure him positive reviews. See Mason, *Literary Advertising*, 92–94.
65. Bernard Barton to Byron, May 24, 1812, JMA, MS.43523. Along with this letter, Barton sent a copy of his poetry collection *Metrical Effusions* (1812), for which he asks Byron to "honour me with a candid declaration of your sentiment respecting it." He implies this may help him secure a future edition of the work.
66. Barton to Byron, May 24, 1812, JMA, MS.43523.
67. Byron to Bernard Barton, June 1, 1812, in *BLJ*, 2:179.
68. Anonymous letter to Byron, n.d., JMA, MS.43523.
69. Anonymous to Byron, postmarked May 26, 1814, NLS, JMA, MS.43523.
70. King, *Writing to the World*, 5.
71. Pearsall, *Atlantic Families*, 11.
72. David Fordyce, *The New and Complete British Letter-Writer; or, Young Secretary's Instructor in Polite Modern Letter-Writing* (London: C. Cooke, [1790?]), 66 and 61, ESTC Number T13268, ECCO.
73. Pearsall, *Atlantic Families*, 57.
74. Murray to Byron, August 29, 1817, in *Letters of John Murray*, 241–242.
75. Barton to Byron, April 15, 1814, JMA, MS.43523.
76. Barton to Byron, April 14, 1814, JMA, MS.43523.
77. Barton to Byron, April 15, 1814, JMA, MS.43523.
78. Smith, "Preface to Volume II," 8.
79. Byron replied with a short letter explaining, "[I]t is not in my power to be of service." Byron to Barton, April 16, 1814, in *BLJ*, 4:97.
80. Sommerset to Byron, [after 1813], JMA, MS.43523.
81. Anonymous to Byron, March 20, 1814, Dublin, JMA, MS.43523; and Sophia Louisa MacDonald to Byron, [1815], Oxford, Bodleian Libraries, Deposit Lovelace Byron 155, fol. 88r.

82. Review of *Manfred, Knight Errant*, 3:1223.
83. Brantlinger, *Reading Lesson*, 8.
84. Scott, review of *Childe Harold*, Canto III and *The Prisoner of Chillon*, 5:2030.
85. Anonymous to Byron, postmarked May 26, 1814, JMA, MS.43523.
86. William Edmund Romedy to Byron, July 21, 1819, JMA, MS.43523. Romedy's letter indicates that he read *Lara* and *The Corsair* first and then "perused the other productions of Lord Byron's pen," including *Childe Harold*.
87. Francis Jeffrey, review of *Sardanapalus, a Tragedy*; *The Two Foscari, a Tragedy*; and *Cain, a Mystery*, *Edinburgh Review* (February 1822), in *RR*, part B, 2:935.
88. Byron to Hodgson, May 12, 1821, in *BLJ*, 8:114.
89. Romedy to Byron, July 21, 1819, JMA, MS.43523.
90. Stauffer, *Anger, Revolution, and Romanticism*, 65–66.
91. Mee, *Romanticism, Enthusiasm, and Regulation*, 62.
92. Review of *Don Juan*, XII-XIV, *Literary Museum* (December 1823), in *RR*, part B, 4:1512. Christensen notes that later in Byron's career, "the degradation of the lord by the poet" became "a well-worn theme of the reviews." Christensen, *Lord Byron's Strength*, 221.
93. Lynch, *Loving Literature*, 136.
94. Review of *Don Juan*, VI-VIII, *John Bull* (July 1823), in *RR*, part B, 3:1220; and review of *Don Juan*, XII-XIV, *Literary Museum*, 4:1512.
95. McDayter, *Byromania*, 5. Though her study focuses on later nineteenth-century celebrities, Marcus similarly notes: "Celebrities by definition attract large followings, but their very popularity usually inspires a vocal minority to resist the general euphoria. What better way to take down the latest celebrity than to cast a newborn star's devotees as gullible, ignorant, and unruly?" Marcus, *Drama of Celebrity*, 90.
96. Brantlinger, *Reading Lesson*, 56.
97. Romedy to Byron, July 21, 1819, JMA, MS.43523; and Sommerset to Byron, [after 1813], JMA, MS.43523.
98. Wilson, review of *Childe Harold*, Canto IV, *Edinburgh Review* (June 1818), in *RR*, part B, 2:896.
99. Marcus, *Drama of Celebrity*, 220.
100. Review of *Cain*, by Lord Byron, *Ladies' Monthly Museum*, 3rd series, XV (January 1822), in *RR*, part B, 3:1254, emphasis in the original.
101. Burke, *Philosophical Enquiry*, 56.
102. Burke, 29.
103. Burke, 29.
104. Review of *Childe Harold*, Canto III, *Portfolio, Political and Literary* (November 1816), in *RR*, part B, 5:1966.
105. Smith, *Theory of Moral Sentiments*, 337.
106. Wilson, review of *Childe Harold*, Canto IV, 2:895.
107. Baillie, *Plays on the Passions*, 73.
108. Smith, *Theory of Moral Sentiments*, 337.
109. Scott, review of *Childe Harold*, Canto IV, 5:2049.
110. Piozzi, *British Synonymy*, 1:217.
111. Josiah Conder, review of *Childe Harold*, Canto III, and *The Prisoner of Chillon, and Other Poems*, *Eclectic Review* (March 1817), in *RR*, part B, 2:742.
112. Conder, 2:743.
113. Smith, *Theory of Moral Sentiments*, 153–154.
114. Josiah Conder, review of *The Corsair* 4th edition, *Eclectic Review* (April 1814), in *RR*, part B, 2:721.

115. Burke is a partial exception here in his considerations of words over painting; however, his ideas about sympathy's relation to printed words versus spoken ones remain obscure. See Burke, *Philosophical Inquiry*, 55–57.
116. Yousef, *Romantic Intimacy*, 78.
117. Yousef, 2.
118. Wilson, review of *Childe Harold*, Canto IV, *Edinburgh Review* (June 1818), in *RR*, part B, 2:895.
119. Review of *Childe Harold* I–II, (2nd ed., 1812), *Christian Observer* (June 1812), in *RR*, part B, 2:569.
120. Jeffrey, review of *Childe Harold's Pilgrimage Canto the Third*, and *The Prisoner of Chillon*, *Edinburgh Review* (December 1816), in *RR*, part B, 2:880.

CHAPTER 3 — LADY CAROLINE LAMB'S FEMALE FOLLIES AND THE DANGERS OF FAMILIARITY

* Lady Caroline Lamb, "Lines to Harriet Wilson," in *Fugitive Pieces and Reminiscences of Lord Byron*, by Isaac Nathan (London: Whittaker and Treacher, 1829), 195.

1. Lamb to John Murray, November 9, 1813, quoted in *Lady Caroline Lamb: A Biography*, by Paul Douglass (New York: Palgrave Macmillan, 2004), 156. For another description of this incident, see Fiona MacCarthy, *Byron: Life and Legend* (London: Murray, 2002), 216–217.
2. Lamb, "Biondetta, 1812," in "Commonplace Book of Caroline Lamb [blue]," JMA, MS.43366, fol. 3r. The entry, ostensibly about a spaniel named Biondetta, is autobiographically charged. "Biondetta" was a pet name Byron used for Lamb.
3. Duncan Wu, "Appropriating Byron: Lady Caroline Lamb's 'A New Canto,'" *Wordsworth Circle* 26, no. 3 (1995): 141; and Gioia Angeletti, "Women Re-writing Men: The Examples of Anna Seward and Lady Caroline Lamb," in *Romantic Women Poets: Genre and Gender*, ed. Lilla Maria Crisafulli and Cecilia Pietropoli (Amsterdam: Rodopi, 2007), 252.
4. James Soderholm, *Fantasy, Forgery, and the Byron Legend* (Lexington: University Press of Kentucky, 1996).
5. Wu, "Appropriating Byron," 140–146; Nicola J. Watson, "Trans-figuring Byronic Identity," in *At the Limits of Romanticism: Essays in Cultural, Feminist, and Materialist Criticism*, ed. Mary A. Favret and Nicola J. Watson (Bloomington: Indiana University Press, 1994), 185–206; Paul Douglass, "The Madness of Writing: Lady Caroline Lamb's Byronic Identity," *Pacific Coast Philology* 34, no. 1 (1999): 53–71; Paul Douglass, "Playing Byron: Lady Caroline Lamb's *Glenarvon* and the Music of Isaac Nathan," *European Romantic Review* 8, no. 1 (1997): 1–24; Rosemary March, "The Page Affair: Lady Caroline Lamb's Cross-Dressing," in Caro: The Lady Caroline Lamb Website, ed. Paul Douglass, n.d., 1–13, https://sites.google.com/sjsu.edu/caro/biography/the-page-affair (accessed May 1, 2021); and Tuite, *Lord Byron and Scandalous Celebrity*, 19–43.
6. Leigh Wetherall Dickson, "Authority and Legitimacy: The Cultural Context of Lady Caroline Lamb's Novels," *Women's Writing* 13, no. 3 (2006): 370.
7. Vicesimus Knox, *Essays Moral and Literary . . . A New Edition in Two Volumes*, 2 vols. (London: Charles Dilly, 1782), 1:155, ESTC Number T92818, ECCO.
8. Caroline George Lamb to Annabella Milbanke, May 7, 1816, Oxford, Bodleian Libraries, Dep. Lovelace Byron 78, fol. 24v. Items from Dep. Lovelace Byron are cited by catalog number and, if applicable, folio. I thank Paper Lion and the proprietor of the Lovelace Byron Papers for allowing me to consult and quote from this collection.

9. Sady Doyle has written "a feminist anatomy of the trainwreck," convincingly arguing for its misogynist roots and gendered applications. Doyle, *Trainwreck: The Women We Love to Hate, Mock, and Fear* (Brooklyn, NY: Melville House, 2017), xxi.
10. Lamb, "Lines to Harriet Wilson," 195.
11. Bourdieu, *Field of Cultural Production*, 37.
12. Coleridge, *Biographia Literaria*, 2:7.
13. Lady Caroline Lamb to Lady Morgan, watermark 1823, London, Victoria and Albert Museum, Forster Collection MS 328, Item 31. Subsequent letters from the Forster Collection are cited as "Forster" followed by call number and item number. Some of the letters are undated; where possible I include relevant contextual information suggestive of a letter's date.
14. Lady Melbourne to Lamb, April 13, 1810, quoted in Douglass, *Lady Caroline Lamb*, 91.
15. Lamb to Lady Melbourne, April 1810, in *The Whole Disgraceful Truth: Selected Letters of Lady Caroline Lamb*, ed. Paul Douglass (New York: Palgrave Macmillan, 2006), 53. Hereafter cited as *Letters*.
16. For more about Lamb's first affair, see Paul Douglass, "Lady Caroline Lamb Before Byron," *Wordsworth Circle* 36, no. 3 (2005): 117–124.
17. For a description of the bonfire where Lamb burned Byron's effigy, see Douglass, *Lady Caroline Lamb*, 138–139.
18. Quoted in Susan Normington, *Lady Caroline Lamb: This Infernal Woman* (London: House of Stratus, 2001), 94.
19. Amanda Vickery, *The Gentleman's Daughter: Women's Lives in Georgian England* (New Haven, CT: Yale University Press, 1998), 54. Ben Wilson similarly observes that a Romantic-era aristocrat could "lead a scandalous private life and retain one's good name as long as the private did not intrude upon the public." Wilson, *Decency and Disorder: The Age of Cant, 1789–1837* (London: Faber and Faber, 2007), 150.
20. Byron to Lady Melbourne, July 6, 1813, in *BLJ*, 3:72.
21. Lamb to Thomas Medwin, November 1824, in *Letters*, 204.
22. Lamb to John Murray, July 17, 1813, JMA, MS.43466. Most letters in the JMA, like this one, are unfoliated.
23. *The Satirist*, quoted in Bernard Grebanier, *The Uninhibited Byron: An Account of His Sexual Confusion* (New York: Crown, 1971), 129. See also Douglass, *Lady Caroline Lamb*, 152–153.
24. "Births," *Bell's Weekly Messenger*, February 5, 1809, 48, The British Newspaper Archive.
25. Lady Melbourne to John Cam Hobhouse, May 28, 1816, JMA, MS.43472.
26. Augusta Leigh to Hobhouse, May 21, 1816, Dep. Lovelace Byron 361, unfoliated.
27. To maintain consistency, I refer to "Annabella Milbanke" rather than "Lady Byron"; some of the manuscript material I cite was written prior to Milbanke's marriage to Byron.
28. For more on *Glenarvon*'s political elements, see Malcolm Kelsall, "The Byronic Hero and Revolution in Ireland: The Politics of *Glenarvon*," *Byron Journal* 9 (1981): 4–19.
29. Robert Wilmot-Horton to Milbanke, quoted in Malcolm Elwin, *Lord Byron's Family: Annabella, Ada, and Augusta, 1816–1824*, ed. Peter Thomson (London: John Murray, 1975), 34.
30. Peter W. Graham, "Fictive Biography in 1816: The Case of *Glenarvon*," *Byron Journal* 19 (1991): 66.
31. *Glenarvon* (London: Colburn, 1816), London, British Library, N.1834 (vol. 1). This particular copy was rebacked in 1946, so it is difficult to know when the key was added. However, the key is written on laid rather than wove paper (though the watermark is not visible), and it appears contemporaneous with the text.

32. *Glenarvon* (London: Colburn, 1816), London, Victoria and Albert Museum, Dyce Collection, D.12.E.28.
33. *Glenarvon* (London: Colburn, 1817), Baltimore, Johns Hopkins University, Milton S. Eisenhower Library, Eisenhower Rare Book Collection, PO4859.L5G5 1817 c.1.
34. Robert Wilmot-Horton to Milbanke, quoted in Elwin, *Lord Byron's Family*, 32–33. Modern editions of *Glenarvon* continue the tradition of character keys, identifying Lamb's fictional characters with their factual counterparts; see *Glenarvon*, ed. Frances Wilson (London: Everyman, 1995), xxxviii.
35. Unsigned review of *Glenarvon*, *British Lady's Magazine* 4 (August 1816): 101.
36. Lamb to Lady Melbourne, May 9, 1816, British Library, Lamb Papers, Add. 45546, fol. 91v.
37. William Lamb to Colburn, May 17, 1816, Forster MS 328, Item 12.
38. For more about the novel's editions, see *Glenarvon* in *The Works of Lady Caroline Lamb*, ed. Leigh Wetherall Dickson and Paul Douglass (London: Pickering and Chatto, 2009), 1:387.
39. Frederick Burwick, *Playing to the Crowd: London Popular Theatre, 1780–1830* (New York: Palgrave, 2011), 5. Burwick also discusses the plays in "Lady Caroline Lamb's *Glenarvon* on Stage," *Wordsworth Circle* 42, no. 2 (2011): 139–143.
40. See "The Turf," *York Herald, and General Advertiser*, April 4, 1818; "The Turf," *York Herald, and General Advertiser*, May 16, 1818; "Racing," *York Herald, and General Advertiser*, June 6, 1818; "Newcastle Races, 1818," *Caledonian Mercury* (Edinburgh), June 29, 1818; and "York August Meeting," *Hull Packet and Original Weekly Commercial, Literary and General Advertiser*, August 18, 1818. These articles were all accessed through the British Library Newspapers database. Naming racehorses after literary characters was not new; Tom Keymer and Peter Sabor note several *Pamela*-themed horses running in the mid-eighteenth century. Keymer and Sabor, *"Pamela" in the Marketplace: Literary Controversy and Print Culture in Eighteenth-Century Britain and Ireland* (Cambridge: Cambridge University Press, 2005), 3.
41. Marcus, *Drama of Celebrity*, 72.
42. Bourdieu, *Field of Cultural Production*, 42.
43. Knox, *Essays Moral and Literary*, 2:351.
44. Notably, critics and lay readers resoundingly found Byron's poem "Fare Thee Well" offensive. Like *Glenarvon*, "Fare Thee Well" shares details not only about the poet but also about others in his circle, particularly his estranged wife.
45. Byron, preface to Cantos I and II, *Childe Harold*, in *CPW*, 2:4.
46. Preface to the 2nd edition of *Glenarvon*, in Dickson and Douglass, *The Works of Lady Caroline Lamb*, 1:353. The preface to the fourth edition of *Glenarvon* (1817) differs from that of the second and third edition. The later preface is mystical in tone and content; it is focalized through Calantha's spirit prior to her decision to renounce her "etherial [*sic*] nature, and to become an inhabitant of the earth." Preface to the 4th edition of *Glenarvon*, in *The Works of Lady Caroline Lamb*, 1:360. Further references to Lamb's works are all from Dickson and Douglass's three-volume *Works of Lady Caroline Lamb* and are cited parenthetically by page number.
47. John Clubbe is the first scholar to draw attention to the extensive revisions to the second edition, in "*Glenarvon* Revised—and Revisited," *Wordsworth Circle* 10, no. 2 (1979): 205–217. Douglass's edition of *Glenarvon* for *The Works of Lady Caroline Lamb* details the variants found in the second and third editions of 1816 and the fourth edition of 1817; *Glenarvon*, 389–451. For more on these revisions, see Paul Douglass, "Twisty Little Passages: The Several Editions of Lady Caroline Lamb's *Glenarvon*," *Wordsworth Circle* 40, no. 2–3 (2009): 77–82; and Ria Grimbergen and Paul Douglass, "On a Special Copy of

Caroline Lamb's *Glenarvon* Recently Discovered in Koninklijke Bibliotheek," *Byron Journal* 37, no. 2 (2009): 151–160.

48. Byron, preface to Cantos I and II, *Childe Harold*, 4.
49. Byron, *The Corsair*, in *CPW*, 3:149.
50. Caroline George Lamb to Milbanke, May 7, 1816, Dep. Lovelace Byron 78, fol. 25r.
51. "Doctor Sir Richard Croft," *Morning Post*, February 19, 1818, Gale Document Number R3209708333, British Library Newspapers.
52. Burke, *Philosophical Enquiry*, 56 and 57; emphasis in the original.
53. Burke, 56.
54. Patricia Meyer Spacks, *Gossip* (Chicago: University of Chicago Press, 1985), 22.
55. Lamb to Milbanke, [Fall 1816], Dep. Lovelace Byron 78, fol. 177r.
56. Nussbaum, *Autobiographical Subject*, 65.
57. Frances Wilson, "'An Exaggerated Woman': The Melodramas of Lady Caroline Lamb," in *Byromania: Portraits of the Artist in Nineteenth- and Twentieth-Century Culture*, ed. Frances Wilson (Basingstoke, UK: Macmillan Press, 1999), 196.
58. Milbanke, May 17, 1816, Dep. Lovelace Byron 118/4, fols. 40–41.
59. Milbanke, "character sketches in notebook dated 1812," Dep. Lovelace Byron 118/2, fol. 1v.
60. Milbanke, fol. 3v.
61. Milbanke, fol. 4r.
62. Milbanke, fol. 1v.
63. Milbanke, fol. 3v.
64. Lamb to Lady Melbourne, [library estimates after October 15, 1812], British Library, Lamb Papers, Add. 45546, fol. 41v.
65. One exception is Elinor St. Clara. She, like other women whom Glenarvon seduces, dies; however, Elinor commits suicide by galloping her horse off a cliff, its eyes covered with a green scarf. Though partially compelled by Glenarvon's betrayal of both herself and the Irish rebels that she helps lead, Elinor's choice suggests more active agency than the deaths of the novel's other doomed women.
66. Unsigned review of *Glenarvon*, *Theatrical Inquisitor, and Monthly Mirror* 9 (August 1816): 122, HathiTrust, https://hdl.handle.net/2027/inu.30000047477272 (accessed May 1, 2021).
67. Caroline George Lamb to Annabella Milbanke, May 7, 1816, Dep. Lovelace Bryon 78, fol. 24v.
68. Judith Noel Milbanke to Milbanke, June 16, 1816, Dep. Lovelace Byron 36, fol. 55v.
69. Sir Ralph was Lady Melbourne's brother, William Lamb's uncle, and Lord Byron's father-in-law.
70. Percy Shelley, quoted in Clubbe, "*Glenarvon* Revised," 207. Godwin and Lamb were friendly correspondents, so it is unlikely he needed Northcote's additional encouragement to read the novel.
71. Edward Bulwer, quoted in Clubbe, "*Glenarvon* Revised," 207.
72. Caroline George Lamb to Milbanke, May 7, 1816, Dep. Lovelace Byron 78, fols. 24v–25r.
73. Lady Cowper to Frederic Lamb, March 31, 18[—] [after 1816], Hertfordshire Archives and Local Studies, Papers of the Lamb Family of Brocket Hall, DE/Lb/F82/31, fol. 2v. Cowper's second marriage made her Viscountess Palmerston, the name that she is perhaps more often associated with today; since the marriage took place in 1837 after Lamb died, I have used "Cowper" throughout.
74. Cowper to Lamb, [1816], British Library, Lamb Papers, Add. 45548, fol. 144r–v.
75. Cowper to Lamb, [1816], British Library, Lamb Papers, Add. 45548, fol. 143v.

76. Smith, *Theory of Moral Sentiments*, 50.
77. Smith, 243.
78. Unsigned review of *Glenarvon*, *Theatrical Inquisitor*, 123.
79. Cowper to Lamb, [1816], British Library, Lamb Papers, Add. 45548, fol. 144v.
80. Smith, *Theory of Moral Sentiments*, 249–250.
81. Cowper to Lamb, [1816], British Library, Lamb Papers, Add. 45548, fol. 143r–v.
82. For more on French and British secret histories, see Brewer, "Personal Scandal and Politics," 84–106.
83. Ina Ferris, "The 'Character' of James the First and Antiquarian Secret History," *Wordsworth Circle* 37, no. 2 (2006): 74. See also April London, "Isaac D'Israeli and Literary History: Opinion and Anecdote, and Secret History in the Early Nineteenth Century," *Poetics Today* 26, no. 3 (2005): 351–386.
84. Gary Kelly, *English Fiction of the Romantic Period, 1789–1830* (London: Longman, 1989), 221.
85. Tuite, *Lord Byron and Scandalous Celebrity*, 30.
86. Unsigned review of *Glenarvon*, *Theatrical Inquisitor*, 125.
87. Nussbaum, *Autobiographical Subject*, 139.
88. Milbanke, "character sketches," Dep. Lovelace Byron 118/2, fols. 1v–2v.
89. Milbanke, Dep. Lovelace Byron 118/4, fol. 7v.
90. Milbanke, fol. 7v.
91. Leo Braudy, "Knowing the Performer from the Performance," in "Celebrity, Fame, Notoriety," ed. Joseph A. Boone and Nancy J. Vickers, special issue, *PMLA* 126, no. 4 (2011): 1072.
92. Smith, *Theory of Moral Sentiments*, 332.
93. Byron, "[To Lady Caroline Lamb]," in *CPW*, 3:17, line 14.
94. "Art. V., [review of] *Glenarvon, a Novel*," *British Critic* 5 (June 1816): 628–629.
95. Unsigned review of *Glenarvon*, *Monthly Review* 80 (June 1816), quoted in Douglass, introduction to *Glenarvon*, xxxii, emphasis in the original.
96. [Elizabeth Thomas], *Purity of Heart, . . . Addressed to the Author of "Glenarvon"* (London: W. Simpkin and R. Marshall, 1816), vi. Thomas's novel went into a second edition in 1817, and there was at least one American edition. Lamb read *Purity of Heart* and appears to have been hurt by it. She described it as "not very witty though meant to be so." Lamb to Lady Melbourne, [after October 1816], British Library, Lamb Papers, Add. 45546, fol. 103r. She sent the novel to Murray, noting of Thomas, "wit & razor edge she has not but a most unkind tongue to make up for it." Lamb to Murray, [1816], JMA, MS.43467. Lamb's correspondence with Colburn also paints a negative picture of the novel: "[T]he Author of Purity of Heart has less idea even of common humour—& liveliness than any one I ever met with." Lamb to Colburn, [1816], Forster MS 328, Item 18.
97. [Thomas], *Purity of Heart*, vi.
98. [Thomas], 67–68.
99. Lamb's letters often reference her horses, one of which she tried to sell to John Murray, using the fact that "his name shall be changed from Cameron to Glenarvon" as a selling point. Lamb to Murray, [1816?], JMA, MS.43467. In a poignant letter to her husband shortly after their separation, she repeatedly begs him to send over her horses, claiming, "my Health depends upon riding." Lamb to William Lamb, postmarked September 12, 1825, Hertfordshire Archives and Local Studies, Papers of the Lamb Family of Brocket Hall, DE/Lb/F32/5, fol. 1v.
100. [Thomas], *Purity of Heart*, 114–115.
101. Lamb to Lady Melbourne, [after May 9, 1816], British Library, Lamb Papers, Add. 45546, 91r; and Lamb to John Cam Hobhouse [1816], JMA, MS.43465.

102. Milbanke, quoted in Douglass, *Lady Caroline Lamb*, 191.
103. Caroline George Lamb to Milbanke, postmarked 1816, Dep. Lovelace Byron 78, fol. 32v.
104. Clara Tuite, "Tainted Love and Romantic Celebrity," *ELH* 74, no. 1 (2007): 78.
105. Tuite, 81.
106. Cowper to Lamb, [1816], British Library, Lamb Papers, Add. 45548, fol. 144r; and unsigned review of *Glenarvon*, *Theatrical Inquisitor*, 125.
107. Lamb to unnamed recipient, [1822], Forster MS 328, Item 32.
108. William Lamb to Colburn, May 17, 1816, Forster MS 328, Item 12.
109. Lamb to William Godwin, April 18, 1822, in *Letters*, 184.
110. Lamb to Amelia Opie, January 1, 1822, in *Letters*, 183. For exciting work on Lamb's female writing circle, see Leigh Wetherall Dickson, "The Construction of a Reputation for Madness: The Case Study of Lady Caroline Lamb," *Working with English: Medieval and Modern Language, Literature and Drama* 2 (2005–2006): 32–36.
111. Lamb to Thomas Malthus, [1821–1822], in *Letters*, 176–177.
112. "Art. III., [review of] *Graham Hamilton*," in *Monthly Review, or Literary Journal, Enlarged: From September to December, Inclusive, 1822* (London: A. and R. Spottiswoode, 1822), 135, HathiTrust, https://hdl.handle.net/2027/inu.30000093224685 (accessed May 1, 2021).
113. "Literature. Graham Hamilton," *Morning Post*, July 4, 1822, Gale Document Number R3209761298, British Library Newspapers.
114. Unsigned review of *Graham Hamilton*, *Blackwood's Edinburgh Magazine* 11, no. 65 (June 1822): 731.
115. Chawton House Library holds the only second edition of the novel that I know of (copy no. 6680). I have been unable to collate it with a copy of the first edition; it may be that the novel is a different issue of the first edition with a new title page, rather than a true second edition.
116. Lamb to Colburn, [May–June 1822], Forster MS 328, Item 20.
117. Lamb to Colburn, dated "rec'd March 12 1822," Forster MS 328, Item 33. See also William Lamb's letter to Colburn on the same subject, March 18, 1822, Forster MS328, Item 35.
118. *Glenarvon* appeared anonymously, but neither Colburn nor Lamb kept her identity secret; she wrote to him, "[I]t is useless to deny it—every one knows who wrote the Book." Lamb to Colburn, [between May 17 and mid-June 1816], Forster MS 328, Item 13.
119. Lamb to Colburn, [1822], in *Letters*, 183.
120. Lamb to Murray, postmarked 1821, JMA, MS.43467; and Lamb to Murray, [1823], JMA MS.43467.
121. Lamb to Colburn, n.d., Forster MS 328, Item 57.
122. Lamb to Colburn, dated "rec'd Mar. 12 1822," Forster MS 328, Item 22.
123. William Lamb to Colburn, March 29, 1822, Forster MS 328, Item 51.
124. Unsigned review of *Graham Hamilton*, *Blackwood's Edinburgh Magazine*, 731.
125. "Art. III., *Graham Hamilton*," *Monthly Review*, 135.
126. Lamb to Colburn, n.d., Forster MS 328, Item 55.
127. Lamb to Thomas Malthus, [1821–1822], in *Letters*, 177.
128. Leigh Wetherall Dickson has also identified possible connections between *Graham Hamilton* and seventeenth-century work by John Ford. Dickson, "A Written Warning: Lady Caroline Lamb, Noblesse Oblige and the Works of John Ford," in *Shakespeare and the Culture of Romanticism*, ed. Joseph Ortiz (Burlington, VT: Ashgate, 2013), 254–256.
129. Douglass mentions that *Graham Hamilton* is "perhaps modelled on Jane Austen's or Fanny Burney's work." Douglass, "Madness of Writing," 65.

130. "Art. III., *Graham Hamilton*," *Monthly Review*, 136n.
131. Stephanie Insley Hershinow, *Born Yesterday: Inexperience and the Early Realist Novel* (Baltimore: Johns Hopkins University Press, 2019), 25–26.
132. Lamb to Milbanke, May 22, 1812, Dep. Lovelace Byron 359, unfoliated.
133. Leigh Wetherall Dickson, introduction to *Graham Hamilton*, in *Works of Lady Caroline Lamb*, 2:xv.
134. Milbanke, "character sketches," Dep. Lovelace Byron 118/2, fols. 1r–1v.
135. See for example, C. Eulenstein, "Elinor's Song. And Can'st Thou Bid My Heart Forget?," in *Lays of Harmony, Popular Vocal Music with Accompaniment for the Guitar* (London: E. Donajowski, [1894]), 2–4. For recordings of Lamb's songs, see Paul Douglass and Frederick Burwick, eds., Romantic-Era Songs, January 20, 2013; http://www.sjsu.edu/faculty/douglass/music/index.html (accessed May 1, 2021).
136. There are several undated editions of Kiallmark's music for "Waters of Elle." The version without lyrics is G[eorge] Kiallmark, *Waters of Elle! Air from Glenarvon, with Variations and Flute Accomp. Ad Lib: Composed & Dedicated to Miss Emily Montague*. London: Chappell and Co. and Goulding, [18??].
137. G. Hime, *Waters of Elle, a Favorite Canzonet, from the Popular Novel "Glenarvon"* (Liverpool: Hime & Son, [1821?]); and G. A. Hodson, *"Waters of Elle," from "Glenarvon"* (Dublin: E. McGullah, [1821?]).
138. The various editions of Klose's songs from *Glenarvon* are undated. The British Library estimates that Klose's setting of *And Canst Thou Bid My Heart Forget* was published between 1820 and 1827. Burwick asserts that the first edition was published in 1820. Burwick, "*Glenarvon* on Stage," 143. However, the song must have appeared earlier. I have located an 1818 advertisement for "The Second Edition of Elinor's Song from Glenarvon; 'And canst thou bid my Heart forget', composed by F. J. Kolse." "New Music," *Morning Post*, October 28, 1818, Gale Document Number R3209713538, British Library Newspapers.
139. F. J. Klose, *And Canst Thou Bid My Heart Forget. Elinor's Song from "Glenarvon"* (London: Mayhew, [1825?]).
140. Caroline Lamb, "To a Friend, On Sending a Fancy Drawing, After Promising Her Own Picture in the Character of a Gypsey," in *The Bijou: Or Annual of Literature and the Arts*, ed. W[illiam]. F[raser]. (London: Pickering, 1828), 89–90.
141. Frances Arabella Rowden, *A Biographical Sketch of the Most Distinguished Writers of Ancient and Modern Time Intended for the Use of Schools and Private Education* (London: Longman, Hatchard, Seely, and Lake, 1820), n.p.
142. Frances Arabella Rowden, *A Christian Wreath for the Pagan Deities: Or an Introduction to the Greek and Roman Mythology* (London: A. J. Valpy, 1820), 146n1.
143. For a more sustained analysis of Lamb's songs, poems in literary annuals, and contributions to didactic works, see Lindsey Eckert, "Lady Caroline Lamb's Recuperative Materiality," in "Romantic Women and Their Books," ed. Michelle Levy and Andrew Stauffer, Special issue, *Studies in Romanticism* 60, no 4 (2021): 451–466.
144. Lamb to Lady Melbourne, [1812–1814], British Library, Lamb Papers, Add. 45546, fol. 75r.

CHAPTER 4 — "THE WHOLE CURSED STORY"

* William Hazlitt, "On Coffee-House Politicians," in *The Selected Writings of William Hazlitt*, ed. Duncan Wu (London: Pickering and Chatto, 1998), 6:182. References to Hazlitt's works are to Wu's edition (hereafter *SWWH*) and are cited by essay title, volume, and page number.

1. For an explanation of periodical culture's expansion in the Romantic period and distinctions between dailies, weeklies, and monthlies, see Jonathan Mulrooney, *Romanticism and Theatrical Experience: Kean, Hazlitt, and Keats in the Age of Theatrical News* (Cambridge: Cambridge University Press, 2018), 27–106.
2. Hazlitt, "On the Pleasure of Hating," in *SWWH,* 8:121; and Hazlitt, "On Novelty and Familiarity," in *SWWH,* 8:287.
3. Hazlitt, "On Novelty and Familiarity," 8:288 and 275.
4. Marcus Tomalin, "'Vulgarisms and Broken English': The Familiar Perspicuity of William Hazlitt," *Romanticism: The Journal of Romantic Culture and Criticism* 13, no. 1 (2007): 28.
5. At the time, divorce in England could be secured only through an act of Parliament, which is why the Hazlitts went to Scotland. The proceedings took several months. Sarah Stoddart Hazlitt's journal offers a powerful account of her travels and divorce in "Journal of My Trip to Scotland, By Mrs. Hazlitt," in *Liber Amoris or the New Pygmalion by William Hazlitt with Additional Matter Now Printed for the First Time from the Original Manuscripts,* ed. Richard Le Gallienne (n.p.: privately printed, 1894), 239–335. For analysis of the journal, see Sonia Hofkosh, *Sexual Politics and the Romantic Author* (Cambridge: Cambridge University Press, 1998), 111–121; and Gillian Beattie-Smith, "Writing the Self: The Journal of Sarah Stoddart Hazlitt, 1774–1843," *Women's History Review* 22, no. 2 (2013): 197–210.
6. This man, John Tompkins, had also been a lodger at 9 Southampton Buildings. Though it appears that Walker never married Tompkins, they did spend their lives together and had children. See Duncan Wu, "Hazlitt's *Liber Amoris*: A Defence," *Wordsworth Circle* 31, no. 1 (2000): 22.
7. Barry Cornwall [Brian Waller Proctor], quoted in Le Gallienne, introduction to *Liber Amoris . . . with Additional Matter,* xiv. The quotation is Cornwall's recollection of a conversation that he had with Hazlitt.
8. Cornwall, quoted in Le Gallienne, introduction to *Liber Amoris . . . with Additional Matter,* xiv.
9. Thomas De Quincey, "Chapter IV: Recollections of Charles Lamb," in *Literary Reminiscences; from The Autobiography of an English Opium-Eater* (Boston: Ticknor, Reed, and Fields, 1851), 1:118–119, HathiTrust, https://babel.hathitrust.org/cgi/pt?id=hvd.hwjvkc&view=1up&seq=15 (accessed May 1, 2021).
10. Hazlitt, *Liber Amoris,* in *SWWH,* 7:32 and 58. Subsequent references to *Liber Amoris* are cited parenthetically by page number.
11. [John Gibson Lockhart?], review of *Liber Amoris, Blackwood's Edinburgh Magazine* (June 1823), in *RR,* part C, 1:167.
12. Hazlitt novelized the events in *Liber Amoris*; it is not nonfiction. However, the similarity between Hazlitt's original letters to P. G. Patmore and those published in *Liber Amoris* indicates the text's proximity to actual events, and it is clear that Hazlitt contemplated publishing his letters about Walker as he wrote them. See Marilyn Butler, "Satire and the Images of Self in the Romantic Period: The Long Tradition of Hazlitt's *Liber Amoris,*" in *Spirits of Fire: English Romantic Writers and Contemporary Historical Methods,* ed. G. A. Rosso and Daniel P. Watkins (London: Associated University Presses, 1990), 162. For more on the nonautobiographical aspects of the novel, see Daniel Robinson, "Taking 'Other Liberties' with Hazlitt's *Liber Amoris,*" *Studies in Short Fiction* 34, no. 2 (1997): 141–149; and Duncan Wu, "Hazlitt's 'Sexual Harassment,'" *Essays in Criticism* 50, no. 3 (2000): 210–211.
13. De Quincey, "Chapter IV: Recollections of Charles Lamb," 1:118.
14. Le Gallienne, introduction to *Liber Amoris . . . with Additional Matter,* xx.

15. Geoffrey Keynes, *Bibliography of William Hazlitt*, 2nd ed. (Surrey, UK: St. Paul's Bibliographies, 1981), 67. As with *Elegiac Sonnets*, questions of how many issues, states, or editions of *Liber Amoris* appeared remain unsatisfactorily resolved. Keynes's descriptions of the book's bindings refer to different colored bindings, which he associates with different issues; hence, his claim that the work was issued three times: once in "pink paper boards and spine," "a later issue in drab paper boards with brown or green spine," and later copies with "a 'secondary binding' of dark green cloth" (67). Given that standardized publishers' bindings were a relatively new feature of books in the 1820s, I am more hesitant than Keynes to equate different colored bindings with new issues. However, in most extant copies of *Liber Amoris* D1 and G8 are cancellations, perhaps indicating the presence of two editions of the work: one censored and one not censored. Unfortunately, exploring further the bibliographic details of *Liber Amoris* is beyond the focus of the present argument.
16. Eva Wiseman, "Our Love-Hate Relationship with TV," *Guardian*, February 17, 2013, http://www.guardian.co.uk/lifeandstyle/2013/feb/17/hate-watching-tv (accessed May 13, 2021). Emily Nussbaum is generally considered the first to have introduced the term *hate-watching* into popular usage. See Nussbaum, "Hate-Watching 'Smash,'" *New Yorker* online, April 27, 2012, http://www.newyorker.com/online/blogs/culture/2012/04/hate-watching-smash.html (accessed May 12, 2021).
17. Le Gallienne, introduction to *Liber Amoris . . . with Additional Matter*, xx.
18. Review of Hazlitt's *Characteristics: In the Manner of Rochefoucault's Maxims*, *Literary Register* (July 1823), in *RR*, part C, 2:553.
19. Review of *Liber Amoris*, *John Bull*, no. 131 (June 16, 1823): 188; and [Lockhart?], review of *Liber Amoris*, 1:171.
20. Review of Hazlitt's *Characteristics*, 2:554.
21. Quoted in Wu, "Introductory Notes: *Liber Amoris*," in *SWWH*, 7:xvii. The criticism lasted even after Hazlitt's death in 1830. Douglass Jerrold's short story "The Metaphysician and the Maid," published in the *New Monthly Magazine* in 1839, parodies *Liber Amoris*. Martin Friedman offers a detailed account of Jerrold's story and its relation to Hazlitt's posthumous reputation in "Hazlitt, Jerrold, and Horne: *Liber Amoris* Twenty Years After," *Review of English Studies* 22, no. 88 (1971): 455–462. The only positive review *Liber Amoris* received was in the *Examiner*.
22. Crabb Robinson, quoted in Howe, *William Hazlitt*, 326. Incidentally, Sarah Walker's father was Crabb Robinson's tailor, so he knew the family (Howe, 306). Crabb Robinson's comments should also be placed in the context of his relationship with Hazlitt; their friendship was strained in 1816 after Hazlitt's criticisms of Wordsworth, though by 1821 they were on tensely formal but polite terms in the Lamb circle. For a succinct exploration of Hazlitt and Crabb Robinson's relationship, see Philipp Hunnekuhl, "Hazlitt and Crabb Robinson: The Common Pursuit," *Hazlitt Review* 6 (2013): 13–34.
23. John Whale, "*Liber Amoris*: Unmanning the Man of Letters," *Nineteenth-Century Prose* 36, no. 1 (2009): 57. Attempts to read *Liber Amoris* alongside Hazlitt's other works often minimize the text's autobiographical revelations, highlight its political elements, or defend Hazlitt's actions. For instance, Jonathan Gross has argued that "*Liber Amoris* is an act of political nostalgia" about the French Revolution rather than primarily a reaction to unrequited love. Gross, "Hazlitt's Worshipping Practice in *Liber Amoris*," *Studies in English Literature, 1500–1900* 35, no. 4 (1995): 710. Kurt M. Koenigsberger reads the text "as a form of libel" that challenges the notions of self and sovereignty. Koenigsberger, "Liberty, Libel, and *Liber Amoris*: Hazlitt on Sovereignty and Death," *Studies in Romanticism* 38, no. 2 (1999): 303–304. Amanda Louise Johnson sees it as an extension of Hazlitt's ideas about monarchy and the sovereignty of subjectivity. Johnson, "William

Hazlitt, *Liber Amoris*, and the Imagination," *European Romantic Review* 25, no. 6 (2014): 743–756. Anahid Neressian argues that the novel is less a roman à clef than a remediation of Hazlitt's journalism, especially the political essay "On the Spirit of Partisanship." Neressian, *Utopia, Limited: Romanticism and Adjustment* (Cambridge, MA: Harvard University Press, 2015), 142–171.

24. Gregory Dart, *Metropolitan Art and Literature, 1810–1840, Cockney Adventures* (Cambridge: Cambridge University Press, 2012), 23.
25. According to Stoddart Hazlitt, "[I]t had often struck him [Hazlitt] that they [the Walkers] had never objected to the girls of the town coming up to him continually, and that Sarah would often send them up when her mother had said he was not at home." Stoddart Hazlitt, "Journal of My Trip to Scotland," 329.
26. Dart, *Metropolitan Art and Literature*, 98.
27. Eliza Haywood, *A Present to a Servant-Maid* (London: T. Gardner, 1743), 44, ESTC Number T76347, ECCO.
28. Straub, *Domestic Affairs*, 36.
29. Catherine Burroughs, "Acting in the Closet: A Feminist Performance of Hazlitt's *Liber Amoris* and Keats's *Otho the Great*," *European Romantic Review* 2, no. 2 (1992): 125–144; and Hofkosh, *Sexual Politics*, 104–121. Again, Walker's complex socioeconomic position doesn't negate the possibility that she may have been romantically and/or sexually interested in Hazlitt; Burroughs entertains this possibility in "Acting in the Closet," 128–129.
30. Hofkosh, *Sexual Politics*, 112.
31. In particular, I have in mind Duncan Wu's work on Walker and Hazlitt. For instance, the entry "stupidity of accusing Hazlitt of 'sexual harassment'" in the index of Wu's biography *William Hazlitt: The First Modern Man* gives one pause, as does his assertion—presumably alluding to Hofkosh and Burroughs—that critics who have written about Hazlitt's potential sexual harassment of Walker and other women "know nothing of the social and sexual norms of Hazlitt's day" and "fail to recognize the anachronism inherent in the application of twenty-first-century American values to the English lower middle class in early-nineteenth-century London." Wu, *William Hazlitt: The First Modern Man* (Oxford: Oxford University Press, 2008), 556 and 328–329. Wu's claim that Walker "did not think herself as harassed or would have reported Hazlitt's conduct to her parents, which she never did," sidesteps the fact that there are no surviving records of what she thought or did, beyond those left by Hazlitt and his circle (Wu, *William Hazlitt*, 329). This rationale, too, problematically equates a lack of reporting with the absence of a hurtful event such as harassment or assault. See also Wu, "Hazlitt's 'Sexual Harassment,'" 199–214; and Wu, "Hazlitt's *Liber Amoris*: A Defence," 20–25.

    Wu is certainly not the only one to take Hazlitt's portrayal of events as fact. Though Dart admits the possibility that Walker may have felt "*obliged* to indulge the residents, as a filial duty," he, like Wu, focuses on Walker's duplicity, and he does not engage feminist work on the novel. Rather, Dart absorbs Hazlitt's view of events, asserting, for instance, "Sarah had been secretly involved with another lodger for much of the time he [Hazlitt] and she had been intimate." Dart, *Metropolitan Art and Literature*, 86, emphasis in original. Relatedly, Charles Mahoney has referred to "Sarah's wantonness" in her interactions with Hazlitt. Mahoney, "*Liber Amoris*: Figuring Out the Coquette," *European Romantic Review* 10 no. 1 (1999): 40. I question such depictions of Walker's supposed "wantonness" and "secrecy." Instead, one might ask why, after Walker's repeated rejections of Hazlitt, he (and his defenders) believed he was entitled to information about her romantic life.
32. Duncan Wu, "Talking Pimples: Hazlitt and Byron in Love," *Romanticism* 10, no. 2 (2004): 168. Dart comes to a similar conclusion: "The book also represented a grave slur on Sarah Walker's character." Dart, *Metropolitan Art and Literature*, 106.

33. Stoddart Hazlitt, "Journal of My Trip to Scotland," 328.
34. Stoddart Hazlitt, 330.
35. Wu, "Hazlitt's *Liber Amoris*: A Defence," 24; and Lucasta Miller, "*Liber Amoris, The Literary Gazette*, and the Poet L.E.L.," *Hazlitt Review* 9 (2016): 29. Elsewhere Wu has relatedly claimed that publishing *Liber Amoris* was "a decision as courageous as that taken by [Byron's character] Sardanapalus." Wu, "Talking Pimples," 168.
36. Hazlitt, "On Coffee-House Politicians," 6:182.
37. Hazlitt, "On Vulgarity and Affectation," 6:138–139.
38. Hazlitt, 6:143.
39. Hill, *Servants*, 6.
40. Jonas Hanway, quoted in Hill, *Servants*, 110, emphasis in the original.
41. Hazlitt, "On the Knowledge of Character," in *SWWH*, 6:276.
42. Hazlitt, 6:277.
43. Hazlitt, 6:278.
44. Hazlitt to P. G. Patmore, postmarked May 31, 1822, in Le Gallienne, *Liber Amoris . . . with Additional Matter*, 218, emphasis in original.
45. Johnson, *Dictionary of the English Language*, s.v. "common."
46. Smith, *Theory of Moral Sentiments*, 18.
47. "Notice of *Liber Amoris*," *Times*, May 30, 1823, Gale Document Number CS50875582, *The Times* Digital Archive.
48. Thomas De Quincey, "Notes on Godwin, Foster, and Hazlitt," in *Coleridge and Opium-Eating and Other Writings*, vol. 11 of *De Quincey's Works* (Edinburgh: Adam and Charles Black, 1863), 303, emphasis in original, HathiTrust, https://hdl.handle.net/2027/ucl.b3311687 (accessed May 13, 2021).
49. Smith, *Theory of Moral Sentiments*, 24.
50. Smith, 147.
51. Smith, 147.
52. De Quincey, "Notes on Godwin, Foster, and Hazlitt," 303. Though De Quincey acknowledged that many readers "expressed disgust for him [Hazlitt] as too coarsely indelicate in making such disclosures," De Quincey himself thought "there was no indelicacy in such an act of confidence, growing, as it did, out of his lacerated heart" (303).
53. Smith, *Theory of Moral Sentiments*, 11.
54. Smith, 34.
55. De Quincey, "Notes on Godwin, Foster, and Hazlitt," 303.
56. Stauffer, *Anger, Revolution, and Romanticism*, 13.
57. Baillie, *Plays on the Passions*, 72.
58. Baillie, 72–73.
59. Hazlitt, "On Novelty and Familiarity," 8:275.
60. Hazlitt, 8:275.
61. Hazlitt, 8:275.
62. "Notice of *Liber Amoris*," 3.
63. Review of Hazlitt's *Characteristics*, 2:553. Though a review of Hazlitt's *Characteristics*, it also addresses *Liber Amoris*.
64. Smith, *Theory of Moral Sentiments*, 18.
65. Cornwall, quoted in Le Gallienne, introduction to *Liber Amoris . . . with Additional Matter*, xiv.
66. Benjamin Robert Haydon to Miss Mitford, September 8, 1822, quoted in Howe, *William Hazlitt*, 318.
67. "Z." [John Gibson Lockhart], "On the Cockney School of Poetry. No. 1," *Blackwood's* (October 1817), in *RR*, part C, 1:51.

68. Smith, *Theory of Moral Sentiments*, 55.
69. [John Wilson], "Hazlitt Cross-Questioned," *Blackwood's* 30, no. 17 (August 1818): 550.
70. Unsigned review of *Liber Amoris, John Bull*, no. 132 (June 23, 1823): 198, emphasis in the original.
71. Review of *Table Talk, Monthly Literary Register* 4 (1 August 1822), quoted in Wu, "Introductory Note: *Table-Talk; or, Original Essays*," in *SWWH*, 6:xiv.
72. [Eyre Evans Crowe], "Hazlitt's *Table-Talk*," *Blackwood's* (August 1822), in *RR*, part C, 1:156, emphasis in the original.
73. See St Clair, *Reading Nation*, 586–587 and 596. Christensen has highlighted the importance of price for Byron's poetry. "Keeping the price of the volumes high," he explains, "was a way not only of appealing to an elite clientele but of *determining* a clientele, and a taste for Byron." Christensen, *Lord Byron's Strength*, 144, emphasis in the original. Hazlitt's critics scoffed at what they saw as his misguided attempts to do something similar.
74. Klancher, *Making of English Reading Audiences*, 13.
75. A modern example of this strategy is the tagline for the UK advertising campaign for Stella Artois beer, which from 1982 to 2007 was "Reassuringly Expensive."
76. "Art. V.—[review of] *Table Talk, or Original Essays*. By William Hazlitt," in *The Quarterly Review. Vol. XXVI. October and January* (London: Murray, 1822), 106, HathiTrust, https://babel.hathitrust.org/cgi/pt?id=njp.32101076520624 (accessed May 21, 2021).
77. Review of *The Round Table* and *Characters of Shakespeare's Plays*, *Edinburgh Magazine* (November 1817), in *RR*, part C, 2:813.
78. Hazlitt, "On Familiar Style," in *SWWH*, 6:217.
79. Hazlitt, 6:217.
80. Robert Ready, *Hazlitt at Table* (Rutherford, NJ: Fairleigh Dickinson University Press, 1981), 67.
81. Hazlitt describes his indigestion in "On Living to One's-Self," in *SWWH*, 6:78. His most obvious references to Walker are in his essay "On the Knowledge of Character." Twentieth- and twenty-first-century critics have recognized Hazlitt's combination of the mundane with the metaphysical and the personal with the philosophical as a touchstone of his style. For instance, according to Uttara Natarajan, "Hazlitt's essayistic practice, like his philosophical theory, recovers the imaginative in the everyday. . . . The real and the ideal evolve one into the other and back again: the quotidian bears a visionary aspect the visionary retains a quotidian form." Natarajan, "Hazlitt's Common Sense," *Nineteenth-Century Prose* 36, no. 1 (2009): 23.
82. "Art. V.—*Table Talk*," in *The Quarterly Review*, 106.
83. Hazlitt, "On Vulgarity and Affectation," 6:140–141.
84. Dart, *Metropolitan Art and Literature*, 10.
85. Fairclough, *Romantic Crowd*, 132.
86. "Z." [Lockhart], "On the Cockney School," 1:49. Hunt, in fact, did know Greek. Often the education of those associated with the Cockney school was more robust than their detractors admitted. Wilson's "Hazlitt Cross-Questioned" in *Blackwood's* similarly attacked Hazlitt's knowledge of classical languages. [Wilson], "Hazlitt Cross-Questioned," 551–552.
87. [Crowe], "Hazlitt's *Table-Talk*," 1:163.
88. Hollander, *Figure of Echo*, 72.
89. William Gifford quoted in Hazlitt, *A Letter to William Gifford*, 5:370, in *SWWH*, emphasis in the original.
90. Thomas De Quincey, "Charles Lamb," in *Leaders in Literature with a Notice of Traditional Errors Affecting Them*, vol. 8 of *De Quincey's Works* (Edinburgh: Adam and Charles

Black, 1862), 134–135, HathiTrust, https://hdl.handle.net/2027/ucl.b3311684 (accessed May 21, 2021).

91. Perhaps De Quincey saw too much of his own style in Hazlitt. Adela Pinch observes that De Quincey's "autobiographical writings therefore are veritable quotation books in which he constantly requites his early experiences; for De Quincey, accounting for himself and quoting seem to be one and the same thing." Pinch, *Strange Fits of Passion*, 174.
92. "Z." [Lockhart], "On the Cockney School," 1:49. Lockhart's comments refer to Hunt, yet similar accusations were made across the "Cockney School" series.
93. Hazlitt, "On Reading Old Books," in *SWWH*, 8:207.
94. Hazlitt, 8:214.
95. Graham Good, *The Observing Self: Rediscovering the Essay* (London: Routledge, 1988), 7. Sonia Hofkosh has also asserted the thing-like quality of Hazlitt's quotations, describing them as "verbal tokens, words that are things." Hofkosh, "Broken Images," *Nineteenth-Century Prose* 36, no. 1 (2009): 37.
96. De Quincey, "Charles Lamb," 134.
97. Review of *The Round Table* and *Characters of Shakespeare's Plays*, 2:811. Reiman notes that there is scholarly speculation that Hazlitt wrote the review himself. Reiman, in *RR*, part C, 2:809.
98. Butler, "Satire and the Images of Self," 160. Robert Ready, "The Logic of Passion: Hazlitt's *Liber Amoris*," *Studies in Romanticism* 14, no. 1 (1975): 51. For more on the novel's intertextuality, see also Robinson, "Taking 'Other Liberties,'" 141–149; Mahoney, "*Liber Amoris*: Figuring Out the Coquette," 23–52; and Neressian, *Utopia, Limited*, 142–171.
99. Butler, "Satire and the Images of Self," 163. Jonathan Gross relatedly suggests that Hazlitt's writing "creates its own object"; "No sooner has Hazlitt 'lost' Coleridge, Napoleon, and Sarah [Walker] as objects of worship, than he has gained them on his own terms as literary commodities: 'My First Acquaintance With the Poets,' *The Life of Napoleon Buonaparte*, and *Liber Amoris*." Gross, "Hazlitt's Worshipping Practice," 712.
100. Hazlitt, "On Reading Old Books," 8:207.
101. Hofkosh, "Broken Images," 47.
102. Crabb Robinson, quoted in Howe, *William Hazlitt*, 326. Part of his objection seems to arise from the difference between a work of fiction and what many Romantic readers saw as a work largely based on autobiographical facts.
103. Baillie, *Plays on the Passions*, 92.
104. Leigh Hunt, "Literary Notices. No. 58. *Lectures on the English Comic Poets*. By William Hazlitt, Esq.," *Examiner* (June 1819), in *RR*, part C, 1:441.
105. Ready, "Logic of Passion," 52. For a reading of H.'s "lines" as a sonnet related to Keats's *Endymion*, see Nersessian, *Utopia, Limited*, 155–159.
106. Wu, "Talking Pimples," 165 and 166.
107. Baillie, *Plays on the Passions*, 92.
108. Edmund Spenser, *The Faerie Queene*, ed. A. C. Hamilton, (London: Longman, 2007), 3.7.15. Citations to the *Faerie Queene* indicate book, canto, and stanza number.
109. Kim Wheatley, *Romantic Feuds: Transcending the Age of Personality* (Surrey, UK: Ashgate, 2013), 105.
110. For details on Hunt's centrality to the Cockney school, see Jeffrey N. Cox, *Poetry and the Politics in the Cockney School: Keats, Shelley, Hunt and Their Circle* (Cambridge: Cambridge University Press, 1998), especially 38–81.
111. "Art. III. *The Story of Rimini; A Poem*, by Leigh Hunt," *Monthly Review* (June 1816), in *RR*, part C, 2:698, emphasis in the original; and Leigh Hunt, *The Story of Rimini, A Poem* (London: Murray, 1816), v and vi. The *Quarterly Review* similarly identified the impropriety of *Rimini*'s dedication to Byron, which exemplified "the vulgar impatience of a

low man . . . to scramble over the bounds of birth and education, and fidget himself into the *stout-heartedness* of being familiar with a LORD." [John Wilson Croker and William Gifford], "Art. IX. *The Story of Rimini, a Poem*, by Leigh Hunt," *Quarterly Review* (January 1816), in *RR*, part C, 2:756, emphasis in the original. These class-inflected critiques echo Adam Smith's description of a vulgar social reacher who "is fond of being admitted to the tables of the great, and still more fond of magnifying to other people the familiarity with which he is honoured there." Smith, *Theory of Moral Sentiments*, 257.

112. "Z." [Lockhart], "On the Cockney School," 1:51. Of course, Francesca was not related to Paolo by blood, but he was her husband's brother.
113. "Z." [John Gibson Lockhart?], "Letter from Z. to Leigh Hunt, King of the Cockneys," *Blackwood's* (May 1818), in *RR*, part C, 1:84.
114. [Lockhart?], review of *Liber Amoris*, 1:166.
115. Gregory Dart, ed., *Liber Amoris and Related Writings* (Manchester: Carcanet, 2008), 226n.
116. Le Gallienne, introduction to *Liber Amoris . . . with Additional Matter*, xxv.
117. Hill, *Servants*, 50.
118. "Notice of *Liber Amoris*," 3.
119. Despite the overlapping themes of a man courting a lower-class woman, Hazlitt's novel does not explicitly reference *Pamela*. However, the notable similarities between the two texts offer another example of Hazlitt's bathetic application of existing literary frameworks to his own failed love. Unlike Mr. B., Hazlitt was not a landowner, member of Parliament, or justice of the peace; he was a lodger in rented London rooms struggling to make ends meet.
120. This not a valuation of Walker's abilities but rather an observation based on contemporary accounts, imperfect as those accounts may be. Walker clearly had some education, since she and Hazlitt maintained a limited correspondence, and he also lent her several books. However, she was certainly not educated to the degree of other women Hazlitt had known, like Dorothy Wordsworth, Mary Lamb, and his first wife. Hazlitt's views on educated women were fraught, to say the least; in *Table-Talk* Hazlitt claims, "I do not care a fig for any woman that knows even what *an author* means. If I know she has read any thing I have written, I cut her acquaintance immediately." Hazlitt, "On Great and Little Things," in *SWWH*, 6:211, emphasis in the original.
121. Stoddart Hazlitt, "Journal of My Trip to Scotland," 275. Of course, it is possible that Bell was trying to flatter Stoddart Hazlitt by criticizing her husband's new love interest.
122. Hofkosh, "Broken Images," 38.
123. Deidre Lynch, "On Going Steady with Novels," *Eighteenth Century: Theory and Interpretation* 50, no. 2–3 (2009): 209.
124. Hazlitt, "The Same Subject Continued [On the Conversation of Authors]," in *SWWH*, 8:34.
125. Hazlitt, "On the Pleasure of Hating," 8:121.

CHAPTER 5 — MEDIATING A MANUSCRIPT ETHOS

* [Letitia Elizabeth Landon], introduction to *Fisher's Drawing Room Scrap-book; with Poetical Illustrations by L.E.L.* [for 1832] (London: Fisher, Son, and Jackson, 1832). Dating annuals sometimes causes confusion. Like calendars today, annuals typically appeared in the autumn before the publication date printed on them, meaning that, for instance, the famous *Keepsake* for 1829 was published at the end of 1828. Readers should keep in mind that, despite the cited publication date, these volumes were typically in circulation the previous year.

The case of the first volume of *Fisher's Drawing Room Scrap-book*, a title that was produced until 1852, is especially complex. It was advertised in 1831, published in December 1831, and printed with an 1831 publication date; this version is now rare, but a copy from the University of Minnesota is accessible through HathiTrust. *Fisher's Drawing Room Scrap-book; with Poetical Illustrations by L.E.L.* [for 1832] (London: Fisher, Son, and Jackson, 1831), HathiTrust, https://hdl.handle.net/2027/umn.31951002225359l (accessed May 21, 2021). The volume was shortly reissued with the same engraved title page (with the original publication date of 1831) and a different letterpress title page (with an updated publication date of 1832). I have encountered entries in some library catalogues stating that the 1831 edition and the more common 1832 version are identical (see, for instance, the University of Maryland's online catalogue). This is inaccurate. While the lists of contents and engravings are the same in both versions, Landon's 1831 introduction was reset for the 1832 volume, resulting in different paragraphing. The 1832 version also has substantive additions to Landon's dedicatory poem "The Princess Victoria." Because of COVID-19 travel restrictions, I have been unable to collate copies in person. Throughout this chapter I cite the more common 1832 version.

1. Landon contributed more than 160 pieces to different literary annuals. She edited *Fisher's Drawing Room Scrap-book* from 1832 to 1839 and wrote the majority of the content published in it. She also wrote all of *Heath's Book of Beauty* for 1833. For more information on Landon's contributions to the annuals, as well as those of her contemporaries, see Katherine D. Harris, *Forget Me Not: The Rise of the British Literary Annuals, 1823–1835* (Athens: Ohio University Press, 2015), 286–320.
2. Lee Erickson, *The Economy of Literary Form: English Literature and the Industrialization of Publishing, 1800–1850* (Baltimore: Johns Hopkins University Press, 1996), 29. Like Erickson, William G. Rowland Jr. points to the decreasing demand for poetry at the end of the Romantic period in *Literature and the Marketplace: Romantic Writers and Their Audiences in Great Britain and the United States* (Lincoln: University of Nebraska Press, 1996). William St Clair offers an alternative view, arguing that the decline in poetry sales may not have been as sharp as Erickson or Rowland suggest. St Clair, *Reading Nation*, 175–176.
3. Katherine D. Harris, "Feminizing the Textual Body: Female Readers Consuming the Literary Annual," *Papers of the Bibliographical Society of America* 99, no. 4 (2005): 575.
4. Erickson, *Economy of Literary Form*, 5.
5. Harris identifies eight characteristics of literary annuals: they were intended to be annual symbols of affection; they were marketed annually in November; the genre would improve with new techniques, tastes, and technologies; eminent authors would be published; they would include original rather than republished works; engravings would have a key place; useful information would be important; and the binding would be fetching. Harris, *Forget Me Not*, 35.
6. [Landon], introduction to *Fisher's Drawing Room Scrap-book* [for 1832], unpaginated. Landon's poems illustrating images—many of them scenes of the British empire—have prompted work on her as an (anti)imperialist figure. See, for example, Jean Fernandez, "Graven Images: The Woman Writer, the Indian Poetess, and Imperial Aesthetics in L.E.L.'s 'Hindoo Temples and Palaces at Madura,'" *Victorian Poetry* 43, no. 1 (2005): 35–52; Vanessa Warne, "'What Foreign Scenes Can Be': The Ruin of India in Letitia Landon's *Scrapbook Poems*," *Victorian Review* 32, no. 2 (2006): 40–63; and Jonas Cope, "Scrapped Sentiment: Letitia Landon and *Fisher's Drawing Room Scrap-Book*, 1832–1837," *Romanticism* 25, no. 2 (2019): 190–204. The threads of imperialism and colonialism in Landon's poems are important, yet Storti challenges scholarly readings of the poet's political interest in imperialism and orientalism. "Landon did not elect to focus

'on a South Indian landscape,'" Storti explains, but rather the "choice was made for her" in the engravings of Indian and other colonial landscapes that her publishers selected for her to write about. Storti, "Letitia Landon," 538.

7. For more on the flexible terminology used for these books, see Deidre Lynch, "Paper Slips: Album, Archiving, Accident," *Studies in Romanticism* 57, no. 1 (2018): 93–95.
8. [Landon], introduction to *Fisher's Drawing Room Scrap-book* [for 1832], unpaginated.
9. Thomas Carlyle, "Signs of the Times," *Edinburgh Review* 49, no. 98 (1829): 442 and 444.
10. Review of *The Literary Souvenir, Blackwood's Edinburgh Magazine* 17, no. 96 (January 1825): 94, HathiTrust, https://hdl.handle.net/2027/chi.28408055 (accessed May 24, 2021). The question of whether the literary annual is a medium or a genre is complex. Taking a lead from new media studies, in which a medium is defined as "that which remediates" and "appropriates the techniques, forms, and social significance of other media," I suggest that annuals' adaptation of diverse media and genres—from engravings, embossed prints, and facsimile autographs to poetry, essays, and short stories—aligns them with the realm of medium rather than genre. Jay David Bolter and Richard Grusin, *Remediation: Understanding New Media* (Cambridge: MIT Press, 1999), 65.
11. I have in mind Bolter and Grusin's emphasis on the embeddedness of media relations within a network of "social arrangements." Bolter and Grusin, *Remediation*, 70. While they are not concerned with nineteenth-century manuscript or print media, their observations about new media apply to decidedly "old" media.
12. Hofkosh, *Sexual Politics*, 87. Relatedly, Samantha Matthews characterizes annuals as "aspirational: a printed, published book that looked like an elegant album belonging to a society lady in a grand country house who could attract celebrity contributors." Matthews, "Albums, Belongings, and Embodying the Feminine," in *Bodies and Things in Nineteenth-Century Literature and Culture*, ed. Katharina Boehm (New York: Palgrave Macmillan, 2012), 113.
13. Matthews, "Albums, Belongings," 111. An expanded and lively historical overview of "albo-mania" and "albo-phobia" in the 1820s can be found in Matthews, *Album Verses*, 127–162.
14. William Makepeace Thackeray, quoted in Vanessa Warne, "Thackeray among the Annuals: Morality, Cultural Authority and the Literary Annual Genre," *Victorian Periodicals Review* 39, no. 2 (2006): 166. Thackeray's comments specifically criticize the reprinting in *Fisher's Drawing Room Scrap-book* of illustrations that had already appeared in other publications; however, Storti has shown that Landon's written contributions to the annuals remixed her previously published poems. Storti, "Letitia Landon," 533–556.
15. William Makepeace Thackeray, "A Word on the Annuals," *Fraser's Magazine* 16, no. 96 (December 1837): 763, HathiTrust, https://hdl.handle.net/2027/nyp.33433081686697 (accessed May 24, 2021).
16. Jerome McGann, *The Textual Condition* (Princeton, NJ: Princeton University Press, 1991), 57.
17. Celeste Langan and Maureen McLane, "The Medium of Romantic Poetry," in *The Cambridge Companion to British Romantic Poetry*, ed. James Chandler and Maureen McLane (Cambridge: Cambridge University Press, 2008), 242.
18. Jackson, *Marginalia*, 67. Relatedly, St Clair claims that manuscript albums "created their own genre, 'verses written in a lady's album.'" St Clair, *Reading Nation*, 225.
19. Judith Pascoe, "Poetry as Souvenir: Mary Shelley in the Annuals," in *Mary Shelley in Her Times*, ed. Betty T. Bennett and Stuart Curran (Baltimore: Johns Hopkins University Press, 2000), 174.
20. *Oxford English Dictionary* online, s.v. "souvenir."

21. For work on Romantic authors and annuals, see Morton D. Paley, "Coleridge and the Annuals," *Huntington Library Quarterly* 57, no. 1 (1994): 1–24; Peter J. Manning, "Wordsworth in the *Keepsake*, 1829," in *Literature in the Marketplace: Nineteenth-Century British Publishing and Reading Practices*, ed. John O. Jordan and Robert L. Patten (Cambridge: Cambridge University Press, 1995), 44–73; Pascoe, "Poetry as Souvenir," 173–184; Stephen Colclough, "'Designated in Print as "Mr. John Clare"': The Annuals and the Field of Reading, 1827–1835," *John Clare Society Journal* 24 (2005): 53–68; and Lindsey Eckert, "'I'll be bound': John Clare's 'Don Juan,' Literary Annuals, and the Commodification of Authorship," *Nineteenth-Century Literature* 69, no. 4 (2015): 427–454. For Victorian authors' relationships with annuals, see Warne, "Thackeray among the Annuals," 158–178; Christine Alexander, "'The Kingdom of Gloom': Charlotte Brontë, the Annuals, and the Gothic," *Nineteenth-Century Literature* 47, no. 4 (1993): 409–436; and Kathryn Ledbetter, "'Begemmed and Beamuletted': Tennyson and Those 'Vapid' Gift Books," *Victorian Poetry* 34, no. 2 (1996): 235–245. For work that moves beyond author-focused studies of annuals, see Margaret Linley, "A Centre That Would Not Hold: Annuals and the Cultural Democracy," in *Nineteenth-Century Media and the Construction of Identity*, ed. Laurel Brake, Bill Bell, and David Finkelstein (New York: Palgrave, 2000), 54–74; Sara Lodge, "Romantic Reliquaries: Memory and Irony in the Literary Annuals," *Romanticism* 10, no. 1 (2004): 23–40; Feldman, "Evidence of Inscriptions," 54–62; Manuela Mourão, "Remembrance of Things Past: Literary Annuals' Self-Historicization," *Victorian Poetry* 50, no. 1 (2012): 107–123; and Harris, *Forget Me Not*.
22. Feldman, "Evidence of Inscriptions," 54–62; Andrew Piper, *Dreaming in Books: The Making of the Bibliographic Imagination in the Romantic Age* (Chicago: Chicago University Press, 2009), 128–138; and Michelle Levy, *Family Authorship and Romantic Print Culture* (Basingstoke, UK: Palgrave, 2008), 170.
23. Samantha Matthews, "Importunate Applications and Old Affections: Robert Southey's Album Verses," *Romanticism* 17, no. 1 (2011): 79.
24. Harris, *Forget Me Not*, 80.
25. I have in mind, for example, Margaret Ezell's arguments about "the replacement of the 'social' author and manuscript practice" by print. Ezell, *Social Authorship and the Advent of Print* (Baltimore: Johns Hopkins University Press, 1999), 142.
26. Matthews, "Importunate Applications and Old Affections," 78.
27. Lynch, "Paper Slips," 102.
28. Lynch, 92–93. The cataloguing of literary annuals, like albums, presents problems. Annuals are catalogued under different subject headings, including "gift books," "annual," and "anthology," and they are sometimes classified as books and other times as periodicals. For more on annuals and cataloguing practices, see Harris, *Forget Me Not*, 18–19.
29. Felicia Dorothea Brown Hemans, Commonplace book manuscript, [18—], Harvard University, Houghton Library, MS Eng 767.
30. For more on extra-illustrated books, see Lucy Peltz, *Facing the Text: Extra-Illustration, Print Culture, and Society in Britain 1769–1840* (San Marino, CA: Huntington Library, 2017). For more on collections of ephemera and collectanea, see Gillian Russell, *The Ephemeral Eighteenth Century: Print, Sociability, and Cultures of Collecting* (Cambridge: Cambridge University Press, 2020). Russell also notes the applicability of the term *assemblage* in relation to Sarah Sophia Banks's volumes of collectanea, which feature tickets to events like balls and, thus, record sociability. Russell, *Ephemeral Eighteenth Century*, 112–113.
31. Samantha Matthews, "From Autograph to Print: *Charles Lamb's Album Verses, with a Few Others* (1830)," *Charles Lamb Bulletin* 154 (2011): 145.

32. Patrizia Di Bello, *Women's Albums and Photography in Victorian England: Ladies, Mothers and Flirts* (Aldershot, UK: Ashgate, 2007), 42.
33. Stephen Colclough, *Consuming Texts: Readers and Reading Communities, 1695–1870* (Basingstoke, UK: Palgrave, 2007), 130.
34. Lynch, *Loving Literature*, 137.
35. Caroline Lamb, Commonplace Book of Caroline Lamb (Green), JMA, MS.43365. The John Murray Archive also holds manuscript volumes owned by Annabella Milbanke (Lady Byron) and Augusta Leigh. See Commonplace Book of Lady Byron, 1809–1815, JMA, MS.43360; and August Leigh, Commonplace Book of Augusta Leigh, 1822, JMA, MS.43369. Relatedly, Hertfordshire Archives and Local Studies holds multiple albums and commonplace books that Lamb kept, including Verses and Sketches by Lady Caroline Lamb, [c. 1813], Papers of the Lamb Family of Brocket Hall, DE/Lb/F64; and Sketches, Stories and Verse by Lady Caroline Lamb, 1803-c1825, Papers of the Lamb Family of Brocket Hall, DE/Lb/F66.
36. Thomas Colley Grattan, *Beaten Paths; and Those Who Trod Them* (London: Chapman and Hall, 1862), 2:138–139.
37. Di Bello, *Women's Albums*, 33.
38. Miss Pipper to Byron, February 28, [18—], JMA, MS.43523. For more on how Byron's poetry made its way into Romantic-era manuscript volumes, see Throsby, "Byron, Commonplacing and Early Fan Culture," 227–244.
39. Robert Southey to Charles Wynn, November 5, 1821, quoted in St Clair, *Reading Nation*, 225.
40. Robert Southey to Grosvenor Charles Bedford, June 10, 1827, quoted in Matthews, "Importunate Applications and Old Affections," 77.
41. Coleridge to J. H. Green, May 30, 1827, in *Collected Letters of Samuel Taylor Coleridge*, ed. Earl Leslie Griggs (Oxford: Clarendon Press, 1956–1971), 6:686.
42. Lynch, "Paper Slips," 95n16.
43. Charles Lamb, "In the Album of a Clergyman's Lady," in *Album Verses, with a Few Others* (London: Moxon, 1830), 43.
44. Pierre Bourdieu, *Distinction: A Social Critique of the Judgment of Taste*, trans. Richard Nice (Cambridge, MA: Harvard University Press, 1984), 76–80.
45. For more about *Album Verses* and its 1836 reprint, see J. C. Thomson, *Bibliography of the Writings of Charles and Mary Lamb: A Literary History* (Hull: J. R. Tutin, 1908), 103–106. For more on *Album Verses* and its critical reception, see Matthews, *Album Verses*, 181–204.
46. The Album of Mrs Birkbeck, London, Birkbeck College, Birkbeck Library. I draw several examples from Birkbeck's album for two reasons: one, her album is typical of the medium; two, while I examined the album in person, it has also been digitized, making it accessible to readers interested in exploring further the works I cite here. See the Album of Anna Birkbeck, Birkbeck Library, https://birkbeck.lunaimaging.com/luna/servlet/BIRKBECKBCM~15~15 (accessed May 25, 2021). Patrizia Di Bello has also written thoughtfully about this album. See Di Bello, "Mrs. Birkbeck's Album: The Hand-Written and the Printed in Early Nineteenth-Century Print Culture," *19: Interdisciplinary Studies in the Long Nineteenth Century* 1 (2005): 26; and Di Bello, *Women's Albums and Photography*, 29–52.
47. Bolter and Grusin, *Remediation*, 232.
48. Ambassador of the Empire of the Sultan, untitled entry, in the Album of Mrs Birkbeck, fol. 120.
49. John Britton, "An Album," in the Album of Mrs Birkbeck, fol. 145.
50. My phrasing adapts the concept of "the romance of orality" used by Penny Fielding and Maureen McLane. See Penny Fielding, *Writing and Orality: Nationality, Culture, and*

Nineteenth-Century Scottish Fiction (Oxford: Oxford University Press, 1996); Maureen McLane, "Ballads and Bards: British Romantic Orality," *Modern Philology* 98, no. 3 (2001): 423–443; and Maureen McLane, "The Use and Abuse of 'Orality' for Art: Reflections on Romantic and Late Twentieth-Century *Poiesis*," *Oral Tradition* 17, no. 1 (2002): 135–164.

51. According to the catalogue notes, "Internal clues point to a possible compiler [of the album] being either Dorothy Benson Harrison or her daughter. Dorothy was born Dorothy Wordsworth hence her moniker of 'Middle Dorothy.' She was very much part of the Wordsworth circle. She was the daughter of Wordsworth's cousin Richard Wordsworth." Catalogue notes on MS Autograph Album [unknown compiler], Grasmere, UK, Jerwood Center, DCMS181. My work on this album would not be possible without the help of Jeff Cowton, who generously drew it to my attention and discussed it with me during my visit to the Jerwood Centre. I also wish to thank Harriette Smale for information about this album and its contributors.
52. O[wen] L[loyd], untitled poem, in MS Autograph Album (unknown compiler), Jerwood Center, DCMS181, unfoliated.
53. Jonathan Culler, "Why Lyric?," *PMLA* 123, no. 1 (2008): 205.
54. Jonathan Culler, "Lyric, History, and Genre," in *The Lyric Theory Reader: A Critical Anthology*, ed. Virginia Jackson and Yopie Prins (Baltimore: Johns Hopkins University Press, 2014), 74.
55. Virginia Jackson analyzes Emily Dickinson's forms of address as well as her deictics, noting that *here* and *there* in Dickinson's poetry point to "the page we hold in our hands (but not exactly that page, of course, once the poem 'is printed' and many pages are delivered into my hands)." Virginia Jackson, *Dickinson's Misery: A Theory of Lyric Reading* (Princeton, NJ: Princeton University Press, 2005), 157. I see the trope of space and remediation that deixis foregrounds not as a characteristic of a particular poet, like Dickinson, but as a key element of album verse more generally. Closer to my own position, Heather Dubrow argues that deixis in sixteenth-century poetry often challenges assumptions about lyric mode. This is particularly the case, she claims, when deictics point to the "here" of a page that may alternately be sung, recited, or printed in different forms. Dubrow, "Neither Here Nor There: Deixis and the Sixteenth-Century Sonnet," in *The Lyric Poem: Formations and Transformation*, ed. Marion Thain (Cambridge: Cambridge University Press, 2013), 30–50. Sylvia Adamson's earlier work on Thomas Wyatt relatedly suggests that he plays with tensions between deixis in speech versus in manuscript; she points out that in writing, the referents of deictics are more opaque than when spoken. Adamson, "Deixis and the Renaissance Art of Self Construction," *Sederi* 16 (2006): 5–29. The strategies that Dubrow and Adamson identify in the sixteenth century are even more complicated in the Romantic period, when the explosion of print and literary commercialization increased the likelihood that the "this" or "here" in a printed poem represented a seemingly private manuscript remediated for a more public audience. Remediated album verse shifts the "you" of a particular poem from a familiar, private audience to an explicitly commercial one.
56. M. H. Abrams, "Structure and Style in the Greater Romantic Lyric," in *Romanticism and Consciousness: Essays in Criticism*, ed. Harold Bloom (New York: Norton, 1970), 207.
57. Piper, *Dreaming in Books*.
58. Martha Noble, untitled poem dated 1841, in the Album of Mrs Birkbeck, fol. 209.
59. Eliza Emmerson, "Lines of Being Invited by a friend to contribute to Mrs. G. Birkbeck's Album," in the Album of Mrs Birkbeck, fol. 93.
60. Samantha Matthews, "'O All Pervading Album!': Place and Displacement in Romantic Albums and Album Poetry," in *Romantic Localities: Europe Writes Place*, ed. Christoph Bode and Jacqueline Labbe (London: Pickering and Chatto, 2010), 103.

61. Wordsworth, "Essays Upon Epitaphs," 2:66.
62. W[illiam]. A[lexander]., "Written in An Album." in *The Literary Souvenir; Or, Cabinet of Poetry and Romance* [for 1826], ed. Alaric A. Watts (London: Hurst, Robinson, 1826), 180; Richard Polwhele, "Impromptu On Being Desired by a Young Lady to Write Some Lines in Her Album," in *Forget Me Not; A Christmas and New Year's Present for MDCCCXXVII*, ed. Frederic Shoberl (London: R. Ackermann, 1827), 94; John Malcolm, "Written in a Lady's Album," in *The Literary Souvenir; Or, Cabinet of Poetry and Romance* [for 1827], ed. Alaric A. Watts (London: Longman, Rees, Orme, Brown & Green, and John Andrews, 1827), 192–193.
63. Meredith L. McGill, *American Literature and the Culture of Reprinting, 1834–1853* (Philadelphia: University of Pennsylvania Press, 2003), 177.
64. Malcolm, "Written in a Lady's Album," 193.
65. My reading of Malcolm's poem differs from David Stewart's. He also observes the poem's emphasis on traces of handwriting, yet ultimately concludes: "These are not moments of transcendence: annual poetry does not claim the ability to escape its physical form." Rather than see poems like Malcolm's "enacting a poetry of doubt," as Stewart does, I see them attempting both to enact the value of materiality so common in album verse and to invite readers to imagine handwriting and sociability behind print. Stewart, *The Form of Poetry in the 1820s and 1830s: A Period of Doubt* ([New York]: Palgrave Macmillan, 2018), 86.
66. Levy, *Literary Manuscript Culture*, 7.
67. M. A. Shee, "An Impromptu, Addressed to a Lady who required a Specimen of the Author's Hand-writing," in *The Literary Souvenir* [for 1827], 328.
68. Tamara Plakins Thornton makes a similar connection about the double meaning of "character formation," in *Handwriting in America: A Cultural History* (New Haven, CT: Yale University Press, 1996), 71.
69. W[illiam]. A[lexander]., "Written in an Album," 180. Lynch also notes that album verses "often draw analogies between the blankness of the as yet uninscribed album and the innocence of the book's (generally female) owner." Lynch, "Paper Slips," 110.
70. Barbara Johnson, *Persons and Things* (Cambridge, MA: Harvard University Press, 2008), 14, emphasis in the original.
71. Charles Lamb, "Verses Written in Lady Barton's Album," in *Christmas Box. An Annual Present for Children* [for 1828], ed. T. Crofton Croker (London: William Harrison Ainsworth, 1828), 15–16; William Elliot, "For ———'s Album," in *The Bengal Annual, a Literary Keepsake for MDCCCXXX*, ed. David Lester Richardson (Calcutta: Samuel Smith, 1830), 275–276; Mrs. Cockle, "Written in a Young Lady's Album," in *The Juvenile Keepsake. MDCCCXXIX*, ed. Thomas Roscoe (London: Hurst, Chance, 1829), 156–157; and J. A. St. John, "Verses Written for a Lady's Album," in *The Juvenile Keepsake. MDCCCXXIX*, 169.
72. Charles Lamb, "In the Album of a Clergyman's Lady," 43.
73. Lodge, "Romantic Reliquaries," 33.
74. Thornton, *Handwriting in America*, 33.
75. S., "On Autographs," in *The Literary Souvenir: Or, Cabinet of Poetry and Romance* [for 1825], ed. Alaric A. Watts (London: Hurst, Robinson, 1825), 384.
76. Coleridge to J. H. Green, May 30, 1827, in *Collected Letters*, 6:686.
77. A.N.L. Munby, *The Cult of the Autograph Letter in England* (London: Athlone Press, 1962), 10.
78. Smith, *Theory of Moral Sentiments*, 257.
79. Harris holds the contrasting view that the signature plates in annuals undermine "the owner's written influence on the work." Harris, *Forget Me Not*, 84.

80. Piper, *Dreaming in Books*, 137.
81. Thomas K. Hervey, preface to *Friendship's Offering, or the Annual Remembrancer A Christmas Present or New Year's Gift for 1824*, ed. Thomas K. Hervey (London: Lupton Relfe, 1824), iv.
82. *Remember Me! A New Year's Gift or Christmas Present, 1825* (London: J. Poole, 1825). I discuss the formatting of pocketbooks more thoroughly in Lindsey Eckert, "Priscilla Wordsworth's Pocketbook Diaries and Interfaces of Subjectivity," *Review of English Studies* 71, no. 300 (2020): 508–527.
83. Austen, *Emma*, 103 and 115. For an example of such albums, see Collection of enigmas, rebuses, conundrums and charades, with answers, 1828, Harvard University, Houghton Library, MS Am 1177.
84. *Friendship's Offering; or the Annual Remembrancer: A Christmas Present or New Year's Gift, for 1825*, ed. Frederic Shoberl (London: Lupton Relfe, 1825), McLean Collection, D 0418 copy 1, 279. In this copy, ten of twenty-five charades have been answered.
85. *Friendship's Offering . . . for 1825*, McLean Collection, D 0418 copy 2, 272. In this copy, sixteen of twenty-five charades and five of the twenty-two riddles have been answered.
86. While many annuals held in libraries are not annotated, I find it difficult to believe that these sanctioned writing spaces were regularly left blank. Minimal marginalia in library copies may reveal more about acquisition practices than how these books were typically used in the nineteenth century. H. J. Jackson has detailed the shifting value placed on marginalia, which in turn has influenced the acquisition practices of libraries and private collectors. Until recently, there was a strong preference for clean copies of books, unless notes had been made by established literary or historical figures. Jackson, *Marginalia*, 235.
87. Walter Benjamin, "The Work of Art in the Age of Mechanical Reproduction," in *Illuminations: Essays and Reflections*, ed. Hannah Arendt (New York: Mariner Books, 2019), 183.
88. The blurring of reader and writer aligns annuals with the miscellanies explored by Piper. "[W]hite space in the miscellanies," Piper explains, "was an invitation to cross the boundaries between reader and author and produce the presence of multiple hands on the page." Piper, *Dreaming in Books*, 129.
89. [Leigh Hunt], "Pocket-Books and Keepsakes," in *The Keepsake for 1828*, ed. Frederic Mansel Reynolds (London: Hurst, Chance, 1828), 16–17.
90. Paula R. Feldman, introduction to *The Keepsake for 1829*, ed. Paula R. Feldman (Peterborough, ON: Broadview, 2006), 9.
91. St Clair, *Reading Nation*, 229.
92. Katherine D. Harris, introduction to *The Forgotten Gothic: Short Stories from British Literary Annuals, 1823–1831*, ed. Katherine D. Harris (n.p.: Zittaw Press, 2012), xxxv.
93. Jackson, *Marginalia*, 235.
94. Feldman, "Evidence of Inscriptions," 56. Again, I want to foreground that current understandings of nineteenth-century inscription practices in annuals are filtered through the shifting values that libraries and collectors have placed on annotated books.
95. Thomas K. Hervey, preface to *Friendship's Offering, A Literary Album* [for 1826], ed. Thomas K. Hervey (London: Lupton Relfe, 1826), vii–viii. Nodding to the complexities of Lamb's love life and difficult marriage, the volume also includes a poem she wrote to her husband, "Verses to the Hon. W. Lamb." Lodge also notes the "Byronic 'reliques'" in *Friendship's Offering*, yet she mistakenly notes that the volume contains an engraving of "a miniature 'taken' by Caroline Lamb." Lodge, "Romantic Reliquaries," 28. Though Hervey mentions the engraving in the preface and in advertisements at the rear of the volume, it seems to have been sold separately.

96. Walter Scott, for instance, received five hundred pounds for the four short stories published in the 1829 *Keepsake*. Wordsworth received the equally impressive sum of a hundred guineas for twelve pages of poetry, which also appeared in *The Keepsake*; Coleridge was paid fifty pounds for his contributions to the same volume. See Manning, "Wordsworth in the *Keepsake*, 1829," 49; and Coleridge to Alaric Watts, September 14, 1828, in *Collected Letters*, 6:761. Other authors were paid far less; for a discussion of the relatively low payments that John Clare received, see Eckert, "I'll be bound," 427–454.
97. Sara Lodge, "By Its Own Hand: Periodicals and the Paradox of Romantic Authenticity," in Milnes and Sinanan, *Romanticism, Sincerity and Authenticity*, 195. In some cases, poems in annuals did arise from familiar relationships. Coleridge's decision to write for *The Keepsake* was influenced by the fact that Southey and Wordsworth also contributed to the volume. See Coleridge to Alaric Watts, September 14, 1828, in *Collected Letters*, 6:761.
98. Alaric A. Watts, preface to *The Literary Souvenir* [for 1825], viin.
99. [Letitia Elizabeth Landon], "The Farewell," in *Fisher's Drawing Room Scrap-book, MDCCCXXXIX, With Poetical Illustrations by L.E.L.* (London: Fisher, Son, 1839), 6.
100. [Letitia Elizabeth Landon], "To Marguerite, Countess of Blessington," in *Fisher's Drawing Room Scrap-book, MDCCCXXXIX*, 52–53.
101. Miss [Maria Jane] Jewsbury, "To L. E. L.—After Meeting Her for the First Time," in *Fisher's Drawing Room Scrap-book, MDCCCXXXIX*, 24–25.
102. St Clair, *Reading Nation*, 32.
103. Bourdieu's understanding of the dialectic of downclassing and upclassing is another way of figuring what I am describing. Bourdieu, *Distinction*, 163–168.
104. Landon, introduction to *Fisher's Drawing Rom Scrap-book* [for 1832], unpaginated.
105. James Hogg to Thomas Pringle, November 27, 1828, quoted in Richard J. Hill, "Scott, Hogg, and the Gift-Book Editors: Authorship in the Face of Industrial Production," *Romantic Textualities: Literature and Print Culture, 1780–1840*, no. 19 (2009): 14.

CODA

* Shelley, "Defence of Poetry," 533.
1. Walpole to Agnes Berry, February 13, 1791, in *Walpole's Correspondence*, 11:196.
2. For more on Canning, see John Treherne, *The Canning Enigma* (London: Cape, 1989); Judith Moore, *The Appearance of Truth: The Story of Elizabeth Canning and Eighteenth-Century Narrative* (Newark: University of Delaware Press, 1994); and Straub, *Domestic Affairs*, 66–82.
3. Shelley, "Defence of Poetry," 533.
4. Shelley, 517.
5. Shelley, 533.
6. Coleridge, *Biographia Literaria*, 2:7.
7. Wiseman, "Our Love-Hate Relationship with TV."

BIBLIOGRAPHY

MANUSCRIPT ARCHIVES

Deposit Lovelace Byron. Bodleian Libraries, Oxford. Dep. Lovelace Byron 36, Dep. Lovelace Byron 78, Dep. Lovelace Byron 118/2, Dep. Lovelace Byron 118/4, Dep. Lovelace Byron 155, Dep. Lovelace Byron 359, and Dep. Lovelace Byron 361.

Lamb Papers. The British Library, London. Add. 45546 and Add. 45548.

Papers of the Lamb Family of Brocket Hall. Hertfordshire Archives and Local Studies, Hertford. DE/Lb/F32/5 and DE/Lb/F82/31.

John Murray Archive. National Library of Scotland, Edinburgh. MS.43465, MS.43466, MS.43467, MS.43472, MS.43508, and MS.43523.

Forster Collection. Victoria and Albert Museum, London. Forster MS 328.

ALBUMS, NOTEBOOKS, AND UNIQUE/ANNOTATED PRINTED BOOKS

Birkbeck Library, Birkbeck College in the University of London

Birkbeck, Anna. The Album of Mrs. Birkbeck. No call number.

Bodleian Libraries, University of Oxford

Milbanke, Annabella. "character sketches in notebook dated 1812." Bodleian Libraries, Oxford. Dep. Lovelace Byron 118/2.

The British Library

Lamb, Caroline. *Glenarvon.* 3 vols. London: Colburn, 1816. N.1834.

Chawton House Library

Lamb, Caroline. *Graham Hamilton.* 2 vols. London: Colburn, 1822. Chawton House Library. Copy no. 6680.

Hertfordshire Archives and Local Studies

Lamb, Caroline. Sketches, Stories and Verse by Lady Caroline Lamb. 1803–c1825. Papers of the Lamb Family of Brocket Hall. DE/Lb/F66.

Verses and Sketches by Lady Caroline Lamb. [c. 1813]. Papers of the Lamb Family of Brocket Hall. DE/Lb/F64.

Houghton Library, Harvard University

Collection of enigmas, rebuses, conundrums and charades, with answers. 1828. MS Am 1177.

Hemans, Felicia Dorothea Brown. Commonplace book manuscript. [18—]. MS Eng 767.

Jerwood Centre, Wordsworth Trust, Grasmere

MS Autograph Album [unknown compiler]. DCMS181.

John Murray Archive, National Library of Scotland

Lamb, Caroline. Commonplace book of Caroline Lamb (Green) MS.43365.

Commonplace Book of Caroline Lamb (Blue). MS.43366.

Leigh, Augusta. Commonplace Book of Augusta Leigh. 1822. MS.43369.

Milbanke, Annabella. Commonplace Book of Lady Byron. 1809–1815. MS.43360

Milton S. Eisenhower Library, Johns Hopkins University

Lamb, Caroline. *Glenarvon*, 3 vols. London: Colburn, 1817. PO4859.L5G5 1817 c.1.

Robertson Davies Library, Massey College in the University of Toronto

Shoberl, Frederic, ed. *Friendship's Offering; or the Annual Remembrancer: A Christmas Present or New Year's Gift, for 1825*. London: Lupton Relfe, 1825. McLean Collection. D 0418 copy 1.

———. *Friendship's Offering; or the Annual Remembrancer: A Christmas Present or New Year's Gift, for 1825*. London: Lupton Relfe, 1825. McLean Collection. D 0418 copy 2.

Victoria and Albert Museum

Lamb, Caroline. *Glenarvon*. 3 vols. London: Colburn, 1816. Dyce Collection. D.12.E.28.

PUBLICATIONS

Abrams, M. H. "Structure and Style in the Greater Romantic Lyric." In *Romanticism and Consciousness: Essays in Criticism*, edited by Harold Bloom, 201–229. New York: Norton, 1970.

Adams, Samuel, and Sarah Adams. *The Complete Servant; Being a Practical Guide to the Peculiar Duties and Business of All Descriptions of Servants*. London: Knight and Lacey, 1825. HathiTrust. https://hdl.handle.net/2027/pst.000005795819 (accessed May 30, 2021).

Adamson, Sylvia. "Deixis and the Renaissance Art of Self Construction." *Sederi* 16 (2006): 5–29.

Alexander, Christine. "'The Kingdom of Gloom': Charlotte Brontë the Annuals, and the Gothic." *Nineteenth-Century Literature* 47, no. 4 (1993): 409–436.

A[lexander], W[illiam]. "Written in an Album." In *The Literary Souvenir; or, Cabinet of Poetry and Romance* [for 1826], edited by Aleric A. Watts, 180. London: Hurst, Robinson, 1826.

Allan, David. *A Nation of Readers: The Lending Library in Georgian England*. London: British Library, 2008.

Allen, James Smith. *In the Public Eye: A History of Reading in Modern France, 1800–1940*. Princeton, NJ: Princeton University Press, 1991.

Anderson, Benedict. *Imagined Communities: Reflections on the Origin and Spread of Nationalism*. Rev. ed. New York: Verso, 2016.

Anderson, Howard, Philip B. Daghlian, and Irvin Ehrenpreis, eds. *The Familiar Letter in the Eighteenth Century*. Lawrence: University Press of Kansas, 1968.

Angeletti, Gioia. "Women Re-writing Men: The Examples of Anna Seward and Lady Caroline Lamb." In *Romantic Women Poets: Genre and Gender*, edited by Lilla Maria Crisafulli and Cecilia Pietropoli, 241–258. Amsterdam: Rodopi, 2007.

Anti-Jacobin Review and Magazine. "Art. V. [Review of] *The Young Philosopher*." Vol. 1 (August 1798): 187–190. HathiTrust. https://hdl.handle.net/2027/chi.16481211 (accessed April 23, 2021).

Arnold, Matthew. "Memorial Verses." In *The Oxford Poetry Library: Matthew Arnold*, edited by Miriam Allot, 94–96. Oxford: Oxford University Press, 1995.

"Art. III., [Review of] *Graham Hamilton*." In *The Monthly Review, or Literary Journal, Enlarged: From September to December, Inclusive, 1822*, 135–143. London: A. and R. Spottiswoode, 1822. HathiTrust. https://hdl.handle.net/2027/inu.30000093224685 (accessed May 1, 2021).

"Art. V., [Review of] *Table Talk, or Original Essays*. By William Hazlitt." In *The Quarterly Review. Vol. XXVI. October and January*, 103–108. London: Murray, 1822. HathiTrust. https://babel.hathitrust.org/cgi/pt?id=njp.32101076520624 (accessed May 21, 2021).

Austen, Jane. *Emma*. Edited by Kristin Flieger Samuelian. Peterborough, ON: Broadview Press, 2004.

———. *Mansfield Park*. Edited by James Kinsley. Oxford: Oxford University Press, 2008.

———. *Pride and Prejudice*. Edited by Robert P. Irvine. Peterborough, ON: Broadview Press, 2002.

Baillie, Joanna. *Plays on the Passions*. Edited by Peter Duthie. Peterborough, ON: Broadview Press, 2001.

Barbauld, Anna Laetitia. "Mrs. Charlotte Smith." In *The Old Manor House*, by Charlotte Smith, i–viii. Vol. 36 of *The British Novelists; with An Essay; and Prefaces, Biographical and Critical*, edited by Anna Laetitia Barbauld. London: Rivington, 1810. HathiTrust. https://babel.hathitrust.org/cgi/pt?id=nyp.33433112069152 (accessed June 1, 2021).

Barker-Benfield, G. J. *The Culture of Sensibility: Sex and Society in Eighteenth-Century Britain*. Chicago: University of Chicago Press, 1992.

Barrell, John. *Imagining the King's Death: Figurative Treason, Fantasies of Regicide 1793–1796*. Oxford: Oxford University Press, 2000.

———. *The Spirit of Despotism: Invasions of Privacy in the 1790s*. Oxford: Oxford University Press, 2006.

Bates, Courtney Alice. "Addressing Each Other: Reciprocal Relationships in American Fan Letters." PhD diss., Washington University, 2011. ProQuest 3450716.

Beattie-Smith, Gillian. "Writing the Self: The Journal of Sarah Stoddart Hazlitt, 1774–1843." *Women's History Review* 22, no. 2 (2013): 197–210.

Beebee, Thomas O. "Publicity, Privacy, and the Power of Fiction in the Gunning Letters." *Eighteenth-Century Fiction* 20, no. 1 (2007): 61–88.

Behrendt, Stephen. "Charlotte Smith, Women Poets, and the Culture of Celebrity." In *Charlotte Smith in British Romanticism*, edited by Jacqueline Labbe, 189–202. London: Pickering and Chatto, 2008.

Bell's Weekly Messenger. "Births." February 5, 1809, 48. The British Newspaper Archive.

Benis, Toby Ruth. "'Likely Story': Charlotte Smith's Revolutionary Narratives." *European Romantic Review* 14, no. 3 (2003): 297–306.

Benjamin, Walter. "The Work of Art in the Age of Mechanical Reproduction." In *Illuminations: Essays and Reflections*, edited by Hannah Arendt, 166–195. New York: Mariner Books, 2019.

Berlant, Lauren. "Intimacy: A Special Issue." In "Intimacy," edited by Lauren Berlant. Special issue, *Critical Inquiry* 24, no. 2 (1998): 281–288.

Bisset, Robert. "The History of Literature for 1799." In *The Historical, Biographical, Literary, and Scientific Magazine. The History of Europe, for the Year 1799*, 1:1–306. London: G. Cawthorn, [1800?]. ESTC Number N52538. Eighteenth Century Collections Online.

Blackwood's Edinburgh Magazine. Unsigned review of *Graham Hamilton*, by Caroline Lamb. Vol. 11, no. 65 (June 1822): 731–733.

———. Unsigned review of *The Literary Souvenir*. Vol. 17, no. 96 (January 1825): 94–101. HathiTrust. https://hdl.handle.net/2027/chi.28408055 (accessed May 24, 201).

Blank, Antje, "Things as They Were: The Gothic of Real Life in Charlotte Smith's *The Emigrants* and *The Banished Man*." *Women's Writing* 16, no. 1 (2009): 78–93.

Bolter, Jay David, and Richard Grusin. *Remediation: Understanding New Media*. Cambridge, MA: MIT Press, 1999.

Bourdieu, Pierre. *Distinction: A Social Critique of the Judgment of Taste*. Translated by Richard Nice. Cambridge, MA: Harvard University Press, 1984.

———. *The Field of Cultural Production: Essays on Art and Literature*. Edited by Randal Johnson. New York: Columbia University Press, 1993.

Brandt, Andrea. "How to Set Boundaries in the Age of Oversharing." *Psychology Today* blog, December 2, 2019. https://www.psychologytoday.com/us/blog/mindful-anger/201912/how-set-boundaries-in-the-age-oversharing (accessed May 30, 2021).

Brantlinger, Patrick. *The Reading Lesson: The Threat of Mass Literary in Nineteenth-Century British Fiction*. Bloomington: Indiana University Press, 1998.

Braudy, Leo. "Knowing the Performer from the Performance." In "Celebrity, Fame, Notoriety," edited by Joseph A. Boone and Nancy J. Vickers. Special issue, *PMLA* 126, no. 4 (2011): 1070–1075.

Bravo, Tony. "In the Oversharing Age, Why Some Parents Won't Post Photos of Their Kids." *San Francisco Chronicle* online, April 18, 2019. https://www.sfchronicle.com/style/article/In-the-oversharing-age-why-some-parents-won-t-13776168.php (accessed May 30, 2021).

Brewer, David A. *The Afterlife of Character, 1726–1825.* Philadelphia: University of Pennsylvania Press, 2005.

Brewer, John. "Personal Scandal and Politics in Eighteenth-Century England: Secrecy, Intimacy and the Interior Self in the Public Sphere." In *Media and Political Culture in the Eighteenth Century,* edited by Marie-Christine Skuncke, 84–106. Stockholm: Kungl. Vitterhets Historie och Antikvitets Akademien, 2005.

———. "This, That and the Other: Public, Social and Private in the Seventeenth and Eighteenth Centuries." In *Shifting the Boundaries: Transformation of the Languages of Public and Private in the Eighteenth Century,* edited by Dario Castiglione and Lesley Sharpe, 1–21. Exeter: University of Exeter Press, 1995.

British Critic. "Art. V., [Review of] *Glenarvon, a Novel.*" Vol. 5 (June 1816): 627–633.

British Lady's Magazine. Unsigned review of *Glenarvon,* by Caroline Lamb. Vol. 4 (August 1816): 101–103.

Burke, Edmund. *A Philosophical Enquiry into the Origin of Our Ideas of the Sublime and Beautiful.* Edited by Adam Phillips. Oxford: Oxford University Press, 2008.

———. *Reflections on the Revolution in France.* Edited by Conor Cruise O'Brien. New York: Penguin, 2004.

Burroughs, Catherine. "Acting in the Closet: A Feminist Performance of Hazlitt's *Liber Amoris* and Keats's *Otho the Great.*" *European Romantic Review* 2, no. 2 (1992): 125–144.

Burwick, Frederick. "Lady Caroline Lamb's *Glenarvon* on Stage." *Wordsworth Circle* 42, no. 2 (2011): 139–143.

———. *Playing to the Crowd: London Popular Theatre, 1780–1830.* New York: Palgrave, 2011.

Butler, Marilyn. "Satire and the Images of Self in the Romantic Period: The Long Tradition of Hazlitt's *Liber Amoris.*" In *Spirits of Fire: English Romantic Writers and Contemporary Historical Methods,* edited by G. A. Rosso and Daniel P. Watkins, 153–169. London: Associated University Presses, 1990.

Byron, George Gordon. *Lord Byron: The Complete Poetical Works.* Edited by Jerome McGann. 7 vols. Oxford: Clarendon, 1980–1993.

Cafarelli, Annette Wheeler. *Prose in the Age of Poets: Romanticism and Biographical Narrative from Johnson to De Quincey.* Philadelphia: University of Pennsylvania Press, 1990.

Caledonian Mercury. "Newcastle Races, 1818." June 29, 1818. Gale Document Number BB3205375116. British Library Newspapers.

Caprino, Kathy. "How Social Media Over-Sharing about Your Child Can Cause Irrevocable Harm." *Forbes,* April 12, 2019. https://www.forbes.com/sites/kathycaprino/2019/04/12/how-social-media-over-sharing-about-your-child-can-cause-irrevocable-harm (accessed May 30, 2021).

Carlyle, Thomas. "Signs of the Times." *Edinburgh Review* 49, no. 98 (1829): 439–459.

Chandler, James K. *Wordsworth's Second Nature: A Study of the Poetry and Politics.* Chicago: University of Chicago Press, 1984.

Cheeke, Stephen. "Being There: Byron and Hobhouse Seek the 'real' Parnassus." *Romanticism* 7, no. 2 (2001): 127–144.

Christensen, Jerome. *Lord Byron's Strength: Romantic Writing and Commercial Society.* Baltimore: Johns Hopkins University Press, 1995.

Clubbe, John. "*Glenarvon* Revised—and Revisited." *Wordsworth Circle* 10, no. 2 (1979): 205–217.

Cochran, Peter. "Byron's Fan Letters." In *The Burning of Byron's Memoirs: New and Unpublished Essays and Papers,* 85–88. Newcastle upon Tyne, UK: Cambridge Scholars, 2014.

Cockle, Mrs. "Written in a Young Lady's Album." In *The Juvenile Keepsake. MDCCCXXIX*, edited by Thomas Roscoe, 156–157. London: Hurst, Chance, 1829.

Cohen, Michèle. "'Familiar Conversation': The Role of the 'Familiar Format' in Education in Eighteenth- and Nineteenth-Century England." In *Educating the Child in Enlightenment Britain: Beliefs, Cultures, Practices*, edited by Mary Hilton and Jill Shefrin, 99–116. Burlington, VT: Ashgate, 2009.

Colclough, Stephen. *Consuming Texts: Readers and Reading Communities, 1695–1870.* Basingstoke, UK: Palgrave, 2007.

———. "'Designated in Print as "Mr. John Clare"': The Annuals and the Field of Reading, 1827–1835." *John Clare Society Journal* 24 (2005): 53–68.

Coleridge, Samuel Taylor. *The Collected Works of Samuel Taylor Coleridge.* Edited by Kathleen Coburn. 16 vols. Princeton, NJ: Princeton University Press, 1971–2002.

———. "Fears in Solitude. Written in April, 1798, During the Alarm of an Invasion." In *Samuel Taylor Coleridge: The Complete Poems*, edited by William Keach, 239–244. New York: Penguin, 2004.

———. Preface to *Poems on Various Subjects*, v–xi. London: G. G. and J. Robinsons; Bristol: J. Cottle, 1796.

Cope, Jonas. "Scrapped Sentiment: Letitia Landon and *Fisher's Drawing Room Scrap-Book*, 1832–1837." *Romanticism* 25, no. 2 (2019): 190–204.

Cox, Jeffrey N. *Poetry and the Politics in the Cockney School: Keats, Shelley, Hunt and Their Circle.* Cambridge: Cambridge University Press, 1998.

Crabb, George. *English Synonymes Explained. . . .* 2nd ed. London: Baldwin, Cradock, and Joy, and T. Boosey, 1818.

Critical Review: Or, Annals of Literature. Unsigned review of *Elegiac Sonnets*, by Charlotte Smith. Vol. 57 (June 1784): 472–473. Google Books. http://google.cat/books?id=lRQFAAAAYAAJ (accessed April 23, 2021).

———. Unsigned review of *The Packet*, by Elizabeth Gunning. Vol. 11 (May 1794): 178–181.

Cuddy-Keane, Melba. "From Man-Mail to Readers' Letters: Locating John Farrelly." *Woolf Studies Annual* 11 (2005): 3–32.

Culler, Jonathan. "Lyric, History, and Genre." In *The Lyric Theory Reader: A Critical Anthology*, edited by Virginia Jackson and Yopie Prins, 63–77. Baltimore: Johns Hopkins University Press, 2014.

———. "Why Lyric?" *PMLA* 123, no. 1 (2008): 201–206.

Curran, Stuart. Introduction to *The Poems of Charlotte Smith*, edited by Stuart Curran, xix–xxix. Oxford: Oxford University Press, 1993.

———. *Poetic Form and British Romanticism.* Oxford: Oxford University Press, 1986.

Currie, Joy. "'Mature Poets Steal': Charlotte Smith's Appropriations of Shakespeare." In *Shakespeare and the Culture of Romanticism*, edited by Joseph M. Ortiz, 99–120. 2nd ed. London: Routledge, 2016.

"D." "Sonnet To Mrs. Smith on Reading Her Sonnets Lately Published." *European Magazine* 9 (May 1786): 366.

Dale, Amelia. *The Printed Reader: Gender, Quixotism, and Textual Bodies in Eighteenth-Century Britain.* Lewisburg, PA: Bucknell University Press, 2019.

Darnton, Robert. "Readers Respond to Rousseau: The Fabrication of Romantic Sensitivity." In *The Great Cat Massacre and Other Episodes in French Cultural History*, 215–256. New York: Basic Books, 1984.

Dart, Gregory, ed. *Liber Amoris and Related Writings.* By William Hazlitt. Manchester: Carcanet, 2008.

———. *Metropolitan Art and Literature, 1810–1840: Cockney Adventures.* Cambridge: Cambridge University Press, 2012.

Daugherty, Beth Rigel. "'You Kind of Belong to Us, and What You Do Matters Enormously': Letters from Readers to Virginia Woolf." *Woolf Studies Annual* 12 (2006): 1–212.

De Quincey, Thomas. "Chapter IV: Recollections of Charles Lamb." In *Literary Reminiscences; from The Autobiography of an English Opium-Eater*, 1:97–134. Boston: Ticknor, Reed, and Fields, 1851. HathiTrust. https://hdl.handle.net/2027/hvd.hwjvkc (accessed May 1, 2021).

———. "Charles Lamb." In *Leaders in Literature with a Notice of Traditional Errors Affecting Them*, 108–160. Vol. 8 of *De Quincey's Works*. Edinburgh: Adam and Charles Black, 1862. HathiTrust. https://hdl.handle.net/2027/ucl.b3311684 (accessed May 21, 2021).

———. "Notes on Godwin, Foster, and Hazlitt." In *Coleridge and Opium-Eating and Other Writings*, 280–312. Vol. 11 of *De Quincey's Works*. Edinburgh: Adam and Charles Black, 1863. HathiTrust. https://hdl.handle.net/2027/ucl.b3311687 (accessed May 13, 2021).

De Selincourt, Ernest, and Chester L. Shaver, eds. *The Letters of William and Dorothy Wordsworth*. Vol. 1, *The Early Years 1787–1805*. Rev. 2nd ed. Oxford: Clarendon Press, 1967.

Di Bello, Patrizia. "Mrs. Birkbeck's Album: The Hand-Written and the Printed in Early Nineteenth-Century Print Culture." *19: Interdisciplinary Studies in the Long Nineteenth Century* 1 (2005): 1–36.

———. *Women's Albums and Photography in Victorian England: Ladies, Mothers and Flirts*. Aldershot, UK: Ashgate, 2007.

Dickson, Leigh Wetherall. "Authority and Legitimacy: The Cultural Context of Lady Caroline Lamb's Novels." *Women's Writing* 13, no. 3 (2006): 369–391.

———. "The Construction of a Reputation for Madness: The Case Study of Lady Caroline Lamb." *Working with English: Medieval and Modern Language, Literature and Drama* 2 (June 2005): 27–46.

———. Introduction to *Graham Hamilton*. In *The Works of Lady Caroline Lamb*, edited by Leigh Wetherall Dickson and Paul Douglass, 2:ix–xxx. London: Pickering and Chatto, 2009.

———. "A Written Warning: Lady Caroline Lamb, Noblesse Oblige and the Works of John Ford." In *Shakespeare and the Culture of Romanticism*, edited by Joseph Ortiz, 245–266. Burlington, VT: Ashgate, 2013.

Dierks, Konstantin. "The Familiar Letter and Social Refinement in America, 1750–1800." In *Letter Writing as a Social Practice*, edited by David Barton and Nigel Hall, 31–41. Philadelphia: John Benjamins, 1999.

D'Israeli, Isaac. *A Dissertation on Anecdotes*. 1793. Facsimile, New York: Garland, 1972.

Dolan, Elizabeth A., and Gillian Andrews. Charlotte Smith Story Map, 2018. https://arcg.is/08POqD (accessed April 23, 2021).

Douglass, Paul. Introduction to *Glenarvon*. In *The Works of Lady Caroline Lamb*, edited by Leigh Wetherall Dickson and Paul Douglass, 1: xxvii–xliv. London: Pickering and Chatto, 2009.

———. *Lady Caroline Lamb: A Biography*. New York: Palgrave Macmillan, 2004.

———. "Lady Caroline Lamb Before Byron." *Wordsworth Circle* 36, no. 3 (2005): 117–124.

———. "The Madness of Writing: Lady Caroline Lamb's Byronic Identity." *Pacific Coast Philology* 34, no. 1 (1999): 53–71.

———. "Playing Byron: Lady Caroline Lamb's *Glenarvon* and the Music of Isaac Nathan." *European Romantic Review* 8, no. 1 (1997): 1–24.

———. "Twisty Little Passages: The Several Editions of Lady Caroline Lamb's *Glenarvon*." *Wordsworth Circle* 40, no. 2–3 (2009): 77–82.

———, ed. *The Whole Disgraceful Truth: Selected Letters of Lady Caroline Lamb*. New York: Palgrave Macmillan, 2006.

Douglass, Paul, and Frederick Burwick. Romantic-Era Songs, January 20, 2013. http://www.sjsu.edu/faculty/douglass/music/index.html (accessed May 1, 2021).

Doyle, Sady. *Trainwreck: The Women We Love to Hate, Mock, and Fear.* Brooklyn, NY: Melville House, 2017.

Dubrow, Heather. "Neither Here nor There: Deixis and the Sixteenth-Century Sonnet." In *The Lyric Poem: Formations and Transformation,* edited by Marion Thain, 30–50. Cambridge: Cambridge University Press, 2013.

Eckert, Lindsey. "'I'll be bound': John Clare's 'Don Juan,' Literary Annuals, and the Commodification of Authorship." *Nineteenth-Century Literature* 69, no. 4 (2015): 427–454.

———. "Lady Caroline Lamb's Recuperative Materiality." In "Romantic Women and Their Books," edited by Michelle Levy and Andrew Stauffer. Special issue, *Studies in Romanticism* 60, no. 4 (2021): 451–466.

———. "Priscilla Wordsworth's Pocketbook Diaries and Interfaces of Subjectivity." *Review of English Studies* 71, no. 300 (2020): 508–527.

Egan, Gerald. *Fashioning Authorship in the Long Eighteenth Century.* London: Palgrave Macmillan, 2016.

Eisner, Eric. *Nineteenth-Century Poetry and Literary Celebrity.* New York: Palgrave Macmillan, 2009.

Elfenbein, Andrew. *Byron and the Victorians.* Cambridge: Cambridge University Press, 1995.

Elliott, J. E. "The Cost of Reading in Eighteenth-Century Britain: Auction Sale Catalogues and the Cheap Literature Hypothesis." *ELH* 77, no. 2 (2010): 353–384.

Elliot, William. "For ———'s Album." In *The Bengal Annual, a Literary Keepsake for MDCCCXXX,* edited by David Lester Richardson, 275–276. Calcutta: Samuel Smith, 1830.

Elwin, Malcolm. *Lord Byron's Family: Annabella, Ada, and Augusta, 1816–1824.* Edited by Peter Thomson. London: John Murray, 1975.

Erickson, Lee. *The Economy of Literary Form: English Literature and the Industrialization of Publishing, 1800–1850.* Baltimore: Johns Hopkins University Press, 1996.

Esterhammer, Angela. "The Scandal of Sincerity: Wordsworth, Byron, Landon." In *Romanticism, Sincerity and Authenticity,* edited by Tim Milnes and Kerry Sinanan, 101–119. Basingstoke, UK: Palgrave Macmillan, 2010.

Eulenstein, C. "Elinor's Song. And Can'st Thou Bid My Heart Forget?" In *Lays of Harmony, Popular Vocal Music with Accompaniment for the Guitar,* 2–4. London: E. Donajowski, [1894].

Ezell, Margaret. *Social Authorship and the Advent of Print.* Baltimore: Johns Hopkins University Press, 1999.

Fairclough, Mary. *The Romantic Crowd: Sympathy, Controversy, and Print Culture.* Cambridge: Cambridge University Press, 2013.

Feldman, Paula R. Introduction to *The Keepsake for 1829,* edited by Paula R. Feldman, 7–25. Peterborough, ON: Broadview Press, 2006.

———. "Women, Literary Annuals, and the Evidence of Inscriptions." *Keats-Shelley Journal* 55 (2006): 54–62.

Fernandez, Jean. "Graven Images: The Woman Writer, the Indian Poetess, and Imperial Aesthetics in L.E.L.'s 'Hindoo Temples and Palaces at Madura.'" *Victorian Poetry* 43, no. 1 (2005): 35–52.

Ferris, Ina. *The Achievement of Literary Authority: Gender, History, and the Waverly Novels.* Ithaca, NY: Cornell University Press, 1991.

———. *Book-Men, Book Clubs, and the Romantic Literary Sphere.* New York: Palgrave Macmillan, 2015.

———. "The 'Character' of James the First and Antiquarian Secret History." *Wordsworth Circle* 37, no. 2 (2006): 73–76.

Fielding, Penny. *Writing and Orality: Nationality, Culture, and Nineteenth-Century Scottish Fiction.* Oxford: Oxford University Press, 1996.

Fletcher, Loraine. *Charlotte Smith: A Critical Biography.* New York: Palgrave, 1998.

Fordyce, David. *The New and Complete British Letter-Writer; or, Young Secretary's Instructor in Polite Modern Letter-Writing.* London: C. Cooke, [1790?]. ESTC Number T13268. Eighteenth Century Collections Online.

Franta, Andrew. "Godwin's Handshake." *PMLA* 122, no. 3 (2007): 696–710.

———. *Romanticism and the Rise of the Mass Public.* Cambridge: Cambridge University Press, 2007.

Friedman, Martin. "Hazlitt, Jerrold, and Horne: *Liber Amoris* Twenty Years After." *Review of English Studies* 22, no. 88 (1971): 455–462.

Gamer, Michael. *Romanticism, Self-Canonization, and the Business of Poetry.* Cambridge: Cambridge University Press, 2017.

Garnai, Amy. *Revolutionary Imaginings in the 1790s: Charlotte Smith, Mary Robinson, Elizabeth Inchbald.* Basingstoke, UK: Palgrave Macmillan, 2009.

Genette, Gérard. *Paratexts: Thresholds of Interpretation.* Translated by Jane E. Lewin. Cambridge: Cambridge University Press, 1997.

George, Mary Dorothy. *Catalogue of Political and Personal Satires Preserved in the Department of Prints and Drawings in the British Museum.* Vol. 6, *1784–1792.* London: British Museum, 1938.

Glavey, Brian. "Lyric Wilt, or, The Here and Now of Queer Impotentiality." *New Literary History* 51, no. 3 (2020): 567–586.

Godwin, William. *Caleb Williams.* Edited by Gary Handwerk and A. A. Markley. Peterborough, ON: Broadview Press, 2000.

Good, Graham. *The Observing Self: Rediscovering the Essay.* London: Routledge, 1988.

Graham, Peter W. "Fictive Biography in 1816: The Case of *Glenarvon.*" *Byron Journal* 19 (1991): 53–68.

Grattan, Thomas Colley. *Beaten Paths; and Those Who Trod Them.* 2 vols. London: Chapman and Hall, 1862.

[Grattan, Thomas Colley]. "The Confessions of an English Glutton." *Blackwood's Edinburgh Magazine* 13, no. 72 (January 1823): 86–93.

Grebanier, Bernard. *The Uninhibited Byron: An Account of His Sexual Confusion.* New York: Crown, 1971.

Griggs, Earl Leslie, ed. *Collected Letters of Samuel Taylor Coleridge.* 6 vols. Oxford: Clarendon Press, 1956–1971.

Grimbergen, Ria, and Paul Douglass. "On a Special Copy of Caroline Lamb's *Glenarvon* Recently Discovered in Koninklijke Bibliotheek." *Byron Journal* 37, no. 2 (2009): 151–160.

Gross, Jonathan. "Hazlitt's Worshipping Practice in *Liber Amoris.*" *Studies in English Literature, 1500–1900* 35, no. 4 (1995): 707–721.

Gunning, Elizabeth. *The Packet: A Novel.* 4 vols. London: J. Bell, 1794.

[Gunning, John]. *An Apology for the Life of Major General G*[unning], *Written by Himself.* London: J. Ridgway, 1792.

Gunning, Susannah. *A Letter from Mrs Gunning, Addressed to His Grace the Duke of Argyll.* 2nd ed. London: printed for the author, 1791.

Harris, Katherine D. "Feminizing the Textual Body: Female Readers Consuming the Literary Annual." *Papers of the Bibliographic Society of America* 99, no. 4 (2005): 573–622.

———. *Forget Me Not: The Rise of the British Literary Annual, 1823–1835.* Athens: Ohio University Press, 2015.

———. Introduction to *The Forgotten Gothic: Short Stories from British Literary Annuals, 1823–1831,* edited by Katherine D. Harris, xvi–xxxvii. n.p.: Zittaw Press, 2012.

Hawkins, Ann R., ed. *Romantic Women Writers Reviewed.* 9 vols. London: Pickering and Chatto, 2011–2013.

Haywood, Eliza. *A Present to a Servant-Maid; Or the Sure Means of Gaining Love and Esteem.* London: T. Gardner, 1743. ESTC Number T76347. Eighteenth Century Collections Online.

Hazlitt, William. *Liber Amoris or the New Pygmalion by William Hazlitt with Additional Matter Now Printed for the First Time from the Original Manuscripts.* Edited by Richard Le Gallienne. n.p.: privately printed, 1894.

———. *The Selected Writings of William Hazlitt.* Edited by Duncan Wu. 9 vols. London: Pickering and Chatto, 1998.

Hershinow, Stephanie Insley. *Born Yesterday: Inexperience and the Early Realist Novel.* Baltimore: Johns Hopkins University Press, 2019.

Hervey, Thomas K. Preface to *Friendship's Offering, A Literary Album* [for 1826], edited by Thomas K. Hervey, v–x. London: Lupton Relfe, 1826.

———. Preface to *Friendship's Offering, or the Annual Remembrancer a Christmas Present or New Year's Gift for 1824*, edited by Thomas K. Hervey, iii–iv. London: Lupton Relfe, 1824.

Hill, Bridget. *Servants: English Domestics in the Eighteenth Century.* Oxford: Oxford University Press, 1996.

Hill, Richard J. "Scott, Hogg, and the Gift-Book Editors: Authorship in the Face of Industrial Production." *Romantic Textualities: Literature and Print Culture, 1780–1840*, no. 19 (2009): 8–19.

Hime, G. *Waters of Elle, a Favorite Canzonet, from the Popular Novel "Glenarvon."* Liverpool: Hime & Son, [1821?].

Hodson, G. A. *"Waters of Elle," from "Glenarvon."* Dublin: E. McGullah, [1821?].

Hofkosh, Sonia. "Broken Images." *Nineteenth-Century Prose* 36, no. 1 (2009): 27–54.

———. *Sexual Politics and the Romantic Author.* Cambridge: Cambridge University Press, 1998.

Hollander, John. *The Figure of Echo: A Mode of Allusion in Milton and After.* Berkeley: University of California Press, 1981.

Howe, P. P. *The Life of William Hazlitt.* London: Hamish Hamilton, 1947.

Hull Packet and Original Weekly Commercial, Literary and General Advertiser. "York August Meeting." August 18, 1818. Gale Document Number BB3205906938. British Library Newspapers.

Hunnekuhl, Philipp. "Hazlitt and Crabb Robinson: The Common Pursuit." *Hazlitt Review* 6 (2013): 13–34.

[Hunt, Leigh]. "Pocket-Books and Keepsakes." In *The Keepsake for 1828*, edited by Frederic Mansel Reynolds, 1–18. London: Hurst, Chance, 1828.

Hunt, Leigh. *The Story of Rimini, A Poem.* London: Murray, 1816.

Jackson, H. J. *Marginalia: Readers Writing in Books.* New Haven, CT: Yale University Press, 2001.

———. *Romantic Readers: The Evidence of Marginalia.* New Haven, CT: Yale University Press, 2005.

Jackson, Virginia. *Dickinson's Misery: A Theory of Lyric Reading.* Princeton, NJ: Princeton University Press, 2005.

Janowitz, Anne. "Amiable and Radical Sociability: Anna Barbauld's 'Free Familiar Conversation.'" In *Romantic Sociability: Social Networks and Literary Culture in Britain, 1770–1840*, edited by Gillian Russell and Clara Tuite, 62–81. Cambridge: Cambridge University Press, 2002.

Jerman, Bernard R. "Disraeli's Fan Mail: A Curiosity Item." *Nineteenth-Century Fiction* 9, no. 1 (1954): 61–71.

Jewsbury, Miss [Maria Jane]. "To L.E.L.—After Meeting Her for the First Time." In *Fisher's Drawing Room Scrap-book MDCCCXXXIX. With Poetical Illustrations by L.E.L.*, 24–25. London: Fisher, Son, 1839.

"J. M." *The Agreeable Variety . . . Containing . . . Discourses, Characters, and Poems, Relating to the Most Useful Subjects*. London: printed for the author, 1717.

John Bull. Unsigned review of *Liber Amoris*, by William Hazlitt. Vol. 131 (June 16, 1823): 188–189.

———. Unsigned review of *Liber Amoris* "(Continued from our last)." Vol. 132 (June 23, 1823): 197–198.

Johnson, Amanda Louise. "William Hazlitt, *Liber Amoris*, and the Imagination." *European Romantic Review* 25, no. 6 (2014): 743–756.

Johnson, Barbara. *Persons and Things*. Cambridge, MA: Harvard University Press, 2008.

Johnson, Samuel. *A Dictionary of the English Language*. 2nd ed. London: J. and P. Knapton, T. and T. Longman, C. Hitch and L. Hawes, A. Millar, and R. and J. Dodsley, 1755–1756.

———. *The Lives of the Poets: A Selection*. Edited by Roger Lonsdale. Oxford: Oxford University Press, 2006.

Jones, Chris. *Radical Sensibility: Literature and Ideas in the 1790s*. New York: Routledge, 1993.

Kaminski, Margot. "Toward Defining Privacy Expectations in an Age of Oversharing." *Economist*, August 16, 2018. https://www.economist.com/open-future/2018/08/16/toward-defining-privacy-expectations-in-an-age-of-oversharing (accessed May 30, 2021).

Keen, Paul. *The Crisis of Literature in the 1790s: Print Culture and the Public Sphere*. Cambridge: Cambridge University Press, 1999.

Kelly, Gary. *English Fiction of the Romantic Period, 1789–1830*. London: Longman, 1989.

Kelsall, Malcolm. "The Byronic Hero and Revolution in Ireland: The Politics of *Glenarvon*." *Byron Journal* 9 (1981): 4–19.

Keymer, Thomas. "Sterne and Romantic Autobiography." In *The Cambridge Companion to English Literature, 1750–1830*, edited by Thomas Keymer and Jon Mee, 173–193. Cambridge: Cambridge University Press, 2004.

Keymer, Thomas, and Peter Sabor. *"Pamela" in the Marketplace: Literary Controversy and Print Culture in Eighteenth-Century Britain and Ireland*. Cambridge: Cambridge University Press, 2005.

Keynes, Geoffrey. *Bibliography of William Hazlitt*. 2nd ed. Surrey, UK: St. Paul's Bibliographies, 1981.

Kiallmark, G[eorge]. *Waters of Elle! Air from* Glenarvon, *with Variations and Flute Accomp. Ad Lib; Composed & Dedicated to Miss Emily Montague*. London: Chappell and Co., [18??].

King, Rachael Scarborough. *Writing to the World: Letters and the Origins of Modern Print Genres*. Baltimore: Johns Hopkins University Press, 2018.

Klancher, Jon. "Configuring Romanticism and Print History: A Retrospective." *European Romantic Review* 23, no. 3 (2012): 373–379.

———. *The Making of English Reading Audiences, 1790–1832*. Madison: University of Wisconsin Press, 1987.

Klein, Lawrence E. "Gender and the Public/Private Distinction in the Eighteenth Century: Some Questions about Evidence and Analytic Procedure." *Eighteenth-Century Studies* 29 (1995): 97–109.

Klose, F. J. *And Canst Thou Bid My Heart Forget. Elinor's Song from "Glenarvon."* London: Mayhew, [1825?].

Knezevich, Ruth. "Females and Footnotes: Excavating the Genre of Eighteenth-Century Women's Scholarly Verse." *ABO: Interactive Journal for Women in the Arts, 1640–1830* 6, no. 2 (2016): 1–17.

A Knight of Chivalry. *A Friendly Letter to the Marquis of Lorn, on the Subject of Mrs. Gunning's Pamphlet*. London: J. Ridgway, 1791.

Knowles, Claire. *Sensibility and Female Poetic Tradition, 1780–1860: The Legacy of Charlotte Smith*. Surrey, UK: Ashgate, 2009.

[Knox, Vicesimus]. *Elegant Epistles: Being a Copious Collection of Familiar and Amusing Letters, Selected for the Improvement of Young Persons, and for General Entertainment. . . . A New Edition Improved and Enlarged*. London: T. Longman et al., 1794. Google Books. https://books.google.com/books?id=Yc5bAAAAcAAJ (accessed May 1, 2021).

Knox, Vicesimus. *Essays Moral and Literary. . . . A New Edition in Two Volumes*. 2 vols. London: Charles Dilly, 1782. ESTC Number T92818. Eighteenth Century Collections Online.

Koenigsberger, Kurt M. "Liberty, Libel, and *Liber Amoris*: Hazlitt on Sovereignty and Death." *Studies in Romanticism* 38, no. 2 (1999): 281–309.

Labbe, Jacqueline M. *Charlotte Smith: Romanticism, Poetry, and the Culture of Gender*. Manchester: Manchester University Press, 2003.

———. "Revisiting the Egotistical Sublime: Smith, Wordsworth, and the Dramatic Monologue." In *Fellow Romantics: Male and Female British Writers, 1790–1835*, edited by Beth Lau, 17–38. Surrey, UK: Ashgate, 2009.

———. "Selling One's Sorrows: Charlotte Smith, Mary Robinson, and the Marketing of Poetry." *Wordsworth Circle* 25, no. 2 (1994): 68–71.

———. *Writing Romanticism: Charlotte Smith and William Wordsworth, 1784–1807*. New York: Palgrave, 2011.

Lamb, Caroline. *Glenarvon*. Edited by Frances Wilson. London: Everyman, 1995.

———. "Lines to Harriet Wilson." In *Fugitive Pieces and Reminiscences of Lord Byron*, by Isaac Nathan, 195–196. London: Whittaker and Treacher, 1829.

———. "To a Friend, On Sending a Fancy Drawing, After Promising Her Own Picture in the Character of a Gypsey." In *The Bijou: Or Annual of Literature and the Arts*, edited by W[illiam] F[raser], 89–90. London: Pickering, 1828.

———. *The Works of Lady Caroline Lamb*. Edited by Leigh Wetherall Dickson and Paul Douglass. 3 vols. London: Pickering and Chatto, 2009.

Lamb, Charles. *Album Verses, with a Few Others*. London: Moxon, 1830.

———. "Verses Written in Lady Barton's Album." In *Christmas Box. An Annual Present for Children* [for 1828], edited by T. Crofton Croker, 15–16. London: William Harrison Ainsworth, 1828.

[Landon, Letitia Elizabeth]. "The Farewell." In *Fisher's Drawing Room Scrap-book MDCC CXXXIX. With Poetical Illustrations by L.E.L.*, 5–6. London and Paris: Fisher, Son, 1839.

———. *Fisher's Drawing Room Scrap-book; with Poetical Illustrations by L.E.L.* [for 1832]. London: Fisher, Son, and Jackson, 1831. HathiTrust. https://hdl.handle.net/2027/umn.31951002225359l (accessed May 24, 2021).

———. *Fisher's Drawing Room Scrap-book; with Poetical Illustrations by L.E.L.* [for 1832]. London: Fisher, Son, and Jackson, 1832.

———. "To Marguerite, Countess of Blessington." In *Fisher's Drawing Room Scrap-book MDCCCXXXIX. With Poetical Illustrations by L.E.L.*, 52–53. London and Paris: Fisher, Son, 1839.

Langan, Celeste, and Maureen McLane. "The Medium of Romantic Poetry." In *The Cambridge Companion to British Romantic Poetry*, edited by James Chandler and Maureen McLane, 239–262. Cambridge: Cambridge University Press, 2008.

Ledbetter, Kathryn. "'Begemmed and Beamuletted': Tennyson and Those 'Vapid' Gift Books." *Victorian Poetry* 34, no. 2 (1996): 235–245.

Le Gallienne, Richard. Introduction to *Liber Amoris or the New Pygmalion by William Hazlitt with Additional Matter Now Printed for the First Time from the Original Manuscripts*, iii–xxvi. n.p.: privately printed, 1894.

Lester, Amelia, and David Haglund. "Memoir in the Age of T.M.I." *Out Loud Podcast, New Yorker*, April 14, 2015. https://www.newyorker.com/podcast/out-loud/memoir-in-the-age-of-tmi (accessed May 30, 2021).

Levy, Michelle. *Family Authorship and Romantic Print Culture*. Basingstoke, UK: Palgrave, 2008.

———. *Literary Manuscript Culture in Romantic Britain*. Edinburgh: Edinburgh University Press, 2020.

Levy, Michelle, and Betty A. Schellenberg. *How and Why to Do Things with Eighteenth-Century Manuscripts*. Cambridge: Cambridge University Press, 2021.

Lewis, W. S., and Dayle Wallace, eds. *Horace Walpole's Correspondence with Mary and Agnes Berry and Barbara Cecilia Seton*. Vol. 11 of *The Yale Edition of Horace Walpole's Correspondence*. New Haven, CT: Yale University Press, 1944.

Linley, Margaret. "A Centre That Would Not Hold: Annuals and the Cultural Democracy." In *Nineteenth-Century Media and the Construction of Identity*, edited by Laurel Brake, Bill Bell, and David Finkelstein, 54–74. New York: Palgrave, 2000.

Lodge, Sara. "By Its Own Hand: Periodicals and the Paradox of Romantic Authenticity." In *Romanticism, Sincerity and Authenticity*, edited by Tim Milnes and Kerry Sinanan, 185–200. Basingstoke, UK: Palgrave Macmillan, 2010.

———. "Romantic Reliquaries: Memory and Irony in the Literary Annuals." *Romanticism* 10, no. 1 (2004): 23–40.

London, April. "Isaac D'Israeli and Literary History: Opinion and Anecdote, and Secret History in the Early Nineteenth Century." *Poetics Today* 26, no. 3 (2005): 351–386.

London Chronicle. "London." February 19–22, 1791.

Luedtke, Janet E. "'Something Special for Someone': Anne Sexton's Fan Letters from Women." In *Rossetti to Sexton: Six Women Poets at Texas*, edited by Dave Oliphant, 165–189. Austin: Harry Ransom Humanities Research Center, University of Texas at Austin, 1992.

Lynch, Deidre Shauna. *The Economy of Character: Novels, Market Culture, and the Business of Inner Meaning*. Chicago: Chicago University Press, 1998.

———. *Loving Literature: A Cultural History*. Chicago: Chicago University Press, 2015.

———. "On Going Steady with Novels." *Eighteenth Century: Theory and Interpretation* 50, no. 2–3 (2009): 207–219.

———. "Paper Slips: Album, Archiving, Accident." *Studies in Romanticism* 57, no. 1 (2018): 87–119.

MacCarthy, Fiona. *Byron: Life and Legend*. London: Murray, 2002.

Mahoney, Charles. "*Liber Amoris*: Figuring Out the Coquette." *European Romantic Review* 10, no. 1 (1999): 23–52.

Malcolm, John. "Written in a Lady's Album." In *The Literary Souvenir; Or, Cabinet of Poetry and Romance* [for 1827], edited by Alaric A. Watts, 192–193. London: Longman, Rees, Orme, Brown & Green, and John Andrews, 1827.

Manning, Peter J. "Wordsworth in the *Keepsake*, 1829." In *Literature in the Marketplace: Nineteenth-Century British Publishing and Reading Practices*, edited by John O. Jordan and Robert L. Patten, 44–73. Cambridge: Cambridge University Press, 1995.

March, Rosemary. "The Page Affair: Lady Caroline Lamb's Cross-Dressing." Caro: The Lady Caroline Lamb Website, edited by Paul Douglass, 1–13, n.d. https://sites.google.com/sjsu.edu/caro/biography/the-page-affair (accessed May 1, 2021).

Marchand, Leslie, ed. *Byron's Letters and Journals*. 13 vols. London: Murray, 1973–1994.

Marcus, Sharon. *The Drama of Celebrity*. Princeton, NJ: Princeton University Press, 2019.

Mason, Nicholas. *Literary Advertising and the Shaping of British Romanticism*. Baltimore: Johns Hopkins University Press, 2013.

Matthews, Samantha. "Albums, Belongings, and Embodying the Feminine." In *Bodies and Things in Nineteenth-Century Literature and Culture*, edited by Katharina Boehm, 107–129. New York: Palgrave Macmillan, 2012.

———. *Album Verses and Romantic Literary Culture: Poetry, Manuscript, Print, 1780–1850*. Oxford: Oxford University Press, 2020.

———. "From Autograph to Print: Charles Lamb's *Album Verses, with a Few Others* (1830)." *Charles Lamb Bulletin* 154 (2011): 143–154.

———. "Importunate Applications and Old Affections: Robert Southey's Album Verses." *Romanticism* 17, no. 1 (2011): 77–93.

———. "'O All Pervading Album!': Place and Displacement in Romantic Albums and Album Poetry"." In *Romantic Localities: Europe Writes Place*, edited by Christoph Bode and Jacqueline Labbe, 99–116. London: Pickering and Chatto, 2010.

McDayter, Ghislaine. *Byromania and the Birth of Celebrity Culture.* Albany: State University of New York Press, 2009.

McGann, Jerome. *The Textual Condition.* Princeton, NJ: Princeton University Press, 1991.

McGill, Meredith L. *American Literature and the Culture of Reprinting, 1834–1853.* Philadelphia: University of Pennsylvania Press, 2003.

McLane, Maureen. "Ballads and Bards: British Romantic Orality." *Modern Philology* 98, no. 3 (2001): 423–443.

———. "The Use and Abuse of 'Orality' for Art: Reflections on Romantic and Late Twentieth-Century *Poiesis*." *Oral Tradition* 17, no. 1 (2002): 135–164.

Mee, Jon. *Romanticism, Enthusiasm, and Regulation: Poetics and the Policing of Culture in the Romantic Period.* Oxford: Oxford University Press, 2003.

Milberger, Kurt Edward. "'The First Impression, You, Yourself, Will Buy': The Gunninghiad, *Virginius and Virginia* and the Art of Scandal at the Minerva Press." *Romantic Textualities: Literature and Print Culture, 1780–1840*, no. 23 (2020): 39–59.

Miller, Lucasta. "*Liber Amoris, The Literary Gazette*, and the Poet L.E.L." *Hazlitt Review* 9 (2016): 27–39.

Milnes, Tim, and Kerry Sinanan, eds. *Romanticism, Sincerity and Authenticity.* Basingstoke, UK: Palgrave Macmillan, 2010.

Mole, Tom. *Byron's Romantic Celebrity: Industrial Culture and the Hermeneutic of Intimacy.* New York: Palgrave, 2007.

———, ed. *Romanticism and Celebrity Culture, 1750–1850.* Cambridge: Cambridge University Press, 2009.

Monthly Magazine. "The Enquirer. No. IX, Question: Ought Sensibility to Be Cherished, or Repressed?" Vol. 2, no. 9 (October 1796): 706–709. HathiTrust. https://hdl.handle.net/2027/chi.16684863 (accessed February 20, 2021).

Moore, Judith. *The Appearance of Truth: The Story of Elizabeth Canning and Eighteenth-Century Narrative.* Newark: University of Delaware Press, 1994.

More, Hannah. "Sensibility: A Poetical Epistle to the Hon. Mrs. Boscawen." In *Sacred Dramas: Chiefly Intended for Young Persons: The Subjects Taken from the Bible. To Which Is Added, Sensibility, A Poem*, 267–290. London: Cadell, 1782.

Morning Post. "Doctor Sir Richard Croft." February 19, 1818. Gale Document Number R3209708333. British Library Newspapers.

———. "Literature. Graham Hamilton." July 5, 1822. Gale Document Number R3209761298. British Library Newspapers.

———. "New Music." October 28, 1818. Gale Document Number R3209713538. British Library Newspapers.

Mourão, Manuela. "Remembrance of Things Past: Literary Annuals' Self-Historicization." *Victorian Poetry* 50, no. 1 (2012): 107–123.

Mulrooney, Jonathan. *Romanticism and Theatrical Experience: Kean, Hazlitt, and Keats in the Age of Theatrical News.* Cambridge: Cambridge University Press, 2018.

Munby, A. N. L. *The Cult of the Autograph Letter in England.* London: Athlone Press, 1962.

Myers, Mary Anne. "Unsexing Petrarch: Charlotte Smith's Lessons in the Sonnet as Social Medium." *Studies in Romanticism* 53, no. 2 (2014): 239–263.

A Narrative of the Incidents Which Form the Mystery, in the Family of General Gunning. London: Taylor, 1791.

Natarajan, Uttara. "Hazlitt's Common Sense." *Nineteenth-Century Prose* 36, no. 1 (2009): 12–26.

Neressian, Anahid. *Utopia, Limited: Romanticism and Adjustment*. Cambridge, MA: Harvard University Press, 2015.

Nicholson, Andrew, ed. *The Letters of John Murray to Lord Byron*. Liverpool: Liverpool University Press, 2007.

Normington, Susan. *Lady Caroline Lamb: This Infernal Woman*. London: House of Stratus, 2001.

North, Julian. *The Domestication of Genius: Biography and the Romantic Poet*. Oxford: Oxford University Press, 2009.

Northeastern University Women Writers Project. Women Writers in Review (database). https://wwp.northeastern.edu/review/ (accessed April 23, 2021).

Nussbaum, Emily. "Hate-Watching 'Smash.'" *New Yorker* online, April 27, 2012. http://www.newyorker.com/online/blogs/culture/2012/04/hate-watching-smash.html (accessed May 13, 2021).

Nussbaum, Felicity A. *The Autobiographical Subject: Gender and Ideology in Eighteenth-Century England*. Baltimore: Johns Hopkins University Press, 1989.

O'Quinn, Daniel. *Staging Governance: Theatrical Imperialism in London, 1770–1800*. Baltimore: Johns Hopkins University Press, 2005.

Paley, Morton D. "Coleridge and the Annuals." *Huntington Library Quarterly* 57, no. 1 (1994): 1–24.

Parsons, Gabrielle. "The Millennial Dating Struggle: Trying to Find Honesty in the Age of Oversharing." *Blavity*, June 13, 2018. https://blavity.com/the-millennial-dating-struggle-trying-to-find-honesty-in-the-age-of-oversharing?category1=community-submitted (accessed May 30, 2021).

Parsons, Nicola. *Reading Gossip in Early Eighteenth-Century England*. Basingstoke, UK: Palgrave, 2009.

Pascoe, Judith. "Female Botanists and the Poetry of Charlotte Smith." In *Re-visioning Romanticism: British Women Writers, 1776–1837*, edited by Carol Shiner Wilson and Joel Haefner, 193–209. Philadelphia: University of Pennsylvania Press, 1994.

———. "Poetry as Souvenir: Mary Shelley in the Annuals." In *Mary Shelley in Her Times*, edited by Betty T. Bennett and Stuart Curran, 173–184. Baltimore: Johns Hopkins University Press, 2000.

———. *Romantic Theatricality: Gender, Poetry and Spectatorship*. Ithaca, NY: Cornell University Press, 1997.

Paston, George, and Peter Quennell, eds. *"To Lord Byron": Feminine Profiles Based Upon Unpublished Letters, 1807–1824*. New York: Charles Scribner's Sons, 1939.

Pearsall, Sarah M. S. *Atlantic Families: Lives and Letters in the Later Eighteenth Century*. Oxford: Oxford University Press, 2008.

Peltz, Lucy. *Facing the Text: Extra-Illustration, Print Culture, and Society in Britain 1769–1840*. San Marino, CA: Huntington Library, 2017.

Perkins, Pam. "The Fictional Identities of Elizabeth Gunning." *Tulsa Studies in Women's Literature* 15, no. 1 (1996): 83–98.

Pinch, Adela. *Strange Fits of Passion: Epistemologies of Emotion, Hume to Austen*. Stanford, CA: Stanford University Press, 1996.

Piozzi, Hester Lynch. *British Synonymy; or An Attempt at Regulating the Choice of Words in Familiar Conversation*. 2 vols. London: G. G. and J. Robinson, 1794. HathiTrust. https://hdl.handle.net/2027/nyp.33433069256968 (accessed May 30, 2021).

Piper, Andrew. *Dreaming in Books: The Making of the Bibliographic Imagination in the Romantic Age*. Chicago: Chicago University Press, 2009.

Polwhele, Richard. "Impromptu On Being Desired by a Young Lady to Write Some Lines in Her Album." In *Forget Me Not; A Christmas and New Year's Present for MDCCCXXVII*, edited by Frederic Shoberl, 94. London: R. Ackermann, 1827.

Quennell, Peter. *Byron: The Years of Fame*. Hamden, CT: Archon Books, 1967.

Raven, James. *The Business of Books: Booksellers and the English Book Trade 1450–1850*. New Haven, CT: Yale University Press, 2007.

Ready, Robert. *Hazlitt at Table*. Rutherford, NJ: Fairleigh Dickinson University Press, 1981.

———. "The Logic of Passion: Hazlitt's *Liber Amoris*." *Studies in Romanticism* 14, no. 1 (1975): 41–57.

Reiman, Donald, ed. *The Romantics Reviewed: Contemporary Reviews of British Romantic Writers*. 9 vols. New York: Garland, 1972.

Remember Me! A New Year's Gift or Christmas Present, 1825. London: J. Poole, 1825.

Roberts, Bethan. *Charlotte Smith and the Sonnet: Form, Place, and Tradition in the Late Eighteenth Century*. Liverpool: Liverpool University Press, 2019.

Robinson, Daniel. "Taking 'Other Liberties' with Hazlitt's *Liber Amoris*." *Studies in Short Fiction* 34, no. 2 (1997): 141–149.

Rose, Mark. *Authors and Owners: The Invention of Copyright*. Cambridge, MA: Harvard University Press, 1993.

Rosenbaum, Susan B. *Professing Sincerity: Modern Lyric Poetry, Commercial Culture, and the Crisis of Reading*. Charlottesville: University of Virginia Press, 2007.

Rousseau, Jean-Jacques. *The Confessions*. Translated by J. M. Cohen. New York: Penguin, 1953.

Rowden, Frances Arabella. *A Biographical Sketch of the Most Distinguished Writers of Ancient and Modern Time Intended for the Use of Schools and Private Education*. London: Longman, Hatchard, Seely, and Lake, 1820.

———. *A Christian Wreath for the Pagan Deities: Or an Introduction to the Greek and Roman Mythology*. London: A. J. Valpy, 1820.

Rowland, William G., Jr. *Literature and the Marketplace: Romantic Writers and Their Audiences in Great Britain and the United States*. Lincoln: University of Nebraska Press, 1996.

Russell, Gillian. *The Ephemeral Eighteenth Century: Print, Sociability, and Cultures of Collecting*. Cambridge: Cambridge University Press, 2020.

"S." "On Autographs." In *The Literary Souvenir; Or, Cabinet of Poetry and Romance* [for 1825], edited by Alaric A. Watts, 383–391. London: Hurst, Robinson, 1825.

Sangster, Matthew. *Living as an Author in the Romantic Period*. Basingstoke, UK: Palgrave, 2021.

Schellenberg, Betty A. *The Professionalization of Women Writers in Eighteenth-Century Britain*. Cambridge: Cambridge University Press, 2005.

Schor, Esther. *Bearing the Dead: The British Culture of Mourning from the Enlightenment to Victoria*. Princeton, NJ: Princeton University Press, 1994.

Scott, Walter. "Memoir of the Early Life of Sir Walter Scott, Written by Himself." In *Memoirs of the Life of Sir Walter Scott*, by John Gibson Lockhart, 1–60. Edinburgh: Robert Cadell; London: John Murray, 1837.

Seward, Anna. *Letters of Anna Seward: Written between the Years 1784 and 1807*. 6 vols. Edinburgh and London: Constable, Longman, Hurst, Rees, Orme, and Brown, William Miller, and John Murray, 1811.

Shee, M. A. "An Impromptu, Addressed to a Lady Who Required a Specimen of the Author's Hand-Writing." In *The Literary Souvenir; Or, Cabinet of Poetry and Romance* [for 1827], edited by Alaric A. Watts, 327–328. London: Longman, Rees, Orme, Brown & Green, and John Andrews, 1827.

Shelley, Percy Bysshe. "A Defence of Poetry." In *Shelley's Poetry and Prose*, edited by Donald H. Reiman and Neil Fraistat, 509–535. New York: Norton, 2002.

Sinanan, Kerry, and Tim Milnes. Introduction to *Romanticism, Sincerity and Authenticity*, edited by Tim Milnes and Kerry Sinanan, 1–28. Basingstoke, UK: Palgrave Macmillan, 2010.

Siskin, Clifford H. *The Historicity of Romantic Discourse*. Oxford: Oxford University Press, 1988.

Smith, Adam. *The Theory of Moral Sentiments*. Edited by D. D. Raphael and A. L. Macfie. Indianapolis: Liberty Fund, 1982.

Smith, Charlotte. *Desmond*. Edited by Antje Blank and Janet Todd. Peterborough, ON: Broadview Press, 2001.

———. *Elegiac Sonnets*. 4th ed., corrected. London: J. Dodsley, H. Gardner, and J. Bew, 1786.

———. *The Poems of Charlotte Smith*. Edited by Stuart Curran. Oxford: Oxford University Press, 1993.

———. Preface to *The Banished Man. A Novel*, 1: v–xi. London: Cadell and Davies, 1794. ESTC Number T70700. Eighteenth Century Collections Online.

Snaith, Anna. "Wide Circles: The *Three Guineas* Letters." *Woolf Studies Annual* 6 (2000): 1–168.

Sodeman, Melissa. *Sentimental Memorials: Women and the Novel in Literary History*. Stanford, CA: Stanford University Press, 2015.

Soderholm, James. *Fantasy, Forgery, and the Byron Legend*. Lexington: University Press of Kentucky, 1996.

Spacks, Patricia Meyer. *Gossip*. Chicago: University of Chicago Press, 1985.

———. *Privacy: Concealing the Eighteenth-Century Self*. Chicago: Chicago University Press, 2003.

Spenser, Edmund. *The Faerie Queen*. Edited by A. C. Hamilton. London: Longman, 2007.

Stanhope, Philip Dormer. *The Art of Pleasing; or, Instructions for Youth in the First Stage of Life, in a Series of Letters to the Present Earl of Chesterfield, by the Late Philip Earl of Chesterfield*. London: G. Kearsley, 1783.

Stanton, Judith Phillips. "Charlotte Smith's 'Literary Business': Income, Patronage, and Indigence." *Age of Johnson: A Scholarly Journal* 1 (1987): 375–401.

———, ed. *The Collected Letters of Charlotte Smith*. Bloomington: Indiana University Press, 2003.

Stauffer, Andrew M. *Anger, Revolution, and Romanticism*. Cambridge: Cambridge University Press, 2005.

———. *Book Traces: Nineteenth-Century Readers and the Future of the Library*. Philadelphia: University of Pennsylvania Press, 2021.

St Clair, William. *The Reading Nation in the Romantic Period*. Cambridge: Cambridge University Press, 2005.

Stewart, David. *The Form of Poetry in the 1820s and 1830s: A Period of Doubt*. [New York]: Palgrave Macmillan, 2018.

St. John, J. A. "Verses Written for a Lady's Album." In *The Juvenile Keepsake. MDCCCXXIX*, edited by Thomas Roscoe, 169. London: Hurst, Chance, 1829.

Stoddart Hazlitt, Sarah. "Journal of My Trip to Scotland, By Mrs. Hazlitt." In *Liber Amoris or the New Pygmalion by William Hazlitt with Additional Matter Now Printed for the First Time from the Original Manuscripts*, edited by Richard Le Gaillienne, 239–335. n.p.: privately printed, 1894.

Stokes, Christopher. "Lorn Subjects: Haunting, Fracture and Ascesis in Charlotte Smith's *Elegiac Sonnets*." *Women's Writing* 16, no. 1 (2009): 143–160.

Storti, Sarah Anne. "Letitia Landon: Still a Problem." *Victorian Poetry* 57, no. 4 (2019): 533–556.

Straub, Kristina. *Domestic Affairs: Intimacy, Eroticism, and Violence between Servants and Masters in Eighteenth-Century Britain*. Baltimore: Johns Hopkins University Press, 2009.

Styles, John. "Involuntary Consumers? Servants and Their Clothes in Eighteenth-Century England." *Textile History* 33, no. 1 (2002): 9–21.

Tanselle, G. Thomas. "The Bibliographical Concepts of *Issue* and *State*." *Papers of the Bibliographic Society of America* 69, no. 1 (1975): 17–66.

Thackeray, William Makepeace. "A Word on the Annuals." *Fraser's Magazine* 16, no. 96 (December 1837): 757–763. HathiTrust. https://hdl.handle.net/2027/nyp.33433081686697 (accessed May 24, 2021).

Theatrical Inquisitor, and Monthly Mirror. Unsigned review of *Glenarvon*, by Caroline Lamb. Vol. 9 (August 1816): 122–125. HathiTrust. https://hdl.handle.net/2027/inu.30000047477272 (accessed May 1, 2021).

[Thomas, Elizabeth]. *Purity of Heart, . . . Addressed to the Author of "Glenarvon."* London: W. Simpkin and R. Marshall, 1816.

Thomson, J. C. *Bibliography of the Writings of Charles and Mary Lamb: A Literary History*. Hull: J. R. Tutin, 1908.

Thornton, Tamara Plakins. *Handwriting in America: A Cultural History*. New Haven, CT: Yale University Press, 1996.

Throsby, Corin. "Byron, Commonplacing and Early Fan Culture." In *Romanticism and Celebrity Culture, 1750–1850*, edited by Tom Mole, 227–244. Cambridge: Cambridge University Press, 2009.

———. "Flirting with Fame: Byron's Anonymous Female Fans." *Byron Journal* 32, no. 2 (2004): 115–123.

Times. "The Marquis of Blandford's Marriage." September 14, 1791. Gale Document Number CS50990382. *The Times* Digital Archive.

———. "Notice of *Liber Amoris*." *Times*, May 30, 1823. Gale Document Number CS50875582. *The Times* Digital Archive.

Tomalin, Marcus. "'Vulgarisms and Broken English': The Familiar Perspicuity of William Hazlitt." *Romanticism: The Journal of Romantic Culture and Criticism* 13, no. 1 (2007): 28–52.

Treherne, John. *The Canning Enigma*. London: Cape, 1989.

Tuite, Clara. *Lord Byron and Scandalous Celebrity*. Cambridge: Cambridge University Press, 2015.

———. "Tainted Love and Romantic Celebrity." *ELH* 74, no. 1 (2007): 59–88.

Vickery, Amanda. *The Gentleman's Daughter: Women's Lives in Georgian England*. New Haven, CT: Yale University Press, 1998.

Wang, Fuson. "Cosmopolitanism and the Radical Politics of Exile in Charlotte Smith's *Desmond*." *Eighteenth-Century Fiction* 25, no. 1 (2012): 37–59.

Warne, Vanessa. "Thackeray among the Annuals: Morality, Cultural Authority and the Literary Annual Genre." *Victorian Periodicals Review* 39, no. 2 (2006): 158–178.

———. "'What Foreign Scenes Can Be': The Ruin of India in Letitia Landon's *Scrapbook Poems*." *Victorian Review* 32, no. 2 (2006): 40–63.

Watson, Nicola J. "Trans-figuring Byronic Identity." In *At the Limits of Romanticism: Essays in Cultural, Feminist, and Materialist Criticism*, edited Mary A. Favret and Nicola J. Watson, 185–206. Bloomington: Indiana University Press, 1994.

Watts, Alaric A. Preface to *The Literary Souvenir; Or, Cabinet of Poetry and Romance* [for 1825], edited by Alaric A. Watts, iii–viii. London: Hurst, Robinson, 1825.

Weisman, Karen. "Form and Loss in Charlotte Smith's *Elegiac Sonnets*." *Wordsworth Circle* 33, no. 1 (2002): 23–27.

Welsh, Alexander. *Strong Representations: Narrative and Circumstantial Evidence in England*. Baltimore: Johns Hopkins University Press, 1992.

Westover, Paul. "Imaginary Pilgrimages: Felicia Hemans, Dead Poets, and Romantic Historiography." *Literature Compass* 2 (2005): 1–15.

Whale, John. "*Liber Amoris*: Unmanning the Man of Letters." *Nineteenth-Century Prose* 36, no. 1 (2009): 55–76.

Wheatley, Kim. *Romantic Feuds: Transcending the Age of Personality*. Surrey, UK: Ashgate, 2013.

Whyte, Samuel. "Lines, by Samuel Whyte, Esq. of Grafton-Street, In Answer to the Foregoing." In *The Protected Fugitives. A Collection of Miscellaneous Poems, the Genuine Productions of a Lady. Never Before Published*, by Henrietta Battier, 202–208. Dublin: James Porter, 1791. ESTC Number T189070. Eighteenth Century Collections Online.

Wilson, Ben. *Decency and Disorder: The Age of Cant, 1789–1837*. London: Faber and Faber, 2007.

Wilson, Frances. "'An Exaggerated Woman': The Melodramas of Lady Caroline Lamb." In *Byromania: Portraits of the Artist in Nineteenth- and Twentieth-Century Culture*, edited by Frances Wilson, 195–220. Basingstoke, UK: Palgrave Macmillan, 1999.

[Wilson, John]. "Hazlitt Cross-Questioned." *Blackwood's Edinburgh Magazine* 3, no. 17 (August 1818): 550–552.

———. "Monologue or Soliloquy on the Annuals." *Blackwood's Edinburgh Magazine* 29, no. 160 (December 1829): 948–961.

Wiseman, Eva. "Our Love-Hate Relationship with TV." *Guardian*, February 17, 2013. http://www.guardian.co.uk/lifeandstyle/2013/feb/17/hate-watching-tv (accessed May 13, 2021).

Wollstonecraft, Mary. *A Vindication of the Rights of Woman and a Vindication of the Rights of Men*. Edited by Janet M. Todd. Oxford: Oxford University Press, 2008.

Wordsworth, William. *A Letter to a Friend of Robert Burns: Occasioned by an Intended Republication of the Account of the Life of Burns, by Dr. Currie*. London: Longman, 1816.

———. *The Prelude: 1799, 1805, 1850*. Edited by Jonathan Wordsworth, M. H. Abrams, and Stephen Gill. New York: Norton, 1979.

———. *The Prose Works of William Wordsworth*. Edited by W.J.B. Owen and Jane Worthington Smyser. 3 vols. Oxford: Clarendon Press, 1974.

Wordsworth, William, and Samuel Taylor Coleridge. *Lyrical Ballads: 1798 and 1800*. Edited by Michael Gamer and Dahlia Porter. Peterborough, ON: Broadview Press, 2008.

Wu, Duncan. "Appropriating Byron: Lady Caroline Lamb's 'A New Canto.'" *Wordsworth Circle* 26, no. 3 (1995): 140–146.

———. "Hazlitt's *Liber Amoris*: A Defence." *Wordsworth Circle* 31, no. 1 (2000): 20–25.

———. "Hazlitt's 'Sexual Harassment.'" *Essays in Criticism* 50, no. 3 (2000): 133–214.

———. Introductory notes to *Liber Amoris*, by William Hazlitt. In *The Selected Writings of William Hazlitt*, by Duncan Wu, 7: xi–xviii. London: Pickering and Chatto, 1998.

———. "Talking Pimples: Hazlitt and Byron in Love." *Romanticism* 10, no. 2 (2004): 158–172.

———. *William Hazlitt: The First Modern Man*. Oxford: Oxford University Press, 2008.

York Herald, and General Advertiser. "Racing." June 6, 1818. Gale Document Number R3211024623. British Library Newspapers.

———. "The Turf." April 4, 1818. Gale Document Number R3211024488. British Library Newspapers.

———. "The Turf." May 16, 1818. Gale Document Number R3211024576. British Library Newspapers.

Yousef, Nancy. *Romantic Intimacy*. Stanford, CA: Stanford University Press, 2013.

Zimmerman, Sarah M. "Varieties of Privacy in Charlotte Smith's Poetry." *European Romantic Review* 18, no. 4 (2007): 483–502.

INDEX

Page numbers in *italics* indicate illustrations.

ABOUT THE AUTHOR

LINDSEY ECKERT is an assistant professor of English at Florida State University in Tallahassee where her research and teaching focus on Romanticism and the history of text technologies.